An Archaeology of Black Markets

Florida Museum of Natural History: Ripley P. Bullen Series

UNIVERSITY PRESS OF FLORIDA

Florida A&M University, Tallahassee
Florida Atlantic University, Boca Raton
Florida Gulf Coast University, Ft. Myers
Florida International University, Miami
Florida State University, Tallahassee
New College of Florida, Sarasota
University of Central Florida, Orlando
University of Florida, Gainesville
University of North Florida, Jacksonville
University of South Florida, Tampa
University of West Florida, Pensacola

An Archaeology of Black Markets

Local Ceramics and Economies in Eighteenth-Century Jamaica

Mark W. Hauser

Foreword by Jerald T. Milanich

University Press of Florida
Gainesville/Tallahassee/Tampa/Boca Raton
Pensacola/Orlando/Miami/Jacksonville/Ft. Myers/Sarasota

Copyright 2008 by Mark W. Hauser
All rights reserved
Printed in the United States of America on recycled, acid-free paper
Parts of chapter 4 first appeared as M. Hauser, and C. R. DeCorse. 2003.
Low-fired earthenwares in the African Diaspora: Problems and prospects.
International Journal of Historical Archaeology 7(1): 67–98.

First cloth printing, 2008
First paperback printing, 2013

Library of Congress Cataloging-in-Publication Data
Hauser, Mark W.
An archaeology of Black markets : local ceramics and economies in
eighteenth-century Jamaica / Mark W. Hauser ; foreword by Jerald T.
Milanich.
p. cm.—(Ripley P. Bullen series / Florida Museum of Natural History)
Includes bibliographical references and index.
ISBN 978-0-8130-3261-0 (cloth: alk. paper)
ISBN 978-0-8130-4902-1 (pbk.)
1. Slavery—Jamaica—History—18th century. 2. Blacks—Jamaica—
History—18th century. 3. Blacks—Jamaica—Economic conditions—
18th century. 4. Pottery—Jamaica. 5. Excavations (Archaeology)—Jamaica.
6. Jamaica—History—18th century. I. Florida Museum of Natural History.
II. Title.
HT1096.H38 2008
972.92'033—dc22   2008018546

The University Press of Florida is the scholarly publishing agency for the
State University System of Florida, comprising Florida A&M University,
Florida Atlantic University, Florida Gulf Coast University, Florida International University, Florida State University, New College of Florida, University of Central Florida, University of Florida, University of North Florida,
University of South Florida, and University of West Florida.

University Press of Florida
15 Northwest 15th Street
Gainesville, FL 32611-2079
http://www.upf.com

I would like to dedicate this book to my friends in the field and finds unit of the Jamaica National Heritage Trust whose tireless efforts help preserve the cultural patrimony of Jamaica.

Contents

List of Tables ix

List of Maps xi

List of Figures xiii

Foreword xvii

Acknowledgments xix

Introduction 1

1. Historical Archaeology of the Caribbean Plantation 13
2. Markets of Contention: Historical and Legal Perspectives on Informal Economies in Eighteenth-Century Jamaica 39
3. Between Urban and Rural 67
4. Routing Pots: Ceramics of the African Diaspora 93
5. Rooting Pots: Jamaican Colonial Ceramics 120
6. Locating Enslaved Craft Production: Petrographic and Chemical Analysis of Eighteenth-Century Jamaican Pottery 160

   Epilogue: Boundaries and Identities 192

   Appendix A. Assignment of Samples from Sites to Ceramic Groups 203

   Appendix B. Instrumental Neutron Activation Analysis of Eighteenth-Century Pottery from Jamaica 205
   Christophe Descantes and Michael D. Glascock

   Bibliography 219

   Index 263

Tables

3.1. Distance in English Miles of Cities from Kingston, along the Postal Roads of Jamaica 73
3.2. Estimated Cost of Posting Packages from Kingston Using Postal Rates Described by Edward Long 73
3.3. Estimated Percentages of Imported, Regional (Identified as Spanish Jars), and Local Jamaican Wares Recovered from Seville Estate 80
3.4. Estimated Percentages of Vessel Forms Recovered from Seville Estate 80
3.5. Estimated Percentages of Imported, Regional (Identified as Spanish Jars), and Local Jamaican Wares Recovered from Juan De Bollas and Thetford 83
3.6. Estimated Percentages of Imported, Regional (Identified as Spanish Jars), and Local Jamaican Wares Recovered from Eighteenth-Century Contexts in Jamaica 90
3.7. Types of Materials Recovered from Domestic Assemblages at Each of the Sites 90
6.1. Distribution of Yabba Sherds, MNVs, and Rim Sherds 166
6.2. A Cross-Tabulation of Groups Represented from Samples Plotted on the Ternary Diagram and Their Provenance 175
6.3. Distribution of Chemical Subgroups 187
A.1. Assignment of Samples (000) from Sites to Ceramic Groups 203
B.1. Principal Components Analysis of 49 Specimens 215
B.2. Mahalanobis-distance-calculated Probabilities and Posterior Classification for Compositional Group 1 Members Using Seven Principal Components 216
B.3. Mahalanobis-distance-calculated Probabilities and Posterior Classification for Compositional Group 2 Members Using Seven Principal Components 216
B.4. Mahalanobis-distance-calculated Probabilities and Posterior Classification for Unassigned Specimens into Groups 1 and 2 Using Seven Principal Components 217
B.5. Compositional Group Membership and Decoration 217

Maps

1.1. The Caribbean region—islands discussed in the text, labeled 16
1.2. Topography and rivers of Jamaica 17
1.3. Location of Jamaican cities, settlements, and estates described in text 18
1.4. The Middle Passage (transatlantic trade in Africans) between the sixteenth and nineteenth centuries 26
2.1. Seventeenth-century street markets located through the historic documents and oral history 44
2.2. Eighteenth-century street markets located through the historic documents and oral history 45
2.3. Nineteenth-century street markets located through the historic documents and oral history 46
3.1. The development of Jamaican roads in the eighteenth century 72
3.2. Locator of sites discussed and roads corresponding to Jeffery's 1776 map connecting these sites to Spanish Town 76
3.3. A plan of Port Royal redrawn from *Plan de la ville de Port Royal* by Jacques Belin (1764) and *His Majesty's Yard in Jamaica* by Nathaniel Watts (1815) 89
4.1. Archaeological sites and regions of investigation in West Africa discussed or referenced in text 99
4.2. Contemporary Ghana showing approximate location of ethno-linguistic groups 104
4.3. Islands in the Eastern Caribbean discussed in the text 109
6.1. Geological map of Jamaica with the location of sites included in petrographic analysis 165

Figures

I.1. *The Destruction of Roehamton Estate in the Parish of St. James in January 1832* by Adolphe Duperly 2
1.1. A view of an estate on San Domingue. Agriculture et economie rustique, economie rustique, sucrerie 27
1.2. *View of Roehampton Estate*, Jamaica 35
2.1. *A Negro Market in the West Indies* 41
2.2. *Marketplace, Falmouth, Jamaica* by Adolphe Duperly 55
3.1. Chronology of sampled archaeological sites in seventeenth-, eighteenth-, and nineteenth-century Jamaica 77
3.2. A plan of St. Jago de la Vega in the island of Jamaica, 1786, by John Pitcarne 86
4.1. Pie charts illustrating the point of origin of enslaved peoples shipped to selected American colonies before 1808 103
5.1. Ma Lou (Louisa Jones) building a yabba in 1984 121
5.2. Munchie (Marlene Roden) forming a yabba in 1998 121
5.3. New Seville ware cup 128
5.4. Pottery sellers in Kingston, Jamaica 135
5.5. Victoria Jubilee Market in Kingston, Jamaica 136
5.6. Jamaica new and old: Women with pots, bowls, and jars on display 136
5.7. *Water Jar Sellers* by Isaac Belisario, 1838 138
5.8. Candy sellers. Late nineteenth century, Jamaica 139
5.9. Glazed Jamaican coarse earthenware 141
5.10. A selection of forms in which glazed yabbas were shaped 142
5.11. Glazed yabba with handle 143
5.12. Glazed Jamaican chamber pot (chimney) 143
5.13. Slipped and burnished water jar with handle 144
5.14. A selection of forms in which slipped yabbas are found 145
5.15. Slipped and burnished vertical pot 146
5.16. Slipped and burnished yabba 146
5.17. Untreated yabba with punctated decoration 147

5.18. A selection of forms in which untreated yabbas are found 148
5.19. Untreated yabba with punctated decoration 149
5.20. Untreated yabba with rouletted decoration 149
5.21. Frequency of raw sherd count of the three types of ceramics over time using Port Royal ceramic collection 151
5.22. Frequency of minimum number of vessels (MNV) of the three types of ceramics over time using Port Royal ceramic collection 152
5.23. Frequency over time of rim sherds of the three types of ceramics over time from Port Royal 153
5.24. Frequency over time of rim sherds of different forms of local ceramics from Port Royal 154
5.25. Variation in rim diameters of yabbas from Port Royal over time 155
5.26. Frequency of decorated ceramics by decoration type over time from Port Royal 156
5.27. Frequency of enslaved coming from different regions of Africa into Jamaica between 1655 and 1808 158
6.1. Distribution of ceramic types on analyzed sites by rim count 167
6.2. Ternary diagram showing the diversity of ceramic recipes of ceramics recovered from control samples 173
6.3. Ternary diagram showing the diversity of ceramic recipes used to make yabbas 174
6.4. Microphotograph taken at 10x of sample 025, which belongs to ceramic group 1 177
6.5. Microphotograph taken at 10x of sample 011 178
6.6. Microphotograph of sample 052 (St. Peter's Church) 180
6.7. Microphotograph of sample 013 (Old Naval Dockyard) taken at 10x 182
6.8. Microphotograph of sample 058 (St. Peter's Church) 184
6.9. Microphotograph of paste from sample 124 (St. Peter's Church) 185
6.10. Distribution of chemical groups across sites 189
7.1. *Indian Girls Cooking Rice outside of House* by Rev. W. Bailey 1907 200
B.1. Bivariate plot of principal components 1 and 2 displaying two compositional groups 210
B.2. Bivariate plot of principal components 1 and 2 displaying two compositional groups and labeled unassigned specimens (+) 211
B.3. Bivariate plot of base-10 logged chromium and sodium concentrations showing the chemical distinctiveness of the two compositional groups 212

B.4. Bivariate plot of base-10 logged thorium and hafnium concentrations showing the chemical distinctiveness of the two compositional groups   213

B.5. Bivariate plot of base-10 logged sodium and arsenic concentrations showing two possible subgroups within compositional group 1   214

Foreword

In 1943, before there was anything known as historical archaeology, the late Ripley P. Bullen, for whom this book series is named, excavated an early-nineteenth-century house site in Andover, Massachusetts, the residence of Lucy Foster, a freed slave and a woman of the African Diaspora. In 1948 Ripley moved to Florida to work in archaeology, and four years later he became curator at what today is the Florida Museum of Natural History.

During his quarter-century at the Museum, Bullen turned part of his archaeological attention to the Caribbean, where he became a major presence. When he died in 1976 he left behind a marvelous legacy of organizations and publications devoted to Caribbean archaeology (see http://www.flmnh.ufl.edu/caribarch/).

Because of his varied interests, I know Ripley would be pleased that the Ripley P. Bullen Series and the University Press of Florida are publishing Mark W. Hauser's book *An Archaeology of Black Markets*, which bridges African Diaspora and Caribbean studies.

Ripley, I suspect, also would be astounded at the growth and contributions of historical archaeology. Though still a relatively young discipline, historical archaeology's field methods and theoretical approaches have proven to be well suited to helping us better understand the peoples of the Caribbean. Drawing on the historical record to provide context, practitioners of historical archaeology can articulate sophisticated research problems, the solving of which gives voice to individuals and groups whose behavior in the past oftentimes is shrouded by the rich, famous, and more powerful.

In this engaging book, archaeologist Mark W. Hauser of the University of Notre Dame does just that. He applies the tenets of historical archaeology to examine the participation of enslaved people of African descent in local markets in plantation-era Jamaica. His methods to gather data include both petrographic and chemical analysis of Jamaican-made ceramics and the interpretation of eighteenth-century texts. The results of that research provide perspectives on social and economic interactions among Jamaicans, including the role of women in the manufacturing of ceramics that were traded over large areas of the island through a system of Sunday "black markets."

Hauser also is able to better discern the contribution of these local markets to the island's economy and the role of the markets in providing a setting for enslaved plantation laborers to exchange and acquire not only material goods, but social information as well.

Since his first participation in an archaeological project in the Caribbean one and a half decades ago, Mark Hauser's fieldwork has taken him to a number of places in that region, including St. John, St. Thomas, Cuba, Martinique, Guadeloupe, Dominica, and Jamaica. He continues his research in the area, examining how enslaved peoples created and transformed the world in which they lived. It is an interesting story, one that historical archaeology is uniquely suited to unraveling. I am pleased that the Bullen Series can include *An Archaeology of Black Markets* among our list of titles.

Jerald T. Milanich
Series Editor

Acknowledgments

I am indebted to many people and institutions that generously gave of their time, offered encouragement, and provided support. Foremost among these are the people of Port Royal who hosted me during my research and proved to be wonderful friends and excellent teachers. Special thanks go to Ms. Dobson, Chief, Ms. Gloria, Bridget and Roger, and Marva. I would also like to thank Marlene Roden (Munchie), from Spanish Town, who took the time to show me how to make a yabba and answered countless questions, oftentimes the same one.

I am most indebted to the Jamaica National Heritage Trust. The Trust as an institution hosted me during my research in 1998 and 2000. The organization was generous with both its facilities and personnel. Foremost I would like to thank Dorrick Gray, my colleague and friend, without whom this project would never have happened. He was a wonderful host and an even better sounding board. His knowledge and experience of colonial period archaeology of Jamaica is rich, and his assistance and generosity with that knowledge was most valuable. I would also like to thank Roderick Ebanks, whose considerable experience and knowledge on the subject helped focus this work. His research on Ma Lou was a constant touchstone by which to gauge my own research. Most important, he introduced me to Marlene Roden and was willing to engage in discussions about this project. I would also like to thank the employees of the Field and Finds divisions of the Jamaica National Heritage Trust, including Silvaneous Walters, Audene Brooks, Rosie Whitaker, Ryan Murphy, Ricardo Tyndall, and Clifton "Joe" McKee. Annie Howard-Brown runs the Finds unit and was very helpful in locating and assisting with the analysis of the Jamaican coarse earthenware. She was a constant source of support; Tyndall, who lived in Port Royal at the time, was always there to keep me company and helped me be welcomed into the community. The stories he told me about his time going between Ocho Rios and Spanish Town selling hardware provided a lot of insight into street sellers. I owe an enormous debt to these individuals not only as colleagues, but as people who welcomed me into their lives and families.

I would also like to thank the officers and members of the Archaeological Society of Jamaica. Mr. Ainsley Henriques, past president, always showed enthusiasm and support for this project and was instrumental in facilitating its completion both behind the scenes and in the open. I am grateful for the assistance and input provided by members of the faculty of History and Archaeology at the University of West Indies, Mona. Philip Allsworth-Jones and I arrived in Jamaica in 1998 at about the same time. He was instrumental in introducing me to the campus and its various faculty and research centers. I would like to especially thank James Robertson, whose knowledge and wonderful generosity with that knowledge helped me frame the initial questions for this book.

Interdisciplinary projects like these are the result of many people's efforts and assistance. This project could not have been accomplished without the institutional support I have received. I would especially like to thank the departments of Anthropology and Earth Sciences at Syracuse University for the assistance, time, and space provided to me to complete this project. Five people were absolutely critical in their generosity of time, patience with endless drafts, and insightful commentary: Douglas V. Armstrong, Theresa A. Singleton, Christopher R. DeCorse, Susan Wadley, and M. E. Bickford. Douglas Armstrong was one of the first to conduct archaeological research on the African Diaspora through archaeology in a systematic fashion in the Caribbean. He was a constant source of support, experience, and assistance. He was instrumental in providing connections with Jamaican colleagues when I was still quite early in the research, read countless drafts of this manuscript, helped frame the initial project this book is in part based on, and was always there to help provide context for this research with his two decades' worth of experience in Jamaican archaeology. His comments were always on the mark and helped establish a link between previous scholarship and future directions of Caribbean archaeology. Theresa Singleton has provided great insight and guidance for this manuscript. Without lengthy conversations about my research during a field trip to El Cafetal del Padre, I believe I would have taken much longer to complete this study. This trip also gave me a chance to see collections in Cuba that broadened my perspective on issues of local coarse earthenware. I have been exceedingly lucky to have Theresa as a mentor and friend. She has continued to be a source of insight and knowledge. Christopher DeCorse has brought to this project a perspective from West Africa. DeCorse is one of the few scholars to engage and publish research both in the Caribbean and West Africa and as such has framed much of his scholarship in relation to the Diaspora. His nearly thirty years of experience in West African archaeology and historic materials provided insight not only into my research but many others'. Specifically, access to Ghanaian collections and his experience have broadened my understanding of material culture in the Atlantic world. Susan Wadley has been a demanding editor who helped bring clarity to this manuscript from a jumbled set of thoughts. Probably she, more than anybody else, has helped me keep in mind the limitations and strengths of this research. Finally, I would like to thank Pat Bickford, who patiently trained me in mineral identification, optical crystallography, and what they can tell us about the geological conditions in which soils and rocks were formed. Beyond teaching me a technique, he has a wonderful gift for parsimony. As a former editor of a journal, Pat was a demanding reader, erasing jargon with joyful glee. He challenged me to ask more interesting questions and convey them in an economic manner.

I would like to thank the Field Museum of Natural History in Chicago. I owe thanks to John Terrell and Chap Kusimba of the Department of Anthropology. They have graciously provided space and facility support during the final stages of research for this project. I would especially like to thank Antonio Curet. Antonio was constantly pushing me to finish this manuscript and has read numerous drafts. His perceptive questions and expertise in the Caribbean and material analysis were invaluable. His ability to both critique thoroughly and gently show the strengths of a piece have made this a better book.

During the writing of this manuscript the members of the University of Notre Dame Africana Studies Department and Anthropology Department welcomed me into their academic communities. I am grateful to many people there, but most especially to Richard Pierce, Emily Osborn, Deborah Rotman, Mark Schurr, Eric Linland, and Sarah Busdiecker. I would especially like to thank my assistant, Emily Kelly, who managed most of the tedious parts of writing a manuscript: entering references into my citation manager, double-checking the bibliography, locating and organizing permissions from libraries and archives, etc. Without her able assistance I would have been overwhelmed right from the beginning. I was lucky enough to have wonderful colleagues as an instructor at DePaul University, including Anna Agbe Davis and Jane Baxter. John Karam was a wonderful source of conversation, acuity, support, and friendship. Amor Kohli continues to be a wonderful colleague and a source of information and conversation about the African Diaspora. I owe many references and citations to his close reading and listening.

Various colleagues have been generous with their time in reviewing aspects of this manuscript, providing insight, and commenting on larger ideas. Friends and colleagues from my days as a graduate student at Syracuse University have continued to be wonderful colleagues, including Samuel Spiers, Natalie Swanepoel, David Babson, and Heather Gibson. I am deeply indebted to François Richard, who was especially helpful in reviewing manuscripts and kindly suggesting references and points of theoretical departure.

Scholars who work in Jamaica and the broader Caribbean have been generous, including Laurie Wilkie, Jay Haviser, Benoit Bernard, Kofi Agorsah, Candy Goucher, David Watters, Jerry Handler, and the late Jim Petersen. In Jamaica, Matthew Reeves graciously allowed me to use his collection, and his dissertation is a wonderful complement to this book. In many ways his research at Juan de Bollas and Thetford opened up the question that I explore here. I am most grateful to James Delle, who has been a constant source of support and an excellent interlocutor. His work in Jamaica has provided a wonderful context within which this research fits. Kenneth G. Kelly has read numerous drafts of this manuscript and gone through pages and pages of analysis. He has constantly driven me to get past the words and to the point. I would also like to thank the anonymous reviewers of the mansucript. Their comments were insightful and helpful. They have helped me broaden the appeal of this project. I would like to thank the University Press of Florida editor-in-chief, John Byram, who believed in and pursued this project, and Eli Bortz, who organized the reviews and offered an immense amount of support. I also thank the project editor, Michele Fiyak-Burkley, and the copy editor, Lisa Williams, for bringing the manuscript into final form.

Such an interdisciplinary project requires the assistance of many organizations. I received a great deal of assistance in locating information from numerous archives. I would like to specifically thank the following libraries for their assistance in locating images used in the text: the National Library of Jamaica, the New York Public Library, the Smithsonian Institution Anthropology Archives, and the Special Collections of Syracuse University.

Financial support for this project was in part provided by the Graduate School at Syracuse University as well as the Maxwell School of Citizenship. I would also like to thank Christophe Descantes and Michael Glascock for assistance with and the analysis of ceramic materials at the Missouri University Research Reactor (MURR). Operating support for the MURR Archaeometry Laboratory was provided by a grant from the National Science Foundation (BCS-0504015). This research was also supported in part by a grant from the U.S. Department of Energy, Office of Nuclear Energy, Science and Technology Award No. DE-FG07-03ID14531 to the Midwest Nuclear Science and Engineering Consortium under the Innovations in Nuclear Infrastructure and Education program. They kindly agreed to allow me to publish the report from the analysis they conducted in 2004. Illustrations were made using a variety of software. Maps were created with ESRI ArcView GIS 9.3 or Macromedia Freehand MX. Charts and graphs were produced using Gigawiz Aabel 2.0.

Finally, I would like those who have supported me through the years. Steven Hackenberger introduced me to archaeology and the Caribbean in 1992, in Barbados. He has always shown interest in my work even though I chose to go into historical archaeology. I would also like to thank Ann Maxwell-Hill, Susan Feldman, and the late Mary Moser, who were and continue to be wonderful role models. Most important, I would like to thank my family: my parents have been endless fonts of wisdom and my brothers, of practicality. My father, William Hauser, took enormous labors to edit this manuscript. Finally, my greatest gratitude goes to Kalyani Menon, who helped me through the toughest parts and was my best editor, proofreader, critic, and inspiration.

Introduction

In 1831 what came to be known as the Baptist War and is now known as the 1831 emancipation war began at Kingston Pen near Maroon Town. It spread throughout the western parishes of Jamaica, involved, conservatively, 20,000 slaves, and led to the destruction of property valued at nearly £1.2 million (see Turner 1998 and Higman 1998). Its aftermath is depicted in a series of lithographs published by Adolphe Duperly (figure I.1). The images depict the seeming chaos brought about by the war on the stylized and pastoral landscape of plantation Jamaica (discussed in chap. 2). Of considerable interest is the manner in which this rebellion was organized. As one of the last rebellions in the Anglophone Caribbean in which enslaved laborers participated, it highlights one of the great ironies of slave-holding Jamaica. Historian Barry Higman (1998) has noted that it was led by slaves who had accumulated a degree of economic and symbolic capital (227). While the enslaved were dispossessed of property, the very success of the plantation economy depended on the enslaved amassing material wealth (2) that ultimately put the planters at financial and political risk.

Likewise, the war could also be read as one of the first great labor uprisings in Jamaica (Turner 1998: 149; Delle forthcoming). There has been a considerable amount of scholarship demonstrating the role that independent production had in fomenting political risk, and how that production was facilitated by the ways in which planters organized labor (Higman 1986b, 1987, 1988, 1996, 1998: 2, 2002, 2005; Trouillot 1988: 376; Berlin and Morgan 1995; Morgan 1995, 1998: 219, 2002; Burnard 2004: 143; Eggerton 2006).[1] In the case of the 1831 emancipation war, in contemporary accounts as well as in historiography, the ability of the enslaved to organize the rebellion was attributed to a confluence of secret trails connecting neighboring plantations; a network of sectarian churches with their provision of space

---

1   This scholarship has also pointed out one crucial irony: while production enabled the enslaved to garner a degree of economic independence, after emancipation access to the provision was contingent on laboring on plantations where laborers were formerly enslaved (see Mintz [1974] 1992; Craton 1985: 128; Turner 1995; Marshall 2003).

Figure I.1. *The Destruction of Roehamton* [Roehampton] *Estate in the Parish of St. James in January 1832* by Adolphe Duperly. The image copies a landscape by James Hakewill in his *A Picturesque Tour of the Island of Jamaica* (1825). Lithographer Duperly, after the 1831–1832 uprising, published this image along with a similar rendition of Montpelier estate in 1833. Courtesy of the National Library of Jamaica.

for proselytizing by lay ministers such as Sam Sharpe, and missionaries acting as "agents provocateurs" (Turner 1998: 153); and a system of street markets in which information could be passed. In this book, I focus on this system of Sunday street markets and explore the temporal and spatial boundaries of its reach.

For the enslaved and freed peoples of African descent in Jamaica, the street markets were part of the indeterminacies of everyday life in which they were able to feed themselves, accumulate cash and material wealth, and pass and exchange news, gossip, and information. As a system of provisioning, the ancillary economic activities of the enslaved through these markets were vital in maintaining the economic viability of the plantation. Though embedded in the economic and political structures of plantation Jamaica, the markets were loci of resistance, places in which the self was refashioned, and arenas for the emergence of social networks in which communities developed. These communities went beyond and transgressed the boundaries imposed on enslaved life by the plantation regime. It is because of these three factors that I call these everyday economic practices of the enslaved black markets.

Approaching Limits and Constraints on Diaspora Archaeology

The archaeology of black markets is important to understanding the existence and scale of informal systems of trade and exchange in Jamaica from the seventeenth to the nineteenth century. The phrase "black markets" has several implied meanings. It is a loaded term that quickly brings to mind informal if not surreptitious markets. In this context, it applies to systems of production and exchange of materials generated by African Jamaicans sometimes eluding the gaze of the planters. Archaeological examination of things produced, sold, and exchanged through this economy provides a mechanism by which we can examine how people actively used the markets to transform their lives and create social networks in response to highly structured plantation life. On the one hand, the ancillary economic activities of the enslaved were "rooted" in the plantation systems of the Atlantic world. On the other hand, these activities mapped "routes" of potentially transgressive networks of information and exchange. It is, therefore, also an implicit reference to Robert Ferris Thompson's *Flash of the Spirit* (1984) and Paul Gilroy's *Black Atlantic* (1993) as well as an attempt to untangle the "roots" and "routes" in the historical archaeology of the African Diaspora in the Caribbean.[2]

Gilroy provides us with the metaphor of the ship as a way to get at the movement of ideas and the connection of separated peoples. This leaves us asking the question: How do these abstract movements get embodied on the ground? An assumption of African Diaspora archaeology has been that there is a materiality behind the metaphor. Tracing this materiality is a challenging task, where the focus on social relations leaves open the tendency,

---

2 Paul Gilroy's *The Black Atlantic* (1993) sought to "decent[er] African-American narratives, bringing the Caribbean, Britain, and Europe into the picture" (Clifford 1994: 316), by exploring alternatives to anticolonial nationalist or pan-African perspectives on the one hand, and antinationalist postcolonial accounts of global contexts on the other. Crystallized in a short article on Diaspora (Gilroy 1994), Gilroy's focus was one that attempted to fix in time and space the flows of ideas throughout the Atlantic world and demonstrate the impact people of African descent had on European modernity. There are critiques, however. Jonathan Friedman (2002) has gone as far as to say that relying on such metaphors has, in practice, moved the discussion away from the enormous tragedy imposed by emergent global capital.

in the words of Bertell Ollman (1993), "to move too quickly to the bottom line, to push the germ of development to its finished form" (17). Without a doubt, the use of Gilroy's Black Atlantic to understand the eighteenth-century Caribbean could be an anachronism that displays the tendency Ollman is warning against. However, Gilroy's method of analysis is extremely salient in that his research does three things. First, it decenters traditional units of analysis where modernity is no longer a uniquely European phenomenon. Second, it plays with scale where temporal and spatial margins of past actors extend beyond boundaries imposed by historically defined slots. Finally, it focuses on mobility of individuals and ideas that they carry with them. My use of Gilroy is not an attempt to trace the roots of the Black Atlantic or even to verify its presence in the past. Rather, beginning with utilitarian clay pots (*yabbas*[3]), I try to demonstrate the links between archaeology and history in helping us to write narrative of Jamaica's past. The clay pots, their making, their use, and their sale, were part of the everyday. Sale of the pottery was not illegal, nor diabolical. Yet, just because the pottery itself was unassuming does not mean it was not exceptional. I view this pottery as a durable expression of the social relations that the enslaved created and operated within. The pottery can be a venue into the cultural experiences of enslaved Jamaicans, the scales of its expression, and the historical forces that shaped it.

The title *An Archaeology of Black Markets* is both ambiguous and patently clear, for just as the markets were selectively known or ignored, the people who participated in them were selectively known and ignored. Michel-Rolph Trouillot (1995) notes that the processes underlying the construction and interpretation of history highlight three distinct realms of human capacity, those of agent, actor, and subject (23). Agents occupy structural positions, and in the case of the eighteenth-century Caribbean, this must be configured in light of slavery and emergent capitalism. Actors are in a constant interface with a historical and social context. Indeed, this study had to be framed very specifically (13–14). Chronologically, it examines the period between 1694 and 1807 and, socially, focuses on the particularities of the Jamaican planters. Subjects are those with the ability to define the terms under which situations can be described (14). It is in this 1831 rebel-

---

3   I refer to *yabba* as both a type and a form. This is consistent with the way that people spoke about Jamaican-made ceramics in general. The form refers to a restricted bowl; the type, a coarse, hand-made, low-fired Jamaican ceramic. Unless referenced as a form, the term *yabba* is implicitly referring to the broader category of Jamaican-made ceramics.

lion, discussed above, where some of the enslaved began to define terms under which their enslaved life could be described.

In order to untangle these realms one must look at, or toward, the silences in historical production and develop methods of reading beyond the text into the various subjectivities of the people whose lives we wish to know a little bit more about (Cohn 1996; Comaroff and Comaroff 1992; Comaroff 1996). Archaeology, with its specific focus on those things that are residues of everyday life, allows us to reshape the historical process to include those subjects of the documentary record that are normally left silent (Little 1994). Note, however, that in Trouillot this process must go hand-in-hand with a simultaneous decentering of historical metanarratives. This supplemental move is what enables us to transcend silences in the domains of narrative and lived history, to shed "alternative" light on the past. Following cues from Ann Stahl (1999, 2001) and Martin Hall (2000), I translate these ideas into the archaeological realm by specifically focusing on the contradictions and ironies implicit in the documentary record and archaeological context. The ability of the enslaved to accumulate material wealth through their own independent production is one such irony.

When conducting research on those who have been silenced in the historical record, we must be wary of imposing contemporary or anachronistic analytical frames on the past. Frederick Cooper (2005) warns that in conducting historical research, we must not do it backward, that is, employing anachronistic concepts and constructs as lenses or frameworks past peoples employed. By applying questions rooted in a specific historicity but applied out of context, we effectively run the risk of describing historical forces ahistorically. Rather, Cooper calls for research with a focus on actors whose everyday life is grounded in symbolically informed socially contingent realities. David Scott, in *Conscripts of Modernity* (2004b), criticizes scholars for providing new answers to old questions and concerns instead of actively seeking to redefine the "problem spaces" of history and identity. Historical archaeology is not immune to these old questions (Stahl 2001: 36). The search for antecedent communities in West Africa through the lens of "colonoware" or "Afrocaribbean Ware" is one such question. While an important goal, it is probably not best accomplished through the lens of utilitarian ceramics. Rather, asking what those utilitarian ceramics can tell us about the economic and social lives of those who made and used them presents a much more compelling fit. A shift of analytical focus to the social lives of things presents its own limitations.

Material culture introduces its own kind of silences (Morrison and Lycett

1997; Cobb 2005) because of the sometimes arbitrary nature implicit in the exercises of classification and interpretation. Indeed, theories of historical narrative like those discussed by Trouillot are not alleviated by the inclusion of material culture; rather, they are complicated by such encounters (Trigger 1980, 1981; Thomas 1991; McGuire 1992; Schmidt and Patterson 1995; Stahl 1999, 2001; Thomas 2000; Schmidt 2006). Archaeologically, the primary problem faced in studying black markets is using material culture to define the muddy and ambiguous distinction between informal and formal (or to redefine the terms of the so-called boundary). Informal economies by their very nature are archaeologically ephemeral, especially if we rely on a definition that emphasizes the transgressive potential of the interactions in relation to a larger economic landscape with symbolic and structural manifestations. There is no easy way to tease from material culture that the sale of objects between two enslaved laborers was potentially dangerous to the plantation on which it occurred or the fact that they were sold on the market square on Saturday rather than Sunday was illegal. Rather, we as archaeologists have to focus on the end results of these informal economies, whether in the distribution of artifacts where they should not be, or the organization of a slave rebellion.

This brings up the final limitation of archaeological analyses of black markets: their participants. In the end, the archaeological pitfall of abstracting beyond the actual people you are interested in learning about is ever present in the analysis of poorly documented institutions in slave society. We can define the participants so broadly as to include all inhabitants of the island, including plantation and administrative elite. However, this would minimize the historical realities of everyday life in Jamaica. On the other hand, we can define participants with so narrow a set of parameters as to make the markets nothing more than functional byproducts of the society itself. In either case, the background perspective and agenda of the interpreter are from the outset crucial in laying out the framework through which the data are analyzed (Franklin 1997a and 1997b; Wilkie 2003; Beaudry 2008).

The participants should be defined relative to one another through relationships of power, but also through the shared sets of meanings that actions in the market drew out. In many ways, we can define who the participants were not. For those that relied on the highly centralized economic model of the plantation, the black markets and the participants were "inappropriate elements" (Douglas 1966) on the orderly and economically productive landscapes of the sugar islands. Their definition of participation is one of opposition, but not necessarily of criminality. Janet Roitman examined the vernacular imaginations of criminality and morality and showed (2004) how economic transactions in the margins create their own pressures on colonial forms of knowledge, which, in turn, help to define and redefine what is perceived as legal or illegal. In many ways, participation in the markets of Jamaica required knowledge of the rules that governed its operation and the maintenance of informal social networks that facilitated exchange. At the center of these networks were higglers: itinerant country peddlers. What is known about these higglers is that they generally were women of African descent. What is also generally known is that whether they were free or unfree, they enjoyed a considerable degree of mobility, a mobility that can be gleaned from their silence in the documentary record.

The archaeological residues of this trade and these traders are found in the things that the enslaved made and the things that they sold. Much of the independent production of the enslaved focused on foodstuffs and wares (baskets and calabashes) that decompose readily in the tropical soils of Jamaica. The picture we get, therefore, is partial, a necessarily biased sample of the commodities the enslaved made and used. Neither divorced from the larger market systems nor merely serving immediate and pragmatic needs, both local pottery and the local economy were tied together. They represent how communities developed and were transformed during the plantation period. An underlying network of economic and social relationships connecting the urban and the rural, the free and the enslaved, the white and the black characterized the local economy. Local pottery represents one of many goods produced with knowledge derived from West Africa and Europe. These semi-industrialized products were then sold at markets and distributed across the island. The enslaved and freed populations involved in local pottery production and distribution demonstrate skills and knowledge of both manufacture and marketing brought from West Africa. Nevertheless, the populations had to adapt these skills to their new social and geographic contexts. The resulting pottery and manufacturing systems are thus unique to Jamaica in the eighteenth century in terms of the specifics of historical, cultural, and geological contexts of Jamaica.

In this particular research, I focus on one of the few archaeological remnants that were manufactured and used by the people I am interested in learning about. Yabbas, a local Jamaican ceramic, were made by peoples of African descent; were used by peoples of African descent; were sold in the markets; and, most important, are archaeologically visible. As such yabbas can provide a reflection of how and whether people expressed their identities in material culture, and how this changed over time. To retrieve and understand the social coordinates of ceramic political economy in Jamaica, material culture must be viewed not only as a residue of everyday life, but also as a unit of analysis. As a commodity, it certainly has its biographies, but those biographies gain clarity only in the context of the life histories of the people who made them, traded them, and used them. In Jamaica the institution framing material transactions among the enslaved was the local market system, and the primary participants of this system were higglers, itinerant peddlers of African descent.

There are numerous books about pots and people (Shepard 1954; Rouse 1964, 1992; Kroeber 1916; Hill 1970; Longacre 1970, 1991; Plog 1980; Howard and Morris 1981; Peacock 1982; Sweezy 1984; Arnold 1985, 1993; Krause 1985; Miller 1985; Rice 1988; Zug 1986; Sinopoli 1988; Vlach 1990; Arnold 1991; Ferguson 1992; Skibo 1992). Ceramics have been one of the major materials used to identify and interpret past behavior. This use is, in part, a result of the plasticity and durability of ceramics as forms of material culture. Their value also stems from what ceramics can tell us about the political economy of past societies in very discrete loci and broad regions. Assemblages associated with eighteenth-century occupations in Jamaica are rich in materials, including ceramics (both local and imported), glass, metals, shell, pipe, etc. Such assemblages are hardly unique to Jamaica or the eighteenth century. The emergent globalization in trade and the centralized production of commodities in a relatively small number of cities make such artifact collections an ubiquitous element in any British settlement in the eighteenth century.

Likewise, a book that explores the transgressive potential of informal and everyday practices is far from new (Scott 1985; Bush 1990; Hall 2000; Browne 2004). States have public discourses, which can be both overt and subtle, which act to make explicit and normalize the social inequality implicit within the society (Foucault 1972; Scott 1985, 1992; Hall 2000: 16). As a manner of subversion, groups disenfranchised from this public discourse enact everyday forms of resistance (see Scott 1985). People on the margin exploit the structural inconsistencies and interstices of society in order to gain respite (if temporary) from the dominant themes of power and control. In highly structured social milieus, such as the plantation in eighteenth-century slave societies, order and power become centralizing concepts in maintaining control over a subservient and subaltern population (Goveia 1965, 1980, [1960] 1991; Patterson 1969, 1982; Dunn 1972, 1993; Bush 1981; Delle 1998, 1999, 2000b; Paton 2001). Bridget Brereton (1999) argues that these technologies have also shaped the archives and our understanding of Caribbean women (see Bush 1981, 1990, 1996; Reddock 1985, 1988; Paton 1996).

Planters, through the apparatus of colonial government, manipulation of organized living and working space, and some economic maneuvering, vied to control and discipline the everyday life of the laborers. In his influential study *Sweetness and Power* (1985), Sidney Mintz focuses on the ways in which planters and merchants tied to the sugar industry shaped both the consumption and the production of sugar (see also Austin and Smith 1992). While in Great Britain merchants were disciplining the consumption of sugar by processing it in ways to make it more appealing for the nascent working class, planters were disciplining enslaved laborers to create the raw materials of its production. This discipline imbued all parts of plantation society, from the industrial sugar works of a society to the independent production of the enslaved. But how effective was this disciplining? In what ways did the colonial regimes, as expressed in the legal codes, and their interpretation by planters and visitors extend to the actual practice of the enslaved?

As many have noted, the internal economy was a locus of independent acquisition, marketing, and production among the enslaved (Hall 1977, 1980, 1985, 1994; Bush 1981, 1990; 1996 Simmonds 1987, 2004; Beckles 1989a, 1989b, 1991, 1995, 1999; Tomich, 1993, 1994; Boa 1993; see the volume edited by Gaspar and Hine 1996; Hall 1999). This economy also presaged a Caribbean peasantry rooted in the houseyard and market (Hall 1959; Mintz [1974] 1992; Craton 1982; Trouillot 1988). The independent production by enslaved laborers on provision grounds and the exchange of those goods were activities on the margins of the planters' figurative and material control (Pulsipher 1990, 1991, 1994; McKee 1999; Pulsipher and Goodwin 1999).

In this way, the markets could be viewed as "a symbolic offensive against the established order" (Beckles 1991: 32) inhabited by "fettered entrepreneurs" practicing a nacent and alternate form of capitalism (35) (see also Beckles 1989b, 1991, 1995). Consequently, the informal markets as a meeting place of enslaved goods and ideas can be viewed as a locus of interaction where the enslaved could transgress the social and geographic boundaries imposed by the plantation.

It is important to keep in mind Sidney Mintz's admonition that "slaves who plotted armed revolts in the marketplaces had first to produce for the market, and to gain permission to carry their produce there" (Mintz

1971b: 321). The markets were not pure negation of the economic realms with which they intersected. Rather the markets were a space where people caught in the indeterminacies of everyday life forged and broke friendships; created solidarities and expressed rivalries; and finally, on occasion, organized armed resistance.

In the end, what makes this book about pots and people unique is that it is about how Africans uprooted from their places of origin and brought to the Caribbean adapted to and transformed the landscape around them using knowledge and skills they brought with them, and then passed the knowledge on to their children. The documentary record, while providing a point of departure into an analysis of slave society, is written from the context of elites. In studying pottery—specifically, the coarse earthenware of the African Diaspora—we have one of the few forms of material evidence that reveals the production, exchange and consumption of enslaved African workers. It is a testimony to their knowledges and practices, written not in texts or elite discourse, but in deeds and clay. Coarse earthenware is, in short, one of the few forms of material culture made and used by the enslaved that survives, in partial form, the archaeological record. It is a lens through which we can see, at least partially, the ways in which a displaced and colonized peoples refashioned familiar ways of doing things in unfamiliar contexts.

Organization of the Book

In the first chapter of this book, I discuss theoretical and historical literatures that have influenced not only the formation of my question, but also the manner through which I attempted to answer it. As with any study of the African Diaspora in the West Indies, one must take into account the large literature in both history and anthropology that examines the intersection between political economy, power, embodiment, and identity. Though I do not dismiss economically oriented histories of the Diaspora, I question the degree to which specific moments, key to economic narratives of Caribbean history, shaped the everyday life of the enslaved. Indeed, central to understanding the Caribbean is the necessity to operate simultaneously at multiple scales of analysis, where global processes, often mistakenly glossed as European modernity, are put in tension with local particularities, often shorthanded as creolization (Orser 1996). The internal market system embodies one such locality but also informs us about how that locality is constantly negotiated.

In chapter 2, I explore both the present literature on the internal markets associated with the African Diaspora and attempt to position the eighteenth-century Jamaican markets within the broad theoretical framework I develop. I suggest that comparing the scales of the economic interactions of the planters with those of enslaved laborers will reveal the degree to which the economic lives of enslaved laborers were impacted by the external economy. The planters leave us a template of an internal economy, which is localized in scale (i.e., between contiguous or neighboring plantations) and is aimed at meeting only those island contingencies that are immediate to the plantation. Since the markets were informal, there is little documentation of their existence, much less the daily routines and commodity flows that orchestrated their operation. What archival evidence we do have comes from a very narrow class of inhabitants. Planters' accounts, slave laws, and newspaper advertisements indicate that at least from the elites' perspective, the independent economic interactions of the enslaved were similarly configured. Because of its focus on material culture and distribution, I employed archaeology to determine this economy's extent and therefore the social relations of this community.

In chapter 3, I explain the historical reasons for confining my study to the eighteenth century and describe the sites from which I draw my study sample. To understand the extent to which enslaved laborers shaped their world, I suggest that understanding the flow of commodities through the internally articulated market systems is crucial. I discuss seven sites—Old Naval Dockyard, St. Peter's Church, Old King's House, Juan de Bollas, Thetford, Seville, and Drax Hall—and isolated eighteenth-century contexts on each of the sites based on associated imported goods. The sites I examine represent both urban and rural milieus and include locations on both the north and the south coasts of Jamaica.

Chapter 4 introduces the material through which I analyze the extent of market relations among the enslaved population of Jamaica. Local coarse earthenware, because it is locally produced and consumed, offers an excellent medium for examining the social relations structuring informal market settings. In this chapter, I briefly summarize the latest research on local earthenwares in the region and suggest an alternative approach. Whereas this material has traditionally been studied as a marker of ethnic or cultural identity, I suggest that it is also the residue of a market system, wherein lie its greatest interpretive insights. This is not to suggest that pottery distributions will map the entirety of the markets or even indicate their complexity. From the documentary record, we know that the markets oversaw the sale of numerous goods and commodities, for which different strategies of distribution could have existed. Most of these goods, however, do not survive the archaeological record. By contrast, pottery is a relatively resistant form of material culture which can supply important hints to the extent of the markets.

In chapter 5, I provide an examination of pottery production in Jamaica over time. This discussion highlights the fluidity of vessel forms and types between the seventeenth and twentieth centuries but also demonstrates how specific types present in the archaeological record display a degree of continuity in form and manufacture. Such discernment is important in understanding the ways in which craft production in colonial Jamaica was organized.

In chapter 6, I explore more thoroughly the potential location of pottery craft production in Jamaica during the eighteenth century. I accomplish this by focusing on ceramic petrography to identify potential clay sources of manufacture and to assess the relative heterogeneity or homogeneity of the ceramics' composition. In turn, such findings can shed light on the scale and intensity of production and distribution of this pottery.

In the epilogue, I examine the significance of my findings. The contribution of this study is twofold. First, it gives depth to our historical understanding of the economic lives of enslaved laborers during the eighteenth century. It shows that enslaved laborers did indeed construct their own economic worlds. Second, it calls into question the totality of colonial regimes of control on slave communities in Jamaica. Certainly, the plantation as an extension of the global economy created the context for the markets. They were also social events with a materiality, and the degree to which slaves created and transformed their own social relationships can be gleaned from a juxtaposition of the ways in which planting elite and administrators wrote about the markets and an analysis of the commodities which traversed the island's economic circuits. There is an irony implicit in the street markets of eighteenth-century Jamaica. On the one hand, it was a necessary complement to the plantation economy in which the planter was doubly subsidized by the slaves' labor to produce export commodities and foodstuffs. In this case, the markets facilitated the provisioning of the enslaved. On the other hand, the markets facilitated the accumulation of material and social capital among the enslaved, providing loci of resistance, enabling a refashioning of self, and setting aside an arena for social networks to develop.

1

Historical Archaeology of the Caribbean Plantation

> The manufacturer, the artisan, and the mechanic, cannot be said to enjoy their leisure; for these must work to ward off famine; and if they take but one day in the week, excepting Sunday, to themselves, it is considered as theft upon their families. . . . The occupations of the negro are not so unremitting; and seven months in the year at least, before six o'clock in the morning, and after seven at night, his personal attendance is seldom required, and it is of course dispensed with. He has every Sunday throughout the year to himself, every other Saturday out of crop, two or three days at Christmas, many day in rainy seasons.
> Beckford 1790 2: 137.

A major facet of American historical archaeology is its focus on "complex societies," especially in the context of European expansion, colonialism, and economic hegemony. Studies of colonial elites in North America have highlighted the monumental architecture along with the symbolic role the organization of space has in supporting and imparting concomitant ideologies (Leone 1984, 1988, 1995; Yentsch, Beaudry, and Deetz 1992; Yentsch 1994). Also, many have noted that while the discipline of historical archaeology can include multiple methodological and theoretical perspectives, its practice within the American context has been to focus on the spread and impact of Europeans, their institutions and practices, on colonized and colonizing peoples in other parts of the world (Deetz 1977, 1996; Posnansky 1984; Schrire 1988; DeCorse 1990, 1996, 2001a; Singleton 1990, 1995, 1998, 2001, 2006; Yentsch, Beaudry, and Deetz 1992; Schmidt and Patterson 1995a, 1995b; Orser 1996; Hall 2000; Mullins and Paynter 2000; Kelly 2004; Schmidt 2006). There are broad analogues between American historical archaeology and the archaeologies of "complex societies," empires, and states as described and practiced by a number of scholars working from varied methodological, theoretical, and area interests (Brumfiel and Earle 1987; D'Altroy 1987, 1992; Brumfiel 1994, 2003; Sinopoli 1994a, 1994b, 2003; Sinopoli and Morrison 1995; Muller 1997; Patterson 1999; D'Altroy and Hastorf 2001; Meskell 2002a, 2002b; Stein 2002, 2005; Smith 2003; Pauketat 2004).

What has made historical archaeology in the Americas such a fertile ground for scholarship is its focus on the social "actors" (Johnson 1989, 1996; Wilkie, 2000a, 2000b; Hall 2000; Wilkie and Bartoy 2000; Silliman 2001; Lightfoot 2005; Voss 2005) as individuals who simultaneously are shaped by and shape a constantly emerging historical context. To be certain, this topic has not been the sole province of American historical archaeology (Dobres and Hoffman 1994; Meskell 1999; Dobres 2000; Dobres and Robb 2000; Pauketat 2000, 2004). The depth and access to the documentary record have enabled scholars working on the rise of the modern period to approach (but not fully realize) intentions of select, oftentimes elite, social actors. As John Terrell pointed out (Terrell 2006), this has led historical archaeologists to engage in three questions which have placed them between and within archaeology and historical anthropology: How do we know what we know; whose history are we actually engaging in; and, more germane, what is history?

The historical archaeologies of the Caribbean are varied in topic and approach. Indeed, trying to place bookends and brackets around where and when the colonial Caribbean exactly is located and begins becomes a task involving extension, generalization, and vantage point (see Ollman 1993 for a discussion of abstraction and Wurst 1999 for its utility in historical archaeology). This is in part because of the centrality of the Caribbean in European colonial designs. The Caribbean was Spain's first beachhead in the Americas. Port cities like Port Royal and Bridgetown were cosmopolitan centers for Anglophone America (Zahedieh 1986a: 570; 1994; 2002). It was a place of enormous wealth production for the royal coffers and merchant capitalism. Indeed, it is important to note that Adam Smith's *Wealth of Nations* was as much a reaction to wealth infused from Caribbean industry as commodity production in Great Britain (Zahedieh 1986b; Williams 1994: 4; Smith [1776] 1994: 136–48, 185, 242, 546–81). Finally, and probably most important for many scholars, it was the site of human tragedy that ensued after European colonization, that is, the devastation of indigenous populations due to forced labor and disease, and the subsequent abduction and transportation of Africans to the Caribbean.

Looking beyond the institution of slavery and predatory capitalism as determining Caribbean creole identities, Laurie Wilkie and Paul Farnsworth (1999, 2005) rightly identify the need for multiscalar approaches to the archaeology of the Caribbean plantation. Wilkie and Farnsworth draw on both Anthony Giddens's (1981: 523; 1979: 61) and Pierre Bourdieu's (1977: 82–86) construction of scale, which place agent and social structure in constant tension. Specifically, they use material culture as a way to render visible the social forces behind regional and oceanic commodity chains and center the intimate everyday activities and choices community members make. Through markets, enslaved Africans on Providence Island actively consume material culture, which in turn shaped their everyday life and helped form a community identity (Wilkie and Farnsworth 1999).

Their research follows a methodological cue from George Marcus' multisited ethnography (Marcus and Myers 1995; Marcus 1998). Methodologically, this approach "designed around chains, paths, threads, conjunctions, or juxtaposition of locations" (Marcus 1998: 23) can become overly cumbersome for the ethnographer (Clarke 2004). As historian Frederick Cooper points out, it potentially leads to "story plucking, leapfrogging legacies, doing history backward, and the epochal fallacy" (2005: 17). It can become especially problematic for the archaeologist where the depth of interpretation that has become the hallmark of historical archaeology is sacrificed for potentially more shallow comparative analysis. In such analysis, the people we are most interested in learning about become nothing more than the agents of abstracted flows. Indeed, if we are to have an "actor up" approach to the archaeology of the African Diaspora, greater attention needs to be placed on the ways in which we specifically define the local, the regional, and the global (or indeed the relevance of these spatialities or fields of spatial experience). Indeed, examining nested scales of material interaction allows us to move beyond the simple dichotomies of the former as a grounded reality, and the latter as a rootless abstraction (see Mbembe 2002 for a discussion of the need to rethink temporalities/spatialities).

For convenience' sake historians and archaeologists alike have used certain moments in history as mile markers or events through which to create epochal periods of believed social stasis. These events include (going backward) independence in the 1960s, emancipation (occurring anywhere between 1838 and 1882), the abolition of the Atlantic trade in Africans (1807), the Haitian Revolution (1791–1804), the American Revolution (1776–1783), the War of Spanish Succession (1701–1713), Northern European entrance into the Caribbean milieu (first and second quarters of the seventeenth century), and, probably most well known, the Spanish Conquest (1492–1504). But how important were these "global" events in shaping everyday lives of actors in Caribbean communities? This seems to be the question that historical archaeologists in the Caribbean constantly refer back to.

A Brief Background on Jamaica

At just over 4,200 square miles, Jamaica is the third-largest Caribbean island. It is situated south of Cuba and west of Haiti and the Dominican Republic (map 1.1). Like other Greater Antillean islands, the geological origin of the island is complex, leading to a diverse physical geography (map 1.2). This geography, including littoral and alluvial plains, large morasses and mountainous expanses, proved fertile ground for emergent agro-industry such as sugar, coffee, indigo, and provisioning (Shepherd 1993; Higman 1996, 1998, 2002; Shepherd 2002; Shepherd and Monteith 2002; Smith 2002; Higman 2005). Because much of the land, in comparison to Barbados, remained unutilized by agro-industry, the topography also provided interstitial spaces that were exploited by planters, enslaved laborers, and maroons. The markets are one such interstitial space.

Originally occupied by Western Tainos, the island was settled by the Spanish after Columbus landed somewhere on the north coast in 1493 during his second voyage to the Caribbean. The Spanish mostly used the island as a provisioning station for providing fresh water, cured pork, and a starchy bread for galleons on the journey between Spain and Panama (Cundall and Pietersz 1919). In 1655, an English force led by Admiral Penn and General Venables took control of what they considered an underuti-

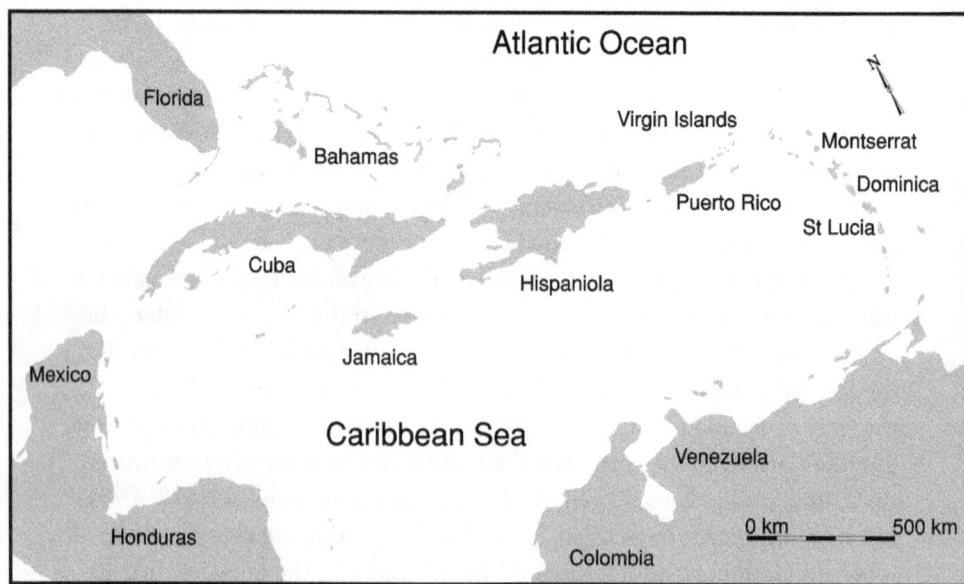

Map 1.1. The Caribbean region—islands discussed in the text, labeled. Illustration by Author.

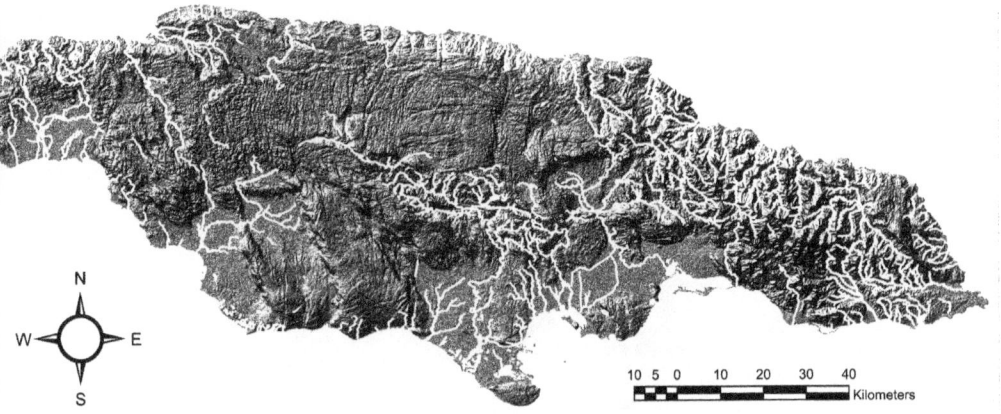

Map 1.2. Topography and rivers of Jamaica. Hillshade calculated using ArcView GIS 8.3, ESRI©, and Global Digital Elevation Model (SRTM), ESRI©. Illustration by Author.

lized Spanish colony, and by the seventeenth century, Jamaica had become the Crown's most valuable possession overseas (Taylor 1965). What made Jamaica, along with the rest of the British West Indian colonies, so important to Britain was the production of staple products like cotton, indigo, and sugar, which placed Britain at the center of the world's economy (for reference to site locations see map 1.3).

To be sure, slavery began almost as soon as Europeans colonized the West Indies. It is important to note, however, that the institution of slavery practiced in the sixteenth century bore only a superficial resemblance to the scale and magnitude of slavery which would occur two hundred years later. On Columbus's second voyage in 1493, Europeans first came into contact with the Western Tainos of Jamaica (Woodward 2006b). Both forced labor under the Spanish and disease contracted from Europeans devastated the populations of Tainos in the Greater Antilles. On Hispaniola (map 1.1) ethnohistorical and archaeological work conducted by Samuel Wilson (Wilson 1990, 1993), Kathleen Deagan and Jose Cruxent (Deagan 1995; Deagan and Cruxent 2002a, 2002b) and Charles Ewen (Ewen 2000) have demonstrated the complexities of interaction between different Tainos polities and European encroachers. Indigenes were forced to work in the gold fields of Cuba and Hispaniola (Rouse 1992: 157). In addition to forced labor, disease also contributed to the massive disappearance of Jamaica's indigenous population (Cook and Borah 1971a, 1971b; Rigau-Perez 1982; Wilson 1990, 1993;

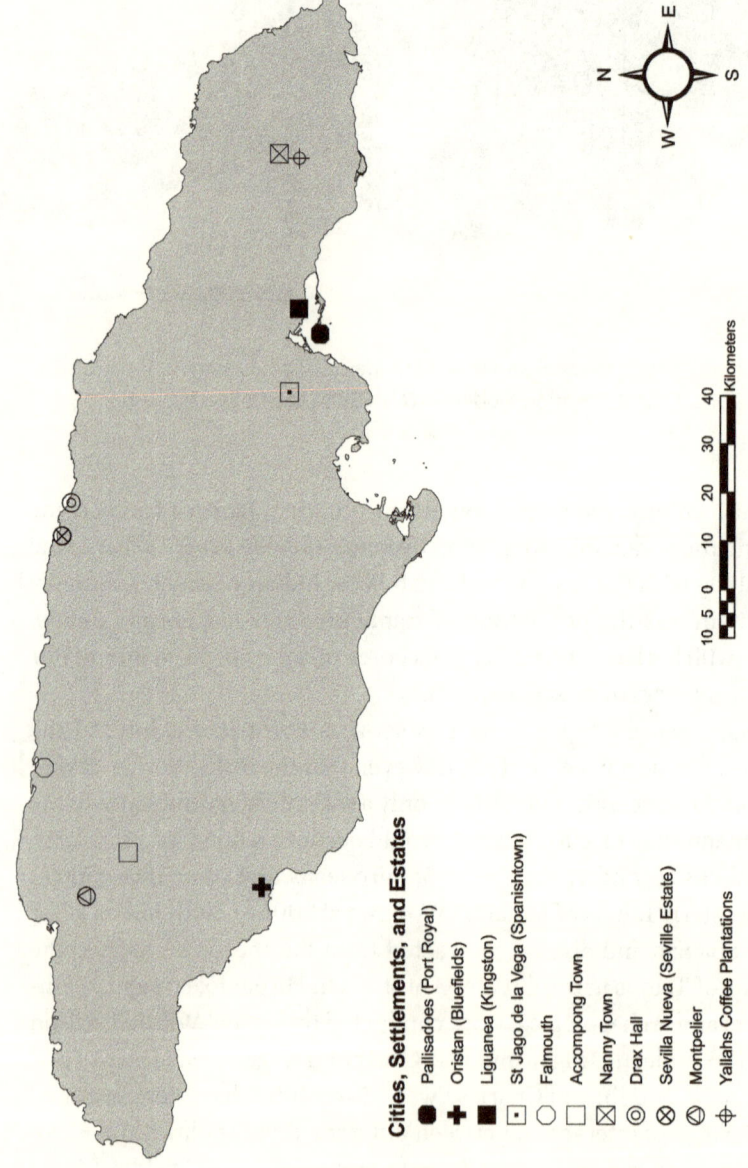

Map 1.3. Location of Jamaican cities, settlements, and estates described in text. Illustration by Author.

Kiple and Kiple 1991; Kiple and Ornelas 1996; Cunningham 1997; Cook 1998).

Rather than being a single polity or people, it is important to realize, those individuals who greeted Columbus and were to be the first colonial subjects of Europe in the Americas were a socially and politically diverse people (Wilson 1990, 1993). Consequently, we have to be careful about how we use the early chronicles of colonization, and be wary of simplistic portrayals of the indigenous people of the Caribbean (Curet 2002). Certainly, the role that the indigenous people had in shaping this Caribbean island in particular and other island societies in general cannot be underestimated. These early interactions, however, are also some of the most poorly documented archaeologically. Our knowledge of the fifteenth century, from an archaeological point of view, has been restricted to the work of a few notable scholars (Deagan 1995; Deagan and Cruxent 2002a, 2002b; Ewen 1990a, 1990b; McEwan 1995; Reitz and McEwan 1995) on Hispaniola and Jamaica (Parrent et al. 1991; Parrent and Parrent 1993; Woodward 1988; 2006a, 2006b). It has invariably focused on the complex interaction among European, African, and indigenous peoples.

The complexity of these interactions has been hinted at by Kathleen Deagan and her students' research at Puerto Real in Haiti (Deagan 1995; Ewen 1990a, 1990b; McEwan 1995; Reitz and McEwan 1995). The investigation of Puerto Real was inspired by Dr. William Hodges, an amateur archaeologist who discovered the site and encouraged its archaeological investigation (Hodges 1995). The project identified the site of the first Spanish settlement in the Americas as well as the nearby site of En Bas Saline (Deagan 1995). The Puerto Real study is an important source of information on early Spanish attempts at settling in the New World. The settlement at Puerto Real was short-lived but important in terms of understanding both the early period of European presence in the New World and the nature of the encounter of three culture areas—indigenous Americans, Africans, and Europeans—and the early development of multicultural identities (Deagan 1995: 455–56).

After Puerto Real, Deagan turned to La Isabela. The archaeological investigation of La Isabella provided an in-depth examination of the first successful colonial European settlement in the Americas (Deagan and Cruxent 2002a, 2002b; see Pantel et al. 1988 for studies of early Spanish colonial sites in Puerto Rico). This study chronicles the details of life and death in an early colonial settlement and addresses issues ranging from house and settlement design to diet and material use. While inspired by the five-hundredth-anniversary observances, Deagan and Cruxent used a combination of archaeological explorations and historical accounts to tell the story not only of the European settlers but also of the social and economic systems that were created and the conditions faced by indigenous and colonist. Columbus had modeled the settlement's economic structure on the *factoría* system and set it up to be a trading center of colonists who would be supported economically through trade with indigenous populations in the region. The study identified the presence of the satellite settlement at Las Coles. This site, located a little more than 1.5 kilometers from La Isabela, included a series of structures including mills and industrial works, and suggests the presence of a complex of sites that provide a more comprehensive understanding of the settlement than had been previously known. The presence of this site also suggests that the selection of La Isabella and related settlement areas was consistent with historic records projecting their economic objectives. The spatial layout of the site is one of its most interesting aspects. Rather than conforming to expectations of a Spanish grid pattern, the town emphasized fortification from external threats (from the indigenous population) and made use of existing geographic and cultural features in the landscape to project authority. Deagan and Cruxent suggest that this town layout is consistent with the Italian architect Francesco di Giorgio Martini (Deagan and Cruxent 2002b).

From an archaeological perspective, very little is known of this early period of contact in Jamaica (Goodwin 1940, 1946; Cotter 1948, 1953, 1964, 1970; Osborne 1974; Woodward 1988, 2006a, 2006b). In the fifteenth century there were three major settlements in Jamaica: Sevilla Nueva, Oristan, and St. Jago de la Vega. During this time, two places in Jamaica were marginally engaged in several plantations growing either sugar or indigo: Oristan and Sevilla Nueva. Jamaicans were also producing provisions for ships on the journey between Panama and Spain (Black 1972), particularly a cassava bread called *bami*. Made out of dried, grated bitter cassava, this loaf originated with the Tainos. Cured smoked pork (now referred to as jerk pork) was also provided to the Spanish. Probably the most extensively studied Spanish-period site has been Sevilla Nueva. The ruined remains of Spain's first colonial seat in Jamaica were visible to English chroniclers in the seventeenth and eighteenth centuries, leading many contemporary historians (Sloane 1707–1725; Knight 1726; Leslie 1740, 1741; Long [1774] 1970; Browne [1759] 1789; Beckford 1790; Edwards 1793; Anonymous 1797) to conclude that England took control of an underutilized and economically unrealized Spanish colony.

Beginning with Charles Cotter's excavations between 1953 and 1968, and followed by Robyn Woodward's investigations of the city between 1987 and 2004, archaeology has demonstrated the significant economic and symbolic investment the Spanish Crown placed into the colonial seat of Jamaica (Woodward 2006a). Robyn Woodward's recent studies of Seville plantation provide an important picture of social and economic systems from the early days of colonial settlement of the region. Woodward's study of a sixteenth-century mill site at Sevilla Nueva, the first capital of Spanish Jamaica, shows the transfer of feudal systems of agricultural production in Jamaica. Sharecroppers worked the lord's land and produced crops that were processed in a central milling operation. The mill and related settlements at Seville project a center of craftspersons, artisans, and agricultural producers.

Africans were first brought to Jamaica during the sixteenth century. In 1513 Juan de Esquivel, complaining about the lack of indigenous labor, requested that the king permit him to bring three enslaved Africans to Jamaica (Cundall and Pietersz 1919: 1). As alluded to above, however, the nature of labor exploitation at Seville was not configured the same way chattel slavery would be implemented two hundred years later. Indeed, as Woodward has argued, the majority of labor at Sevilla Nueva seems to have been configured around artisanal production and low-intensity agricultural production (Woodward 2006a). Woodward highlights the lack of imported materials and the reliance on local indigenous production alongside European artisans to highlight the isolated nature of this settlement (Woodward 2006b: 172). In the second quarter of the sixteenth century, Spain, through the mechanism of the Asiento, turned to Africa in order to meet the demand for labor (Klein and Engerman 1978; Knight 1990: 63), in part because of a preexisting network of trade between Portugal and African polities (Rawley 1981).

Beginning in the early part of the seventeenth century, England and France began to exert economic and political power in the Caribbean through direct and indirect means (Helms 1983, 1986; Kiple and Ornelas 1996; see Paquette and Engerman 1996; Emmer 1998). In the subsequent century, with either royal charter to begin joint stock corporations such as the Dutch West Indies Corporation or royal monopolies to begin merchant ventures, there was extensive fluidity in political boundaries, economic ties, and demographic trends (Emmer 1998; van den Boogaart 1998). Archaeology of these early mercantile and agro-industrial activities has been restricted to a limited number of studies, with probably the most classic study being the multiple excavations of Port Royal (discussed below). The emergent urban landscape is one that has been discussed by numerous archaeologists. Edward Chappel has described early mercantile contexts in Bermuda with a specific focus on the built environment. Indeed, the architectural landscape of early British port cities in the last quarter of the seventeenth century reflected an exuberance which placed Caribbean agro-industry and mercantile activities at the center of the emergent global economy (Chappel 1994: 146; Robertson 2001: 75). In an upcoming book chapter, Fredrick Smith and Karl Watson (forthcoming) look at early urban settlements on Barbados. The cities' positions, they argue, were not inevitable. Barbados's centrality in England's colonial agenda in the West Indies came from enormous effort among local merchants to facilitate trade and "celebrate" the urbanity of Bridgetown. They argue that systems of difference based on color emerge as important in the eighteenth century, but, as Smith and Watson argue, the diversity of the Bridgetown street made it a perceived commercial success.

In 1654, as part of Oliver Cromwell's western design, Admiral Penn and General Venables embarked on a mission to take control of Hispaniola at the port of Santo Domingo, a mission which was by their reckoning a miserable failure. On May 10, 1655, the same fleet landed at what is today called Passage Fort in Kingston Harbor (Taylor 1965: 50) and by the sixteenth had gained control of the seat of power, Villa de la Vega, which today is the city of Spanish Town (ibid.). This expedition was not the first attempt by the English to gain control in Jamaica. Sir Anthony Shirley (in 1597), Captain Newport (in 1603), and Captain William Jackson (in 1643) all landed raiding parties and held hostage settlements in Jamaica (Robertson 2005: 35). In 1655, the campaign led by Penn and Venables established a permanent presence of English colonists though a guerilla war, would continue for several years, especially in the environs of Spanish Town (ibid.: 42). In order to secure the island, the English enlisted the aid of escaped slaves, known as maroons, under the leadership of Juan de Bollas (ibid.: 43).

The period between 1655 and 1692 in Jamaica has often been described as a mercantilist chapter in Jamaica's history. While Spanish Town continued to be the political seat of the island, considerable settlement and investment occurred at the end of a sandy spit protecting Kingston Harbor, known as Port Royal (Pawson and Buisseret [1975] 2001). Sugar technology had been successfully introduced in other English colonies in the Caribbean. The plantation as the focus of the Jamaican economy would not really take off for two decades. A lack of investment and labor prohibited the full exploitation of Jamaica's arable land.

The settlers of Jamaica during the first two decades were mostly drawn from colonies in the Lesser Antilles where the land had already been claimed. Port Royal was home to an array of peoples from Europe, Africa, and the Americas, working as traders, sailors, military personnel, artisans, and laborers (free and enslaved). The population of Port Royal supported the merchants and a bourgeoning hinterland economy based on cattle and sugar production (Pawson and Buisseret [1975] 2001). Since sugar required technological and financial investment, the early poor settlers set up pens and less economically intensive agricultural production such as cotton and cocoa (see Dunn 1972: 149).

Given the proximity to Cuba, Hispaniola, and the Honduran and Miskitu coasts, political and economic ties were strengthened as Jamaica, and specifically Port Royal, grew into one of the largest transshipment ports for enslaved Africans in the Western Caribbean. Concomitant with this growth in trade was a growth in contraband, privateering, and piracy. Zahediah estimates that 1,500 persons were engaged in privateering in a population of approximately 8,500 (Zahedieh 1986b: 212,). A considerable amount of archaeological research has been conducted in Port Royal for this early time period. This research has ranged from amateur investigations focused on the "Pirate Port" to intensive and systematic investigations in order to recover and recreate the seventeenth-century port city landscape. Most notable among this research was a multi-year project conducted by Donny Hamilton that resulted in a number of articles focusing on merchant and craft production of Port Royal inhabitants, and a number of theses and dissertations specializing in specific sets of material culture (Wadley 1985; McClenaghan 1988; Gotelipe-Miller 1990; Franklin 1992; Heidtke 1992; Darrington 1994; Hailey 1994; Trussel 1994; Smith 1995; Dewolf 1998; Fox 1998; Winslow 2000; Donachie 2001).

While Port Royal's decline as a mercantile hub began in the 1680s and continued well into the 1720s (Pawson and Buisseret [1975] 2001), the earthquake in 1692 is often used as a marker in the shift from a mercantile economy to an agro-industrial one. The change in physical landscape, where nearly one-third of Port Royal was submerged by Kingston Harbor, and continuing through the 1694 attempted French invasion of the island, there was a marked shift in the historiography, if not the actual political economy, of Jamaica, from one focusing on mercantilism to one which is preoccupied with the plantation presence. Certainly English plantations were operating on the north coast of Jamaica as early as the 1680s.

The Jamaican Plantation: 1690s–1840s

In figurative and material ways, the plantation had become the dominant economic institution of Caribbean colonial life by 1713. But what exactly was a plantation? For some, most notably historian Eric Williams (1970, 1994) and economist Lloyd Best (1967, 1998), it was a site of European venture capital rooting historical and modern inequities in transoceanic trade and resource extraction. C.L.R. James interjects into this historiography an interwoven analysis of the French and Haitian Revolution, where colonial frameworks and their legacies create complex and shifting class structure (James 1963). For James, colonial historiography needed to privilege class analysis over racial constructions. Still others, including historians David Eltis (1997, 2000) and Robin Blackburn (1988, 1997), take a counterintuitive approach to plantation slavery. They argue that it had less to do with economic rationalism than with economic racialization. For others, including Fernando Ortiz and Sidney Mintz, the plantation was a site where the roots of European industrial capitalism were embedded, and workers and enslaved peoples underwent processes of transculturation (Ortiz 1940) or creolization (Mintz 1992; Mintz and Price 1976, 1992).

The Plantation Economy

This slave regime has been discussed in various ways, not least of which is economic. Lloyd Best (Best and Levitt 1967) posited the "pure plantation model" as a way of describing the series of relationships that existed between colony and colonizer, owner and enslaved, and planter and laborer. The pure plantation model is an attempt by Caribbean economists to apply dependency theory on a localized scale within the Caribbean. At the center of this economy is the plantation, which Best claims "is a globally integrated peripheral economy" (Best 1998: 12). The plantation is peripheral to industrialized metropoles, such as London, to which are exported commodities such as sugar and rum. In return, the plantations receive manufactured goods and processed foods. The plantation itself has peripheries that service the commodity-exporting plantation by providing provisions, labor, and energy. Best states, "It is a loosely knit but tightly managed joint stock corporation, of which the business is overseas investment in trade, carriage and production" (Best 1998: 27) "where the hinterland is called on to adjust . . . or they must substitute home production for imports" (Best and Levitt 1967: 26).

Given the constraints of this system, where "the economy remains, as it has been, passively responsive to metropolitan demand and metropolitan investment" (Best 1968: 36), a flexible set of relationships was required to support the plantation. Ancillary economic activity such as local pottery production of sugar wares and ceramic utensils and provision production would meet shortfalls in the supply of imports from chandlers, factors, and creditors. Probably the most compelling critique of this pure plantation model is that it treats the informal economic activities of the enslaved merely as a function of estate production developed to minimize costs in carriage and overseas transport. While the model was posited from a Keynesian economic model, the actors in this approach to plantations were economically rational actors anticipating the liberal economics of Adam Smith. It is important to understand these activities in their own context and examine how they may have impacted social, economic, and political relationships on the island.

By the eighteenth century, the sugar industry was the cornerstone of Jamaica's economy (Sheridan 1965, 1968, 1973: 215, 1976), and slavery was the primary means of labor (Williams 1970: 136). It was more expedient to use enslaved labor instead of wage labor (Williams [1944] 1994: 6). The Atlantic trade in Africans had become a central mercantile activity in the seventeenth century, such that as early as "the 1640s the two sections [New England and the West Indies] established the famous triangular trading pattern that made the island and mainland settlements economically interdependent and kept them in close touch" (Dunn 1972: 336). The Atlantic trade in Africans burgeoned in the eighteenth century, both because of the high mortality rates of enslaved laborers and because planters felt it was cheaper to purchase more enslaved than to ameliorate their lives (Williams 1970: 137). Through this "slave trade," 11 to 12 million people were taken from West Africa and brought to plantations in Central and South America, the West Indies, and the southeast United States (Eltis 2001; Lovejoy 1981). These enslaved laborers were required to fuel an economic system whose backers attempted to minimize the input costs (see map 1.4). Trevor Burnard calculates that 1,083,369 were transported with the intention to sell in Jamaica (Burnard 2001: 13).

This slave economy effected lasting structural change in the social milieu of the West Indies. Richard Dunn claims, "The plantation system lasted without significant alteration throughout the eighteenth century, continued

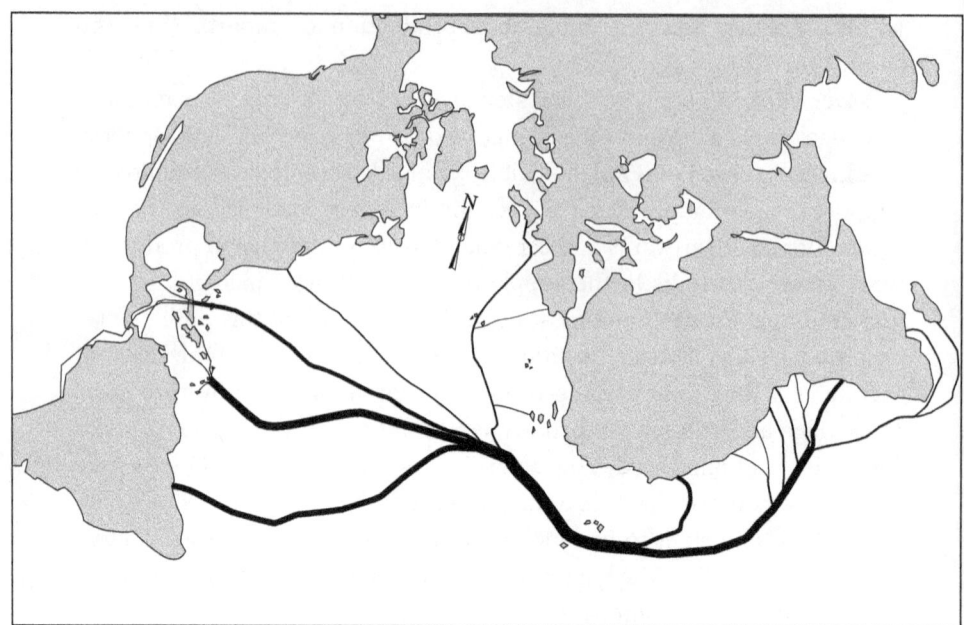

Map 1.4. The Middle Passage (transatlantic trade in Africans) between the sixteenth and nineteenth centuries. Thickness of line is in proportion to population size as synthesized from Thomas (1999); Curtin 1969; Lovejoy (2001); Burnard (2001). Burnard and Morgan (2001). Illustration by Author.

in modified form even after enslaved laborers were freed in the nineteenth century, and still survives in large measure in Jamaica, Barbados, and the Leeward Islands today" (Dunn 1972: 334). The plantation was a regime that required strict structural control over the daily lives and economic world of the people who provided the plantation's labor.

The planters, in laying out estates, building mills devoted to processing, and placing villages, were preoccupied with streamlining costs in legal and physical ways. French encyclopedist Denis Diderot published his *Encyclopédie* between 1751 and 1772, in which he outlines and illustrates an eighteenth-century version of a "how-to" on various trades and industries. Among his descriptions were an illustration of a *sucre*, or a sugar plantation, which describes every industrial detail from the processing of sugar to the layout of an estate (see figure 1.1).

Certainly, Barry Higman's work on plats (manuscript estate plans) between 1750 and 1880 in Jamaica, is one of the earliest attempts to engage these concepts through the built and altered landscape of Jamaican estates and pens (Higman 1986a, 1986b, 1987, 1988). Higman, an economic historian and historical geographer, illustrates the complex relationship between the emergent technologies of British cartography and the rise of colonialism and capitalism (Higman 1988). These plats were in themselves a mechanism through which colonial regimes marked and controlled agro-industrial production (1986a). Higman noted that the organization of space within a plantation varied depending on region, sources of power (wind, water, or cattle mills) and commodities produced (1986b, 1987, 1988). Indeed, while notable differences exist in patterns for coffee- and sugar-estate layouts (1986b: 73), a unifying and significant factor in the industrial layout for the sugar estate (1986a: 17) and coffee estates (1986b: 76) was an economy of movement (1986a: 17), thus placing these specific localities within larger capitalist regimes of production. At Lucky Valley estate in Clarendon parish, for example, the village where the enslaved laborers lived was moved to a location central to the cane fields, a move which anticipated increased output in the 1770s (Higman 1987).

The role of economic efficiency required by capital investment from metropole, and the ways it impacted the spatial organization of estates and pens and how this in turn informs Caribbean history, is echoed in the

Figure 1.1. A view of an estate on San Domingue. Agriculture et economie rustique, economie rustique, sucrerie, p. 18:1:11 pl. 1. Denis Diderot 1762 *Recueil de planches, sur les sciences, les arts libéraux, et les arts méchaniques : avec leur explication*. (Housed at Syracuse University Special Collections).

work of Dale Tomich in Martinique. He pays attention to the ways in which history is interwoven with space and scale by showing how oceanic scales and capitalist development are refracted within the locally articulated slave economies (Tomich 1990, 1991, 1993, 1994, 1995). He argues that "on a world scale, the processes of capitalist development simultaneously unify and differentiate temporal and spatial relations" (Tomich 2004: 136) but that this generalization must be done "by specifying relations, establishing their historical interconnections and contexts, and ordering narrative accounts" (55). In a sense the place where this intersection occurs are the provision grounds.

The Plantation Colony

The plantations were colonial outposts of European capitalism. They were also the site of colonization for forced labor. This institution of plantations provided the impetus for the abduction and sale of nearly 12 million individuals brought from sub-Saharan Africa. Of those millions, nearly 42 percent were brought to the Caribbean to work in the sugar, coffee, and indigo agro-industries. Sidney Mintz (1985) has argued that the sugar plantation provided a model for emergent European industrialization. It was also a context in which enslaved peoples of African descent refashioned the world they were entering using organizing frameworks brought from West Africa and applied in new economic contexts

What remains important is the centrality of the Caribbean in the rise of European modernity. As David Scott has argued, "Caribbean peoples... were the first overseas conscripts of modernity" (Scott 2004a: 192; also see Scott 2004b and Trouillot 2003). Indeed, it is commonly argued that in the post-conquest period, the Caribbean was a laboratory of European modernity in which emergent empires experimented with strategies of production, methods of distribution, and technologies of control. These technologies include the manipulation and production of space through cartography, the racialization and (class)ification of colonized and Diaspora peoples, and a series of legislative mechanisms that dictated trading relationships in efforts to make colonial control complete.

Probably the most well-documented study of the ways in which European colonialism and capitalism became inscribed on the landscape comes from James Delle's work on blue mountain coffee plantations in Jamaica (Delle 1998, 1999, 2000a, 2000b, 2001; Delle et al. 2000). Delle set out to define the ways in which European ideologies interwoven in emergent capitalism were inscribed on these colonial landscapes. Arguing against approaches in economic history where economic efficiency was the primary measure of analysis (Clement 1997; Higman 1986a, 1986b, 1987, 1988), Delle joins a series of scholars in demonstrating the ways in which European capitalism regimented the daily lives of colonial subjects (Delle 1999, 2000a). While Delle's project has been criticized at various points for its top-down approach (Wilkie 1995; Wilkie and Bartoy 2000), Delle highlights the need to not leave the "global" and its concomitant ideologies unexplored. While not explicitly analyzing resistance in terms of the archaeological record, Delle provides a context for examining resistance through an analysis of documents relating contested spatialities (Delle 1998: 204).

Theresa Singleton (2001, 2006) in her analysis of Cafetal del Padre has not only explored the spatial organization of early nineteenth-century Cuban coffee plantations to control the actions of enslaved laborers but also discussed the potential resistance of those same laborers (2001: 110). What sets this coffee plantation and similar ones apart from Anglophone and Francophone analogues on other islands is the presence of masonry walls encapsulating the village. This is similar to institutionalized, prison-like dormitories and pens used on other plantations on the island called *barracones*. Constructed in the 1840s as part of a larger trend to avoid rebellions, runaways (102), and capture by raiders (106), the walls enclosed a laborer village which could be watched from the great house. Drawing on Delle's (1998) analysis of coffee plantations and his use of Foucault, Singleton suggests that the enclosure and surveillance were technologies of control employed at this plantation. The presence of a bell tower and evidence of stairs suggest that planters were provided with a vantage point through which to observe the enslaved (2001: 106).

Within the *barracone*, Singleton states, there is little evidence of "slave-induced modifications either to the excavated structure or to the yard area" (108), but their material life does shed some light on cultural resistance. Like the cases presented in Jamaica, these materials allow archaeologists to infer that enslaved "acquired these objects through purchase or trade, and therefore represent, to some extent, their personal tastes in self-presentation" (108). Modification of these goods, as in the case of a small ceramic disk similar to those identified by Armstrong as game pieces at Drax Hall (1990: 137), suggest that these goods might be a result of divination practices in the quarters of the enslaved (110). As both authors argue, the ability to move away from systems of classification imposed on them by the planting class, and to refashion themselves in their own terms through self-presentation, is a form of resistance. This resistance only gains clarity in opposition to a plantation system organized around control.

While some generalizations can be drawn on the structure and practice of everyday plantation life, twenty-five years of archaeological analysis of plantation sites in the Caribbean have pointed to the necessity of placing the plantation within the historical, political, and geographic context of the islands in which they operated. Indeed, in the organization of plantation labor, different empires had different regimes through which they managed their enslaved populations. For example, while it was common practice in the English-speaking Caribbean to separate recently arrived enslaved individuals with similar linguistic backgrounds, in the Spanish- and French-speaking Caribbean such individuals tended to be grouped together (Craton and Walvin 1970; Tomich 1994; Ortiz 1940, 1994: 7).

The Plantation Community

The colonial Caribbean has been defined as a context of analysis for community-oriented studies of transplanted peoples in which, "the Caribbean . . . because of 'the particular circumstances' of its history, contains within itself a 'culture' different from, though not exclusive of Europe" (Braithwaite 1969: 113). Indeed, while much scholarship has moved away from pan-African attributions ascribed by Melville Herskovits (1933, 1936, [1941] 1990; Redfield, Linton, and Herskovits 1935) and Robert Farris Thompson (1974, 1984, 1990, 1993), practices, beliefs, and technologies learned in different communities in Africa have become generally accepted as shaping the ways in which communities formed in the Caribbean (Mintz 1992; Mintz and R. Price 1992; Mintz and S. Price 1985; cf. Lowenthal 1972, 1977) and how the everyday lives of their members were expressed in material culture (Beckwith 1929; Handler and Lange 1978; Thompson 1984, 1993; Price and Price 1999). While some have questioned the degree to which this material culture would be archaeologically visible (Handler and Lange 1978), almost three decades of archaeological research in Jamaica have demonstrated that the enslaved brought with them ways of doing things which were transformed in New World contexts (Agorsah 1992, 1994; Armstrong 1983, 1990, 1991a, 1991b, 1999, 2003; Armstrong and Kelly 2000; Goucher 1990, 1993, 1999).

One of the major trends in defining and describing the plantation has been to move away from examining it as primarily an economic institution and to focus on the village where the enslaved lived as the site of community formation within the Caribbean. This approach, while eschewing economically deterministic models of human interaction, focuses on the creativity of enslaved individuals in transforming the world around them within the context of macro-social processes. It is a view of the plantation which is very much influenced by the work of Fernando Ortiz (1985) and his concept of transculturation. Influenced by his analysis of Cuban music, Ortiz argues that Caribbean folklife is a "counterpoint" to colonial histories. Transculturation develops when ideas, things, and practices "foreign" to Cuba merged and converged to form a particular social fabric. Ortiz argues that transculturation

> expresses the different phases in the transitive process from one culture to another, because this process does not only imply the acquisition of culture, as connoted by the Anglo-American term *acculturation*, but it also necessarily involves the loss or uprooting of one's preceding culture, what one could call partial *disculturation*. Moreover, it signifies the subsequent creation of new cultural phenomena that one could call *neoculturation*. (Cited in Taylor 1991: 91)

In a sense, the plantation is an engine placed in the Caribbean by European capitalism, which not only processes raw sugar cane into sugar but also processes disparate communities into a single creolized identity.

There is considerable resonance with Ortiz's ideas and those of anthropologists Sidney Mintz and Richard and Sally Price, who in the 1970s championed the idea of transformation, especially as a model for creolization. Employing a linguistic model of creolization, they propose that African cultural materials were retained, but that these materials were merely contributing factors to the new cultural forms that were created (Mintz and Price 1992: 20–21). While the metaphor of language is compelling, it potentially belies the fluidity of such processes in unique and changing social contexts (Singleton 1998: 177; Trouillot 2002: 198–205). Indeed, it is within these settings that interpersonal and intimate histories emerge.

A major trend in historical archaeology has been the attempt to move beyond the evidence of the colonizer. Top-down approaches examine laborer villages in terms of the control of the planting elite (as stated above, also see Pulsipher 1994; Delle 1998; Pulsipher and Goodwin 1999; Singleton 2001). Other scholars have attempted bottom-up approaches examining plantation villages as sites in which enslaved laborers used West African lifeways and applied them in innovative ways (Armstrong 1990; Higman 1998; Armstrong and Kelly 2000; Armstrong and Hauser 2004, 2007). The place, organization, and construction of spaces associated with enslaved life have been a focus of study by many scholars, including the examination of house yards and provision grounds. While scrutiny of these areas forms a particular problem in terms of their identification, delineation, and recovery (Delle 1998: 143), villages and house yards within them have been a fertile ground for examining how enslaved laborers adapted to and transformed the social environment into which they entered (Armstrong 1990: 88; Delle 1998, 2000a; Higman 1998: 144; Pulsipher and Goodwin 1999).

Douglas Armstrong's work on the north coast of Jamaica has provided an excellent case study of ways in which enslaved Africans created and transformed the landscape around them (Armstrong 1990, 1999; Armstrong and Kelly 2000). Based on research conducted between 1980 and 1983, Armstrong's research at Drax Hall was one of the first archaeologically grounded examinations of an enslaved laborer village in the Caribbean. His analysis focused on the house yards of the enslaved, the places where they ate, drank, socialized, and played (Armstrong 1990: 87). Employing Sidney Mintz's concept of transformation, Armstrong argues that in lieu of simplistic notions of transplantation of practices, the enslaved used referents brought with them or passed down from West Africa and applied them in untraditional ways (Armstrong 1990: 10). In the case of Drax Hall, this is most apparent in the material life of the enslaved (138) and their food ways (210).

Indeed the concept of transformation is central to much of Armstrong's work, whether it relates to identity or power. Armstrong's work at Seville estate is probably the clearest example of this negotiation. Seville, a sugar plantation which operated between the 1690s and the late 1800s, is located only a few miles from Drax Hall. What was unique about Seville is that between 1720 and 1800, the village and its organization had changed significantly. While the early village was laid out on principles of order and surveillance and organized in two parallel rows (Armstrong and Kelly 2000: 380), the new village was laid out and organized by the enslaved. While it was organized by principles of efficiency described by Higman above, the layout and location of the new village allowed for a greater degree of autonomy among the enslaved (Armstrong and Kelly 2000: 391). Douglas Armstrong and Kenneth Kelly (2000) suggested that while designed plantation landscapes in Jamaica sought to impose order upon people as well as the natural environment, archaeological evidence for the day-to-day use of houses and yards suggests defiance against such order through adapted African household practices (2000: 392).

Probably one of the most interesting archaeological studies of late has been Barry Higman's historical and archaeological analysis of Montpelier estate in western Jamaica (1998). In this study, Higman attempts to reconstruct the changing landscapes of village life between the eighteenth and twentieth centuries. What is impressive in his analysis is his ability to weave the individual lives of freed and enslaved Jamaicans into broader social and historical contexts. Specifically, by examining the independent production of enslaved workers, Higman demonstrates how their actions shaped larger historical and social events (most specifically the 1831 rebellion).

The Plantation in Between

The archaeology of enslaved life has tended to focus on scales that have been necessarily limited to single plantation communities. Hinted at in Higman's work and certainly coming to fruition in other studies is a refashioning of the enslaved community so that it extends beyond the estate grounds. Such analysis focuses on the provision grounds of the enslaved and their activities at market. Historical archaeologists have become increasingly concerned with regional analysis focusing on the interconnections between different archaeological sites in order to develop a better sense of social relations. This development is due in part to the realization of many years of research and subsequent topical and theoretical syntheses. However, it also is a shifting concern in research toward fluidity of landscape and translocality. As a world area, the Caribbean highlights the need for broader regional analyses where tensions between local specificities and global/translocal processes are mediated. The circuits of commodities coming into and leaving the island, as well as those commodities in circulation within the island, speak to more than the economic coordinates of merchant capitalism. They are reflective of the social lives behind things and the intimate connections between communities that were not overtly mediated by the plantation structure.

While the grown and processed commodities of the Caribbean plantation, as well as the industrial goods produced to provision them, are easily reconciled in the larger economies in which Caribbean folk operated, there were other goods in circulation, stylizing the plantation as a pastoral scene. As many archaeologists have argued, the ability to control production and exchange of social goods, of which these painted representations are one example, was a way in which elites reproduced existing social relations. To be certain, such social goods existed in many media and spectra in eighteenth-century plantation society. Colonial representations of plantation life depicted landscapes as devoid of processes that reflect the control over people, goods, and land that planters thought they had. As W.J.T. Mitchell describes, eighteenth- and nineteenth-century landscape paintings "circulate as a medium of exchange, a site of visual appropriation, a focus for the formation of identity" (Mitchell 1994a: 2).

Nineteenth-century landscapes of the Caribbean emphasized a pastoral environment devoid of the impacts of industrial sugar production and demands of enslaved labor. In the eighteenth century artists and their patrons had developed what Mimi Sheller has described as a "scenic economy" (Sheller 2003: 37). Artists catered to a market in which "the plantocracy favoured a selective depiction of reality" (Honychurch 2003: 1). For the planters the orderly nature of plantation space and the products of labor became important signifiers not only of their economic success but of the power of their colonial efforts to bring about control in an untamed tropical landscape (Pratt 1992: 56; Sheller 2003: 38).

Romanticized views are drawn throughout the Caribbean, including by Johan Heinrich Stobweisser of Cedar Hall plantation in Antigua, Beinecke's panorama of a sugar plantation in St. Vincent and St. Lucia, and Frederick von Scholten's depiction of sugar estates on St. Croix and Carolina estate in St. John. There is one exception to the romanticized depiction of the plantation landscape. William Clark, in his *Ten Views of the Island of Antigua* (1823) depicts the industrial aspects of plantation labor, including scenes from the boiling house, distillery, almost anticipating the stylized industrial art of the 1930s. Still evident, however, is the organized and surveyed nature of the plantation.

In Jamaica, the scenic economy reaches its height through painters such as James Hakewill and Isaac Belisario, and photographers like Adolphe Duperly. Probably one of the best-known sets of landscapes is Hakewill's *A Picturesque Tour of the Island of Jamaica* (1825). Deflecting his gaze from the realities of the highly industrialized sugar plantation, James Hakewill, in his paintings of nineteenth-century rural Jamaica, presents a necessarily idealized landscape. An example given in this text is a copy from his landscape of Roehampton (figure 1.2) estate, reproduced in 1832. This landscape was not published in his 1825 volume but has significance in its manipulation by Duperly in the next decade (see figure I.1). In these landscapes the work and effort of the enslaved are resident in the manicured estate grounds but are invisible in the actual labor. Street markets, as depicted in daguerreotypes and photographs discussed later in this book, created tension and anxiety. They introduced into the colonial order, as represented landscapes

Figure 1.2. *View of Roehampton estate, Jamaica, based on James Hakewill's* Picturesque Tour of Jamaica, printed by R. Martin. Courtesy of the New York Public Library.

painted between 1820 and 1840, disorderly subjects. The disorder of these markets seems to not only be metaphorical, but also have a material reality behind it.

Since the 1980s cultural geographer Lydia Pulsipher has directed a major field project with Conrad M. Goodwin at Galways plantation, the results of which have inspired studies of "the human landscape surrounding Galways" (Pulsipher 1994: 203). Combining oral history with archaeological survey, this research focused on ways in which enslaved laborers took the most marginal pieces of land on plantations, "where they first seized the right to grow their own food crops and then expanded production to sell surplus crops on market" (ibid.). More important, they have explored the "ideational role" of gardens as places in which the enslaved not only escaped the surveillance of the planter but also "construct[ed] a decent life for themselves within a hostile system" (Pulsipher 1994: 217; cf. Pulsipher and Goodwin 1999: 15, 2001). This system was one in which order and observation were mechanisms through which planters and overseers exerted authority and were able to enforce regimens of slave life. Spaces which fell outside of planters' scrutiny enabled the enslaved to impose their own order onto West Indian landscapes in the form of gardens (Pulsipher and Goodwin 1999) and creole economies (Pulsipher 1990).

Early in Jamaica's plantation period we see reference to setting aside land for the enslaved so that they might provision themselves. Hans Sloane visited Jamaica in 1687 and 1688 and published his account between 1707 and 1725. He describes:

> They have Saturdays in the Afternoon, and Sundays with Christmas Holidays, Easter call'd little or Piganinny, Christmas, and some other great Feasts allow'd them for the Culture of their own Plantations to feed themselves from Potatos, Yams and Plantains, etc., which they plant in Ground allow'd them by their Masters, beside a small Plantain-Walk they have by themselves. (Sloane 1707–1725, 1: lii)

Then in the latter part of the eighteenth century, we see that the provision grounds moved beyond merely supplying enslaved laborers with produce for personal consumption but enabled enslaved laborers to earn cash. Parliamentarian Bryan Edwards, who lived in Jamaica in the second and third quarters of the eighteenth century, published his *History, Civil and Commercial, of the British Colonies in the West Indies* in 1793 and recorded:

> The practice which prevails in Jamaica of giving the Negroes land to cultivate, from the produce of which they are expected to maintain themselves (except in times of scarcity, arising from hurricanes and droughts, when assistance is never denied them) is universally allowed to be judicious and beneficial; producing a happy coalition between the master and the slave. The Negro who has acquired by his own labour a property in his master's land, has much to lose, and is therefore less inclined to desert his work. He earns a little money, by which he is enabled to indulge himself in fine clothes on holidays, and gratify his palate with salted meats and other provisions that otherwise he could not obtain; and the proprietor is eased, in a great measure, of the expense of feeding him. (Edwards 1793 2: 123)

Edwards goes on to say in a subsequent footnote: "At the same time, it will be necessary to secure to the Negroes by law, the little property or peculium which their own industry may thus acquire" (Edwards 1793 2: 139). However, Howson shows in Antigua and Montserrat that the congeniality between the owner and the enslaved laborer in their internal economies just might be overstated. She found at least two references where enslaved laborers would conceal their own possessions from planters and white people, because enslaved laborers thought that white people would steal the goods (Howson 1995: 41). In their "free time" the enslaved were producing goods that were not only supplemental but vital to the overall economic and social well-being of plantation Jamaica.

Such studies point to the need to examine plantation life through the activities of the enslaved which were not limited to the plantation but extended beyond it. Indeed, tracing the movement of goods produced and/or exchanged by the enslaved requires a "multi-scalar" approach that reveals the complexity of identity formation in the Caribbean context (Wilkie and Farnsworth 1999, 2005). We need to examine how archaeologies may operate "at multiple spatial scales, ranging from the household to the quarters to the plantation" and beyond (Wilkie and Farnsworth 2005: 3). As Carol Allen has argued, the concept "creole" implies, among other things, a "nativisation or indigenization, marking the point of recognition of that new type as belonging to the locale . . . which does not become fixed in form . . . making context and point of view crucial to understanding" (Allen 2002: 57). Understanding the ways in which people experienced locality becomes an important point of departure in developing effective scales of analysis.

Studying In-between Sites

What is missing in this archaeology of the "in between" is a mechanism to talk about the various archaeological contexts of Jamaica simultaneously. I am not the first to question the totalizing effects of the colonial system's control and its impact on the material life of Caribbean peoples. Indeed, it is somewhat of a cliché to say that all plantations are idiosyncratic and all plantation islands are socially and historically unique. But at what level can comparisons be drawn? By focusing on institutions developed and appropriated by the enslaved, we can begin to see the ways in which locality is refashioned. The market system through which the enslaved participated was one such institution in that it linked the urban with the rural, the elites with the laboring class, plantation enslaved with artisans of the town.

The archaeology of colonial plantations in the Caribbean has highlighted the need to operate simultaneously at multiple scales of analysis. On the one hand, the everyday experiences of enslaved life were in part shaped by the particular social contexts of the community in which enslaved lived. On the other hand, the emergent structures of hierarchy concomitant with globally oriented commodity production also framed the social relations in which these actors operated. It seems that, yes, there was a refashioning of self, and indeed, as highlighted by the 1831 rebellion, there was resistance. In part, the everyday lives of the enslaved were also about the very elementary process of creating society, irrespective of imposed systems. These social networks they forged were present within plantation communities, but they also went beyond the plantation. There is also the remarkably ill-defined and ambiguous space of actions in between, where self-fashioning and overt resistance grade into each other. These self-fashionings are indeed made possible in part by the plantation system yet also act as media for the bending or attrition of rule. This is where markets are important, because they take us away from the structure/agency, power/resistance dyads, toward something infinitely more complex and less overdetermined by either set of polar forces.

2

Markets of Contention

Historical and Legal Perspectives on Informal Economies in Eighteenth-Century Jamaica

> Kingston at this time pays one hundred pounds yearly to a police officer, who as a retail shopkeeper himself, will feel the force of what follows.... If he should observe that this useful and deserving class of citizens, have their trade interfered by schoals of idle and disorderly slaves who infest our streets and lanes, obstruct the common pathway and keep extensive shops in the piazzas (to the constant annoyance of the foot passengers and the peace of the inhabitants) for the sale of beef, pork, herrings, saltfish, shads, salmon, bread, flour, rice, corn meal, biscuit and every possible article of edible commerce—even to our horses' grass—how can this hired officer pass by such flagrant breaches of our laws without remembrance to our duty?
>
> The miscreants here described, who live free from rent and taxes, and who frequently recruit their stores with the spoils of the night, can well afford to undersell the honest white traders. Negroes in general will most assuredly prefer that mode of purchase where tenfold advantages offer, that is, in buying stolen goods from their own colour, rather than give a full and fair price to the merchants of this commodity.
>
> *Columbian Magazine* 1798 4: 1 in Simmonds 1987: 36.

The world abducted Africans were entering in eighteenth-century Jamaica was not new, in that economic institutions, regional political powers, and regimes of social organization all had strangely familiar but distant analogues in Africa. Certainly, at the beginning of the Atlantic trade in Africans, there was a large and vital transcontinental and regional trade in West Africa with its own centers of gravity, set of symbolic networks, and forms of wealth (Posnansky 1973; DeCorse 2001b). Likewise, while there is debate about the ways in which slavery as an institution was configured within West African societies (see Kopytoff and Miers 1977; Lovejoy 1983; Meillassoux 1991; Piot 1996; Shaw 2002; Klein 2002; Lovejoy and Curto

2004), there were systems of inequality where marginalized and/or alienated peoples were considered fungible. Indeed the cultural matrixes of West Africa were as much "forged during the long encounter with Europe... and thus owe their meaning and shape to that encounter as much as anything 'indigenous'" (Piot 1996: 1).

What made European colonization in the Caribbean different was the time frame. While there were factors, merchants, and some fortified presence in West Africa, it is questionable whether Europe approached the same levels of territorial control in the twentieth century that they had in the Caribbean in the eighteenth century. In the Caribbean, where projects of colonization had essentially been completed by the eighteenth century, technologies of control had reached near totalizing effects. The system of chattel slavery became an all-encompassing ideology where laborers became divested of their humanity (Patterson 1969, 1982; Mintz and Price 1992; Burnard 1996, 2001, 2004; Morgan 2006). Likewise, regimentation of trade through treaties, legal statutes, and precedent governed all levels of economic interaction, at least in theory.

Yet, when one examines the economic activities of the enslaved, it appears as if the topography of colonial control is uneven. The opening epigraph, written by an anonymous author, along with contemporary illustrations of market scenes in the British Caribbean (see figure 2.1) describe some of the economic activity of Afro-Jamaicans in the eighteenth century. As Sidney Mintz and Richard Price point out, institutional forms such as the activities described in the passage "could have served as a catalyst in the processes by which individuals from diverse societies forged new institutions, and could have provided certain frameworks within which new forms could have developed" (Mintz and Price 1992: 14). The above passage suggests that while the impact of European capitalism on colonial subjects was encompassing, it was not circumscribed. While there were regimes of economic control, the practice of market participants was somewhat contrary to colonial expectations. We must therefore ask, in what ways did these same colonial subjects structure the Atlantic world?

The market system, as one of these institutional forms, was at the nexus of the global and the local. Its analysis speaks to issues of structure and agency, production and consumption, hegemony and resistance. There is, however, a tendency to oversimplify the system as a single institution. The internal market system has often been depicted, as in the opening epigraph, as an enterprise operating on the margins of legality. The internal economy, however, was more complicated than a single black (illegal) market. It

Figure 2.1. *A Negro Market in the West Indies.* Drawing by W. E. Beastall and G. Testolini, London, 1806. Courtesy of the National Library of Jamaica.

comprised a complex array of interactions that focused around the planter, the merchant, the freeperson, and enslaved laborers. By understanding the complexity of the system and delineating its many facets, tensions are revealed which point to the different scales people engaged in the local economies of Jamaica.

Whether the nature these markets took on was the result of underlying systems of valuation and exchange that Africans brought with them, or whether it was the result of more generalizable processes, as suggested by Mintz (1983), remains unknown. What is known is that by the eighteenth century, the internal market system figured centrally in Jamaican economic and social lives. The social importance of the combination of street markets, higglers, and small-scale trade is one of the reasons why these institutions have figured so prominently in the historiography of the African Diaspora. In the eighteenth century, few other institutions were as explicitly impacted by the rural and urban freed and enslaved. Everybody in Jamaica was dependent on the internal economy, some to a greater extent than others. It is in these markets that we see a struggle over the valuation of local goods, to prevent "engrossing" the price of staples. We also begin to see the attempt to define "Indian, Mulatto, or Negro" participants in the internal economy as perpetrators of market disorder.

Market Demands: Complicating the Internal Economy

The internal economies were a mix of both formal and informal market activity taking place in multiple venues. In this book, I am primarily interested in the more informal and poorly documented transactions. Informal market activity has been part of anthropological and sociological literature for some time but was first expressed as economically rational, partially articulated with larger global processes in 1972 by Keith Hart (Hart 1973). Hart, in his discussion of urban migration in Ghana and the ways "surplus labor" makes due, argues that we have to invest rationality into the motivations of economically disenfranchised peoples. There have been numerous critiques of this dualistic formulation, because as a systematizing tool it can leave silent issues of power and exploitation (Bromley 1978). Ultimately, it is important to understand that informal economies are not a symptom or pathology of underdevelopment, but rather a locally informed intersection with broader economic systems. In her discussion of débroulliards in Martinique, Katherine Browne looks at the ways in which cultural logics embed economic practices of Martiniquais (Browne 2004). These logics are grounded in the historical and social fabric of the plantation Caribbean and are deployed in mediating their identities of being simultaneously French and Caribbean. Informal economy, therefore, becomes a wonderful site of analysis in that it operates simultaneously at multiple scales.

The local street markets and transient sellers of the West Indies have been the focus of considerable scholarship. Marketing systems have been discussed by scholars interested in the economic existence of enslaved laborers in the southeastern United States (see Berlin and Morgan 1995), including South Carolina (Campbell 1993, 1995; Olwell 1996), Virginia (Schlotterboeck 1995), Louisiana (McDonald 1993, 1995, 1996), and in the Caribbean, including Martinique (Tomich 1990: 214, 1991, 1993; Browne 2004), St. John (Olwig 1977, 1985; Hall 1992; Hauser and Armstrong 1999), Barbados (Beckles 1989a, 1989b, 1991, 1999; Custinger 1991), and Jamaica (Katzin 1959a, 1959b, 1960, 1971; Mintz 1960, 1983, [1974] 1992; Norton and Symanski 1975; Bush 1981, 1990, 1996; Durant-Gonzales 1983; Simmonds 1987, 2004; Armstrong 1990; Mintz and Hall [1970] 1991; Turner 1991, 1995; Higman 1996, 1998; Reeves 1997; Ulysse 1999). As many of the above authors have suggested and demonstrated, the growth and vitality of this economy was due in large part to the independent production of the enslaved.

Of these varied writings, the most influential was probably Sidney Mintz and Douglas Hall's "On the Origins of the Jamaican Internal Market System" ([1970] 1991). In this article, Mintz and Hall argue that a system of Sunday markets, which were the focus of this economy, were essentially English in origin and created as a mechanism to help facilitate the provisioning of the enslaved. As such they could be seen as ancillary economic activities to the larger plantation system. While there have been numerous critiques looking either at West African antecedents to West Indian market practices (Beckles 1989b, 1991) or the degree to which colonial law had a totalizing effect on enslaved independent production (Tomich 1990, 1993, 1994, 1995, 2004), the strength of Mintz and Hall's argument rests in their demonstration of the market demand for economic activities which fell outside of the colonial economies of the West Indies.

Richard Sheridan, who spent much of his career exploring the economic history of Jamaica and plantation society, highlighted the crisis faced by planters in supplying manufactured goods and foodstuffs for themselves and the enslaved laborers. He argued that planters relied on a series of complementary strategies, including the importation of manufactured goods through formal colonial trade networks, development of regional cabotage, or intercoastal, trade with neighboring colonies, reliance on contraband trade with Dutch and North American merchants, and dependence on internally grown provisions in Polinks and provision grounds (Sheridan 1965, 1976). To be certain, the last two strategies were by far the most important in a planter's economic success but were also the most precarious. The beginning of the American Revolution put an enormous burden on internally grown provisions. Hurricanes and inclement weather would result in poor crops and island-wide privation.

There were, after all, certain economic constraints. The plantation economy, as it was articulated in Jamaica, was never designed to meet all the needs of the population. It can be shown that early on Jamaica depended on a diversified economy and agriculture. Yu Wu has demonstrated in his dissertation on Jamaican trade that the imported commodities coming into Jamaica fluctuated dramatically between 1688 and 1769. Wu examined the Naval Office shipping lists charting the imports of beef, pork, fish, flour, corn, and other provision commodities from North America, Europe, and the rest of the Caribbean and translated these commodities into calories

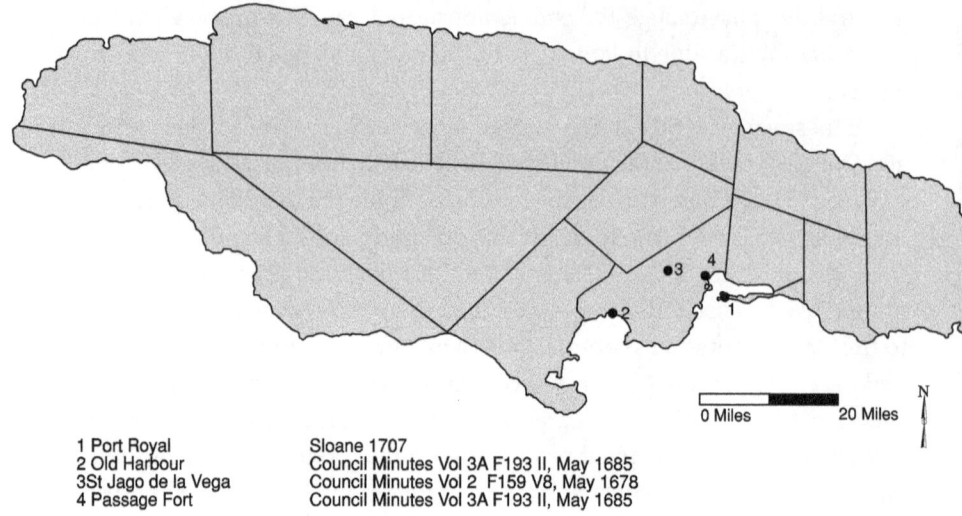

Map 2.1. Seventeenth-century street markets located through the historic documents and oral history. Illustration by Author.

of energy consumed (Wu 1995: 530). Wu found that the amount of calories available to an individual, regardless of race, class, or gender, ranged between 263 calories and 688 calories per day (547). If the calories were devoted to only the white population of Jamaica, the calories fluctuated between 607 and 3,214 calories per day (548). The calories available to the enslaved population ranged between 97 and 506 calories per day (ibid.). Two conclusions can be drawn from this analysis: first, the imports did not come anywhere close to meeting the caloric demands of the local population (551). Second, and possibly more important, the nearly 50 percent fluctuation in imported provisions on a year-to-year basis would indicate that planters needed to involve themselves in some kind of internal economic exchange.

The growth of legal markets can be geographically demonstrated over time in Jamaica either through their establishment in the acts of the assembly, parish vestries, and city councils or through their mention in the accounts of planters and travelers to the island. In the seventeenth century, the markets are located in Spanish Town, Rivermouth (which I suspect was Old Harbour), Spanish Town, and Port Royal. They are clustered around the Liguanea and seem to have taken part in provisioning the port city of Port Royal (map 2.1). By the end of the eighteenth century (map 2.2), we see markets all along the coastal areas of Jamaica and some on the major

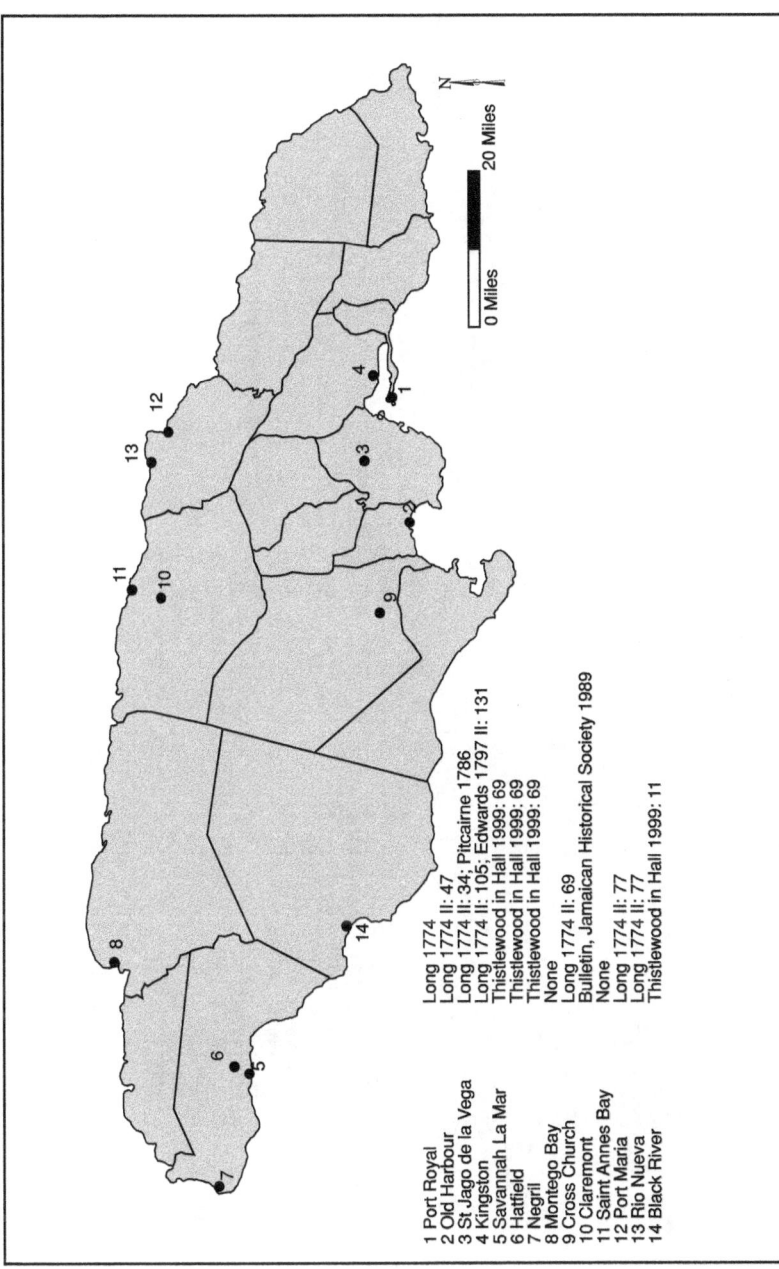

Map 2.2. Eighteenth-century street markets located through the historic documents and oral history. Illustration by Author.

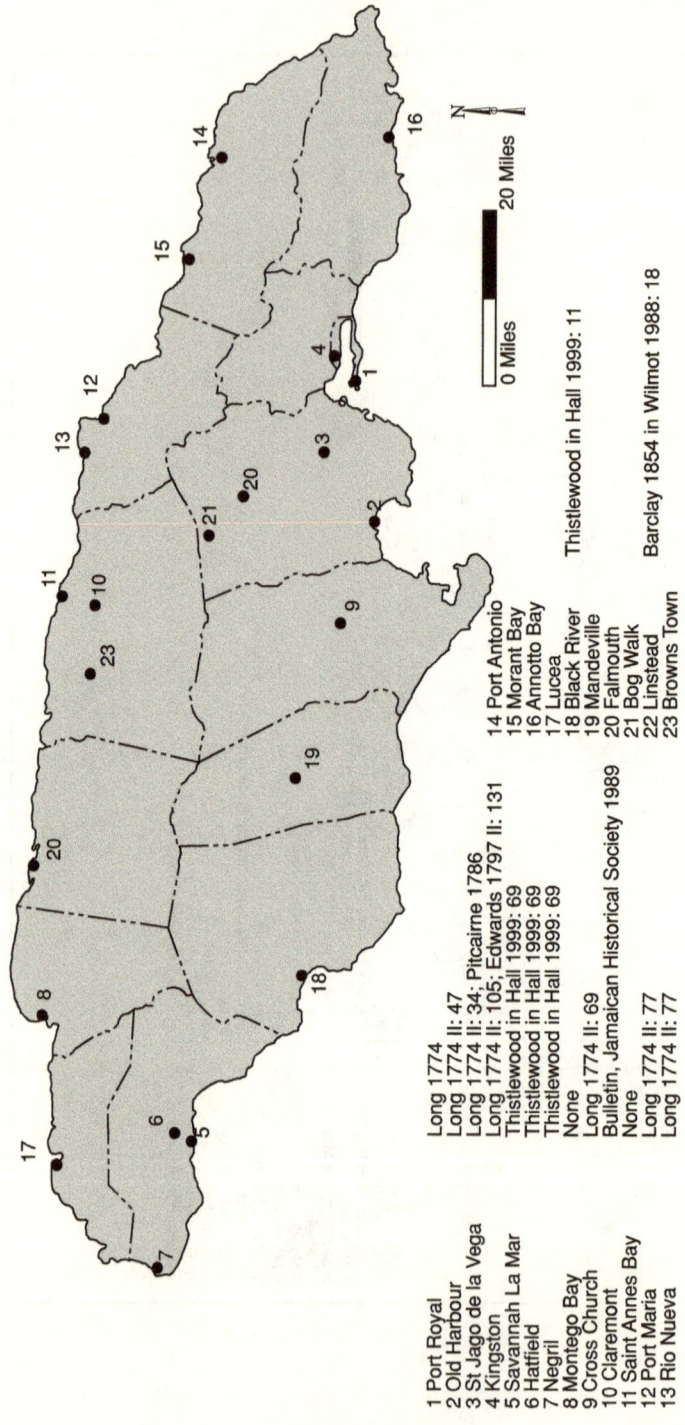

Map 2.3. Nineteenth-century street markets located through the historic documents and oral history. Illustration by Author.

inland routes. The growth in the number of markets and their distribution can be seen as an index to the shifting economic basis in Jamaica. The increasing importance of plantations precipitated the florescence of markets across the island. The distribution of markets changed after the eighteenth century. By the nineteenth century, more of the Jamaican interior gained access to markets (map 2.3). This was in part a factor of the establishment of the free village system and the settlement of towns. It also reflects the island-wide economic move inland toward coffee plantations. The growth in the number and size of the markets demonstrates their importance in the lives of the Jamaicans.

As many have noted, the "internal" economy of plantation Jamaica (Higman 1996; Shepherd 1993, 1996, 2000, 2002a, 2002b; Shepherd and Monteith 2000, 2002) was a complex entity involving multiple loci of production, modalities of exchange, and valences of consumption. It was a complex set of economic behaviors that included barter and trade among the enslaved within the plantation, itinerant peddlers, merchants, wholesalers, and a series of Sunday street markets. The commodities sold in these markets were produced locally on the provision grounds of enslaved laborers, or by artisans within the towns of Jamaica. Most important, as Barry Higman (1996) has noted, it was comprised of two partially overlapping spheres, one dominated by the planter, the other by the enslaved. In short, the internal market system encompassed a range of activities that cannot be reduced to any single institution or set of participants.

Planters proved to be one locus of the internal economy, the enslaved were the other. Patrick Browne, an Irish-born physician, visited Jamaica in 1756 and published in *Civil and Natural History of Jamaica* ([1759] 1789) over thirty years later. Like Hans Sloane's work (1707–1725), this volume is primarily concerned with the natural history of Jamaica, but Browne does spend some time discussing the social structure of Jamaica. He delineated five classes of inhabitants in eighteenth-century Jamaica: planters, settlers, merchants, dependents, and slaves. He describes the planters as

> men of extraordinary fortunes, but for the most part, though rich, and in easy circumstances, are seldom out of debt; for their charges attending sugar settlement, are very considerable, and constant; interest of money very high, and their natural propensity to increase their possessions, constantly engaging them in new disbursements and contracts. (Browne [1759] 1789: 22)

Planters through their managers or lawyers were required to take part in an island economy when provisions and supplies from London did not meet the demands of the plantation population. This included legal transactions between planters, commercial transactions between planters and merchants, and informal transactions between planters and merchants through higglers, or country-sellers, and enslaved laborers. The most informal transactions within the internal economy did not involve the planter, but rather involved the planter's enslaved. Enslaved laborers operated through higglers, bought and sold commodities in markets, and exchanged goods amongst themselves. Presented below are the forms of transaction that occurred in the internal market system from its most formal aspects to its least formal aspects.

One of the planters' uses of the internal system entailed the exchange of livestock and commodities, and the jobbing out of enslaved labor between planters (Higman 1996: 215). Higman notes that often these exchanges took place between planters who employed the same attorney. Cattle, for example, would be moved between plantations, pens, and the abattoir. On the plantation, the cattle would be used for chattel to help drive the machinery or aid in the production of sugar. Cattle would then be moved to another owner's pen to be fattened up so that they might eventually be sent to the butchers in the city. Higman (1991: 128, 1996: 225) also examined commodity production. He noted that while much of the sugar and coffee grown on the island was meant for export, a significant proportion of these commodities was also grown for on-island consumption. The transfer of commodities between plantations was also handled through lawyers. Finally, the labor of their enslaved was transferred between plantation owners (Higman 1996: 223). At the center of this economy were agents or a group of lawyers who administered plantations and the planters' accounts. They kept accounts and balances since this economy operated more on the level of credit and barter than on cash and capital.

Aside from the documented transactions between plantations, planters would also engage in commercial transactions with island merchants to meet so-called Island Contingencies (Howson 1995: 131). This class of people Patrick Browne distinguished into factors, merchants, and peddlers: "the former transact business chiefly for European merchants, and others that supply the market with different sorts of commmodities at their own risque; as well as for different planters, for who they are naturally concerned . . ." (Browne [1759] 1789: 24).

Some planters built this into their system by employing a diversified economy in managing their plantations. If we look at the flow of cattle, planters who owned many plantations would instruct their managers to shift livestock from one holding, which might be a cattle pen, to another holding, which might be a sugar plantation. In order to feed the stock, they might have a third that grew fodder for the cattle (Shepherd 1993). Provisioning was handled similarly. A planter might own a property for growing staples that he would then send to other estates he owned to feed the enslaved. These transactions were handled primarily through the estate managers.

Planters also engaged in external trade that was not necessarily mediated through wholesalers or merchants within the towns of Jamaica. As Kamau Braithwaite (1971: 93) notes, Jamaica relied heavily on the North American colonies in order to provision the plantations. Richard Sheridan cites a London sugar merchant named Richard Glover, who stated that unfettered trade between the islands and the northern colonies was "absolutely necessary for their support and maintenance of their plantations" (Glover 1775, cited in Sheridan 1976). Richard Pares has pointed out that much of this trade was contraband to avoid "clogs upon free movement" by "human contrivance" (Pares 1956: 64–65). As Verene Shepherd (2000, 2002) has pointed out in her detailed analysis of economic practices among elites in Jamaica, the planters undertook a considerable amount of trade in cattle with the Spanish colonies of Cuba and Puerto Rico to the detriment of pen-keepers in Jamaica (2002: 177).

A final component of the "internal" economy involving the planting class, oftentimes indirectly, was the actual town markets. As a mechanism to provision either themselves with victuals or their enslaved with provisions, the planters could not ignore this necessary economic activity. The first laws in Jamaica regarding the internal/informal economy seem to be concerned primarily with where and when the markets could take place and what could be sold there on certain days. Mintz and Hall ([1970] 1991) and Mintz ([1974] 1992) cite an 1895 document that illustrates this:

> Whereas the settlement of our Island of Jamaica is much hindered or obstructed for want of a Faire or Market for the sale and buying of Horses, Mares, Mules, Assinegoes, Cowes, Bulls, and other Cattle and Many other necessities for the use of our subjects there and whereas our Towne of Snt. Jago de la Vega in our Island is commodiously situ-

ated for the keeping of which a Faire or Market in our said Towne ... four times in every year ... for the sale of Horses, Mares, Mules, Assinegoes, Cowes, Bulls, and all or other Cattle and all or any other goods and commodities whatsoever of the groweth or produce of our said Island and all or any goods, wares, merchandizes whatsoever with all liberties ... according to the usage of our kingdome of England. (Institute of Jamaica 1895: 146 in Mintz [1974] 1992: 195)

In 1678, the Council of Jamaica recorded in its minutes the following law for the Spanish Town market:

For setting of market on everyday from six to eleven for fish, food, and herbs and Tuesday Thursday and Saturday for flesh and sometimes at the parade place. (Council Minutes, vol. 2 159V 8, August 1678)

Markets were vital for the political economy of the Jamaican colony, especially in regard to the health of the body politic. In the 1699 "Act to make person a body politic and directors for the Bath of St Thomas the Apostle," provisions were made that a market be established to sell and butcher meat and "sundry provisions" (Jamaica 1716: 275). While the planter-class was protected, to a certain degree, by its status and station in Jamaican society, the settlers, Browne's second class of Jamaicans, were not. He states that settlers differ

from the former [planters], only in degree ... but the inconveniency of carriage and the frequent scarcity of flower; among those that cannot purchase considerable quantity at a time, often oblige them to substitute plantains, cassada [sic], or yams, in the room of bread. (Browne [1759] 1789: 23–24)

Settlers might have come to Jamaica as overseers or dependents to the planting class, but they eventually were able to purchase property and become landed.

Thomas Thistlewood, a planter whose life on Jamaica is an exemplar of this class of people, emigrated to Jamaica in 1750, where he became an overseer at the Egypt estate near Savanna-la-Mar. Eventually, Thistlewood managed to save enough money and purchase his own estate in St. Lucy's parish, where he eventually died in 1786. His diary of over 10,000 pages has been edited by Douglas Hall. In this diary, one gets a very real sense of the different strategies planters had to engage in to survive.

Thistlewood was a skilled horticulturalist who would grow European vegetables. From this garden, Thistlewood would make ketchup to sell to the taverns in Savanna-la-Mar (Hall 1999: 121). He was also able to sell the produce from these gardens to other plantations. In his diary we have firsthand descriptions of such transactions: "A girl from Mr. Meyler's came to buy garden stuff. Wrote to Mr. Meyler, and sent two watermelons, some tomatoes, green peas, dry peas, and dry kidney beans to plant as a present" (Thistlewood in Hall 1999: 164). He maintained a higgler who would sell items for him on other plantations or at the market in Savanna-la-Mar, Negril, or Hatfield Gate (Thistlewood in Hall 1999: 69). For example, in 1767 Thistlewood's chief higgler "sold at Savanna La Mar for me, 14 eggs, 2 bitts; Indian kale, 2 bitts; Cabbage & savoys, 3 bitts" (Thistlewood in Hall 1999: 156).

While these planters and settlers engaged in their own internal economic practices, what poorer settlers like Thistlewood tell us is that they needed to engage in market activities dominated by the enslaved. The higglers, such as the one engaged by Thistlewood, were more than servants; they were necessary personnel with a command of local geographies and costs of goods. The fact that Thistlewood needed to engage a higgler for these transactions tells us that for Englishmen who had been residents of Jamaica for some time, the market spaces were ultimately unfamiliar terrains. For the planting class the markets ultimately became a social space of enslaved laborers and higglers, in which they were outsiders. In contrast, the enslaved were able to co-opt these markets and make them their own.

Internalizing the Informal Economy

This system of street markets and higglers has been generally conceived of as linking the provision ground of enslaved people to a broader world of commodities, both imported and local. It has generally been considered on the gray side of formality and generally the social space of the free and enslaved African Jamaican. Historian Richard Sheridan (1965) called this economy the dual economy, which stands in direct opposition to the broader economy of imported commodities. Braithwaite (1971) has called it a "Creole economy," through which a group of entrepreneurs positioned themselves into a higher class standing in postslavery and postcolonial Jamaica.

For the majority of people living in Jamaica, the class Browne identifies simply as "Negroes," the locus of market activity was a series of Sunday markets and itinerant peddlers. This aspect of Jamaica's local economy has been researched and discussed much more widely and has become identified with the internal economies of Jamaica. As I will demonstrate below, there was legal allowance on the island for street markets which imperfectly meshed with social precedents of market-day activity in West Africa and Europe. This is not to say it was not under considerable scrutiny. It was subject to constant proscription by the planter class. The transactions were usually conducted through cash or barter and, most important, were largely undocumented.

To an archaeologist interested in the African Diaspora, the informal economy as a site of community formation, a place of economic struggle, and a locus of displacement makes it an obvious starting place to see the ways in which enslaved laborers created and transformed the world around them. Equally important, however, are the political struggles embedded within the operation of these markets. Indeed, in looking at Diaspora, migration, and globalization, Jonathan Friedman argues that we have to move beyond the metaphor of dwelling and movement in routing of "maps/histories" and take into account the "real issues of social displacement" (Friedman 2002: 22). Although identifying what today we would call informal market activities as peasant economies, the earliest literature (Mintz 1955; Katzin 1960; Mintz 1960, 1971a, 1971b, 1978, 1983, [1974] 1992) on street vendors highlights many of same issues. The economy was one which was described as monopolistic by planters. Yet, for market participants, it was very competitive. These participants are, for the most part, unenumerated in the documentary record. Sidney Mintz and Douglas Hall ([1970] 1991) understood the ambiguity of these actors when they tackled this textual "invisibility" as they traced the genesis of the internal market system in seventeenth- and eighteenth-century Jamaica. One aspect of this economy, which has not been the focus of study, was its scope and scale. Such understanding is useful in positioning the impact of this creole community on the larger economic system.

It is important to emphasize that when we theorize and define the informal economy and subsequent black marketing, it is not defined in terms of legality. To do so would place barriers on economic interactions that were necessarily fluid and had the potential of extending beyond colonial boundaries. In his analysis of African street markets in New York City, Paul Stoller (Stoller 1996, 2001) points out that the markets were metaphorical and material sites of struggle over the economic landscape of New York City, where zoning legislation and market regulation became mechanisms through which to enumerate economic subjects that the mayor's office presumed and later advertised to be undermining civil society (Stoller 1996, 2001). These same politics played out in eighteenth-century Jamaica.

Taking a cue from Stoller's work, we should define informal economic activities in terms of their transgressive potential and theorize the economies beyond island-specific ways. This enables an understanding of the imperfect fit between local economic demands and the broader colonial landscape of the plantation society that the black markets exploited. This larger economic landscape depended on systems of control which maintained both symbolic and structural manifestations, including the structuring of plantation space (Delle 1998, 1999, 2000a; Delle, Mrozowski, and Paynter 2000; Singleton 2001), its representation in contemporary art (Honychurch 2003), and legal regimentation of the actions of the enslaved (Simmonds 2004).

The problem remains that, by their very nature, informal economies are poorly documented. That being said, the nature of economic interaction between subaltern groups can be culled from the documentary record, although in a partial manner only. To tease out information on informal economies in the past, scholars have generally relied on anecdotal accounts, laws and regulations, and the assumption (not necessarily misplaced) that enslaved laborers exploited both the spatial and structural interstices of slave society. Hillary Beckles (1989b, 1991) argues that Mintz and Hall, in their assertion that the markets were born out of English commercial and legal precedent, fail to take into account that laws establishing markets might be reacting to existing economic practices rather than anticipating market demands. As Elsa Goveia has noted, the West Indian slave laws reflected "the political traditions of the European colonizers and the political necessities of a way of life based upon plantation slavery" (Goveia [1960] 1991: 75). They reflect the immediate needs of those who have power to enact laws and can therefore be used as a way to gauge those activities.

In this way, it can be argued that the slave laws reflect the ideology of the planter and at least an attempt to maintain the status quo. Certainly, as Elsa Goveia argues, the Code Noir comprised "laws of subordination" (Goveia [1960] 1991: 76). Laws regarding the street markets could, therefore, be read as the way the planters tried to subordinate the markets. In Jamaica, there are numerous published digests, abstracts, and accounts of laws passed during the eighteenth century. Most of these laws contain within them both provisions for market activities undertaken locally and provisions for the regulation of the enslaved. In addition to the actual legal code, we have its interpretation by at least one individual, Edward Long.

In Jamaica, attempts at regulating market activities by enslaved laborers can be seen as early as the seventeenth century:

> ... some little disturbance ... had happened at Passage Fort on Saturday night last with the Negroes at this Market which if not prevented might in time grow.... Upon consideration whereof the Board being of Opinion that the liberty given to Negroes to give a Market at the River Mouth and Passage Fort every Saturday had been an Occasion of that disturbance. (Council of Jamaica 1685)

These "little" disturbances highlight a general disorder that many elites perceived as a product of informal economic activities. As Lorna Simmonds (2004: 279) argues, the establishing of markets was as much a reaction against the unstructured and unconfined market activities as it was an attempt to facilitate provisioning. While one mechanism to reduce this disorder was to proscribe and limit the participants' activities, elites also legislated market spaces and places as a way to impose order and, at the same time, benefit from the relief on provisioning afforded by the markets.

In 1793, as an attempt to regulate market activity of the enslaved, the Jamaican assembly passed an act "for and towards erecting and establishing places of public mart or markets, in the towns which they think most fit and convenient" (Jamaica 1793: 34 Geo. 3 cap. xviii). The vestry of Westmoreland parish established one such market at Savanna-la-Mar. Speaking of this city in 1781, Thomas Thistlewood tells us that a robust market of provisions and wares already existed, but "few provisions today at market. My Negroes bought pumpkins for the most part" (Thistlewood in Hall 1999: 283). For Thistlewood, granting his laborers access to this market was a vital element in his provisioning the enslaved, but it was ultimately a space in which he remained an outsider.

Even after the establishment of these formal markets, they remained problematic for the planter. The sociality of the street markets is nicely captured in the Duperly print of the Falmouth market in the mid-nineteenth century (figure 2.2). This print depicts a Sunday market. It was one in a number of daguerreotypes published in Adolphe Duperly's *Daguerrian Excursions* in 1844. This tour served two purposes; it was a manner to introduce a new technology to a potential customer base that previously patronized artists like James Hakewill and Isaac Belisario. Second, it was an attempt to display the everyday life of Jamaica. The silver plates were exposed in Jamaica and later processed in Paris. The technique developed

Markets of Contention 55

Figure 2.2. *Marketplace, Falmouth, Jamaica* by Adolphe Duperly, Daguerrian Excursions in Jamaica (Kingston, Jamaica, 1843). Courtesy of the National Library of Jamaica.

by Daguerre and employed by Duperly required a considerable amount of time for the plate to be exposed; thus, it was ideal for landscapes but rather ill suited for market scenes (Robertson 1985: 17). In the specific shown here it explains why there is an almost photographic quality of the built landscape, while the market participants were later inked in. The combination of techniques was later distributed en masse through lithography.

In a sense, we have in this print an "accurate depiction" of the area around the water cistern combined with Duperly's impression of the actual higglers. One is at first struck by the number of people. Women who seem to be wearing their best clothes dominate the market. All of the images depict a bustling sea of humanity. In a system built of surveillance, isolation and control, this market provided anything but that crucial element. Immediately obvious in this scene is the masonry cistern that acts as center to the market and to Falmouth. While providing a noticeable landmark, it obstructs the views of anyone wishing a clear view of the market. Other systems of control were in place but far less effective. In a sense, this highlights the point and potential of spatialities of these markets. Technologies of control, however effective and sophisticated, are not exclusively about repression but always outline a set of practices that delimit a horizon of possibilities (and not only constraint) for the subjects they purport to fashion (see Foucault 1972).

By regulating the economic activities of the enslaved, attempting to draw revenue from these activities, and formalizing the spaces in which the transactions could take place, the assembly of Jamaica was attempting to create an internal economy. In other words, it was trying to create a framework of economic transactions that could ultimately be governed by the planting class and surveilled by officers of the law. All attempts, however, to anglicize the markets resulted in impromptu "Negro markets" popping up on market day.

Internalizing the Other

The disorder associated with the markets ultimately stemmed from identities that planters, visitors, and administrators describing Jamaica assigned to enslaved laborers participating in the market: thieves, cheats, and runaways. The way in which landscape reflects and shapes structural roles of actors and the ways those roles are mediated through identity has been elucidated by numerous scholars. Ken Olwig defines landscape as the "nexus of law and cultural identity" (1996: 63) and can therefore be operationalized as having:

> a double role with respect to something like ideology: it naturalizes a cultural and social construction, representing an artificial world as if it were simply given and inevitable, and it also makes that representation operational by interpellating its beholder . . . in some more or less determinate relation to its givenness. (Mitchell 1994a: 2; see also Gosden and Head 1994: 114–15)

The regulated nature of markets and the marginal aspect of its participants allow us to view the local economies of the Caribbean in the eighteenth century as one such landscape.

Edward Long was born in Cornwall, was educated as a barrister, and emigrated to Jamaica in 1757. While in Jamaica, he was appointed to the court of the admiralty and gained considerable experience with the Jamaican legal structure. In his three-volume *History of Jamaica*, Long provides one of the most detailed accounts of slave society and, more important, discusses the details the mechanisms of colonial government. Of primary concern to Long is the orderly deputation of enslaved Africans, a community he argues has natural predilections toward laziness and comprehends little if "anything of mechanics arts or manufacture" (Long [1774] 1970: 476). Through the filter of this racist bias, he provides a detailed summary of various codes and how they might better regulate civil disorder among the enslaved.

In legislative terms, the enslaved were never trusted with property. In 1662 and 1678, laws attempted to abate the practice of stealing imported consumables and selling them back in the street markets. During the eighteenth century, this reaction to the sale of stolen items is iterated and reiterated in a succession of codes concerning peddling, including laws passed by the Assembly in 1711, 1730, 1735 (Jamaica 1743), 1749 (Jamaica 1786), 1786, 1788, and 1793 (Jamaica 1793). In essence, these laws permit "Mulattoe, Indian, or Negro" (Jamaica 1738) to hawk "provisions, fruits, and other enumerated articles"[1] (Long [1774] 1970), "provided the persons have a Ticket from the Master or Owner of such Goods" (Jamaica 1738: 294), "in which Ticket is to be expressed their Name, from whence, and whither going" (Leslie 1740), and "upon complaint and conviction before a justice, to be whipped by order of such justice" (Long [1774] 1970).[2]

In these laws, we see not only a circumscription of economic activity among the enslaved, but also an identification of opposition between black and white markets: those run by property-owning (renting) merchants who must pay taxes, and those who are not subjected to the same demands. In the preamble of Act 106 of the 1735 code, we see these politics play out:

> Whereas divers Mulattoes, Indians, and Negroes, have of late been frequently employed in hawking and selling, from Place to Place, all Manner of Goods, Wares, and Merchandize which are commonly used and sold in this island; which Practice tends to manifest Prejudice of Trade, and great Discouragement of House-keepers, who are subject to Parochial Duties, Taxes, and Rents for their Houses: be it

---

1 "Hawking about and selling goods except provisions, fruits and other enumerated articles to be punished, on conviction before a magistrate, by whipping, not exceeding thirty-one lashes" (Long [1774] 1970 2: 487).

2 "A slave, selling in any public place, or market, any other goods than such as properly belong to his owner, or for his owner's use, and that are not expressed in a ticket, upon complaint and conviction before a justice, to be whipped by order of such justice" (Long [1774] 1970 2: 489).

> therefore enacted ... That no Mulattoe, Indian, or Negro whatsoever, shall hawk, or carry about to sell, from Place to Place, or shall sell in any open Street or Market, any sort of Goods, Wares, or Merchandize whatsoever. (Jamaica 1738: 223)

The participants are seen as parasitic to the overall economic well-being of the island, even though it is well known, or at least generally understood, that the division in economic activity is not so rigid.

Market sellers, who did not have to pay taxes or rent, were seen as predatory. In the minds of authors like Edward Long, Bryan Edwards, and William Beckford, they seditiously profited from the hard work of poor white settlers and dependents who played by the rules. By championing the cause of settlers and dependents, administrators successfully embedded and imbued the market with connotations of illegality and conspiracy. Indeed, many administrators blamed factor, planter, and slave. Describing the differences between merchants and peddlers, Patrick Browne states:

> The Merchants import their own goods, and run the risque of the markets; but generally turn to pedlars in the disposal of them; the business was, indeed, beneficial while they could supply the neighboring markets ... and the next class [pedlars] is entirely engrossed by the factors, who generally import such commodities as are commonly wanted at a plantation. (Browne [1759] 1789: 24)

In this case, hardworking merchants are undermined by the collusion of wholesalers and peddlers who cornered the market on imported commodities and imposed inflated prices of (on?) settlers and dependents.

With regard to local produce, price inflation was not so much the result of collusion as the combination of planter apathy and the opportunism of the enslaved. In 1719, Governor Lawes said:

> If it were possible to regulate the markets, so that Poor Men and their Families might be able to live and settle among Us, it would be one good Way to multiply our people, who are much too thin, and the Rich and Wanton forsake Us every Day. (C.O. 137: 13, p. 65. Cited in Pitman [1917] 1945: 109)

He continued to voice concern in 1720:

> The impossibility of their continuing to live here under the prices that govern your markets; which, to my knowledge, has obliged several

families to leave us, for the sake of living cheaper in the Northern Colonies. (C.O. 137: 13, p. 89. Cited in Pitman [1917] 1945: 109)

In 1730, Col. Robert Hayes complained of the local economic conditions to a fellow officer, "I'll assure you half a Crown in England will go farther than a Pistole here; for my cook which is a very indifferent one fifty; & every thing dear in proportion, you May judge what a pleasant situation I am in" (C.O. 137: 19, s. 118. Cited in Pitman [1917] 1945: 109).

There were attempts by the Jamaican Assembly to ameliorate the condition of settlers and dependents by proscribing the buying up of provisions in order to control the market. The 1735 code maintained express provisions to prevent inflation,

> for better preventing of hawkers and forestallers of the market as go a considerable way out of the respective Towns in this Island to meet such persons as bring in Plantation-provisions and other Stock, and do buy up and engross the same; by which Means and the prices of Provisions of all kinds are greatly advanced. (Jamaica 1743)

In 1793 the code had not changed significantly from the 1735 provision:

> If any Mulatto, Indian, or Negro, go out of the towns, to meet persons in plantation bringing provisions and other stock, and buy them up, to revend or engross, they are to be whipped at discretion of the magistrate. (Jamaica 1793)

What is interesting about both the 1735 and the 1793 codes is that they assume a predatory economic practice on the part of indigenous actors or actors of African descent.

There is a vast literature about attempts to enumerate a population in order to define and identify it in abstract terms and eventually control it (see J. Morgan 2002). Certainly, the concept of political arithmetic had been around since the seventeenth century (see Petty [1669] 1970). What is remarkable about these activities is that enumerative technologies in place (while thought to be totalizing by their proponents) were never complete in their task. Certainly, one mechanism employed to keep count on the population of sellers was tickets.

Tickets were basically permission slips given by the master to travel outside the plantation and visit markets. If an enslaved laborer was bringing anything to market, the ticket should have those items listed on it. They ensured, at least in theory, that goods sold at the markets were not stolen. Officials were ideally supposed to check the tickets as they entered the marketplace. Similarly, officers of the law would check for tickets when walking past individuals going to market.

It seems that in the eighteenth century this was an enforced law. Thomas Thistlewood gave tickets out as a boon for a job well done or a celebration: "Gave Jackie, Lewie, Johnie, Margaritta & Phibbah tickets to go to Roaring River to buy Provisions. Also to Hector & Peter—Pero—Sarah, Cubbah, Abba, Eve—Dover to Paradise" (Thistlewood in D. Hall 1999: 101). Tickets were also a means through which the population in general could be controlled. Sellers were asked to produce a ticket, and if they could not, the owner of the goods would be fined, and the enslaved carrying the goods would be whipped (Jamaica 1735).

In an analysis of slave courtroom practices in eighteenth-century St. Andrews parish, Diana Paton demonstrates that laws regarding theft and sale of private property were thoroughly enforced. Of the 222 cases brought before the slave court, 94 were charged with the offense of theft. Of those, 28 were acquitted, 11 were put to death, and the rest were either transported, mutilated, or flogged (Paton 2001: 946). Many of the more severe penalties concerned the theft of livestock, but the other items reported as stolen include "other produce," "clothing," and "cash" (Paton 2001: 929).

A second mechanism through which the Assembly of Jamaica and the common council of Kingston attempted to control the market, and to collect revenue from this poorly enumerated activity, was to issue licenses. In 1786, the ninety-fifth Act of the Assembly attempted to rectify this and established that "Every hawker and Peddlar . . . pay to the Church-wardens, a duty of twenty pounds a year, for obtaining a licence; and if travelling with a beast of burden . . . more" (Jamaica 1786: 10). Certainly, the colonial government had access to considerable revenue stemming from the duties and taxes levied on white-market sales by merchants. They did not have similar access to revenue from the informal economy.

The vestries were supposed to collect this revenue and improve conditions for the poor within their parish. This practice of licensing continued well into the nineteenth century. It probably was more effective as a method of monitoring and enumeration than as a method of revenue generation. It certainly did not assist in making the life of dependents any better.

Both the enslaved and freed market participants most likely inflated prices for their own gain. But to say this was done in the absence of competition assumes that the enslaved were an internally consistent class of people, who did not compete with each other. The enslaved and freed people of African descent who participated in the market were subject to similar pressures of supply and demand as European merchants in Jamaica (Sheridan 1976). These pressures also include the same social and cultural capital deployed in maintaining economic relationships. Because the various actors were aggregated into a single class and set in opposition to the minority of European-descended planters, settlers, and dependents, they were viewed as having a monopoly. This "monopoly" was born out of the participants' ability to move between urban and rural milieus and engage with multiple sectors of Jamaican society. Most important, however, the regulation of markets, and the planters' dependency on the enslaved and freed populations of Jamaica to operate them, created a set of social relations in which the activities these individuals participated in were inevitably on the margins of legality, thereby making the operators ultimately transgressive.

Embodying the Local

Stuart Hall argues that identity is "produced in specific historical and institutional sites within specific discursive formations and practices, by specific enunciative strategies." (S. Hall 1996: 4). Market activity undertaken by higglers embodied the local economy, in that the trade was one of island-produced goods and the islands' shores circumscribed the flow of the commodities. The higglers themselves were also local, in that they had mastered the various physical and economic geographies of Jamaica. They could move seamlessly between plantation and city and between provision ground and market. This mobility allowed the higglers to develop an expertise in the various demands and supplies for local produce on the island—a knowledge not shared by the planter. In a sense, they were a very localized version of what Mary Helms has described as "long distance specialists of various sorts who make it their business to go away and return with tangible and intangible rewards" (Helms 1988: 3). For the enslaved, circumscribed by the obligations of laboring on plantation grounds six days a week, the distances traversed by higglers were great. Conversely, for the planters who did not know the provision ground trails or the unwritten rules of the informal trade, the higglers' knowledge was equally "esoteric." Such knowledge made a higgler a potentially dangerous sort of person who could control the market and pass information outside the gaze of the planter.

When Adam Smith wrote *The Wealth of Nations*, he argued that higgling (the bargaining of prices up) and haggling (the bargaining of prices down) were two elements in a homeostatic system that results in the imperfect valuation of commodities and labor:

> In exchanging indeed the different productions of different sorts of labour for one another, some allowance is commonly made for both. It is adjusted, however, not by any accurate measure, but by the higgling and bargaining of the market, according to that sort of rough equality which, though not exact, is sufficient for carrying on the business of common life. (Smith [1776] 1994: 1.5.5)

In the absence of haggling, or bargaining the price down, a monopoly on the part of sellers is complete. Because of their mastery of the interstitial spaces of Jamaica, and their ability to move between and beyond the bounded localities of Jamaica, higglers, at least from the perspective of the planter, were able to create an imbalanced hold on the market for island produce.

Implicit in the definition of *higgler* is an opprobrium in which the actors have mastered "the 'art of bargaining' in the absence of competition" (Brown 1994: 66). The term, derived from the older form, *to haggle*, has been in use in the English language at least since the seventeenth century. In 1797, Thomas Sheridan's dictionary, *A Complete Dictionary of the English Language,* defined a higgler as "one who sells provisions by retail." According to the Oxford English Dictionary, early in its use, connotations of the word included the linking of urban populations with hinterland goods (see DeFoe 1895 [1756]: 140) and the "forestalling" of those goods for a captive set of consumers (see Ellis 1744: 70; Henry Fielding's *Tom Jones* 1791: 168). Today, the term is considered a Jamaican one, at least in Jamaica (see Cassidy and LePage 1967: 225), and indeed was in common usage when Sidney Mintz (1955), Sidney Mintz and Douglas Hall (1970), as well as Margaret Katzin (1959a, 1959b, 1960), wrote their initial articles describing the origins and practice of the internal market system. In the eighteenth century, however, it does not seem to be a term used to class this specific group of itinerant country peddlers linking the provision grounds with the city markets. In the eighteenth century, a variety of terms are used, including *hawkers, peddlers,* and *forestallers* (Jamaica 1735). It is not until the very end of the eighteenth century and the early nineteenth century that higgler is used to describe this petite bourgeoisie (Kingston Ordinances 1803 cited in Simmonds 2002: 289).

While the higglers were unenumerated, they were not unnoticed. Many of the transgressions that were legislated by the Assembly of Jamaica and the common council of Kingston, as described in the previous chapter, were embodied in descriptive accounts by the country peddlers who would come to be known as higglers. In 1797 they were described by an anonymous author:

> In the towns there is a species of occupation very agreeable to the indolent and desultory disposition of the negroes. They are sent abroad by their owners, to work out as it is called, for which liberty they are obliged to pay a certain rate per week or month. This practice, although prohibited by law, prevails to the great distress of the other negroes, and the poorer sort of white inhabitants. Turned loose on the community, they are guilty of every kind of fraud and forestalling, to make up their respective allotments. (Anonymous 1797: 702)

Whether they were enslaved and colluding with unscrupulous, unnamed planters, as in this passage, or they were freed persons colluding with the enslaved, hawkers and higglers attracted a considerable amount of attention from the white public at large.

As many have noted, urban freed women were not a homogeneous class of people. They were employed as nurses, cooks, and washerwomen, or employed themselves as shopkeepers, tavern keepers, seamstresses, and higglers (Bush 1981; Simmonds 1987, 2004; Boa 1993; Socolow 1996; Brereton 1999). The status afforded each of these occupations speaks to the degree of visibility these women have in the documentary record. Higher-status women, such as tavern keepers and shopkeepers, were visible due to their perceived extravagance in behavior and clothing (Burton 1993: 71). Those that were less well-off, such as higglers and washerwomen, were the constant topic of newspapers such as the *Jamaica Courant*, the *Royal Gazette*, and the *Jamaica Mercury*. In these newspapers, the hardships and misfortunes of these women are regaled (Boa 1993: 6). Also described are the various ways in which these traders undermined local established traders and soon "ruin[ed] the towns" (Simmonds 1987: 34).

There was incredible concern over the higglers' ability to inflate costs, but also over the degree to which planters began to rely on them. An often-discussed example of this is the way in which Thomas Thistlewood relied on Phibbah (the enslaved woman responsible for market activities, and his mistress), to the point where some have argued that an inversion in power relations occurred (Burnard 2004: 217). It is important to keep in mind, however, that no matter how much power these enslaved and freed women were able to accumulate, they were ultimately subjected within a highly regimented society. Such interdependency reveals a central irony of enslaved independent production: even though planters saw themselves as in control of the situation, they in fact were aware they were missing key information.

Indeed, much of the perceived power of these itinerant peddlers came from their ability to negotiate the geographies in between the plantation and the city, and to dictate the costs of goods. The higglers, as I asserted before, had begun to take possession of the interstitial spaces of plantation Jamaica. While there were full-time higglers, this was often a "second job" for many seamstresses, nurses, and washerwomen. While anchored in particular locales, these women often traveled considerable distances. In the case of three higglers, they would travel ten to fifteen miles in a given day (Mullin 1994).

In a discussion of these accounts, Michael Mullin tracks the movement of three part-time higglers noted in the *Royal Gazette* (Mullin 1994: 305). Mimba would travel in the hinterland of St. Andrew's parish between Wagwater and Above Rocks, most likely haggling with enslaved laborers and planters on estates. No mention is made of her coming to market on Saturdays or Sundays. Others, like Bella, moved principally between "the three towns" (cited in ibid.), namely Spanish Town, Port Royal, and Kingston. A third would move between estate and city, linking Fort Augusta, Spanish Town, and plantations in the environs.

From what can be gleaned from the accounts, the range of movement was quite limited. Indeed, if enslaved laborers ventured too far from their estates, they could be arrested for stealing and running away. Similarly, laws governing and taxing itinerant merchants could have also limited freed higglers. In combination with the 1785 Licensing Law discussed above, the Assembly also passed a transient tax in 1785. In this law transient traders are defined as, "All person who shall arrive at the said town . . . , with goods or merchandize for sale, and who are not taxed upon the parish-rolls." In this case it was incumbent upon the vestries to enumerate and tax these individuals: "Justices and Vestry of said town [Kingston, Spanish Town, Montego Bay, Savanna-la-Mar] or Parish, may, and are hereby authorized and required, to asses and tax such transient as often as they shall arrive at the said town" (Jamaica 1789: 78).

The transient traders were most likely a range of merchants and peddlers employing either cabotage, waterborne traffic, or road carriage. They were required to swear a series of oaths regarding their ownership of the goods, thus mitigating the possibility of theft but also telling us that this law was not intended for the enslaved. It did, most likely, extend to the higglers, and restrict monetarily their freedom of movement. In the case of Bella, mentioned earlier, she could be taxed three times—St. Catherine's parish, Kingston parish, and Port Royal parish. Her mobility and her ability to profit from stolen goods marked her as worthy of attention:

> They are the receivers and vendors of stolen goods and occasionally thieves themselves; the most honest part of their employment being to monopolize roots, greens, fruit and other edibles, which they produce from the country Negroes, and retail at exorbitant prices. An evil long and severely felt, yet not withstanding the Legislature has provided a concise and easy method of prevention, they are suffered to proceed without interruption. (Anonymous 1797: 702)

As is indicated in this passage and the chapter, there was much concern about the higglers, but they were also vital in maintaining Jamaica's economic health. Higglers linked the rural with the urban, the elites with the laboring class, and the house yard of plantation enslaved with the tenements of the freed persons and enslaved of the city. The above author is silent as to the gender of the higglers. However, following the work of scholars like Barbara Bush (1990) and Lorna Simmonds (1987, 2004), we can assert that these higglers were predominantly women during the time that this description was penned. This leaves open the possibility that the perceived disorder that markets introduced was also a gendered one. Following Mary Douglas who famously defined dirt as "matter out of place," we can use statements, like those written above, to suggest that for Edward Long and the anonymous author, women's participation may have been "out of place," thus contributing to their perception of disorder in these markets.

Conclusion

While the informal markets were, by and large, contributing to the political economy of the island, many white residents, like the above author, felt that the participants were able to circumvent burdens of the state and undermine the political economy through their trade in stolen goods. Within the context of eighteenth-century Jamaica, many of these market activities were discouraged and proscribed (Higman 1996, 1998; Simmonds 1987, 2004). Also within the context of the pre-emancipation Jamaica, the primary participants in the markets were women of African descent (Mintz and Hall 1970; Hall 1980; Bush 1981, 1990; Beckles 1991; Boa 1993; Turner

1995; Paton 1996, 2001). As was highlighted in the previous chapter, it is not the intention of this book to paint a picture of a single economic system that stood in opposition to the emergent capitalist structure. Rather, I am studying through the material and documentary record the complex set of economic behaviors undertaken by myriad participants but focused on the system of Sunday markets and higglers.

The internal market systems of the Caribbean introduced disorder into the colonial landscapes, a disorder that is evident in contemporary illustrations. It initiated economic instability, at least from the planters' perspective, and its participants and their practices were discordant with administrator expectations. The transgressive nature of these markets went far beyond the collection of petty cash through the sale of goods. They were places of tension, where the enslaved introduced disorder to the slave regime. This disorder existed on an abstract level, providing a level of economic agency from the plantation economy (see Olwell 1996 for a similar phenomenon in South Carolina), but it also provided a real and material means for resistance (Higman 1998). But this was a disorder, which, to some extent, is born of and necessary to the formation of the capitalist state and operation of its economies. Finally, while there has been much written about the transgressive potential of the Sunday markets, they were ultimately venues in which social networks among the enslaved were established. In the next chapter, I look at the ways the markets provided an arena for enslaved to transcend the boundaries of the plantations and develop social networks outside of the plantation milieu. Specifically, I examine the ways in which these markets potentially linked six communities in the central part of Jamaica, represented by seven archaeological sites. While these communities were connected through a series of postal roads, the distances between them were greater than an enslaved laborer's limited range of movement on a market day.

3

Between Urban and Rural

On Sunday they carry their riches to market, for such the produce of a good ground to an industrious negro may with propriety be called; and if they have only this day in the week, as is commonly the case throughout the crop, they must go to the mountains early in the morning to search for provisions, that they may be in time to barter or to vend them at the well-known town, and to which they will repair, although it be ten, or even a more considerable number of miles from the plantation; and it is astonishing what immense weights they will carry upon their heads at this extended distance, with what cheerfulness they will undertake the length and with what spirit and perseverance they will overcome the fatigue of the journey.

Beckford 1790 2: 153

Ann Stahl (2002: 827; see also Stahl 2004) has argued that in the archaeology of colonial contexts, archaeologists must focus on the "embodied forms of practical knowledge which framed colonial relations" (2002: 827). For Stahl, taste proved to be an ideal form of embodied knowledge through which to see how colonial relations shaped ways of doing things in Banda—a region in western Ghana. Stahl suggests that where European capitalism seems to shape the choices of colonial subjects, certain courses of action and social logics that preceded these global transformations played a key role in mediating and translating the latter's expressions in colonial settings. The colonial relations surrounding market activity were complex. As is indicated in the opening quote, the livelihood of the enslaved depended on their ability to grow provisions, make crafts, or barter services. These activities went beyond the physical boundaries of the plantation and acted to connect various communities throughout Jamaica. Yet, for the most part, as archaeologists our analytical scope on plantation life has been single-sited. The social relations of slavery in eighteenth-century Jamaica must be viewed beyond the confines of the plantation. Our units of analysis must allow for the possibility that potentially alternate relations were configured in set-apart places like the provision grounds and market spaces.

Beginning with Sidney Mintz's article (1955) on the Jamaican internal market system (see also Mintz 1960, 1978, 1983; Mintz and Hall [1970] 1991), there has been an analytical primacy given to local economies by anthropologists and historians alike. As an institution, local economies reveal the variegated circuits through which people interacted. Whether the markets proved to be a symbolic affront to the plantation order (see also Beckles 1989a, 1989b 1991, 1995) or the embodied manifestation of an emergent proto-peasantry dependent on land they did not own (Mintz 1978, 1983; Mintz and Hall 1991), the markets were contested sites. As such, the analysis of local economies including street markets and higglers gets at the ways in which people did things in emergent global economies. It is in this ground-up approach to political economy that archaeologists of the Diaspora in the Caribbean have begun to move the debates of field from issues of migration into issues of interaction.

The question I am asking is similar to questions asked by those studying empire and political economy in other world areas: in what ways do domestic and local economies intersect with broader imperial economic systems? This book is an attempt to describe the "diverse economic systems and strategies, which varied with the nature of the good being produced and its context of production" (Morrison and Sinopoli 1992: 335) and the ways in which colonial relations conditioned or framed the consumption of colonial subjects (Stahl 2002). To be certain, the analysis of political economy through archaeology has demonstrated the need to imbricate production, exchange, and consumption within political systems and relationships of power (Cobb 1993; Sinopoli 1994a, 1994b, 2003: 1; Sinopoli and Morrison 1995; Muller 1997; Stein 1998: 356, 2002, 2005; Patterson 1999: 156; Pauketat 2004; Stahl 2004; see also O'Donovan 2002).

There has been considerable interest of late in linking the provision grounds of the enslaved laborer with a broader world of commodities exchanged in internal economies. These connections have been studied through examinations of differential access to imported materials (Tomich [1990] 1991; Howson 1995; Reeves 1997), consumption patterns of enslaved laborers (Wilkie and Farnsworth 1999; Wilkie 2000a; Loftfield 2001; Wilkie and Farnsworth 2005), as well as the scale and impact of local economies manifested in the presence of imported goods. In many ways, this approach has provided a unique bridge between the individual and particular archaeological contexts of plantation laborers, and a series of economic phenomena. This research strategy has been developed by looking at regional intra-island systems of trade through the distribution of island-specific material culture.

For anthropologists, historians, and archaeologists, the Jamaican local economic system has been seen as central to understanding the social dynamics of eighteenth-century plantation society. There is, however, a tendency to oversimplify the system as a single institution, as was highlighted in the last chapter. The internal economy, however, was more complicated than a black market. It comprised a complex array of interactions that focused on the planter, the merchant, the freeperson, and enslaved laborers. By understanding the complexity of the system and delineating its many facets, tensions are revealed which point to questions concerning its scale and scope. By understanding the distribution of commodities that flowed through these markets, we can illustrate, at least partially, the scales of this economy.

Distancing Trade

The infrastructure of roads, waterways, and small ports affected the operation of the planters, the positioning of the plantation, the development of the markets, and, ultimately, the ability of enslaved communities to access these markets. Transport in Jamaica was accomplished either by small coastal craft traveling between major towns along Jamaica's coast, canoes which negotiated the riverine systems of western Jamaica, and a growing road network. By the nineteenth century, Jamaica's infrastructure had grown to the degree that it included an extensive railroad that traveled between Kingston and Montego Bay, and Kingston and Port Antonio. In the eighteenth century, two factors mitigated the distance involved in local economic interaction: first, there was a well-traveled road connecting Kingston, Spanish Town, and Saint Ann's Bay; and second, there was water traffic in the western part of the island.

Traveling by canoe was a very important mechanism through which planters' goods were transported between the plantation and the small coastal ports. In western Jamaica, dominated by river systems like the Black River and the Martha Brae drainages, canoes were especially important, as they were used to traverse great distances. Canoes were either imported from Jamaican dependencies like the Mosquito Coast and the Bay of Honduras (Long [1774] 1970 1: 506) or were constructed locally out of cottonwood by African Jamaicans (Sloane 1707–1725 2: 72; Thistlewood in Hall

1999: 145). Provisions for the plantation would often be delivered by canoe. Thistlewood mentioned:

> About 1 p.m. the canoe came. Received by her, 2 firkins of butter from Meyler's wharf, a small barrel of herrings, and a half a barrel of beef; also received an old grindstone about 22 inches & a half dr. from Mr. Wheatley. (Thistlewood in Hall 1999: 87)

Although, as discussed in the last chapter, laws restricted the use of canoes by enslaved laborers; in western Jamaica, it was the most expedient way for the enslaved to visit the street markets on Sunday. Planters like Thomas Thistlewood also allowed his enslaved to use canoes to travel back and forth between Savanna-la-Mar and Egypt (Thistlewood in Hall 1999: 145).

Cabotage, using vessels that ferried between the smaller ports of Jamaica and the major ports of Kingston and Port Royal, was one of the major mechanisms through which local trade and carriage was expedited. This intercoastal trade employed small vessels, including sloops and schooners, and would have been one of the ways the planters shipped goods in their local internal economy. An anonymous writer noted this of trading boats in the eighteenth century:

> As there are generally many vessels in the harbour, they afford a tolerable trade to the canoes, in which ready prepared coffee and chocolate, bread, fried fish, fruit, &c. are sold. This is not only a useful business, but commendable, from giving employment to disabled Negroes who are fit for little else than making a fire, rowing or steering a boat. (Anonymous 1797: 702; also in Higman 1976: 12)

In 1774, Edward Long estimates that at least sixteen sloops and schooners were trading between Kingston and Jamaica out ports (St. Ann's Bay, Morant Bay, Montego Bay, etc. . . .) (Long [1774] 1970 1: 504). In some cases, masters permitted enslaved laborers to transport goods between distant markets and the plantation by boat. Barclay writes:

> Slaves at Holland estate, have or had lately, a coasting vessel, which they employed in carrying plantains, yams, eddoes and corn, from the estate's warf to Kingston, a distance of sixty to seventy miles. (Barclay [1826] 1969: 272)

While most of the slaves did not have access to canoes, it was one form of transportation linking the interior of Jamaica and the coast and different ports with Kingston.

The final form of transportation was by road. Indeed the importance of well-maintained roads in linking the provision grounds with the market was not lost on some of the planters. In 1790, William Beckford complained:

> Those roads, in particular, that lead to the greatest number of pieces [of land], and that serve as general communication to the foot of the mountains, to the pastures, to the works, and market, should in my opinion, be carefully and substantially paved. (Beckford 1790 1: 171)

Edward Long thought that during his life in Jamaica significant changes were made to the road system, "But by the vast improvements of the roads within these few years, particularly in the mode of constructing them, the carriage of goods and merchandize in general with half the number of horses formerly required" (Long [1774] 1970 1: 465).

Historic maps of Jamaica show how the road network grew during the eighteenth century. Some of the traffic between plantations and between markets occurred through networks of roads in Jamaica, although this was hampered by varying degrees of repair (Goodwin 1946: 98–99). Six maps drawn in the seventeenth and eighteenth centuries demonstrate the development of the road networks in Jamaica. These include *Tabula Iamaicae Insulae* by Edward Slaney (1678), *Neiuwe Kaart van het Eyland Jamaica* by Herman Moll (1710), *A New and Accurate Map of the Island of Jamaica* by Emanuel Bowen (1744), *Carte reduite de l'isle de la Jamaique pour servir aux vaisseaux du Roy* by Jacques Nicholas Belin (1753), *A Correct Map of Jamaica* by Georg Ehret (1757), the map found in Browne's *History of Jamaica* (1759), *A Correct Map of Jamaica* by an Anonymous Cartographer in 1760, found in the *Royal Magazine,* and *A Correct Map of Jamaica* by Thomas Jefferys (1768) and republished in Edward Long (1774) (map 3.1).

There are differing degrees of accuracy, precision, and scale in the rendering of the maps. There are also shifting emphases; the anonymous map was apparently drawn to illustrate a revolt by enslaved laborers (Pedley 1979; Reitan 1985). In the case of Jeffery's maps there is considerable variation in what were identified as roads. As a whole, however, the maps show an increasing investment into the infrastructure of Jamaica. Not only did the roads allow greater access between the rural and the urban, they also provided an alternative to water transport between the west with the east and the north and the south. Importantly for the enslaved of the plantations, they linked their provision grounds with the local markets.

Matthew Reeves (1997: 166) notes that by foot, Linstead and Old Harbour were respectively four and ten hours away from Juan de Bollas. Below, I have transcribed the distances between Kingston and various secondary

72   An Archaeology of Black Markets

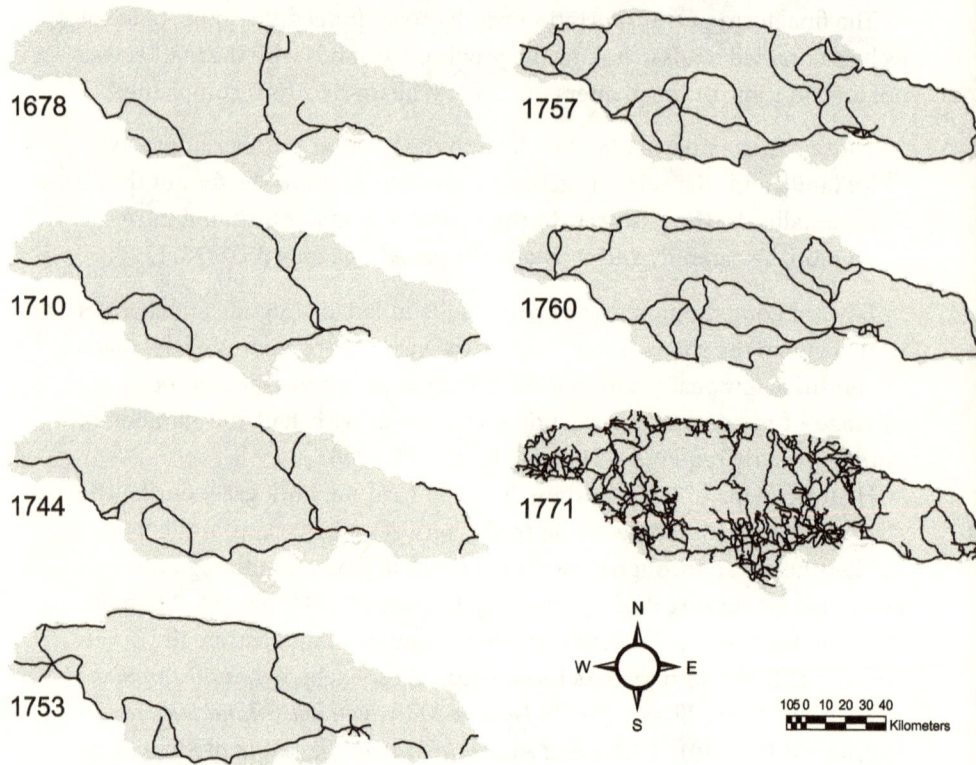

Map 3.1. The Development of Jamaican roads in the eighteenth century. Drawn with varying degrees of accuracy from the seventeenth to the nineteenth century. *Tabula Iamaicae Insulae* by Edward Slaney (1678), *Neiuwe Kaart van het Eyland Jamaica* by Herman Moll (1710), *A New and Accurate Map of the Island of Jamaica* by Emanuel Bowen (1744), *Carte reduite de l'isle de la Jamaique pour servir aux vaisseaux du roy* by Jacques Nicholas Belin (1753), *A Correct Map of Jamaica* by Georg Ehret (1757), the map found in Browne's *History of Jamaica* (1759), *A Correct Map of Jamaica* by an Anonymous Cartographer in 1760 found in the *Royal Magazine*, and *A Correct Map of Jamaica* by Thomas Jefferys (1768) and republished in Edward Long ([1774] 1970). Maps courtesy of the National Library of Jamaica. Illustration by Author.

towns in Jamaica compiled by Edward Long ([1774] 1970) (table 3.1). I have converted these distances into the postal rate (table 3.2) recorded by Long for one ounce of postage ([1774] 1970 2: 231). The distances used to create these various postal zones include 0–60 miles, 61–100 miles, and 100–200 miles. The distances between various towns were considerable and often required more than one day's travel on foot.

Table 3.1. Distance in English Miles of Cities from Kingston, along the Postal Roads of Jamaica

Southside Post	Distance	Northside Post	Distance	Windward Post	Distance
Spanish Town	18	Spanish Town	18	Aeolus	20
Old Harbour	30	Salt Gut	58	Petersfield	26
Clarendon Cross	42	St. Ann	78	Morant Bay	31
St. Elizabeth	79	Rio Bueno	98	Port Morant	38
Lacovia	92	Marthabrae	115	Bath	44
Black River	104	Montego Bay	140	Amity Hall	51
Savanna-la-Mar	129			Manchineal	60
Lucia	154			Port Antonio	71

Source: Synthesized from Long [1774] 1970 2: 231.
Note: The terms for the postal routes—Southside Post, Northside Post, and Windward Post—are Long's.

Table 3.2. Estimated Cost of Posting Packages from Kingston Using Postal Rates Described by Edward Long

Southside Post	Cost	Northside Post	Cost	Windward Post	Cost
Spanish Town	A	Spanish Town	A	Aeolus	A
Old Harbour	A	Salt Gut	A	Petersfield	A
Clarendon Cross	A	St. Ann	B	Morant Bay	A
St. Elizabeth	B	Rio Bueno	B	Port Morant	A
Lacovia	B	Marthabrae	C	Bath	A
Black River	C	Montego Bay	C	Amity Hall	A
Savanna-la-Mar	C			Manchineal	C
Lucia	C			Port Antonio	C

Source: Long [1774] 1970 2:233.
Notes: The terms for the postal routes—Southside Post, Northside Post, and Windward Post—are Long's. Costs are as follows: A = 1 shilling 10.5 pence; B = 2 shillings 6 pence; C = 3 shillings 9 pence.

The markets on the north coast were even farther away. St. Ann's Bay is approximately sixty miles from Spanish Town. The distance between market and plantation, and between plantations themselves, was considerable. In 1790, William Beckford describes what a market day might have looked like for the enslaved:

> They prepare their land, and put in their different crops on the Saturdays that are given to them, and they bring home their provisions at night; and if their grounds be at a considerable distance from the plantation, as they often are to the amount of five or seven miles, or more, the journey backwards and forwards makes this rather a day of labour and fatigue, than of enjoyment and rest; but if, on the contrary, they be within any tolerable reach, it may be said to partake of both. (1790 2: 152)

Within the central corridor of Jamaica, the parishes connected by the north–south postal road, this would have meant that the markets of Spanish Town, Kingston, and Port Royal would have been inaccessible to the enslaved working on plantations in St. Ann's parish and St. Thomas of the Vale parish.

Even with the system of roads and river transport, the distances that the enslaved would have had to travel would have been unmanageable. Higglers could have been the primary means through which the enslaved got their goods to market and were able to acquire material possessions. Certainly, the anecdotal accounts indicate that the reach of these higglers and the flow of commodities through the markets were localized around parish towns. Indeed, as I demonstrated in chapter 2, the planters' island-based economic interaction gives us a sense of how they defined local trade. The trade was localized to small neighborhoods focused on cabotage or intercoastal trade ports (Higman 1996, 2005). Was this the reach of the informal economy? Did it follow similar spatial parameters? Or did the enslaved move beyond the gaze of the planter? We know from the accounts, the laws, and the prosecution of the laws regarding the enslaved that they were mobile, but how mobile were they?

Urban and Rural Slavery in Eighteenth-Century Jamaica

Analysis of urban and rural contexts in the archaeology of the African Diaspora, with very few exceptions (Crane 1993; Hauser 2001), has often been disconnected. In part this is a result of archaeological phenomena that reflect concomitant ideologies of British divisions between rural and urban (Williams 1970; Johnson 2006), and their impact on cultural landscapes of the colonial world (Hall 2000). It also reflects arbitrary analytical constructs within historical archaeology (Wurst 1991). In history, scholars such as Betty Wood have labored to show the connections between urban and rural communities in terms of informal economies (Wood 1987, 1995). Archaeological analyses of class in rural settings show that the distinction of urban and rural can be somewhat of a false dichotomy, where the urban is categorized as commercial and the rural is identified as pastoral or agricultural (Wurst 1991). Indeed, within the Jamaican context the sugar plantation was a highly industrialized process with specialization in labor and equipment (Mintz 1985). In part this is an issue underlying the theoretical approaches used, but it is also an issue of scale where social relations of the island need to be addressed from a regional level (Crumley and Marquardt

1990, Marquardt 1992; Wurst 1999). While it is important to include in such analyses multiple sites, research designs necessarily have to demonstrate the potential interrelatedness between these phenomena (Hauser 2006, 2007). Rather than taking the dichotomies of urban and rural for granted, more attention should be paid to unraveling the nature of social relations both within and between rural and urban contexts in Jamaica.

Street markets and higglers linked both urban and rural spheres of Jamaica in the internal market system. Eighteenth-century Jamaica's rural and urban spheres were distinct but complementary. The enslaved population living on plantations was able to gain access to capital by selling produce grown on provision grounds. With the growth of the urban areas of Jamaica, and an emergent artisan class, there was an increased need for goods that free residents could afford. In Jamaica, seven sites represent either urban and rural milieus and have had extensive archaeological testing conducted. These sites include Seville, Drax Hall, Juan de Bollas, Thetford, Spanish Town, Old Naval Dockyard, Port Royal, and Saint Peter's Church, Port Royal (map 3.2).

There are three reasons why I chose to look at these sites. First, the sites are located in four regions of Jamaica. In the eighteenth century these regions would have corresponded to Port Royal parish, St. Catherine parish, St. John parish, and St. Ann Parish. While they were in discrete parishes, the sites were linked to each other through a system of roads, highlighted in map 3.2. Second, the sites are ideal candidates because they have been systematically excavated and provide excellent chronological control. On the whole these sites represent an occupational history that extends from the seventeenth century to the twentieth century. Each of the sites studied has a discrete archaeological component associated with the eighteenth century (see figure 3.1). Third, and most important, occupants of these sites would have lived in either rural or urban contexts in the eighteenth century. Four of the sites were rural industrial works, including Seville estate. Each of these was a sugar estate at one point. Juan de Bollas, however, during the last quarter of the eighteenth century was also a provisioning estate. Three sites were urban, including Old King's House, the residence of the governor of Jamaica, Old Naval Dockyard, the headquarters for the West Indian Naval Squadron, and Saint Peter's Church.

The Rural Experience

The experience of the enslaved was marked by difference. This difference was expressed not only in the framework of black and white Jamaica, where

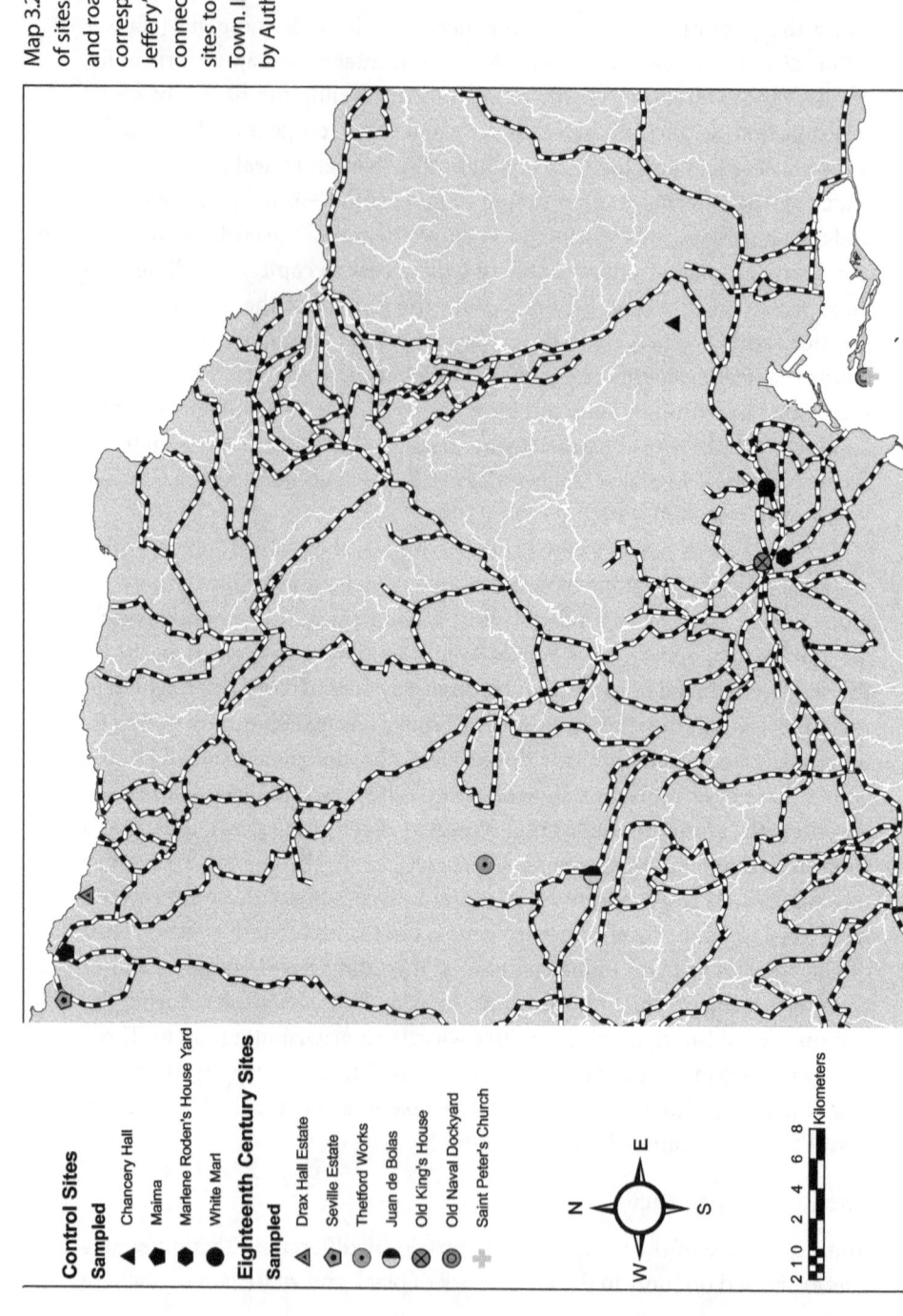

Map 3.2. Locator of sites discussed and roads corresponding to Jeffery's 1776 map connecting these sites to Spanish Town. Illustration by Author.

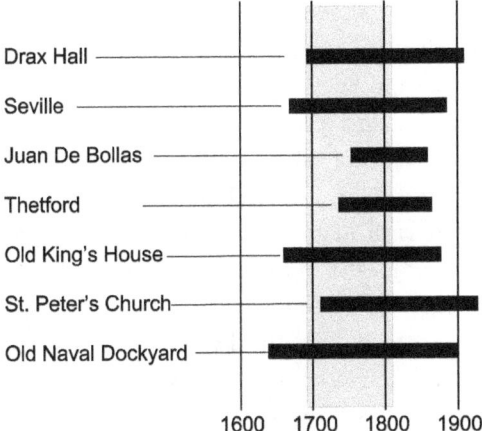

Figure 3.1. Chronology of sampled archaeological sites in seventeenth-, eighteenth-, and nineteenth-century Jamaica. Chronology is based on documented occupation as well as associated material culture. Illustration by Author.

the aggregation of newly arrived enslaved laborers was necessary in resolving the material and ideological contradictions of plantation slavery (Mintz and Price 1992: 20), but also in the way that the everyday life of the enslaved varied depending on social status, class, and gender. The life of the urban enslaved and the life of the rural enslaved varied considerably in degrees of mobility, ways in which their lives were regimented, and the contexts in which they labored. Some of this difference could have been refracted along familiar "idioms of social relations" such as kinship (Mintz and Price 1992: 66), but as Stephen Silliman (2001) points out, there are multiple ways in which laboring peoples lived their social relations.

Archaeology has shown that there were other ways in which difference was expressed in social relations on plantations in Jamaica. Much of this work has focused on the role of landscape in both marking and shaping these social relations (Delle 1998, 1999, 2000a, 2000b); other studies have focused on the goods consumed by plantation laborers (Armstrong 1991a, 1999, 2003; Armstrong and Kelly 2000; Reeves 1997). James Delle, following a body of scholarship on women and slavery, argued that the simultaneous emphasis on the role of enslaved women as producers and reproducers provided another axis through which social differences were expressed (Delle 2000: 178). Similarly, the regimentation of labor, depending on the kinds of goods being produced (e.g., sugar, coffee, indigo, cotton) marked ways in which the enslaved population was internally differentiated (Reeves 1997; Delle 1999, 2000b).

In this analysis, I examined material culture from four plantation sites: Drax Hall, Seville, and Thetford—all sugar estates—and Juan de Bollas, a provisioning estate. Drax Hall (1980) and Seville (1988–1993) were examined by Douglas Armstrong of Syracuse University. In examining both sites, Armstrong focused on the enslaved laborer villages of both plantations. He attempted to define the transformation in African Jamaican ways of life by documenting shifts in the patterns of material culture. This included looking at patterns of consumption and reuse in the case of Drax Hall, and patterns of space and settlement organization in the case of Seville. Examination of the two estates Juan de Bollas and Thetford was part of a Ph.D. thesis by Matthew Reeves at Syracuse University in 1997. Reeves's goal, in this study, was to distinguish the social lives of two communities of enslaved laborers who worked under different plantation systems. Differences in the organization of labor, Reeves hypothesized, would structure the lives of the community. Differences would be apparent in health conditions and social stratification (Reeves 1997: 6).

Drax Hall was a sugar estate throughout most of its incarnations. It is approximately half a kilometer east of St. Ann's Bay on Runaway Bay. In the eighteenth century, St. Ann's Bay would have been the closest market town for enslaved laborers. By the postal road, the plantation is situated approximately fifty-eight miles from Spanish Town. The enslaved population lived in a village southeast of the great house. Like most plantations in Jamaica, the land was divided between cane fields, pasture for cattle, and provision grounds. Also like most plantations, it was arranged to maximize the economic efficiency of its operation. Because of the planned nature of the community that lived at Drax Hall, the components associated solely with enslaved labor could be analyzed in relationship to the great house.

At Drax Hall, the owners maintained approximately 320 enslaved through the course of its operation during the eighteenth century (see Armstrong 1990: 43). Most of the enslaved population in the eighteenth century was of African descent, a majority being Jamaica-born Creoles. By the nineteenth century, the majority of the enslaved population was born on the island (47). While the majority of the enslaved labored in the fields and the factory under a gang system, there were some artisans, skilled laborers, and domestics (41). The estate owners also managed a large force of enslaved artisans, including smiths, sawyers, and carpenters. The enslaved domestic workers included twenty house servants, who worked as housekeepers, seamstresses, cooks, washwomen, and watchmen (ibid.).

The residents of the great house included the owners of the plantation, as well as some of the domestic servants. In 1691, William Drax, a son of a well-established Barbadian planter, consolidated properties on the eastern side of St. Ann's Bay to form Drax Hall Plantation (Armstrong 1990: 24). Over the course of the plantation's occupation, there were more than nineteen owners (282). Archaeology of plantations presents an interesting interpretive challenge. In the village contexts, it can be assumed that the majority of the domestic assemblage recovered from the house yards of the enslaved is associated with the people who lived there. However, the material residues of the residents of the great house are a little bit more complicated. The archaeological residues of great houses represent not only the owners and overseers of the plantation, but also the refuse of those who worked in the great house. In this case, the twenty house servants would have contributed significantly to the refuse of the great house.

Comparison of material goods recovered from various components of the estates shows a parallel assemblage in which a range of imported, regional, and island-made goods is represented. Assemblages at Seville plantation highlight the accumulation of material wealth among the enslaved. Seville estate is located about one kilometer west of St. Ann's Bay on Jamaica's north coast. It is located on the major coastal road that connects Ocho Rios with Montego Bay. In the eighteenth century, it would have been approximately sixty-one miles from Spanish Town. Like Drax Hall, the plantation was also a sugar estate and was initially organized to maximize the economic efficiency of the plantation. The great house rests on the top of a hill leading up into the mountains and has a commanding view of St. Ann's Bay. The plantation is located near a stream that provided fresh water to the plantation and the fields, and power to the sugar works. Seville was first owned by Richard Hemming in 1670, and it was continually occupied up until the 1890s. Maps of the plantation, which date between 1721 and 1791, show significant changes in the spatial layout of the plantation. The early enslaved village existed southeast of the planter's residence. The 1791 map shows a new location for the village. Because of the different locations, Seville presents spatially discrete areas for enslaved communities.

Armstrong excavated five house areas with discrete eighteenth-century components. These five house areas had a total of 13,739 sherds of imported European ceramic material. These sites also contained 1,336 Jamaica-produced ceramics and 2,734 regional ceramics (Spanish jars). What is evident from these numbers (see table 3.3) is the simple fact that the enslaved laborers of plantations were able to acquire through the local economy a vast amount of material goods. While there is some variation between the estate

Table 3.3. Estimated Percentages of Imported, Regional (Identified as Spanish Jars), and Local Jamaican Wares Recovered from Seville Estate

	House Areas					Great House	Total
	1.15	1.16	1.18	1.19	1.2		
European ceramics	70	77	59	82	74	82	74
Jamaican ceramics	9	8	15	6	9	3	9
Spanish jars	21	14	27	13	17	14	18

Note: House areas at Seville estate are as identified by Douglas Armstrong (1991b, 1992, 1999).

Table 3.4. Estimated Percentages of Vessel Forms Recovered from Seville Estate

	House Areas					Great House	Total
	1.15	1.16	1.18	1.19	1.2		
Beverages	6	5	8	10	5	21	6
Storage	17	12	15	18	14	2	14
Serving bowls	70	77	74	62	71	28	70
Serving plates	7	5	3	10	10	42	8
Chamber pots	1	1	0	1	1	7	1

Note: House areas at Seville estate are as identified by Douglas Armstrong (1991b, 1992, 1999).

house and the laborer's village, the percentage of imported European, regional, and Jamaican-made ceramics is comparable. Moreover, these goods are similar to, but probably used differently than, those found at the great house of the estate (table 3.4).

The house yards all have a much higher percentage of serving wares that are in the shape of bowls. This is consistent with observations of domestic assemblages found elsewhere in the Caribbean (Farnsworth 1992), and could be attributed either to differences in food ways (Anderson 1971; Deetz 1996) or to distinctions of class and status (Howson 1995). Regardless, it seems that the residents of both the estate house and the laborer's village are accessing or employing similar market strategies in provisioning the household. Most likely the imported ceramics are purchased either at the town market, or peddled by traveling wholesalers as described in the documentary record. The manner in which the enslaved purchased locally made goods was most likely through the informal sector of Jamaica's local economy.

In addition, enslaved laborers at Drax Hall and Seville had access to trade conducted by small vessels traversing the waterways like those described above. This traffic employed small boats such as the one identified by the Caravel Project and excavated by Greg Cook in 1995 in St. Ann's Bay. While there is no direct evidence that this specific wreck took part in such contraband, trade sloops like these were largely responsible for the sanctioned and illegal interisland trade undertaken in the eighteenth century. What about estates that had more restricted venues to market? Thetford is located in a part of St. Catherine parish that used to be part of St. John parish. It would have been on the border of St. Thomas in the Vale. In the eighteenth century, Old Harbour would most likely have been the town to which the enslaved would go to market. It would have been approximately thirty-six miles from Spanish Town using a combination of trails and the post road. Juan de Bollas is located on the hilly slopes of Juan de Bollas Mountain. It is presently in St. Catherine parish but is close to both St. Ann's parish and Clarendon parish. While it was closer to market than Thetford estate, the inhabitants of the estate still had to rely on the road system of Jamaica.

Throughout Thetford's occupation, it was used as a sugar estate. Thetford estate was a property that emerged from the disintegration of Francis Price's estate, Worthy Park, purchased in 1670 when his son divided the estate among his three daughters. In 1725, Thomas Fuller, who married one of the daughters, consolidated portions of Worthy Park to form Thetford estate (Reeves 1997: 38). In 1795, Peke Fuller purchased the adjacent Murmuring Brook estate and added to an already large holding that included Thetford, Thetford Mountain, and Dodd's Valley, a cattle pen. The property remained in the family and operated as a sugar estate until 1841. During the early nineteenth century, Thetford managed nearly two hundred enslaved laborers (Reeves 1997: 360–67).

In 1731, Juan de Bollas was operating as a sugar works. It continued to operate as a sugar plantation until 1770, when it became the Clarke family home. During this time period, the plantation maintained approximately fifty-five enslaved laborers (Reeves 1997: 33). From 1770 until 1797, it became a provisions estate. In 1797, the home was sold to Samuel Queneborough. He had introduced coffee as a crop to Juan de Bollas (Reeves 1997: 34). In 1815, upon Queneborough's death, control of the estate passed into the hands of Samuel Shand, until 1823, and then William Queneborough Wright until 1838.

As in most sugar estates, there were systems of hierarchy within the enslaved population structured loosely around the gang system. There were 287 enslaved laborers working on Thetford in the early nineteenth century. For the most part, enslaved laborers on Thetford estate worked as gang labor. Men and women participated evenly in this labor system, for the most part. As with most estates, however, the enslaved population was also engaged in domestic and artisanal labor. Enslaved labor employed in either of these was in the minority, although men above the age of thirty-five were often moved into occupational roles (Reeve 1997: 97). The enslaved population at Thetford included artisans such as coopers, carpenters, sawyers, basket makers, rope makers, and blacksmiths (Reeves 1997: 100).

Provisioning and coffee plantations required a different intensity of labor than sugar plantations. Labor was not year-round, but seasonal. The enslaved laborers that worked Juan de Bollas would be jobbed out on nearby plantations such as Guanaboa Vale. During the period of sugar production, Juan de Bollas maintained fifty-five enslaved laborers. During the period of coffee growth, however, the enslaved population increased dramatically, to 275 persons. In 1815, ninety people were taken to the sugar estate at Guanaboa Vale, and in 1817, fifty-six were removed. For the most part, these enslaved laborers enjoyed a better standard of life than those on the sugar estates, with nearly 10 percent more children surviving childhood (Reeves 1997: 60). For the most part, labor participated in the process of growing coffee by either harvesting or maintaining the grounds.

What becomes apparent in the examination of the assemblage associated with laborers at this estate is that there was a degree of internal differentiation among the enslaved that was in part related to the systems of labor employed on each of the plantations. This internal differentiation was manifested in the ways in which the enslaved managed their own labor on the provision grounds. This allowed some to accumulate greater amounts of wealth than others. Eighteenth-century deposits underlying two early nineteenth-century house yards at Thetford estate contained slipware, tin-glazed earthenware, Jamaican-made ceramics, and some metal fragments. At Juan de Bollas, fifteen units dated to the last quarter of the eighteenth century. These units have been designated house area 23 (Reeves 1997: 296). Twenty-three units excavated dated to the early nineteenth century. These structures were designated house areas 21, 22, and 24. In table 3.5, I have synthesized data from Reeves's dissertation highlighting the percentages of ceramic types from eighteenth- and early-nineteenth-century deposits.

What is remarkable about these data are the consistently distinct assemblage patterns between the two plantations. Comparing these data with those from Seville, we see an even more interesting trend, the lack of Spanish jars. This could possibly be attributed to environmental conditions. But it can also be attributed to access to different resources. It appears from these data, and to summarize Reeves's conclusions, that laborers on the Juan de Bollas plantation had much greater access to European wares

Table 3.5. Estimated Percentages of Imported, Regional (Identified as Spanish Jars), and Local Jamaican Wares Recovered from Juan De Bollas and Thetford

	House Areas at Juan de Bollas				House Areas at Thetford		Total
	21	22	23	24	42	43	
European ceramics	75	71	75	71	54	23	51
Jamaican ceramics	25	29	25	29	46	77	49
Spanish jars	0	1	0	0	0	0	0

Note: House areas at Juan de Bollas and Thetford are as identified by Matthew Reeves (1997: 290–314, 375–405).

than did their counterparts on Thetford estate. This conclusion reached by Reeves is important in that it demonstrates the ways in which the life of plantation enslaved laborers was also marked by difference. This difference manifests itself in their access to resources that were acquired from higglers and markets in the neighboring towns. So, to some extent, the "embodied knowledge" of slave consumption—at least on these two plantations—was actively molded by the economic environment.

The Urban Experience

The notable towns of eighteenth-century Jamaica included Kingston, Spanish Town, Port Royal, St. Ann's Bay, Savanna-la-Mar, and Montego Bay. The most prominent of these were Kingston, Spanish Town, and Port Royal. Edward Long (1774) calculates that rents in the towns of Kingston and Spanish Town were by far the dearest, approximately £50 per year. Port Royal was relatively inexpensive. Long estimates that rents averaged about £25 per year. These estimates (evaluations) really refer to the rents that white settlers, merchants, and dependents would have paid and do not refer to the large enslaved population of the towns. However, they do give us a sense of the varied conditions of the three principal towns in which the urban enslaved operated.

The enslaved of the towns considered themselves distinct from and, in some cases, superior to those working on the plantations (Williams 1826: 27). In 1832, some 24,984 of the 312,876 enslaved laborers lived in the principal towns of Jamaica (Higman 1995: 58). The eighteenth-century urban experience was far more complicated than the rural experience described above. There has been very little written by historians or archaeologists about enslaved life in Caribbean urban contexts. Most of the research on urban Jamaica has focused on commerce and power (Higman 1991; Burnard 2002; Robertson 2005). Additionally, there have been a few studies which have tried to understand the life of enslaved and freed women (Simmonds 1987, 2004; Boa 1993). For methodological reasons discussed below, knowledge about the life of the urban enslaved is difficult to ascertain.

This paucity of knowledge flows in part from attempts by the Assembly of Jamaica to zone or regulate enslaved living spaces. The conditions in which people lived varied considerably. For those living in the "negroe" yards, the houses were sometimes depicted as a public risk. The risk these yards represented was often depicted as tangible. In a law passed on December 19, 1770, the assembly stated that, the "negroe huts and houses" in Kingston, Port Royal, and Spanish Town were "a refuge and receptacle for thieves, loose, idle, and runaway negroes, and other slaves, belonging to the said towns and other parishes" (Jamaica 1792: 88). The law reveals a real and palpable fear on the part of the planters. Access to these houses was seen to provide "an opportunity of forming cabals and conspiracies, dangerous to the public peace and security" (ibid.).

Eighteenth-century Spanish Town was the seat of power and a commercial district. The population of the town included English, French, Spanish, Jews, and Africans. In 1794, 2,760 African Jamaicans lived in Spanish Town. Of this population, 800 were free and 1,960 were enslaved (Long [1774] 1970 2: 28). The free African Jamaicans were professionals, either in the service industry or in trade. Free women easily found work as higglers or tavern owners and free men as artisans and soldiers in Spanish Town. The economic position of the African Jamaicans afforded them considerable access to the markets, and they were able to afford "at least a saddle horse or two" (Long [1774] 1970 2: 33).

The archaeology of urban enslaved life is difficult to access because, unlike plantations where there are spatially discrete areas corresponding to the material remains of enslaved life (the village and the house yard), urban contexts are complicated by the fact that enslaved people and the people who controlled their life lived in very close quarters (Crane 1993; Yentsch 1994; Mullins 1998; see also Young 2000 and Shackel, Mullins, and Warner 1998). This provides an archaeological context which mirrors those of great house plantation settings, in the sense that it is difficult to distinguish the assemblages of the planters from those of the enslaved working in the great house. In such cases, one must view the material assemblage as an aggregate of elite and enslaved behavior. Importantly, however, the domestic utilitarian assemblage was probably controlled as much by the servant staff as it was by the planters themselves. Below, I look at two loci of urban life: Spanish Town through the lens of Old King's House, and Port Royal through the lens of Old Naval Dockyard and Saint Peter's Church. In each of these cases, we see an assemblage informed by the close proximity of various classes of white settlers and their domestic servants.

The most obvious example of this comes from the assemblage recovered from Old King's House. Located in Spanish Town (see figure 3.2), King's House was the residence of the governor of Jamaica and the seat of colonial power on the island. Notable residents of King's House included Henry Morgan, Sir William Beeston, and Lady Nugent. King's House not only was the residence of the governor, but also housed a large number of enslaved servants over time. Governors maintained a large number of enslaved people. For example, Captain Henry Morgan, prior to 1692, kept fourteen servants, some of whom were housed in Port Royal while others resided in Spanish Town (Dunn 1972: 181). In 1812, King's House palace held thirty-three enslaved domestics.

Developing an architectural history of the building is difficult, since documentation of renovation to Old King's House is sparse (Cundall 1929; Mathewson 1972a; Robertson 2005). Evidence of its construction history can be gleaned from a blueprint recovered by the Public Works Department in the early twentieth century and a map of Spanish Town drawn in the mid-eighteenth century. In 1700, Beeston built some apartments and offices for his administrative staff (Mathewson 1972a, 1972b: 4; Cundall 1929). In 1761 King's House underwent a major renovation, including the construction of the Georgian facade now extant in Spanish Town (Cundall 1929: 4). In 1872, the seat of government was moved to Kingston, and the governor's residence moved to the newly constructed residence in St. Andrew parish. In 1925, the residence burned down, leaving only the Georgian facade extant.

What we see in the archaeological record are not simply the cultural remains of the governor and his family. It is more likely that much of the assemblage was created by the refuse of the servants who worked for the governor, took care of his horses, dressed him, his children, and his wife, and, finally, cooked meals for the family and any state function held at the residence. In short, while the dominant individual in the household was white, the majority of the household were either African or Creole. They purchased the wares in which the meals were cooked. In all likelihood, they also discreetly ate from the same wares as the rest of the family. In other words, the trash in the midden analyzed is the aggregated trash of the whole household: African, Creole, and European.

Port Royal provides a similar urban context with some notable distinc-

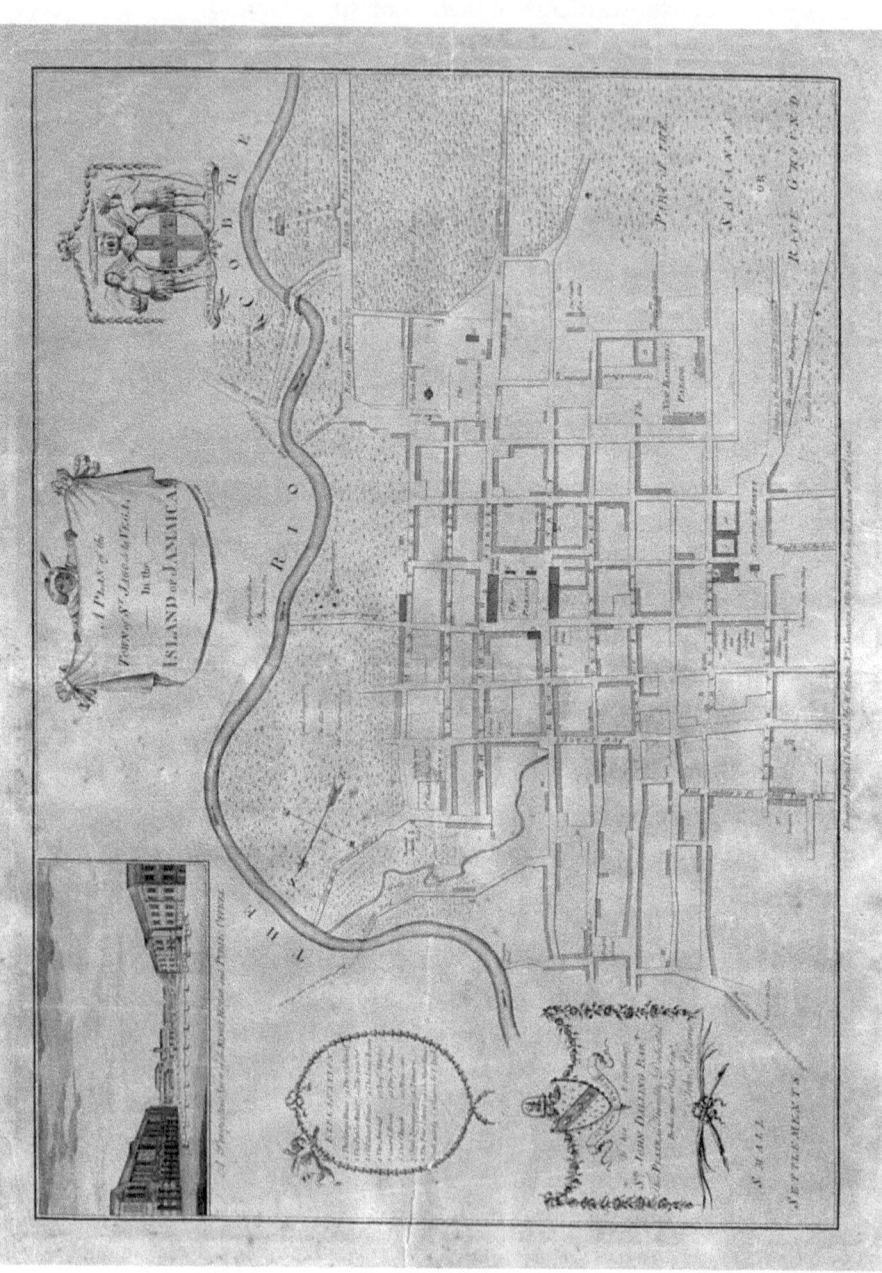

Figure 3.2. A plan of St. Jago de la Vega in the island of Jamaica, 1786, by John Pitcarne. King's House is located in the center of the map. The market is also highlighted in the lower right of the map. Courtesy of the National Library of Jamaica.

tions. The two sites I analyzed were the Old Naval Dockyard and Saint Peter's Church. While both of these sites were inhabited by both people of African and European descent, these inhabitants were not nearly as well off as their Spanish Town counterparts. First, as members of the governor's household, the servants and family had access to a greater array of material goods. Second, by the eighteenth century, Port Royal had fallen on hard times, and its inhabitants were mostly servicing either the naval squadron or the commerce directed at Kingston.

Port Royal was cosmopolitan during the seventeenth century. By 1692, the city was home to peoples of African descent (including creoles from Barbados and Nevis), English, Scottish, Welsh, Irish, Spanish Jews, and Gypsies (Burton 1999: 15). The population of Port Royal at this time has been estimated at 9,000 people, 5,000 of whom were freemen recruited from Kitts and Nevis and Barbados (Watts 1987: 216). The enslaved labor of Port Royal, working as domestics and artisans, numbered about 2,500 (Pawson and Buisseret [1975] 2001: 185). The condition of their houses was different from the town houses of the artisans they worked for. In 1692, John Pike describes a "'Negroes' house that is daubed with Mortar and thatched, eves hanging almost to the ground" (cited in Cadbury 1971: 20).

From 1692 to 1905, Port Royal's economic status gradually shifted from the richest British city in the Americas to a naval station and a fishing village. In 1774, Edward Long describes the city:

> The inhabitants are chiefly supported by the money spent here by the garrison and the squadron; by the gaines made by wherries that ply for fare in the harbor; their turtle fishery, which is considerable; the pilotage of ships in and out; and by their votes of representatives. (Long [1774] 1970 2: 149)

Here we see more evidence of the commodity chains involved in the internal economy of Jamaica. The highly prized turtle meat was fished and sold by Port Royal fishermen on the Pedro banks. It was then turned around and sold through the official markets at Passage Fort or Kingston, or it entered into the informal trade of the island. The pilots and the canoe men described by Long were responsible for linking the three principal towns of Jamaica, Port Royal, Spanish Town (through Passage Fort), and Kingston. As such, they were probably well situated to take advantage of the trade in legally imported goods as well as contraband trade evading the Kingston customs house. By 1836, when the admiral's headquarters were moved to Canada, Port Royal had essentially become a fishing village (Phillippo 1843:

66). Soon it lost its vestry status and became incorporated into St. Andrew parish.

Philip Mayes began his research in the Old Naval Dockyard as salvage archaeology in response to potential tourist development of the town (Mayes 1972: 11). Mayes excavated this area from 1968 to 1971 and produced a rigorous and well-organized study of the city. In his excavation, Mayes was able to detail and recover material from the navy's "negro huts and houses" and "negro kitchen" (1972: 23–43). The individuals residing in these quarters were primarily responsible for much of the manual labor required in maintaining the squadron's presence and feeding the attached sailors. The quarters can be seen on a nineteenth-century plan of the dockyard drawn by Nathaniel Watts (Watts 1815).

St. Paul's Church was destroyed in the 1692 earthquake. It was not rebuilt until 1726. In 1720, the church was rededicated as St. Peter's Church. This church is highlighted in the 1758 Bellin map of Port Royal as "A" (Bellin 1758). I have combined both plans in map 3.3. In this map both St. Peter's Church and the Old Naval Dockyard are highlighted in the overall town plan. The church is highlighted with an "A" and the huts of the dockyard are highlighted with a "B."

Priddy believed that the area was essentially a "squatter's settlement" (Brown 1996: 23) between 1692 and 1726, and probably gives a fairly good picture of the kinds of settlements that existed on this plot during the intervening time period. In 1731, a law was passed by the Assembly allowing town wardens to tear down a "great number of negroe huts and hovels in the front of said town, towards the sea, which renders it very liable to be set on fire" (Jamaica 1735: 143). In 1726, the land became the site of the parish church and was occupied by the clergyman and his servants. Anthony Priddy began work near St. Peter's Church in the 1970s to minimize the impact of the construction of a parking lot. This site was excavated thirty years ago, and institutional memory is quite poor. Only a few of the members working for the Jamaica National Heritage Trust now remember the excavation in any great detail. I therefore had to establish the chronology of the site through the fragmentary notes collected and through a mean ceramic dating of the imported ceramics excavated.

The inhabitants of St. Peter's Church and Old Naval Dockyard, like those who lived in Old King's House, included both freed and enslaved laborers. The people that lived there were African, Creole, and European. Unlike in the plantation context, where the laborers lived in spatially segregated, archaeologically definable components, the inhabitants of St. Peter's Church

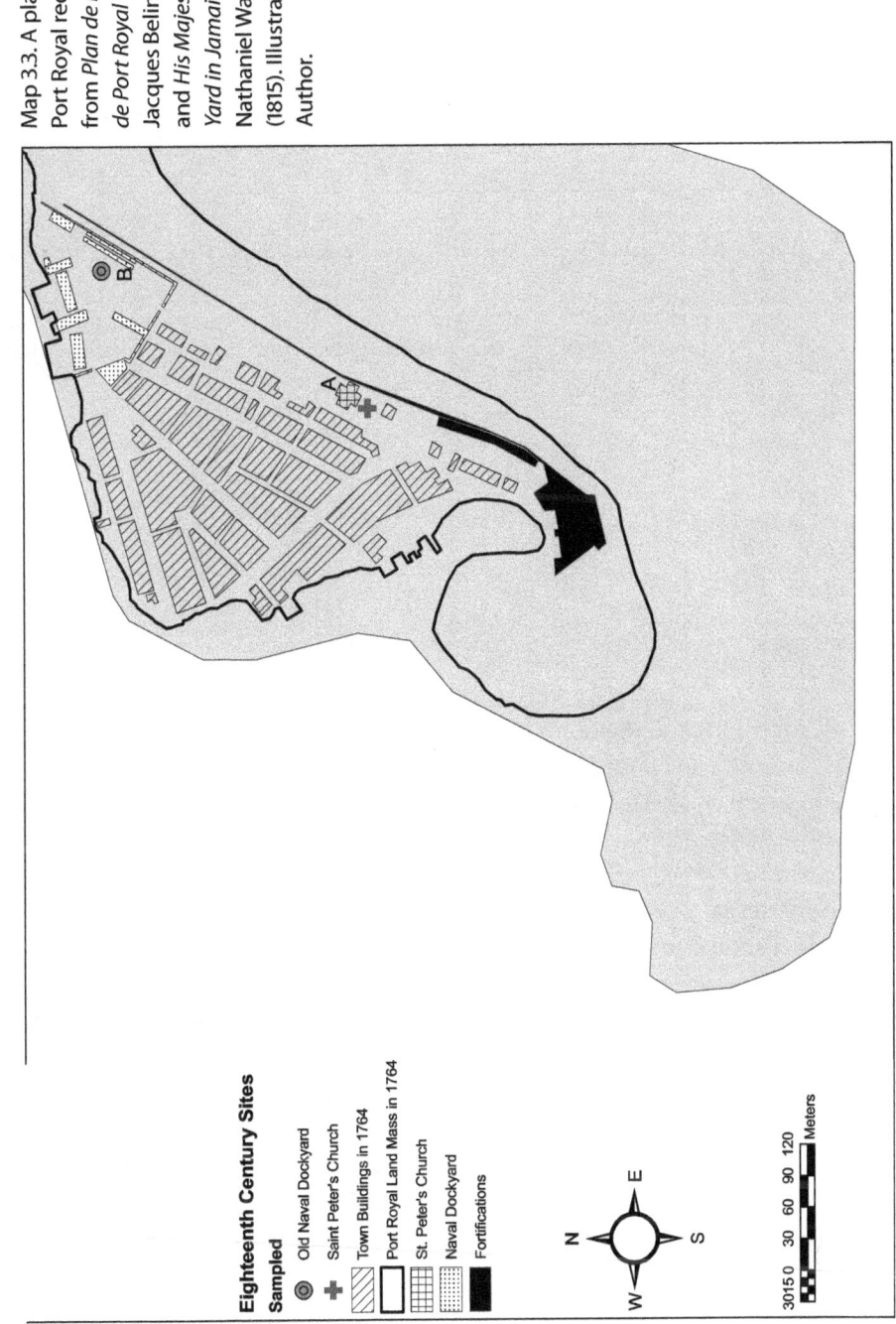

Map 3.3. A plan of Port Royal redrawn from *Plan de la ville de Port Royal* by Jacques Belin (1764) and *His Majesty's Yard in Jamaica* by Nathaniel Watts (1815). Illustration by Author.

Table 3.6. Estimated Percentages of Imported, Regional (Identified as Spanish Jars), and Local Jamaican Wares Recovered from Eighteenth-Century Contexts in Jamaica

	Old King's House	Old Naval Dockyard	St. Peter's Church	Total
European ceramics	81	78	66	78
Jamaican ceramics	13	18	18	16
Spanish jars	4	4	12	5
Other	2	0	4	1

Table 3.7. Types of Materials Recovered from Domestic Assemblages at Each of the Sites

	Jewelry	Glassware	Tobacco Pipe	Local ceramic[a]	Porcelain[b]	Tin glazed ceramics[c]	Cream Colored wares	Slip ware
Seville	X	X	X	X	X	X	X	X
Drax Hall	X	X	X	X	X	X	X	X
Juan de Bollas	X		X	X		X		X
Thetford	X	X	X		X	X	X	
Old King's House	X	X	X	X	X	X	X	X
Old Naval Dockyard	X	X	X	X	X	X	X	X
St. Peter's Church	X	X	X	X	X	X	X	X

[a] regional and island-made.
[b] English and Chinese.
[c] primarily Dutch.

all contributed to the domestic assemblage. However, also like Old King's House and Old Naval Dockyard, many of the cooking wares were probably purchased and used by the domestic servants in preparing the meal for the entire household (table 3.6).

The household assemblages detailed in table 3.6 point to several interesting patterns. First, the occupants of King's House had an assemblage of ceramics similar to that of the great house at Seville estate. This is not surprising, since the residents of both houses were equally well off and had a large staff of domestic servants. While the ceramic assemblages of the people who lived at Old Naval Dockyard and St. Peter's Church were similarly distributed, the actual ceramics were of a poorer quality. The diversity of goods the enslaved had access to through the local economy is highlighted in table 3.7. The difficulty is in disentangling those goods that were bought and sold through the informal sector of Jamaica's local economy. While many of the goods listed in the table could have been purchased through higglers and ad hoc street markets, they were more likely purchased from legal and licensed peddlers and merchants.

Ultimately, the explanation of this assemblage, along with the assemblages previously detailed, can in part be reduced to function. The Jamaican ceramics recovered from these sites were primarily used as cooking vessels. Only a few notable examples of their functions have been detailed in the archaeological record. Ceramics used as serving wares or as items of display tended to be imported wares. The utility of the local ceramics as a functional equivalent to iron cooking pots explains their ubiquity on archaeological sites in the eighteenth century and also explains some of the ceramics' attributes, to be discussed in the following chapters.

Conclusion

As I have discussed in this chapter, the rural and urban enslaved were linked to each other through roadways and waterways. This infrastructure, in effect, linked these disparate communities. It also provided the means through which people residing at these different sites could access a system of formal and informal markets throughout Jamaica. Indeed, the assemblages discussed in this chapter in relation to the various sites testify to the active participation of individuals in these market systems. The markets were a meeting place of people and commodities. They were the points where imported and local goods were exchanged and sold. The enslaved and freed people who lived and worked in each of the contexts discussed above were able to accumulate material wealth through their interaction in the internal economy.

As I mentioned in the introduction of the book, there is no easy way to elicit which archaeological materials were purchased through formal and which through informal means. We know that the enslaved engaged in both realms of economic interaction. We also know that most of the goods bought on the ad hoc markets or through the intercession of higglers were items of local manufacture or local produce. Ubiquitous on each of these archaeological sites are yabbas, a Jamaican-made utilitarian earthenware. As such, these ceramics offer an ideal medium to examine the extent and circulation of commodities in the informal economy of Jamaica.

While there has been a considerable amount of research on these markets, no one has attempted to spatialize their reach. In many ways, some scholarship had assumed that this system was supplemental to the planters' interests in both figurative and geographic terms. What I wanted to know was whether or not this market system was a series of markets localized in scale supplementing neighboring plantations, as has been intimated by the historical and archaeological literature, or whether we could look at this economy as markets regionally linked by higglers, with its own center of gravity. I started off with the supposition that social networks would be resident in the internal marketing system and that the extent of these systems could be traced through material culture.

4

Routing Pots

Ceramics of the African Diaspora

> Upwards of ten thousand assemble every Sunday morning in the market of Kingston, where they barter their provisions, etc., for salted beef and pork, or fine linen and ornaments. . . . Some of them find time on these days to make a few coarse manufactures, besides raising provisions, such as mats for beds, bark ropes of strong and durable texture, wicker chairs and baskets, earthen jars and pans ready for sale.
> Edwards [1793] 1972 1: 125.

As can be gleaned from the above quote, the material culture of enslaved individuals was rich. Through the markets they were able to acquire locally grown and imported provisions that were incorporated into their meals, and social goods through which they displayed status and refashioned self. Of particular interest to me in this quote, however, are the "few coarse manufactures." While all of the goods listed in the quote speak to the independent production of the enslaved, the coarse wares represent direct evidence of manufacture by peoples of African descent outside of the plantation context.

The "earthen jars and pans" that Bryan Edwards refers to are the focus of the second part of the book. These kinds of earthenware have received considerable attention in the archaeology of the African Diaspora and have been called "colono-ware," "colonoware," "Afro-Caribbean ware," "yabbas," and "Criollo ware." In reality they were only one aspect of the independent production of the enslaved and comprise a small portion of the archaeological assemblage. The attention, however, is not misplaced. They are one of the few types of material culture that were predominantly made, used, and traded by enslaved laborers, probably women, and that survive the archaeological record. As such they can speak to the silences implicit in the documentary record about the social relations and networks that the enslaved created as they negotiated their lives and worlds. They become a material way through which the archaeologist can glean insight into the ways in which the enslaved transformed the world around them.

As Leland Ferguson suggests, what attracts people to focus on this class of ceramics are the implicit and "complex processes of colonial creolization: [where] demography and culture varied from place to place" (Ferguson 1992: 22). They are, in effect, an "intercultural artifact" (Singleton and Bograd 2000). In a sense, both Ferguson and Singleton and Bograd argue that we need to simultaneously examine the routes of the people responsible for making and using the pottery (oceanic) and the roots of its production and use (situated context) (Orser 1996). These pots are as oceanic in scope as European industrially produced ceramics. At the same time, their meaning and use are as highly contextual. These ideas are what Ferguson refers to as the "Colono ware concept" (1992: 22).

A danger emerges, however, when this concept becomes reified into an archaeological type. It takes the complex histories of peoples making and using the pots and ossifies those dynamics into a single system of analytical value. Focusing on the routes of the diasporas requires a shift in perspective, where the scale of analysis is regional and the focus is on the interactions between people and places—and the ways in which they are differently materialized in objects and their uses. In this way, the pottery is no longer used analytically as a marker of identity, but rather is a residue of independent production, use, and sale, which can reveal the complex social networks of the enslaved.

Aggregating Pots

There has been an effort to create a generalized category of ceramic through which meanings can be interpreted. Oceanic and regional analyses of the ceramics made in communities touched and affected by the African Diaspora highlight the idiosyncrasies of these ceramic traditions (DeCorse 1999; Hauser and Armstrong 1999; Hauser and DeCorse 2003). Simply put, the range of pottery traditions categorized as "colono-ware" is not a single type, except as a useful device for archaeologists to categorize "other ceramics." As I discuss below, theoretically it assumes a unity of diasporic peoples and experiences. It is, in a sense, an archaeological artifact of the aggregation of peoples of the Middle Passage. Methodologically, it is also untenable. Simply put, systems of distinction, difference, and similarity apparent in one context vary considerably in others.

The significance of African beliefs and traditions that enslaved Africans brought with them to the Americas and their role in shaping American cultural traditions cannot be overstated. The Atlantic trade in Africans, beginning in the sixteenth century, paralleled the expansion of Western Europe. It began as a means of replacing indigenous labor decimated by disease, and it became the foundation for the emerging plantation economies of the Americas. As a result of the Atlantic trade, 12 to 15 million Africans were taken to the Americas (see references and discussions in Anstey 1975; Inikori 1982; Hair 1989; Lovejoy 1989; Manning 1990; Thornton 1998; Craton 1997; Eltis and Richardson 1997; Gomez 1998, 2005; Eltis 2000). The origins, destinations, and specifics of these individuals' enslavement varied greatly. People were taken from many parts of West and Central Africa and transported through coastal ports ranging from Gorée Island in the Senegambia to factory outposts on the coast of Angola. A large majority of this captive labor force were taken to Brazil. However, significant proportions were also transported to the American Southeast, the West Indies, and the Spanish Main.

The Atlantic trade in Africans has been a major focus of historical and cultural research over the past six decades. Examination of African continuities in the Americas, pioneered by Melville Herskovits, has emerged as one of the central foci of this work. Prior to Herskovits's research, African Americans were viewed as having been stripped of their cultural heritage by the disruptive effects of the Atlantic trade in Africans. Writing in the racially segregated 1930s and 1940s, Herskovits argued that patterns of behavior in African-descended populations should not be understood on the basis of misinformed notions of biology, but rather should be seen as representative of cultural traits that could be traced back to West Africa (Herskovits 1933, 1936, 1941; Redfield et al. 1935). Such traits included language, music, food, and elements of material culture.

Since the 1930s, models of cultural change have become more nuanced, and the specifics and complexities of the Atlantic trade more thoroughly documented. The details of work by Sidney Mintz ([1974] 1992) and Richard Price and Sally Price (1980), to name a few, have focused more specifically on the ingenuity of displaced Africans in translating underlying cultural frameworks within new social landscapes. Mintz and Price assert that because "social systems have been highly responsive to changing social conditions, one must maintain a skeptical attitude toward the claims that many contemporary social or cultural forms represent direct continuities from the African homelands" (Mintz and Price 1992: 52). Rather, it was an underlying grammar of "value systems and cognitive orientations" that dictated the material expressions of African peoples in the Americas (Mintz and Price 1992: 55; also see DeCorse 1999: 146–49; Posnansky 1984: 198–99, 1999). Issues of historical and cultural context and change were emphasized in these studies. These crucial concepts must be taken into account to draw an adequate picture of the symbolic and social meanings of material culture in the African Diaspora.

Analogy is one of the fundamental tools of the archaeologist, and it has been used frequently in building interpretations of African American sites and material culture. These inferences draw on the ethnographic record to demonstrate how archaeological materials fit within past sociocultural contexts. These connections must be drawn guardedly. In creating an analogical argument, it is crucial to demonstrate "the principles of connection—the considerations of relevance" (Wylie 1985: 101; also see Stahl 1993). In other words, how does the analogue relate to the subject in the archaeological record?

Ethnic identity and its construction figure prominently in many discussions of transatlantic analogies. Some archaeologists have described the examination of ethnicity as too difficult to cull from the archaeological record or, indeed, disentangle from its modern context (e.g., Atherton 1983: 96; DeCorse 1989a: 137–38; MacEachern 1996, 1998; Singleton and Bograd 1995: 24; Trigger 1995: 277). However, archaeology's potential to connect the past with the present, and the increasing political and legal implications of such study, ensures that this will remain a central focus of archaeological research. Numerous publications illustrate the continuing centrality of this issue to archaeology and the problems that confront its analysis (e.g., McGuire 1982; Shennan 1989; Singleton 1995: 130–34; Singleton and Bograd 1995: 24–29; Stark 1998; Franklin and Fesler 1999; Jones 1999; Orser 2001). Interpretive frameworks range from analysis of stylistic representations of identity (Wiessner 1983; Conkey 1990; Burke 1999) to functional variants of cultural modes (Sackett 1990). What these approaches share is an appreciation of the complex interplay of the sociocultural factors concerned and their material representations. Speaking of identity, ethnicity, and archaeology, Sian Jones writes that "group identity is not a passive and straightforward reflection of a distinct culture and languages," but rather these concepts must be understood in "the cultural contexts and social relations in which they are embedded" (Jones 1999: 224–25). Ultimately, identity and ethnicity are contextual (Jones 1997: 72).

Unfortunately, the search for African analogues in American populations is challenged by the great heterogeneity in African ethnicity represented in the African Diaspora, nuances in the specifics of enslavement and trade, and the complexities of the historical events that have shaped the modern Atlantic world. Given these factors, and the influences of European and Native American societies on historically enslaved American and Caribbean societies, we cannot talk about a single diasporic African context that shaped the identity of African-descended populations in the Americas (Posnansky 1984; Hill 1987; Ferguson 1992: 22; DeCorse 1999: 132, 135–37; Hauser and Armstrong 1999: 72). Study of the African Diaspora defies the simplistic equation of historical antecedents and modern-day expressions. Archaeological inferences must take this into account, as well as the entire range of material culture represented and the multivariate meanings conveyed by the objects present.

Jamaican ceramics, yabbas, are classified in a broader category of ceramics, sometimes called Colono ware, sometimes called Afro-Caribbean ware. In many ways the term used to classify this broader group of ceramic has been the cause of debates focusing on the identity of the potters who made them. In describing this broad range of material culture, I prefer to employ Ferguson's term "Colono ware" in that it betrays the "more complex processes of colonial creolization" (Ferguson 1992: 22). Taken as a localized ceramic material whose production, distribution, and use are affected by the emergent Atlantic economy, we should extend the geographic distribution of these creolized wares to include not only Brazil, the North American colonies, and the Caribbean, but also the settlements and factories located along the West African coast. In this formulation, the identity(ies) of the potters and their antecedents become less important. What become paramount are issues of political economy, social transformations, and local responses to global colonialism and capitalism.

With the preceding in mind, many studies of the archaeology of the African Diaspora and the theoretical basis for the analogues employed have often been problematic. Historical archaeologists have tended to be uncritical of the analogical arguments used and naive in their consideration of historical context. Some research has attempted to link culture-specific historical descriptions of sociocultural phenomena or material culture from Africa to very different sociocultural contexts in the Americas (e.g., Ferguson 1992; Heath 1999; Petersen, Watters, and Nicholson 1999; Wilkie 1999). Such interpretations open a realm of possibilities rather than a world of probabilities. It is possible that meanings associated with decorations, such as the Bakongo cosmogram, reflect the rooting of New World cosmologies with Angola. However, it becomes probable that the individuals shared these ideas when the material was routed through situated and mapped histories.

Discussion of the African context, both in terms of data from the supposedly relevant parts of Africa and in terms of the evidence for connections with specific parts of the Americas, is essential. Yet such discussions are often very limited, and in some instances the allusions to African cultural, social, technological, and material patterns are drawn from secondary sources or isolated primary sources of uncertain validity or relevance. This problem is compounded by the fact that in many instances the data on the relevant areas of Africa during the appropriate time periods of the Atlantic trade are very inadequate (Posnansky 1984: 198; see discussion and references in DeCorse 1999 and 2001a, 2001b). Coupled with poorly suited methodologies and limited sample sizes, some studies obfuscate rather than clarify the dynamics of African American culture.

West African Ceramic Traditions: Colono Wares on the African Atlantic?

While there has been a florescence of literature on West Africa during the time of the Atlantic trade (see DeCorse 2001a, 2001b), part of the problem with attaching ethnic identities to material culture has to do with the state of knowledge about archaeological analysis in West Africa by North Americanists and Caribbeanists. Research in Africa, because of the geographic extent and the logistics of systematic fieldwork, leads to uneven research coverage. There are, in a sense, islands of intense fieldwork separated by large relatively underexamined regions (map 4.1) (see DeCorse 1999; Posnansky 1999). For instance, while coastal Ghana and the Banda region have had a florescence of archaeological activity since the 1960s, other areas of the country have yet to be subjected to the same degree of primary and comparative analysis. To some extent, research has been dominated by work on the Asante kingdom, which emerged as an important power during the eighteenth and nineteenth centuries. However, the coast and hinterland of this area incorporate a great deal of diversity.

As in many world areas, there have been numerous ceramic studies conducted, of varied theoretical sophistication and methodological rigor, in West Africa (Bellis [at Twifu Hemang] 1972; Crossland 1973, 1989; David 1972; Posnansky 1961, 1973, 1976a, 1976b, 1982, 1987; Crossland and Posnansky 1978; Effah-Gyamfi 1979, 1985, 1986; Krause 1978; Posnansky and

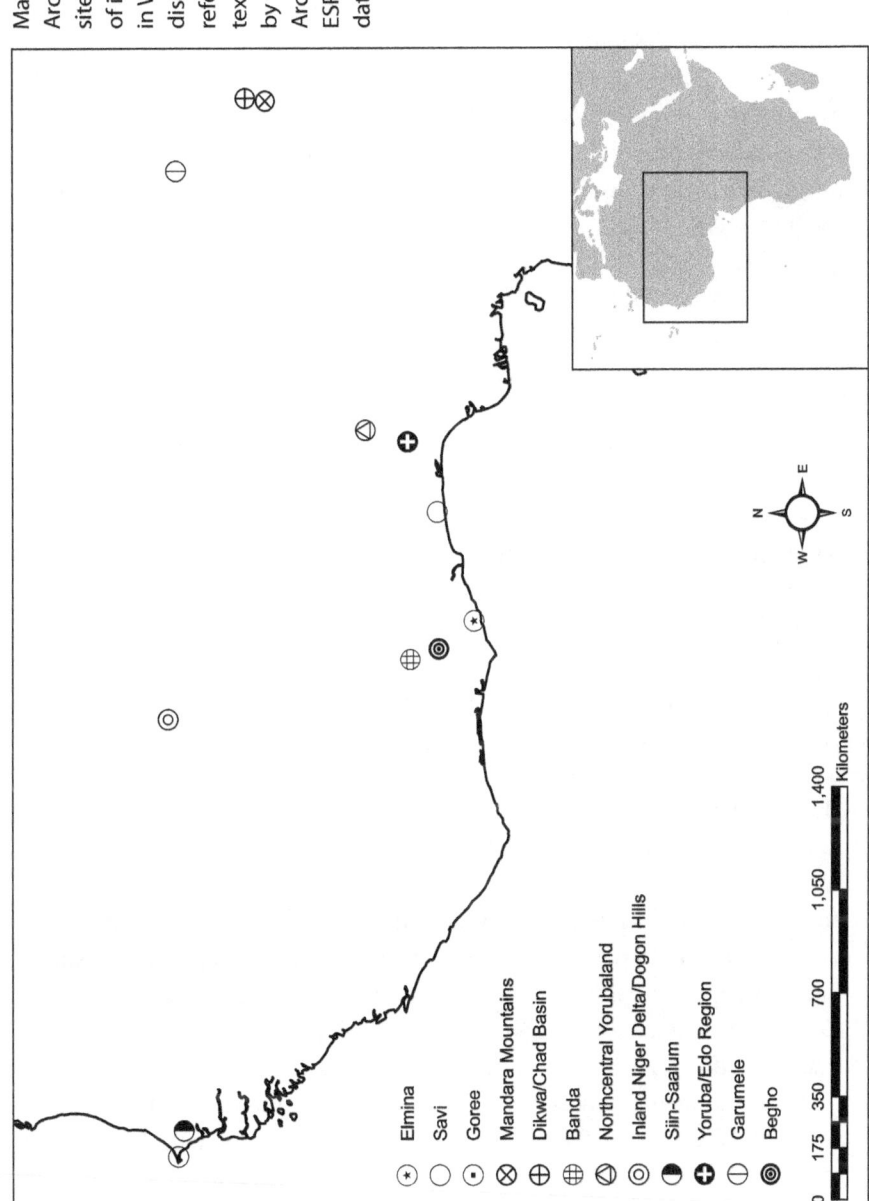

Map 4.1. Archaeological sites and regions of investigation in West Africa discussed or referenced in text. Illustration by Author using ArcView GIS and ESRI Continent data.

DeBarros 1980; Anquandah 1982, etc.; Ebanks 1984, 2003; Agorsah 1985, 1990; David et al. 1988; 1991; Sterner and David 1991; Gosselain 1992a, 1992b, 1998, 2000; Berns 1993; Akinade 1995; McIntosh 1995; Allsworth-Jones 1996; Bredhwa-Mensah 1996; Cruz 1996; Frank 1998; LaViolette 1995, 2000; Stahl and das Dores Giaro da Cruz 1998; McIntosh and Bocoum 2000; David and Kramer 2001; Decorse 2001; McIntosh and Thiaw 2001; Stahl 2001; das Dores Giaro da Cruz 2003; Cunningham 2005). An exhaustive review of the literature is beyond the scope of this book. Rather, I would like to highlight some of the lessons and cautionary tales that can be derived from analysis of this West African material to help understand the intersection of pottery and identity.

Traditionally, Caribbeanist archaeologists have looked to West Africa as a reservoir of cultural antecedents for New World ceramic traditions in the colonial period. This scholarship has sought confirmation of historical connections in comparisons of decorative inventories and stylistic motifs between African and Caribbean ceramics. This is problematic for a number of reasons. First, ethnoarchaeological research in Africa has shown that stylistic repetoires are sensitive to changing tastes and commercial interface and thus flow across social boundaries irrespective of social identity (Hodder 1982; David et al. 1991; Gosselain 1992a, 1998; Sterner et al. 1992; MacEachern 1998). By contrast, the actual technological choices, learning networks, and manufacturing techniques tend to be more conservative dimensions of social groups and in this way seem to be in closer correspondence with social boundaries. In short, they can be more reliable indicators of social identity and group belonging, whether articulated linguistically, culturally, or ethnically (Gosselain 1998, 1999, 2000; Haour 2000, 2005; Haour and Galpine 2005).

Second, the model of the reservoir is limited in that it uncritically presumes a certain endurance and stillness in modes of material expression and ceramic practice in both production and use. Research to date in West and Central Africa has shown that continuity in cultural practice is something to be empirically demonstrated rather than taken for granted (Stahl 1993: 236). Archaeological and ethnoarchaeological studies have illustrated that, if anything, African social boundaries underwent a great deal of social transformation and negotiation in the past five hundred years (for Senegal, see Richard 2007; for Cameroon, David, Sterner, and Gavua 1988; David et al. 1991; Sterner 1991, 1992; Sterner and David 1991; MacEachern 1994, 1998; for Nigeria, see Ogundiran 2001, 2002; Usman 2004; Usman, Speakman, and Glascock 2005; for Niger, see Haour 2005; for Chad, see Gronenborn 1998; Gronenborn and Magnavita 2000; for Ghana, see DeCorse 1989a; das Dores Giaro da Cruz 1996, 2003; Stahl and das Dores Giaro da Cruz 1998; Tetrault and DeCorse 2001; Hauser and DeCorse 2003). The list of studies conducted on sites directly impacted by the Atlantic trade is far shorter (for Savi, see Kelly 1996, 1997a, 1997b, 2001, 2002, 2004; Norman 2004; Norman and Kelly 2004; Kelly and Norman 2006; for Ghana, see DeCorse 1989b, 1992, 1993, 1994, 1996, 2001a, 2001b). Therefore, the mapping of contemporary social, linguistic, and political boundaries onto those that may have existed at given points of the Atlantic period becomes precarious. Concomitantly, the equation of material expressions with identity irrespective of historical context leads to spatial and temporal anachronism and ossification of social process.

Recent scholarship has begun to underscore the need to produce analyses of material culture sensitive to the historicity of social practice and technological tradition (das Dores Giaro da Cruz 1996, 2003; Stahl and das Dores Giaro da Cruz 1998). Specifically, research has emphasized the need to look at political economic forces and the way in which over time they shape material culture and the production systems in which it is embedded. These particular questions have been examined through an array of complementary methodologies emphasizing strategies of production, the circuit of pottery distribution, and the multiple scales in which people, objects, and ideas intersect. Exemplary in this line of research has been the work of Maria das Dores Giaro da Cruz in Banda, Ghana. Following a longitudinal approach to sites associated with the eighteenth and nineteenth centuries, Cruz used a combination of ethnographic research and compositional analysis to track changes in the centers of ceramic production and distribution. Relating these changes to the political economic transformations in the area, she was able to track reconfigurations in the domestic economies, social relations of production, and gender strategies. She thereby demonstrates that far from being an age-old craft and resistant expression of material culture, pottery making was a dynamic industry sensitive to historical circumstances and repeatedly refashioned in the face of events that refashioned the political geography of the Gold Coast in the nineteenth century (das Dores Giaro da Cruz 2003). It is this very analysis of the entanglements of political economy, historicity, and material culture that scholars of the Diaspora should seek to emulate in the Atlantic world. These observations have direct application to the Jamaican context and its historical connections (real and imagined) to the African mainland, Ghana in particular.

Ceramics in Coastal Ghana

There have been some suggestions that in Jamaica, the Akan-speaking peoples contributed significantly to its material and linguistic landscape (Cassidy and LePage [1967] 1980; Mathewson 1972a; Alleyne 1988; cf. DeCorse 1999; Burnard 2001; Hauser and DeCorse 2003; Stewart 2003; Kouwenberg forthcoming).[1] These linkages, to some extant, are borne out by historic evidence (Curtin 1969; Lovejoy 2001). According to Burnard and Morgan, however, enslaved Africans imported to Jamaica were bought at the Gold Coast, the Bight of Benin, the Bight of Biafra, West Central Africa, and the Senegambia (see figure 4.1). While the plurality of enslaved were purchased on the Gold Coast, they were not in the majority (Burnard and Morgan 2001; see also Burnard 1996, 2001)

There have been more specific identifications of stylistic influence from specific ethnolinguistic groups, such as the Shai Hills people (Ebanks 1984). These conclusions belie the fluid nature of identity formation and internal migrations with West Africa. Approximately the size of South Carolina and Georgia combined, modern Ghana stretches from the West African savanna to coastal forest. Presently, approximately fifty ethnolinguistic groups with varying degrees of social cohesion are found within the country (Kropp Dakubu 1988) (map 4.2). Although the nature of population movements and sociocultural transformations during the period of the Atlantic trade are not well documented, available evidence suggests that there has been a fair degree of stability in terms of the distribution of some ethnolinguistic groups and coastal polities (Hair 1967; DeCorse 1994: n37, 2001a: 18–20).

West African societies did not, however, remain frozen in time. There was tremendous change in sociopolitical institutions, trade patterns, and settlement organization as the region was increasingly enmeshed in a world economic system dominated by Europe. At the core of a variety of economic, social, and political transformations were the labor requirements of the emerging plantation economies of the Americas and the structural

---

1 Conversely, some scholars have argued that in the second half of the eighteenth century, there was an Igboization of the Jamaican enslaved population, an ethnogenic process in which there was an "essential reality of Igbo as a nation in the diaspora" (see Chambers 1997: 20, 2000; Thornton 1998: 192–97; 201; c.f. Northrup 2000; Morgan 1997).

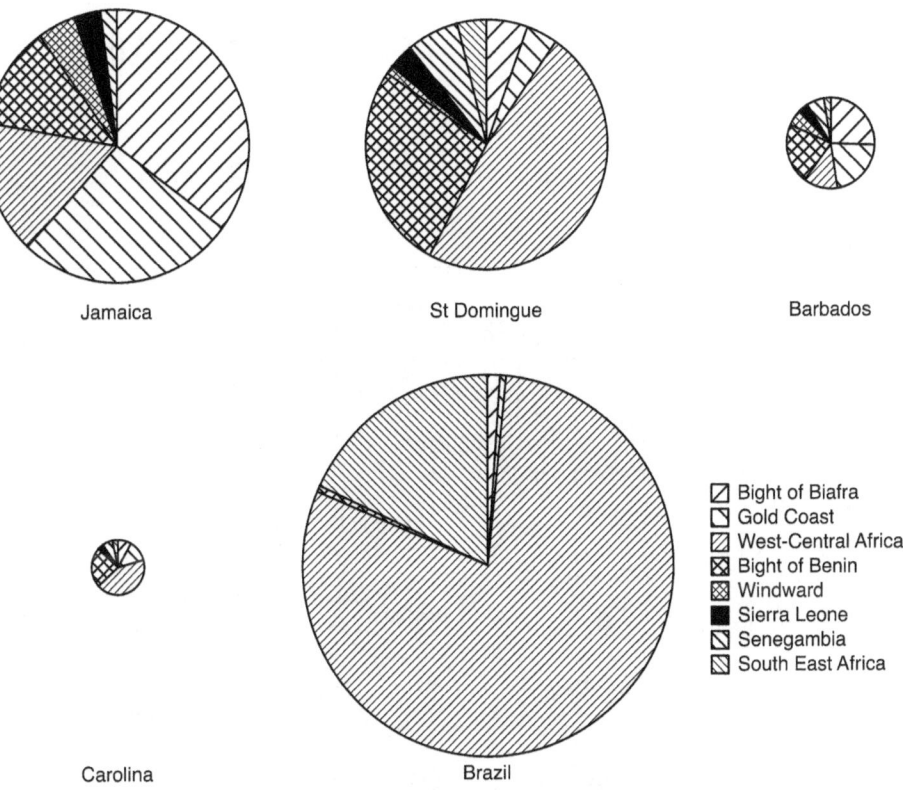

Figure 4.1. Pie charts illustrating the point of origin of enslaved peoples shipped to selected American colonies before 1808. The size of the chart is in linear proportion to the number of people. As a point of reference, the number used for Jamaica is 759,463. The data for this chart are taken from table 2 (Burnard 2001: 21), uses numbers from David Eltis et al. *The Trans Atlantic Trade 1562–1867: A Database*.

changes that made it possible to supply African labor. Along the Gold Coast, there was a trend toward urbanization and increasing craft specialization in the trading enclaves associated with European outposts. New or incipient states such as Elmina emerged and expanded their influence over surrounding settlements. In the hinterland, fortified towns and refuges from slave raiding appeared (DeCorse 2001a, 2001a: 18–31).

While it is worthwhile to underscore underlying continuities in worldview, there was also change in African religions, at least in terms of certain rituals and their material expression (e.g., DeCorse 2001a: 178–91). In general, there is a great deal of similarity within the Akan language family,

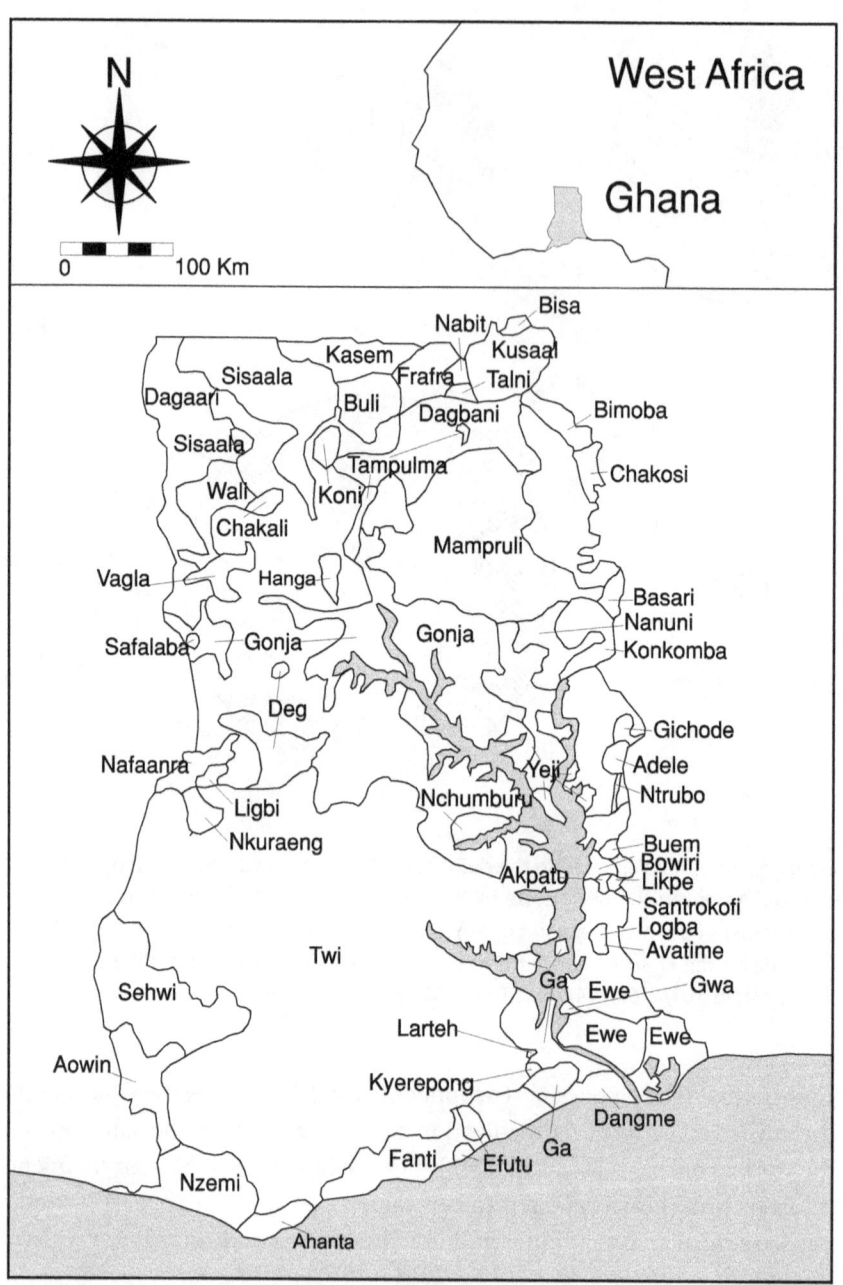

Map 4.2. Contemporary Ghana showing the approximate location of ethno-linguistic groups (adapted from Murdock 1959 and Kropp Dukubu 1988). Illustration by Author.

which can in turn be contrasted with neighboring groups. Akan sociocultural organization is matrilineal, and the clan elders enforce ideological and ritual conformity. However, patrilateral ties of various kinds crosscut and complement this overarching matrilineal framework. Beginning with the earliest Portuguese incursions in the late fifteenth century, there were attempts to convert the local inhabitants to Christianity, with varying success. Converts were often criticized by Europeans for their continued adherence to indigenous beliefs, and instances of mass conversions to Christianity, which do occur in other parts of Africa, did not take place (cf. DeCorse 2001a: 244 n. 17). Nevertheless, some aspects of Christian ritual may have been incorporated into indigenous beliefs to varying degrees, and new practices emerged.

Islam has also been noted as an important influence on some African cultures, and of possible significance in examining cultural patterns in the Diaspora (Meyers 1999: 219). Introduced into North Africa in the eighth century AD, Islam spread to West Africa via the trans-Saharan trade. Many West African populations are at least nominally Muslim, yet the advent of Islam in individual areas was varied in terms of the timing, the forms of Islam represented, the mode of introduction, and the influences on indigenous cosmologies (see discussion and references in Trimingham 1978; Bravmann 1980, 1983; Hiskett 1984; Insoll 2003). In many instances it impacted indigenous practices to only a limited degree or was adapted and transformed to be incorporated into local cosmologies. With regard to Ghana, there is no question that the region was part of broader trade networks by the second millennium AD, in some cases Islamic Mande traders making up a discrete quarter within a settlement (Posnansky 1987: 17–20). However, with regard to the Akan coast, evidence for Mande traders is negligible, and evidence for the influence of northern Islamic migrants on local traditions scant (Hair 1994: 53–54 n. 33, 55–56 n. 37; DeCorse 2001a: 49). The varying modes of introduction and the syncretic nature of West African Islam is in many respects similar to the advent of Christianity, which in some cases was substantially earlier, while Islam did not reach portions of the West African coast and hinterland until the nineteenth century.

Importantly, what this distinction suggests is that the material culture associated with these various peoples varies in both time and space. Archaeologically and ethnographically observed ceramic industries differ in terms of manufacture, vessel forms, and decoration, even in neighboring areas. For example, Akan ceramics are produced by slab molding, while the pottery of the adjacent Ewe is coil-built (DeCorse 2001a: 118–20; Tetrault and DeCorse 2001). Although there may be some similarities in utilitarian vessel forms, these account for only a subset of a wide range of vessel types. This diversity is matched by substantial differences in the sociocultural contexts in which the ceramics were produced (see discussion and references in DeCorse 1999: 138–39). Nor were ceramic industries static through time. Assemblages from throughout southern Ghana reflect substantial change during the post-European-contact period. In addition to greater amounts of European trade materials in the artifact inventories, there is change in house construction, metalworking, and craft production. Ceramics of the seventeenth through twentieth centuries are different from earlier pottery in terms of vessel forms, decoration, and the manufacturing techniques represented (DeCorse 2001a: 116–18). With the expansion of the Asante, aspects of Asante culture became incorporated into other areas. Hence, typically Asante-style carinated, smudged, and modeled vessels appear with increasing frequencies in coastal assemblages in the later eighteenth and nineteenth centuries (DeCorse 2001a: 122).

In addition to the diversity of the region, the other issue that presents a problem with simple identification of ethnicity in the Diaspora has to do with the way the Atlantic trade in Africans worked in Africa. The impact of the Atlantic trade in Africans on the Ghanaian coast and hinterland is just now being evaluated, but it is clear that enslaved peoples from throughout the region, representing many ethnic groups, were brought to the Americas. Although the numbers of individuals shipped from the coast are comparatively well documented, their precise origins and ethnicities are poorly known. People became associated with the area of the coast through which they passed, regardless of their actual origins (Lovejoy 1989). Hence, some enslaved peoples were referred to as "Cormante" or "Kormantin," a reference to a relatively small fort and associated African settlement on the central Gold Coast (Van Dantzig 1980: 21–22), which could not possibly have produced the vast numbers of captive Africans that supposedly came from there. In fact, both the Portuguese and the Dutch prohibited the taking of enslaved Africans from entrepôts such as Elmina and their immediate hinterlands, not because of abolitionist concerns, but because this was seen as disruptive to trade (DeCorse 2001a: 27). Many enslaved Africans were brought to the coast to be held for shipment to the Americas, as well as to meet local labor demands and for sale to local African merchants. As early as the 1470s, substantial numbers of enslaved laborers were taken from coastal Nigeria to the Gold Coast (Rodney 1969; Vogt 1973; DeCorse 2001a: 34–35;). Occasionally, people from coastal settlements like Elmina may have been sold into debt slavery (panyarred), but the majority of captives came from much farther afield in the hinterland or other parts of West Africa. "Elmina" or "Mina" slaves were reportedly the instigators of the St. John revolt of 1733 (Pope 1969: 134–35), but it is more likely that these were Adangme and Akwamu men and women from the eastern Gold Coast sold to agents of the Danish West India and Guinea Company following the breakup of the Akwamu state (Kea 1996; DeCorse 2001a: 27–28).

Given the preceding, it is likely that the captive Africans from the Ghanaian coast that reached Jamaica during the seventeenth and eighteenth centuries brought varied cultural backgrounds and life experiences with them. There may have been some commonalities, or at least familiarity, with certain languages and agricultural practices, such as shifting hoe cultivation. Yet the specific cosmologies, cultural practices, and technologies the Ewe, Fante, Krobo, and Ga would have brought with them across the Atlantic were distinct. Within the context of the Diaspora, this heterogeneity further mitigated the survival of direct continuities and contributed to the variation in individual regional and island patterns seen today. Today, African-descended populations make up the majority (90%) of Jamaica's population. Our understanding of specific phenomena is contingent on recognizing the complexities of the past and the genesis of a unique constellation of features that became "Jamaican."

The attempt to create a generalized category of ceramics is problematic in two ways. First, it reproduces the aggregation of African peoples that came about in the Middle Passage, thus making homogeneous an ethnically, linguistically, and religiously diverse group of people. Second, it belies the complex histories that existed for each of the peoples living in different parts of the Atlantic world. It is not enough to say that the Caribbean followed a different historical trajectory than the southeast United States. Rather, the ceramics produced by peoples unable to afford or gain access to, or unwilling to import, utilitarian wares are residues of complex, locally situated, yet regionally informed histories.

Pottery of the Caribbean

As I have argued above, the ways in which Jamaican ceramics have been analyzed by archaeologists has been to look for their roots. In the Caribbean and southeastern United States, much of the discussion of ceramics associated with African production and use has focused on issues of the identity of the people who made and used the pottery. In a regional and oceanic perspective, these ceramics are diverse, with only a few superficial similarities. What unifies this disparate group of ceramics are not methods of manufacture, designs and decoration, or even form and function. Rather, they are groups of ceramics made by peoples of African descent who employed skills brought from Africa in combination with skills introduced by Europeans and Amerindians. These techniques required adaptations to local demands of material, function, and manufacture. How should we make this pottery a useful analytical category? Where do we draw the line between the particularity of island contexts and a system of analysis that speaks to broader issues of colonization, displacement, and independent production?

Some scholars believe this disparate group of ceramics can be classified as one "regional creolized pottery tradition" (Heath 1999: 217; see also Petersen, Watters, and Nicholson 1999: 189), because "continuity can be well demonstrated spatially" (Petersen, Watters, and Nicholson 1999: 191). The assumption here is that the underlying technological, cultural, and historical contexts of ceramic production and its use were comparable across the Caribbean. This assumption is problematic, because emerging evidence suggests that, despite superficial similarities and the generally low firing temperatures likely represented in the wares' manufacture, there is a great deal of difference in the technological attributes present, as well as the contexts in which the vessels functioned (Hauser and DeCorse 2003). While there may be some continuity in form in the British and Dutch islands of the eastern Caribbean, these similarities end when one approaches the western Caribbean, including the British West Indies, the francophone islands, and the Spanish-speaking Caribbean (map 4.3). On these islands, though enslaved and freed Africans both produced and used ceramics, the potteries represented differ considerably from the ceramics some would identify as "Afro-Caribbean." In fact, superficial similarities aside, there is substantial variation in the formal attributes of assemblages from places such as Jamaica. Rather than similarity in manufacture or decorative inventory, it is the association with enslaved laborers that has been used to unite this disparate group of ceramics.

Review of historic period pottery traditions illustrates some of the differences present in the manufacture, decorations, and contexts represented, as well as the varying amounts of information available on the various traditions. While islands in close proximity do share some similarity in ceramic types and forms, as in the case of Barbuda and Antigua, most similarities in the ceramic traditions are restricted to similarities in form and low firing

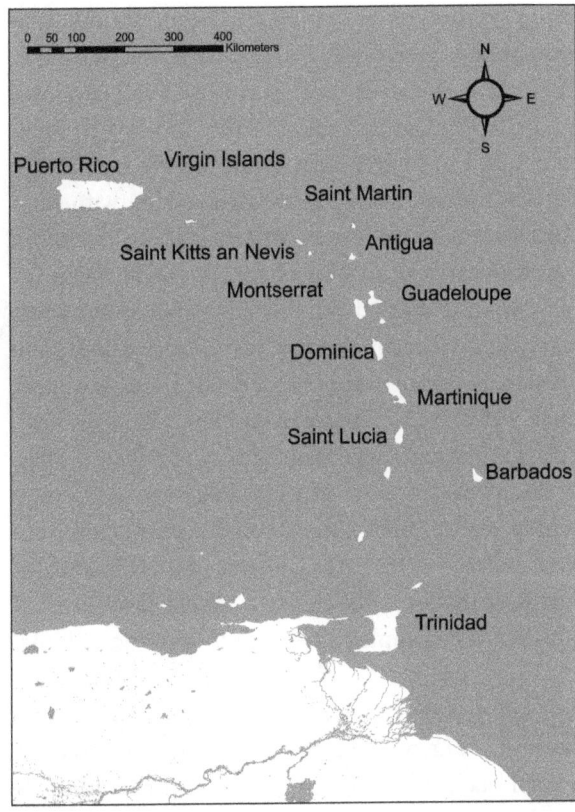

Map 4.3. Islands in the Eastern Caribbean discussed in the text. Illustration by Author.

temperatures. In addition, the varying degrees of analyses undertaken and the small size of some assemblages call into question the utility of making broad generalizations. The material reviewed below includes descriptions of local ceramic traditions as described in ethnographic accounts or inferred from archaeological collections. What does emerge from this brief review of the archaeological and ethnographic literature is that the pottery traditions found on islands today as well as those represented in the archaeological record emerge from complex histories of interaction and displacement.

As some have pointed out (Wilson 1997; Hofman and Bright 2004), indigenous peoples did not just die out and cease to impact and transform the Caribbean basin. The complexity of interaction between European, African, and Amerindian is probably best highlighted in the Greater Antilles, and specifically Hispaniola. With regard to Haiti, Gartley refers tangentially to earthenware imported from the Dominican Republic (1979). He describes the pottery as well made, with a polished exterior surface treatment and a red-orange paste, but the precise type of manufacturing method(s) employed have not been determined (Gartley 1979: 47). In Santa Domingo, a handful of sherds of distinctive wheel-thrown, kiln-fired local ceramics have been reported (Vega 1979: 43; García Arévalo 1986: 53), which seem to differ with local pottery found in Puerto Real, Haiti (Smith 1995: 352). The latter is an interesting assemblage from contexts associated with early historic to relatively recent contexts, including 23,267 sherds. Smith (1995), who examined the ceramics, described a series of locally made wares including Christophe plain ware, red slipped ware, unidentified plain ware, unidentified decorated ware, and modern "Haitian" ware. Christophe plain ware, the focus of his analysis, is comprised of thick-walled, undecorated, coarse earthenware (Smith 1995: 345). These were generally coil-built, low-fired utilitarian vessels, including bowls, jars, ollas, and collared ollas. The ceramics were most likely low-fired in an inconsistent environment (Smith 1995: 361). The highly varied collection of non-European ceramics recovered from Puerto Real points to the heterogeneity of this class of ceramic. Again, this heterogeneity makes it difficult to establish a single class of ceramic. It ultimately belies the complex interaction between colonial peoples.

In the Eastern Caribbean there is a considerable amount of evidence that enslaved African laborers and indigenous Caribbean peoples interacted, intermarried, and influenced each other. There has been a considerable amount of research into pottery production in the Eastern Caribbean and on St. Lucia specifically (McKusick 1960; Vérin 1961, 1963, 1967; Heath 1988: 125–31; Beuze 1990; England 1994; Hofman and Bright 2004). While Verin and McKusick highlighted the Amerindian influences on the colonial pottery found in Northern part of the island, Heath focused on the potential African influences. An ethnographic and archaeological study of pottery recovered in St. Lucia by Corinne Hofman and Alistair Bright (2004) highlights the problems associated with broad categories employed by archaeologists in the analysis of "folk" pottery. Through a careful analysis of pre-Columbian Suazoid pottery from multiple archaeological sites, historic Island Carib pottery, and modern folk pottery, Hofman and Bright were able to demonstrate the ways in which each tradition of pottery contained differences reflecting social and cultural environments (2004: 27). At the same time the assemblages reflect the multiple influences including Antillean (Suazoid), South American (Island Carib), and West African (contemporary folk pottery) and acknowledge "a blend of traditions" (2004: 29). Chronologically, the study spans the past 1,800 years. It is important to note, however, that this analysis relies primarily on a review of secondary literature, ethnographic accounts, and ethnographic observation. It is thus difficult to assess when transformations in pottery technology, design, and use took place.

Of primary interest to scholars of the African Diaspora is their discussion of folk pottery; the last in the sequence of discussion. This pottery is formed using a coiling technique, smoothed, and polished. It is fired in an open pit with local wood (Hofman and Bright 2004: 27). Seven forms were identified by Pierre Verin using creole nomenclature including "Terrine," "Canari," "Tesson," "Kastol," "Le Leshwit," "Krish," "Jé," "Shodie," "Plate," and "Potaflé" (Vérin 1961; Hofman and Bright 2004: 21). This pottery, the techniques used to manufacture it, and the forms into which they were made are similar to those found in Martinique, suggesting the possibility of regional interactions.

In Martinique and Guadeloupe, there have been several archaeological and ethnographic studies of pottery manufacture on the island, including an ethnographic examination of low-fired coarse earthenwares made by a local potter named Madame Trime (Beuze 1990); an archaeological analysis of wheel-thrown utilitarian ceramics at Trois Ilets (England 1994), and an archaeological analysis of industrial potteries devoted to the production of sugar wares in Les Saintes (Gabriel 2003). From a combination of archaeological data and documentary evidence, the pottery traditions of Martinique and Guadeloupe are recovered from deposits dating to as early as the mid-eighteenth century.

More recently Kenneth Kelly has recovered numerous Caribbean-made ceramics from sugar estates in southern Martinique (Crève Coeur), in Basse-Terre, Guadeloupe (Grande Pointe) and in Grande Terre, Guadeloupe (La Mahaudière). A combination of documentary evidence and associated archaeological materials places these contexts in the eighteenth and nineteenth centuries (Kelly and Hauser in press). At Crève Coeur, the domestic assemblage of enslaved labor generally consists of three types of island-made ceramics. The first type of ceramics is related to the industrial processing of sugar. These ceramics are a thick-walled, wheel-thrown earthenware. The paste is coarse, orange red, and contains large grog, broken limestone, and detrital inclusions. Its surface is untreated. These ceramics are found in forms that include drip jars and sugar cones. The second type of ceramic is a utilitarian ware associated with household cooking and serving. It also appears to be wheel-thrown and is thin-walled. These ceramics have been recovered in archaeological excavations at La Mahaudière and

Grande Pointe by Kelly, and also salvaged from construction sites in Basse-Terre and St. Martin by Antoine Chancerel and Christian Stouvenot. The third kind of ceramic is a hand-built ceramic similar to those described by Beuze (1990) in her ethnographic description of the potter Madame Trime in the commune of St. Anne in Martinique. This is a coil-made, thick-walled ceramic. The surfaces are evened and smoothed using a scraper and a rag (Beuze 1990). It appears to be fired in an open pit with highly variable cores and surface clouding. It is both slipped and burnished. This third kind of ceramic is similar to the folk pottery described in St. Lucia. In fact, the terms used to classify the pottery are the same as those used in St. Lucia.

The similarities between the pottery on St. Lucia and Martinique speak to the level of interaction that must have occurred between the two islands in colonial contexts. Beyond the detailed description of types and manufacture that the authors of these studies have provided, these projects reveal the diversity of ceramic manufacture and strategies of trade in which enslaved artisans in the Eastern Caribbean were involved. This diversity emerged out of a history that included the patchwork of traditions that influenced enslaved potters in the eighteenth century. Similar to islands of the Eastern Caribbean, though from distinct colonial legacies, the histories of Saba, St. Martin, Antigua, Barbuda, St. Eustatius, Nevis, and St. Kitts are interconnected. There has been a considerable amount of work on local ceramic traditions in the northeastern Caribbean that reflects these interactions.

In Antigua, Handler described a tradition of pottery manufacture characterized by a red slip, clouding, and a relatively low-luster burnish (Handler 1964: 151–52; also see Handler and Lange 1978: 3; Gartley 1979: 47). There are archaeological examples of fragmented body sherds from eighteenth- and nineteenth-century contexts, as well as comparative studies of ethnographic forms by Heath (1988: 141). The modern method of manufacture includes pinch pulling and scraping (Handler 1964: 151), and this may be comparable to the techniques represented in archaeological examples. Ethnographic evidence for open hearth firing (Handler 1964: 152) and coring and clouding in archaeological samples (Nicholson 1990) indicates that this pottery was low-fired in inconsistent environments. In the eighteenth century, the Antiguan pottery forms identified primarily consist of round-bottomed, hemispherical bowls and round, red-slipped griddles (Nicholson 1990; Watters 1997). Notably, the griddles are one of the few instances from the British West Indies where this form, normally associated with Amerindian contexts, is present in historic sites of the African Diaspora. The presence of this type of pottery made in this form speaks again to the complicated histories and interactions between indigenous Caribbean populations and African-descended populations.

Antiguan ceramic forms represented ethnographically include cooking pots, monkey jars, flowerpots, and coal pots (Handler 1964: 151; Heath 1988: 114). The three later forms are late-nineteenth- and twentieth-century and represent a subset of the range of shapes found archaeologically. These forms seem to appear in archaeological contexts in nearby islands but in ceramics with different fabrics.

On St. Eustatius, there are similar forms in nineteenth-century sites. Barbara Heath examined 1,924 archaeological ceramics from three sites primarily dating to the eighteenth and nineteenth centuries (Heath 1988: 149). The vessels are found in a variety of forms, including cooking pots, dishes, monkey jars, teapots, dry storage jars, liquid storage jars, and jugs produced by coiling and hand-modeling (186, 206). In addition, firing environments of archaeological ceramics were inferred to be, on the whole, variable, and Heath (186) notes that vessels were produced in both reduced and oxidizing environments. Surface treatments ranged from red painted to burnished to untreated and do not seem to be linked to specific vessel forms or type of manufacture (ibid.). Heath argued that the similarity in form represented an underlying tradition of ceramic manufacture. This is certainly possible. It is also likely that the similarity in shapes derives from interaction between the enslaved populations of the island where the potters are essentially borrowing and copying from one another.

This interaction can be discerned through careful examination of the constituent materials making up the pottery. In neighboring Montserrat, for example, there is evidence that the enslaved from different plantations were trading pottery. Local pottery from Montserrat, represented by 20 low-fired earthenware sherds from the Harney slave cemetery, has been discussed by Watters (1987, 1988). These ceramics were coil-made and undecorated. Variable coloration, coring, and clouding indicate that the ceramics were inconsistently fired (Petersen and Watters 1988: 169), probably in the open. Because the paste inclusions are consistent with Montserrat's geological environment, Watters concluded the pottery was made on the island (Watters 1987). Howson's (1995) work at Galways plantation, also on Montserrat, has described an assemblage of local coarse earthenware that comprises approximately 47 percent (total number not stated) of the total ceramic assemblage (Howson 1995: 336). Howson noticed that, macroscopically, the inclusions found in these ceramics are similar to those in the ceramics discussed by Watters (236). These observations could point to a single site of manufacture and trade between populations, or the use of the same clay source. Importantly, however, both Watters's and Howson's research suggest a degree of intra-island trade between and among enslaved from different plantations.

Not only did trade occur within island contexts, it also occurred between islands. To the north, low-fired earthenware from Barbuda has been excavated from Codrington Castle (Watters 1997). The twenty-two vessels are represented by thick-walled, smoothed body sherds, and the assemblage was comprised mostly of utilitarian pots with no decorative treatment. The lack of any historic documentation, and the similarity in temper with the Antiguan pottery discussed above, suggested to Watters that the vessels were most likely imported (Watters 1997: 284). The importing of these ceramics bespeaks a trade between islands in which potters could learn to copy and steal ideas from their neighbors. More important, it speaks to an interdependency that emerged in the northeastern Caribbean among the planters and the enslaved of different colonies.

Analysis of pottery from the Virgin Islands (Danish, British, and Spanish) bespeaks a lively interisland as well as intercolonial trade. In the U.S. Virgin Islands, "Afro-Cruzan" ware, described on the basis of thirty-one sherds from six plantation sites in St. Croix, is a hand-molded, inconsistently low-fired, unglazed or untreated earthenware (Gartley 1979: 47). Vessel surfaces were smoothed and evened. While there has been further exploration of this type of pottery in St. Croix by Stephen Lenik (2004), there has been little exploration of the production of this kind of ceramic. Similar earthenwares have been recovered from late-eighteenth- and nineteenth-century contexts by Douglas Armstrong on the East End of St. John (Hauser 1998; Hauser and Armstrong 1999), and on St. Thomas by Gary Vescelius (Gartley 1979: 47). Elizabeth Kellar (2004) has also recovered coarse earthenware from her excavations of eighteenth-century contexts at Adrian estate, also on St. John. Vessel forms include simple restricted bowls and everted pots (Hauser 1998: 35–36) or olla-shaped vessels (Gartley 1979: 48). However, the assemblages recovered thus far are still quite small, consisting of a total of 118 sherds from East End, and some 200 sherds from Adrian.

Recent longitudinal studies of 630 ceramics from Cinnamon Bay, an early cotton estate on the north coast of St. John, have challenged the assumption that indigenous ceramics and ceramics made by people of African descent can easily be distinguished. This site preliminarily dates from the early eighteenth century and continued to be occupied until the late nineteenth century (Armstrong, Hauser, and Knight 2005: 744). What is remarkable about these ceramics is their heterogeneity. A second point of interest stems from the similarity between coarse earthenware recovered from early historic contexts of the site and Taino pottery recovered from the adjacent prehistoric site (Hauser and Armstrong 2004). Much of this similarity can be explained by a similar paste, which is probably the result of both groups exploiting a similar, or the same, clay source. Much of the pottery was irregular in texture but contained fine white shell and quartz inclusions. However, there are some analogues between the two types of pottery that are striking. Some of the lips recovered from the prehistoric site are folded, similar to those recovered from the Taino settlement. Similarly, there is one instance in which the form of the pottery was in the shape of an olla. While these attributes do not indicate an ethnic affiliation with Taino potters, the presence of these attributes does indicate a more complex interaction between peoples of African descent and the Taino than studies of other historic potteries have indicated. The presence of these attributes might indicate that peoples of African descent were influenced by the Taino pottery they found and incorporated some stylistic elements into their own traditions. Furthermore, it might even indicate interaction between the two groups.

Similarly, in Puerto Rico we find an equally complex history of interaction resident in the pottery. Puerto Rican low-fired earthenwares, identified as criollo wares by Brian Crane (1993) and Carlos Magana (1999), have been recovered from San Juan. The collections examined were not explicitly demarcated but were primarily recovered from eighteenth- and nineteenth-century urban contexts (Magana 1999: 131). Criollo ware is divided into three form types, ollas, cazuelas, and ringfooted (Magana 1999: 136), which also reflect differences in paste and manufacture. The tempers/paste(s) of the ollas and cazuelas are characteristically highly variable coarse sands, quartzites, and grog temper (Magana 1999: 136). The firing environment is variable, with paste discolorations indicating both reducing and oxidizing environments (Magana 1999: 136). There also tends to be appliqué decoration around the belly of the vessel (Magana 1999: 136). In contrast, the ringfooted criollo ware is a coarse, handmade, sand-tempered ceramic, some with micaceous inclusions (Crane 1993: 115). The vessels seem to be coiled, with the bases being modeled or hand-molded (Magana 1999: 136). Crane examined 654 sherds of criollo ceramics, which made up approximately 16 percent of his total study collection of Puerto Rican Criollo wares and Colono wares from South Carolina (Crane 1993: 92). They appear to have been low-fired, but in a consistent environment (Crane 1993: 117). They were all burnished, except for vessels with a heavy micaceous wash (Magana 1999: 136). Decorations include stamping and rouletting (Magana 1999: 140). Crane tentatively suggests manufacture was by enslaved peoples of African descent influenced by Taino practices, but he also argues that the complexity of identity within Puerto Rico makes it difficult to ascribe manufacture to one ethnic group (Crane 1993: 115).

In Cuba, there are several traditions of local pottery manufacture, most of which enslaved laborers were either directly or indirectly manufacturing. Some locally made utilitarian pottery is identified as Ceramica Ordinaria, subsuming storage jars, roof tiles, floor tiles, and sugar molds, as well as Mexican red-painted ware, Feldspar Inlaid ware, El Morro ware and others (Pratt Puig 1980: 18–33). Some of the ceramics identified as Ceramica Ordinaria are comparable in manufacture, surface treatment, decoration, and form to some that have been identified as Afro-Jamaican. The Cuban ceramics, however, were not necessarily produced by peoples of African descent. One subset, in fact, consists of partially glazed or unglazed coarse earthenwares of uncertain manufacture. They have been recovered from Maroon sites and date to the nineteenth century; they are therefore associated with African Diaspora populations (La Rosa Corzo 1991).

Also included in the group are distinctive nineteenth-century, low-fired earthenwares that have been attributed to Amerindians. The archaeological examples recovered are restricted to a few pieces from the Guanabacoa suburb of Havana. Cuban estate holders continued to import Native American labor from the Yucatán well into the nineteenth century, and contemporary documentary accounts describe the manufacture of ceramics by the Guanabacoa Amerindians (Theresa Singleton personal correspondence, July 5,2001). Stylistically, the ceramics are comparable to Afro-Jamaican ceramics in that they are devoid of a decorative inventory and occur in utilitarian forms. Lacking more information on the historical context of ceramic production in both Havana and the Yucatán makes it difficult to be certain about their origin. It is possible that peoples of African descent also manufactured some of these ceramics (Antonio Sandrino conversation, March 8, 2000). The forms discussed are common throughout the Caribbean and thus highlight the difficulties in attributing ethnicity solely on the basis of form. A term to describe these hand-built ceramics, which has gained favor with some Cuban archaeologists, is *ceramicas de transculturacion* (Singleton personal correspondence July 5, 2001). This term is very similar to Ferguson's rationale behind the classification "Colono ware" and implies a creolized manufacturing tradition.

This brief review illustrates that there is little that one can identify as a common attribute in historic Caribbean pottery. If one were to assign general characteristics to this form of material culture, they would be threefold. First, it does not look like European or aboriginal pottery. Second, the pottery is primarily utilitarian in function. Third, the pottery is stylistically generalized. In other words, there is little to no decorative inventory. What decoration does exist seems to be idiosyncratic to the island or potter. Surface treatment is also generalized. Though a few attributes are apparent in some places, such as glazing, slips, and smoothing, these attributes are far from ubiquitous. The complexity of colonial processes and the idiosyncrasies of creolization require a particularistic approach to these ceramics with mindful observation of the institutions that might bind them (Ferguson 1992: 22).

Local historic pottery from the Caribbean is quite diverse. The research highlighted the need to discuss the ceramics within the historical particularities of the contexts in which they were found. What this review illustrates is how idiosyncratic the pottery is to each of the islands. In the Caribbean, low-fired earthenware is ubiquitous in contexts associated with the African Diaspora. The particularities of locally produced pottery in the Caribbean inhibit broad categorical lumping. Variation between and within islands suggests that the pottery should be treated particularistically through a systematic approach. Following Emerson and Pauketat (Emerson and Pauketat 2002: 106), I suggest that we need to view these ceramic assemblages as embodying the flows of commodities and movement of peoples and ideas, rather than as residues of antecedent identities. Certainly, those identities were important to the people who made and used these ceramics, but those identities were ultimately the product of the social networks in which the enslaved were rooted.

Conclusion

The African Diaspora was not only a movement of people from one continent to another. It was, more important, a displacement born from emergent European capitalism that affected and transformed local communities. We see the effect of the Diaspora in the systems of belief, the political economies, and the material residues of communities on either side of the

Atlantic in the eighteenth century, continuing into the present. It is important not to forget this broader field of power when we approach the Diaspora—a forced displacement of people.

This did not have the effect of stripping culture from people, but rather it created contexts in which people had to reform social networks, reshape themselves, and use their skills and knowledge in order to make do in wholly new contexts. People brought these skills and knowledge with them. That does not mean, however, that they did not continue to learn, to adapt, and to appropriate technologies, ideas, and meanings. As Karen Olwig has pointed out in her analysis of USAID and its effect on Nevisian potters, pottery production has been transformed by "the historic integration of Afro-Caribbean culture," tourism, and recent demands in regional utilitarian production (Olwig 1990: 8, 12, 13). The pottery seen in the Caribbean today is a diverse patchwork of traditions and techniques that reflects the diverse origins of those who made and continue to make the pottery.

The point of the preceding discussion is not to deny African influence in American ceramics. We know that African-inspired features have been found in many American societies. Certainly the fact that coiling and slab manufacture, as opposed to wheel-throwing or molding, are the predominate types of manufacture in many Caribbean low-fired earthenware traditions is notable, as is the occurrence of a suite of decorative techniques that may be found in African ceramics. The issue is whether it is possible to delineate correlations with specific parts of Africa—namely the Gold Coast—or an Islamic decorative tradition. We know that African cultures were not transplanted en masse to remain static and unchanged in the Americas. This factor, combined with the extremely limited contemporary data for many areas of Africa, as well as ambiguities about ethnicities of enslaved Africans in the Americas, allows only the most tenuous statements to be made about continuities. The multiple displacements, the disruptive nature of enslavement, and the melding of different cultures (numerous African, European, and Native American) makes direct connections unlikely and, in fact, unexpected. Indeed, the multiple colonial histories and heterogeneous populations involved require a more nuanced understanding of creolization and its material residues. Studies must recognize the productive and creative power of these displaced people struggling to create meaning and fashion their worlds anew in far-flung colonial contexts. Methodologically, such studies must begin with a strong grounding in the historical contexts represented and a recognition of the dynamic and innovative nature of African American societies. It is only within the context of local and regional interactions that this variation and change in pottery assemblages becomes meaningful.

Frederick Cooper (2005: 17) warns about establishing causalities through an analysis of only a partial field of actors and agents, something he calls leapfrogging legacies. Certainly cautioning against these leapfrogging legacies is as salient in the analysis of pottery as it is in text (DeCorse 1999; Hauser and DeCorse 2003). By aggregating this variegated class of material culture into a single type, we belie the complex, regionally informed interactions that brought about their use. In the next chapter I look at the diversity of island-made pottery in Jamaica. This diversity speaks to the multiple forces shaping enslaved independent production. Most important, the diversity speaks to the different industries that the enslaved engaged in to meet the market demand for their wares, imported, grown, or manufactured. The eighteenth century presents a unique time period in which to understand the informal economic sector in Jamaica. The eighteenth century saw a dramatic increase in the enslaved population through importation. It also saw increasing intensification of the sugar industry. We also have documentary evidence, which adds texture to our understanding of the markets. We don't have an understanding of this economy's scope or scale. Archaeological sites excavated from the 1960s until the 1990s present a body of data through which to understand the scope of this market system. By establishing the variability and relative provenance of the ceramics, we can understand the scale of commodity flow through the street markets of Jamaica.

5

Rooting Pots

Jamaican Colonial Ceramics

> The economic crisis of recent years, compounded by the rapid proliferation of cheap, readily available pots and plates, has led to the almost-extinction of the Afro Jamaican ceramic in Jamaica. Most potters have died or have given up potting. Out of the sizable communities in which most yards made pots for markets as far as 50–60 miles away, there are now only three practicing potters.
>
> Ebanks 1984: 31.

In this opening quote, Jamaican archaeologist Roderick Ebanks is describing the particular difficulties that were faced by Jamaican potter Ma Lou (figure 5.1). Today, Munchie, her daughter, is the last remaining potter to work in a ceramic tradition that is analogous to, if not descended from, the archaeological ceramics recovered from domestic contexts associated with eighteenth-century enslaved laborers. Munchie learned her craft from her mother (figure 5.2), who in turn had learned it from her own mother (Ebanks 1984). While the documentary and archaeological records are relatively silent on the actual identity of the potters who made Jamaican colonial ceramics, a combination of ethnographic, archival, and archaeological analysis can establish that women of African descent were making the majority of colonial ceramics used in eighteenth-century domestic contexts. The knowledge used to excavate and process the clay, build the vessel, and fire these pots was passed down from mother to daughter. This tradition of pottery manufacture was not isolated or changeless, as is implied in the above quote. It was affected by the distribution of labor, the importation of functional equivalents, and most importantly the systems of distribution that brought the pottery to market and eventually into the kitchens of the people who used them.

The focus of this chapter is the yabba, a coarse, sometimes low-fired earthenware. Yabbas are generally associated with the independent production of African Jamaicans and are recovered from archaeological contexts

Figure 5.1. Ma Lou (Louisa Jones) building a yabba in 1984. Photograph by and courtesy of Roderick Ebanks.

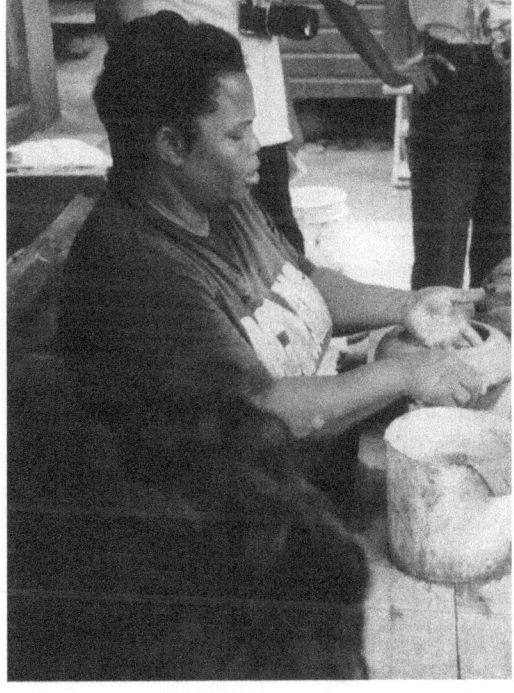

Figure 5.2. Munchie (Marlene Roden) forming a yabba in 1998. Photograph by Author.

with laboring and enslaved peoples of African descent. As such they are one of the few forms of archaeologically recovered material culture that are directly related with enslaved independent production, trade, and use. Based on insight gained from the ethnographic record, we can go further and say that it represents the independent production of enslaved women. This production was rooted in a larger web of social networks and commodity production.

As many archaeologists and ethnoarchaeologists have argued, the process through which systems of technical knowledge are passed from one generation to the next, from one community to another is inherently complex and social. The knowledge is simultaneously explicit and implicit, where the routine of craft production is punctuated by specific active decisions made by the potter (Dietler and Herbich 2000; Gosselain 1992b; 1998, 2000; Stark 1998; Dobres 2000; David and Kramer 2001). The women who made these pots used systems of knowledge and ways of doing things that they learned from their mothers and, in some cases, brought with them from Africa and employed in new economic tasks. The pottery they made had to respond to the demands of the informal markets in which they were sold. This pottery can be seen, therefore, as a material embodiment of the social networks that linked generations of women and communities of enslaved laborers within informal and formal political economy.

Rooting the Archaeological Discussion

Before I discuss the archaeological ceramics, I would like to turn briefly to the ways in which these ceramics have been approached by archaeologists. It is not enough to say they were colonial ceramics produced in Jamaica, in that such a classification belies a broad spectrum of ceramics produced in Jamaica as early as the fifteenth century and continuing up until today. Jamaican colonial ceramics were diverse in manufacture, function, and decorative inventory. This diversity was in part a function of the shifting political economy of the island; it is also a function of the diverse influences informing and shaping the potter's craft. Various authors have attempted to link this diversity with specific antecedent populations.

Yabba actually refers to the form rather than to the specific method of manufacture or decoration of Jamaican historic ceramics. I will be using *yabba* as a classification of type, unless I am explicity describing the form. The precise etymology of the word remains uncertain, and other, non-Akan, West African or Caribbean origins remain possibilities. The term itself is believed to be either derived from the Twi word *ayawa*, meaning "earthenware dish," or a local "Taino" word for "Big Mouth" (Mathewson 1972b: 55). Mathewson was most likely relying on Cassidy's and, later, Alleyne's (1988) arguments that the Akan and Ewe groups were predominantly responsible for many of the structural similarities found within the British island-based "creoles." While Kouwenberg (forthcoming) has argued that Jamaican creole patois has multisubstrate origins, she has also identified that *yabba* is most likely derived from Twi (Kouwenberg, personal communication 2007). Regardless of the term's origin, its use implies a link between a contemporary African Jamaican yabba pottery tradition that was practiced in Spanish Town by potter Ma Lou and now her daughter, Munchie, and archaeologically recovered low-fired earthenwares. This Jamaican-made pottery has been described in archaeological contexts by several scholars, including Mathewson (1972a), Mayes (1972), Ebanks (1984), Armstrong (1990), Pasquariello (1995), Reeves (1997), Meyers (1999), Higman (1998). The classification of this pottery in a consistent framework proved to be challenging, in that yabbas were ultimately not a single type of ceramic, nor were they made into a single form. The ceramic type yabba, identified by the above authors, is varied in manufacture, decorative inventory, and surface treatment.

Almost from their initial discovery, Jamaican earthenwares were associated with Afro-Jamaicans. In her classic study of Jamaican folk life, Martha Beckwith describes yabbas as "hand turned and covered with a rude glaze" (Beckwith 1929: 47). Philip Mayes (1972: 101) and Duncan Mathewson (1972b: 55, 1973:26) were the first archaeologists to identify locally produced low-fired Jamaican ceramics in seventeenth-, eighteenth-, and nineteenth-century contexts, and both researchers classified these wares as "yabbas," employing a traditional Jamaican term for locally produced Jamaican earthenware. Much of the work on this particular form of pottery has tended to focus on its "Africanness" and demonstrations of long-term processes such as creolization or syncretism. While these are interesting endeavors, such arguments tend to gloss not only the fluidity of identities and social networks, but also the materials' potential in unpacking those social relations.

Richard Meyers (1999: 202) argued that "decorative attributes consistent with West African pottery traditions can be isolated" in a seventeenth-century Port Royal assemblage. Meyers's conclusions, based on a small subset of the earthenwares recovered from Port Royal, are compared with disparate ceramic traditions of uncertain relevance to the Jamaican material.

Meyers focuses on the analysis of decoration, specifically the techniques employed. Out of the nine hundred sherds in the study collection, twenty-eight were decorated with stamping, punctation, incision, and/or grooving. These techniques, Meyers claims, represent African traditions. He draws a link between the Port Royal potters and potters from Jenne-jeno in Mali, Qsar es-Seghir in northern Morocco, and Abodum, Twifo Heman, Elmina, and New Buipe, Ghana (Meyers 1999: 212–15).

Ethnoarchaeological research, in Africa particularly, has shown that decoration is often a poor index of "ethnic belonging" (David et al. 1991; Sterner 1992; MacEachern 1998). By contrast, technical knowledge and manufacturing modes, because they tend to be more "conservative" and less subject to contingencies of contact (although that's not true all the time), are sometimes a more reliable expression of "social identity" (whether manifested in cultural, linguistic, kinship, or political terms) (Gosselain 1992b, 1998). Meyers's argument is that stamping as a decorative technique diffused from northern Africa into Mali through Islamic expansion, then into Ghana through the northern trade, and then across the Atlantic through slavery (Meyers 1999: 215). Although a long-distance, north–south trade did exist in West Africa, Meyers admits his scenario to be mere speculation. Nevertheless, it seems that his entire argument rests on this unlikely series of connections (Hauser and DeCorse 2003).

Earlier attempts at similar arguments (Ebanks 1984: 36) have been criticized (Hill 1987; DeCorse 1999). The failure of these arguments rests on the inability of the authors to draw credible historical and cultural connections and lines of relevance, or indeed to recognize that the African societies from which ceramic traditions supposedly originated were becoming increasingly "creolized" themselves or transformed from one or two centuries of immersion in changing Atlantic political economies. To examine seventeenth-century Jamaican low-fired earthenware through a West African lens, we should use as our analogue seventeenth-century West African ceramic traditions. We focus on those portions of West Africa where the enslaved potters of the Americas likely originated and establish spatial and temporal continuity between the technological and stylistic elements employed by the West African potters from whom the analogy is drawn and the Caribbean potters to whom the interpretation is applied. Having done this, we can look at constellations of attributes that may suggest continuities in the traditions. As discussed in the previous chapter, African potting traditions are extremely varied, incorporating a tremendous diversity in manufacturing technique, decorative inventory, and the sociocultural context of production (Hauser and DeCorse 2003). Modern, ethnographically described, potting traditions may provide some insight, but the relevance of forms and meanings derived from a modern context to archaeologically recovered assemblages from earlier periods would have to be established through the direct historical approach. This becomes especially difficult when one considers transformations in African societies during the post-European-contact period and, further, that in various American settings "social and cultural characteristics—and, some would say, individual idiosyncrasies of their inhabitants—cannot be accounted for, or even described, without reference to colonialism" (Trouillot 1992: 22). The strongest analogies, therefore, are made by comparing contemporaneous ceramic traditions from the areas for which historical connections can be documented (Hauser and DeCorse 2003).

In colonial Jamaica, there is no single ceramic tradition or potential antecedent to the pottery tradition that became popular in the eighteenth century. Most likely there were multiple influences derived from Africa, indigenous America, and Europe (Hauser and DeCorse 2003). Published data regarding the number of peoples of African descent versus Europeans on Jamaica provide a demographic context which makes the manufacture by African Jamaicans probable. Drawing on ethnographic and documentary data, we can develop an analogy linking at least some of the pottery production to Afro-Jamaicans.

During the course of the Atlantic trade in Africans between 1655 and 1808, some 759,463 enslaved laborers were brought to and remained in Jamaica (Dunn 1972: 235–37; Burnard 2001: 21). Of the 3,432 voyages recorded in the Transatlantic Slave Trade Database (Eltis, Behrendt, and Richardson 2000), Trevor Burnard estimates that 1,083,369 were intended to be brought to Jamaica and that 168,165 people either died in the passage or disembarked (Burnard 2001: 13). During the early part of English settlement (Thornton 1955: 404), the failed Royal Adventurers Trading into Africa and its successor, the Royal Africa Company, supplied very small numbers to Jamaica (Bennett 1964: 63). In 1661, documents recorded 514 enslaved laborers. In 1664, Governor Modyford augmented this number by 800 with laborers from Barbados (Dunn 1972: 154). There were 9,500 laborers in 1673; 45,000 in 1703; and 210,894—working on 710 plantations—in 1787 (Edwards [1793] 1972: 237; Pitman [1917] 1945: 373; Sheridan 1973: 210). Between 1688 and 1755, the number of enslaved peoples retained in

Jamaica, rather than resold to other colonies or islands, steadily increased in the African Diaspora (deported) population on the island (Wu 1995: 376).. By 1713, the population of enslaved laborers increased to 55,000 (Dunn 1972 :164 fn).

Given the size of this population, the nature of plantation society, and the labor requirements of the island, African-descended populations likely played a central role in Jamaican craft industries, including ceramic production (Hauser and DeCorse 2003). An analogous ceramic might give us some clue. The Port Royal red clay pipe industry in the seventeenth century was controlled by a European, John Pope. According to Taylor (1688), however, "the Negroes make tobacco pipes" out of a "red claie" on the Liguanea Plain (cited in Pawson and Buisseret [1975] 2001: 105).

In Barbados, the pottery industry had its roots primarily in plantation contexts and involved the production of wares designed to assist the capital production of the estate—primarily ceramic sugar pots and cones (see Handler 1963b). This industry certainly utilized African labor and may well have drawn upon knowledge of pottery production or even skilled artisans captured from Africa, but it was modeled in more decidedly European potting traditions and technologies and was initially centered in plantation workshops and kilns, like the one at Codrington estate Barbados (Loftfield 2001). It has been assumed that domestic-based ceramic industries began to emerge at the beginning of the nineteenth century. They did so in clay-rich but otherwise extremely marginal lands—a rather dangerous area prone to landslides. Production was by a community of potters who were of Africa descent, but the wares they produced project a local, Barbadian permutation that involved African heritage and potting practices derived from the industrial pottery works that had been in operation on the estate combined with design elements that reflect local needs and emerging traditions (see Handler 1963b).

Thomas Loftfield does suggest, however, that there was a seventeenth-century tradition of domestic pottery production that employed artisan laborers (2004). This pottery tradition would have been contemporary and slightly earlier than the tradition which begins as early as the seventeenth century in Jamaica. A pottery tradition that would have been used by inhabitants that are for the "most part Europeans, some Creolians, born and bred in the Island Barbados, the Windward Islands, or Surinam, who are the Masters, and Indians, Negros, Mulatos, . . . [etc.], who are the Slaves." (Sloane 1707–1725: xlvi). It is possible, and I think likely, that the pottery tradition we find in seventeenth-century contexts of Port Royal was made in Jamaica by émigrés from Barbados. Indeed, the internal dimensions and flows of the Caribbean also have to be considered in developing the appropriate analogues for archaeological ceramics.

The final groups to potentially influence eighteenth-century potter production were pre-conquest indigenous Jamaicans. This influence would have been indirect. At the same time, given a certain degree of continuity in population between indigenous peoples, enslaved Africans under the Spanish, and freed Maroons under the British (Agorsah 1992), it remains a distinct possibility. In the sixteenth century at New Seville, there is a broad range of utilitarian ceramics in use by Spanish colonizers and their workforce, indigenous Jamaicans. These ceramics include forms of pottery resembling pre-Columbian Taino ceramics as well as a creolized ceramic identified by Woodward as "New Seville ware" (Woodward 2006b: 170). Both wares contain a sand micaceous paste and are decorated with a burnish. Both wares were handmade, as opposed to wheel-thrown. The distinguishing characteristic of the New Seville ware is its use of European forms, such as pedestal cups, pitchers, and jugs (see figure 5.3). Indeed, one of the forms present in this archaeological assemblage is an inverted bowl that anticipates the later shape of yabbas (Woodward 2006b: 170).

I am not suggesting that eighteenth-century yabbas were derived from Taino ceramics; rather, I would like to highlight one potential influence. By the time the enslaved laborers of seventeenth- and eighteenth-century Jamaica were making and using pots, this ware was no longer produced. That does not mean, however, that eighteenth-century enslaved Jamaicans were not aware of this pottery. In 1707 Hans Sloane writes:

> On these Red Hills, four Miles from Town [Guanoboa], lived Mr. Barnes a Carpenter. . . . Half a Mile from his Plantation, ten years ago, he found a Cave in which lay a human Body's Bones all in order, the Body having been eaten by Ants. The Ants Nests we found there, the rest of the Cave was fill'd with Pots or Urns, wherein were Bones of Men and Children, the Pots were Oval, large, of redish dirty colour. On the upper part of the Rim or Ledge there stood out an Ear, On which were made some Lines, the Ears were not over an Inch square towards the top it had two parallel Lines round, being grosly cut in the Edges near. The Negroes had remov'd most of these Pots to boil their Meat in. (Sloane 1707–1725: liv)

Figure 5.3. New Seville ware cup, the Cotter Collection, Jamaican National Heritage Trust. Photograph by Author.

The pottery that Sloane is referring to was made by indigenous Tainos several centuries before its use by enslaved laborers. This tells us that the enslaved were reusing pottery from pre-conquest contexts and that we should be mindful of not assuming that ceramics recovered from colonial contexts are colonial ceramics. It also shows us that while indigenous Jamaicans had died off by the sixteenth century, their pottery might still influence pottery production in eighteenth-century Jamaica.

Documentary Evidence of Colonial Ceramics

There is relatively little information on ceramic production or distribution in the documentary record of Jamaica. This evidence is largely anecdotal from the accounts of planters and visitors to the island. All told, I have been able to glean only five accounts mentioning pottery manufacture, and two more mentioning its sale (Edwards [1793] 1972; Sloane 1707–1725; Long 1794; Anonymous 1797; Phillippo 1843). Complementing these accounts are contemporary ethnographies on the remaining potters working within the tradition, similar to those found in the archaeological record. Both these forms of evidence point to a complex system of production reliant on kinship ties, and a method of distribution that included sale at Sunday markets. Below, I detail documentary evidence from the eighteenth and nineteenth centuries and ethnographic evidence recorded by Roderick Ebanks in the 1970s.

Writers documented the production and use of Jamaican-made ceramics in the seventeenth century. In 1687, Hans Sloane makes brief reference to the use of earthen jars as musical instruments (Heath 1999) but goes on to record:

> Pots for refining sugar were made at the Liguanea, and though more brittle and dearer than when bought from England, they were made here to supply the present needs of the planters, the clay of which they are made is dug up near the place. (Sloane 1707–1725)

Sloane extols the actual pots, saying,

> There are very good Bricks and Pots made here of the Clay of the Country, to the easie making of which the few Rains, as well as plenty of Fire-wood conduces much. (Sloane 1707–1725: xlviii)

Sloane goes on to record that these pots were a standard fixture in the house yard of the enslaved:

> The Negroes Houses are likewise at a distance from their Masters, and are small, oblong, thatch'd Huts, in which they have all their Moveables or Goods, which are generally a Mat to lie on, a Pot of Earth to boil their Victuals in, either Yams, Plantains, or Potatoes, with a little salt Mackerel, and a Calabash or two for Cups and Spoons. (xlvii–xlviii)

Even in the seventeenth century, it is clear that the enslaved were provisioned with locally made and imported provisions. The pottery as one component of the kitchen goods of the enslaved was one that was made locally.

In the eighteenth century, written evidence describes in vague ways pottery manufacture. An anonymous writer in 1797 describes the domestic utensils of enslaved African Jamaicans, in the *Columbia Magazine*:

> Some negroes are expert in manufacturing pots and other common vessels on which they bestow a coarse glazing. Their pans (called Yab-

bas) are convex at the bottom without a ring as ours. (Anonymous 1797: 252; also in Armstrong 1990: 293)

In 1774, Edward Long described these pots as "a better sort of earthenware, manufactured by the Negroes" (Long [1774] 1970 3: 851). These pots were used primarily for cooking in the following manner: "The trivet for supporting the vessel in which he prepares his food, consists of three large stones" (Anonymous 1797: 252; also in Armstrong 1990: 292). These types of pottery can be defined as coarse, internally glazed, restricted, direct rimmed vessels. They are ubiquitous in the archaeological record of Jamaica and can be found as early as the seventeenth century.

Through a discussion of the clay sources used that appears in the same archival record, we know that the pots were manufactured locally. Speaking of the local clay sources on the island, Edward Long states:

> The first is used in claying muscavado Sugars as, well as for a better sort of earthenware, manufactured by the Negroes. The second is more frequent, and supplies the inhabitants with water jars, and other convenient vessels for domestic use. It is likewise most proper for tiles, and drips. (Long [1774] 1970 3: 851)

Edward Long is describing the alluvial soils found in the Liguanea plain around Kingston. In 1843, James Phillippo describes another source of clay used to manufacture these ceramics: "Particles of golden mica have been found in districts near the source of the Rio Cobre, and sometimes, near Spanish Town, it has been incorporated with the potter's clay" (Phillippo 1843: 72). This source of clay, and the potters Phillippo is referring to, matches up with the ethnographically described contemporary potters.

The problem with the documentary record is that it is sparse, ambiguous, and vague. It concentrates on the cataloguing of local manufacture, rather than on those who manufactured it. As such, from the documents alone it is impossible to ascertain who was actually making the pots, other than people of African descent. Questions left unanswered include: Who among the enslaved made these pots? How were they made? How did people learn how to make these pots? And, most important, in what context were they made?

The strongest evidence of local production is ethnographic. Two contemporary descriptions exist for yabbas. In research conducted for his master's thesis, Roderick Ebanks interviewed, and documented pottery manufactured by, Ma Lou, Ms. Louisa Jones. The industry responsible for production of Jamaican pottery today is concentrated in family compounds and organized around female members of the family (Ebanks 1984). Roderick Ebanks recorded in 1984:

> Fanny Johnson [Ma Lou's mother] was a potter, as was her mother before her. The yard in which Mother Lou was born contained a large external family of maternal aunts and their children. All of these aunts made pots, and almost every yard in the district was occupied by a family of potters. By the time Ma Lou was nine she and her female cousins had begun to learn pottery from her mother, three aunts, and uncle's wife. (Ebanks 1984:33)

Born in 1911, Ma Lou had learned her skill from her mother, and pottery formed a family enterprise. Ma Lou had to become a domestic servant in the 1950s when the economy crashed:

> Ma Lou continued to perfect her skills until the end of the 1940s, when the introduction of the aluminum pot all but destroyed the potting industry, which appears to have relied heavily on cooking pot sales to sustain it. (Ebanks 1984: 31)

During this time, Ma Lou claimed, she lost much of the skill she had developed as a young child.

Beginning in the 1970s, a growing involvement by the middle class in Jamaican arts and heritage revived interest in yabbas, especially those that evoked linkages to African traditions. Ma Lou began making yabbas again for sale at craft markets and cultural expositions in Kingston. Her work became a celebrated embodiment of Jamaica's art and heritage (Francis-Brown 1983; Morgan 1989), and Ma Lou was sometimes mentioned in the same sentence as master Jamaican ceramicist Cecil Baugh. It is during this time that Roderick Ebanks conducted most of his interviews with Ma Lou.

Ma Lou passed away in 1992, and her daughter, Munchie, took up her trade. Moira Vincentelli has recently interviewed and recorded the production of pottery by Munchie, Marlene Roden (2004). Munchie learned the trade from her mother, a transmission of knowledge that seems to be rooted in kinship ties focused on matrifocal house yards (Ebanks 1984: 3; Vincentelli 2004: 125). This transmission, at least from conversations I had in 1999 and 2007, does have some material evidence.

In 1999, when I asked Munchie how I would be able to tell the differences between her mother's pottery and her own, she laughed. She then went on to tell me that her mother's mark was made pressing her pinky fingernail into the rim three times. Munchie made four marks. I then asked if her daughter would make five. She laughed and said, "No—maybe my son," and pointed to her son, who was arranging pottery to sell to me. In her house yard all the children helped her collect the clay and fuel, prepare the clay, and sometimes shape the pottery. In 2007, Munchie was still selling pottery, though not making as much. Her son still had interest, but as Munchie said, no one comes by to buy yabbas anymore. While the focus of pottery manufacture was certainly around these two women, a host of individuals are involved in the production and sale of the pottery. It can be inferred from the above quote that the other individuals might have been members of the potters' family.

In the eighteenth and nineteenth centuries, there is evidence that labor required for independent production by the enslaved was distributed through the family. In 1790, William Beckford describes the working of provision grounds:

> Upon these occasions they move, with all their family, into the place of cultivation; the children of different ages are laded with baskets, which are burdened in proportion to their strength and age; and it is pleasing to observe under what considerable weights they will bear themselves up, without either murmur or fatigue. The infants are flung at the backs of the mothers, and very little incommode them in their walks or labour. (Beckford 1790 2: 155–56)

The proximity of family members was crucial in the passing down or transmission of technical knowledge required to produce pottery. To successfully make a living from this craft production, the potters would have to develop a mastery of the local resources to manufacture the pottery as well as meet the functional demands of the pottery's potential users.

Using both modern accounts as well as my field notes, the sequence of techniques and choices that make up the production process can be developed. There is evidence that in the past women participated in and organized the manufacture of the pottery I am examining. Today, the house yard continues to be the center of production and the location from which most of the resources are extracted. Clay is excavated from Munchie's property that lies in an alluvial wash of the Rio Cobre outside of Spanish Town. She would knead the clay, removing large pieces of gravel and organic material. The clay is then mixed with sand and gravel taken from her property (Vincentelli 2004: 126).

The potter would then flatten the clay with her fist into a single slab and press it into a mold (Ebanks 1984: 33). This mold was a broken base of a yabba called a "keke" (Marlene Roden personal communication 1999). Once the base of the pot was begun, she would then create coils that would be added to the side walls of the pottery (Ebanks 1984: 33). After the initially shaping of the pottery, the potter would continue to shape the vessel by pulling up vertically and finalizing the shape of the vessel (Vincentelli 2004: 126). She would then use a metal tool to scrape the inside of the vessel, hollowing out and thinning the walls of the yabba. During this process, large inclusions would be plucked from the clay, and the walls of the vessel would be patched using the scraped clay (field notes August 23, 1999).

The pottery was then smoothed with a piece of polished wood covered in a local, laterite-rich soil (Ebanks 1984: 33, Vincentelli 2004: 126). This soil would provide a red slip-like surface. The pots were dried for one to two days (Ebanks 1984: 34). The potter would then burnish the dried pots using one of a variety of polishing stones (Vincentelli 2004: 127). The potter would then press her pinky nail onto the rim of the pot as a maker's mark. Ma Lou marked the pot with three strokes, and Munchie with four. Finally, the pots were fired in an open pit lined with dry sticks (Vincentelli 2004: 126) and stacked with green wood (Ebanks 1984: 35) and any other combustible material.

From there the pots would, ideally, be sold. Today, Munchie sells her ceramics using two strategies. First, she sells them out of her house yard. Second, she relies on the tourism bureau. In reality, these strategies are unsuccessful. Munchie finds herself at an impasse:

> She makes functional wares that are no longer needed for the purpose for which they were designed. Her method of working—the distinctive quality of her work which is potentially marketable—is not clear at the point of sale. You have to know about it, see it demonstrated or have it explained. The shapes of her pots are elegant and generous but the thick walls and the undecorated rustic quality make them hard to sell in a gallery context. Limited capital means that transport is relatively expensive, and more sophisticated marketing is beyond the potter's resource. (Vincentelli 2004: 126)

Potters working in the eighteenth century would have faced similar logistical demands. Below, I discuss the distribution of pottery in the informal markets of Jamaica, so that we can begin to evaluate the movement of materials, and indeed people and information, through these networks across Jamaica.

As was indicated in the excerpt from Bryan Edwards that began chapter 4, this pottery was one of many things that were sold on the ad hoc informal market of the towns. A 1711 legal code indirectly refers to the sale of pots on the street markets: "This restraint is construed to extend only to beef, veal, mutton and saltfish; and to manufactures, except baskets, ropes of bark, earthen pots and such like" (Long [1774] 1970 2: 487). As a commodity, these pots were used instead of iron cooking pots and imported earthenwares. Edward Long states that the cost to transport an iron cooking pot in 1771, during a time of peace, was figured at 4 shillings, and a hogshead of earthenware, "if very large," was 15 shillings (Long [1774] 1970: 1: 391). During the seventeenth and eighteenth centuries, yabbas were used for a variety of purposes, including the cooking of pepper pots or stews (Sloane 1707–1725: xix; Anonymous 1797: 252).

The potters probably did not sell the pottery on the markets themselves. Evidence of this comes from the ethnographic notes on the production and circulation of Jamaican-made pottery in the twentieth century. On January 13, 1970, Henia and Jerome Handler conducted several interviews with Cecil Baugh, a master Jamaican potter. In this interview, Baugh described how he first became interested in making pottery and how he learned the craft. During this discussion he alluded to both the glazed and slipped Jamaican ceramics. He said that yabba "should only be applied to bowls, large or small, of earthenware" (Henia Handler notes, January 13, 1970, courtesy of Jerome Handler). Several days later Baugh went on to describe potters living along Mountain View Road in Kingston.

> If a woman was good at making yabbah she might produce several dozen a day. They were given to people to sell in town, "mostly Syrian," who would carry them down and make "100 percent profit." A small yabbah about five inches high, 8 inches across were sold to the seller at a shilling a dozen. The seller would sell them for 2 pence or threepence a piece. (Henia Handler notes, January 15, 1970, courtesy of Jerome Handler)

In the manufacture and distribution of yabbas, the potters could potentially earn up to several shillings for "the Syrian," but the potter would get only a very small percentage of the profit. Essentially the potters would earn for a dozen what a market woman would earn for a single piece.

Probably the most dramatic evidence of the sale of colonial ceramics comes from a series of nineteenth-century watercolors, daguerreotypes, and photographs. One photograph (figure 5.4) depicts a group of sellers on

Figure 5.4. Pottery sellers in Kingston, Jamaica, unknown photographer, late nineteenth/early twentieth century. Courtesy of the Smithsonian Institution National Anthropological Archives. Neg. 92-246.

the side of Port Royal Street at the turn of the century. It is apparent from the photograph that several types of pottery are being sold in the markets. Two types of pottery are present on the right-hand side of the photo. The first is a chimney pot. Chimney pots are handmade, internally and externally glazed, coarse chamber pots with attached loop handles. This photograph appears to be the only documentary evidence of chamber pots, even though the form does appear in the archaeological record.

The second type of pottery on the right-hand side of the photograph is the glazed yabba. These vessels appear in other pictorial evidence, such as a turn-of-the-century photograph depicting the Victoria market (figure 5.5). At the entrance gate, one can see an individual standing next to a pile of upturned glazed pottery. Predating this photograph is a mid-nineteenth-century ink drawing of women selling pottery on the side of an unknown street (figure 5.6). In the lower right-hand corner of the photograph, one can discern pottery vessels similar to those depicted in the first photograph.

The pots on the left-hand side of figure 5.4 functioned primarily as water-storage devices. The tall pot illustrated is a form commonly called a

Figure 5.5. Victoria Jubilee Market in Kingston, Jamaica, unknown photographer, late nineteenth/early twentieth century. Courtesy of the National Library of Jamaica.

Figure 5.6. Jamaica new and old: Women with pots, bowls, and jars on display. Mid-nineteenth century. Courtesy of the National Library of Jamaica.

"Spanish jar." These are coarse, tall, untreated, thick-walled, wheel-thrown, everted rimmed jars. This type of pottery also appears in the 1838 Belisario print titled *Water Jar Sellers*. This watercolor depicts a Spanish jar being carried on the head by the shorter man in the background (figure 5.7). It is important to note that the accompanying description to this watercolor describes the difficulty of obtaining fresh water on the island. In 1838 Belisario writes:

> It may not be generally known to our readers, that we are not wholly indebted to Britain, or the Spanish main for Water-jars—those in ordinary use are manufactured at Potteries near the City, and if they are not capable of producing vessels as tastefully moulded, or as fine in quality as those imported, their wares claim at least a decided preference in the porous natures of their surface, being unvarnished in most instances—such rough appearance may not be pleasing to the eye; but the water on that account is rendered much cooler from the free admission of air: However we may favor these plebian utensils, it must be observed, they are not presentable at the sideboards or tables of respectable families, nor are they usually admitted to the priveledge of entrée. (Belisario 1838: no.3)

These types of pottery were used to collect and store water. References to them are found in documentary sources such as the following anonymous source: "Their water jar is raised from the ground, on a stem of a small tree with three prongs, fixed in the corner of their house" (Anonymous 1797: 252; also in Armstrong 1990: 293). These vessels were common items sold on the market. Belisario goes on to describe the hawkers:

> The characters represented in the print are apprentices, who sally forth daily with the description of jars above alluded to for sale in a wooden tray, called by them a bowl. In England, a hawker of such things would convey them in a small hand cart. . . . A humourous kind of appeal is made to the public, to include a sale of the jars in some such style—"Who want to cool him heart, who want to cool him heart? must come make me cool um one time" and then pretending to have been called by a customer, smartly replies, "I comming Mam, no se me da ya?" (Belisario 1838 no. 3)

These vessels are also common to the archaeological record; and, for the most part, it has been assumed that these vessels were imported from the Spanish colonies of Cuba, Puerto Rico, and Hispaniola. To be sure, vessels in Havana at the Gabinete de Arqueologia I examined and archaeological

Figure 5.7. *Water Jar Sellers* by Isaac Belisario, 1838. Courtesy of the National Library of Jamaica.

materials I examined more closely from Port Royal, Seville, and Old King's House were alike in paste and form.

Below the "Spanish jars" in the Port Royal Street photograph (figure 5.4) are vessels commonly referred to as "monkey jars." Monkey jars are slipped or untreated, coarse, low-fired, tea-pot-shaped vessels. Monkey jars do not appear in the archaeological record until well into the nineteenth century (cf. Heath 1999: 213), and then only as a small component of any assemblage (Armstrong 1990, 1991c, 1998; Reeves 1995; Delle forthcoming; Higman 1998; Mayes 1972). The Belisario print suggests, however, that monkey jars were present at least as early as 1838. The watercolor depicts a very stylized version of a monkey jar carried on a tray by the man in the foreground (figure 5.7). These vessels were used primarily to store, cool, and serve water while working in the fields (Ebanks 1984).

To the left of the "monkey jars" in the Port Royal Street photograph are "water pots." These are slipped or untreated restricted pots with everted or inverted rims. We believe these pots were primarily used for water storage, transportation, and drinking. A turn-of-the-century photograph entitled *Candy Sellers* depicts women on the side of a country road selling various goods (figure 5.8). In the background of this photograph is a woman standing and drinking from a vessel that appears to be similar to those vessels depicted in the Port Royal Street photograph. These vessels are also depicted in the Belisario watercolor (figure 5.7). Although this type of pottery is highly varied in shape, the depiction of them in the watercolor is heavily stylized in this watercolor, and attributes such as small size, tall neck, and flat bottom are not the norm of the pottery.

Matching the pottery in these accounts with those recovered archaeologically is a difficult task. When one interrogates the domestic assemblage of the enslaved, one is confronted with the variety of materials—materials

Figure 5.8. Candy sellers. Late nineteenth century, Jamaica. Courtesy of the National Library of Jamaica.

that neither the written accounts nor the ethnographic analogues speak to. The preceding images do speak to the variety and types of ceramics one encounters in the archaeological contexts of seventeenth-, eighteenth-, and nineteenth-century Jamaica. In describing, cataloguing, and analyzing the archaeological ceramics of English colonial Jamaica, I used these images, and specifically the photograph of Port Royal Street, as a starting place.

Colonial Jamaican-Made Ceramics

Coarse earthenware excavated from historic contexts includes both imported and locally produced ceramics. Coarse earthenware identified as locally produced (yabbas) was primarily utilitarian in function, had little decorative inventory, was handmade, and came in three varieties: glazed, slipped, and untreated. These ceramics, while varying in frequency, have been recovered as early as the seventeenth century. Many of these ceramics recovered archaeologically have analogues in the documentary record. Due to the heterogeneity of coarse earthenware recovered from archaeological contexts of Jamaica, I could not assume that coarse earthenware was necessarily Jamaican-made. To assist in untangling the various kinds of pottery, I employed the photograph of Port Royal Street as my starting place.

There are basically five types of Jamaican-made coarse earthenware and several types of imported coarse earthenware recovered from the archaeological record of Jamaica. Of them, glazed yabbas are the most common, then slipped yabbas, and untreated yabbas appear in a very small frequency. In much smaller numbers were sugar wares recovered from domestic contexts. The imported coarse earthenware includes recognizable British types, as well as Spanish types, including two varieties of Ceramica Ordinaria—Spanish jars or common Ceramica Ordinaria—and Mexican red-painted ware. The local coarse earthenware could be found in a myriad of forms over the seventeenth, eighteenth, and nineteenth centuries but have been predominantly open and restricted bowls, inverted and everted pots, and rarely chamber pots, a primarily urban form. Monkey jars and coal pots were recovered from later nineteenth-century contexts.

Glazed Yabbas

Glazed yabbas appear to be made in a tradition similar to that described by Roderick Ebanks as syncretic wares. Breakage patterns in the sherds indicate that the pots are coil-made. Finger marks indicate that the pots are pulled even into a final form, smoothed externally. These pots are relatively

Figure 5.9. Glazed Jamaican coarse earthenware. Yabba from the Marx Collection, Port Royal, Jamaica. Photograph by Author.

well-fired earthenware but seem to come from variably fired environments (figure 5.9).

The paste is fine and relatively hard. I describe it in the catalogue as irregular in texture. The clay was on the whole well sorted. The clay is yellowish red to gray. Coring is not common, and when it is present, it commonly indicates an oxidizing environment. The clay contains quartz and feldspar inclusions. These inclusions were recorded as fine in size and subangular in texture. Some occasional large white limestone inclusions were noted, but these were also subangular. These inclusions are visible through the glaze of the ceramic.

Diagnostic of this type of ceramic is a glaze. The glaze appears to be fluxed with lead. Because of the variable firing environments, the glaze varies from a clear yellowish color to an opaque emerald green color. The glaze is commonly applied internally. On certain forms, it is common that the glaze is applied partially to the external rim of the pot. Less common, the glaze is also found externally, only on certain forms. Glazed yabbas were

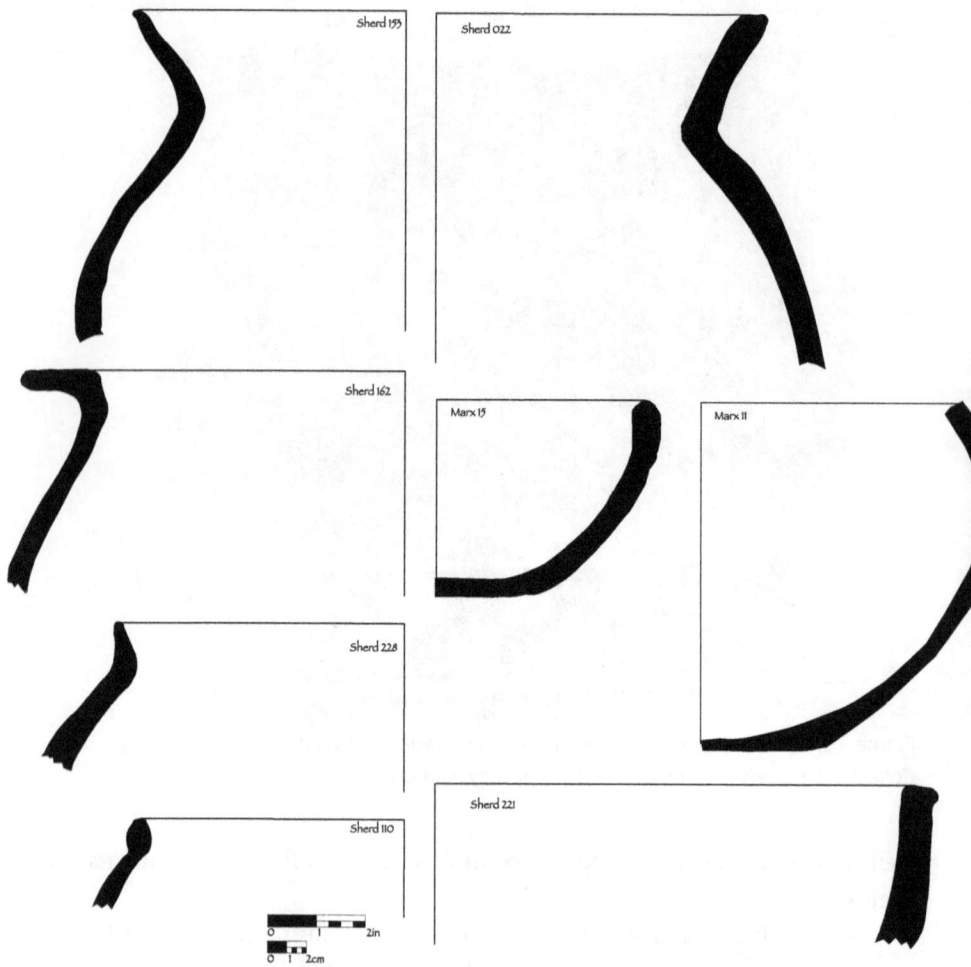

Figure 5.10. A selection of forms in which glazed yabbas were shaped. Illustration by Author.

produced in a variety of forms (figure 5.10). By far the most dominant form is restricted bowls (figure 5.11). This form commonly had a slight carination toward the lip of the bowl. Also found were open bowls, and chamber pots (figure 5.12).

Slipped and/or Burnished Pottery

Slipped and/or burnished yabbas are indistinguishable from pots made by Ma Lou and Munchie. Breakage patterns in the sherds indicate that the pots are coil-made. Finger marks indicated that the pots are pulled even into a

Figure 5.11. Glazed yabba with handle. Yabba from the Marx Collection, Port Royal, Jamaica. Photograph by Author.

Figure 5.12. Glazed Jamaican chamber pot (chimney). Yabba from the Marx Collection, Port Royal, Jamaica. Photograph by Author.

Figure 5.13. Slipped and burnished water jar with handle. Yabba from the Marx Collection, Port Royal, Jamaica. Photograph by Author.

final form, smoothed externally. These pots were fired at a lower temperature than the glazed yabbas. The firing environments were highly variable, as evident from the clouding and coring (figure 5.13).

The clay is coarse and relatively friable. I describe it in the catalogue as hackly in texture. The clay was poorly sorted and is yellowish red to yellowish brown. Coring is extremely common and indicates a reducing environment. The clay contains quartz and feldspar inclusions. These inclusions were recorded as medium in size and subangular in texture. Occasional large white limestone inclusions were noted; these were also subangular. These inclusions were not visible through the slip of the ceramic.

Diagnostic of this type of ceramic is a slip. Because of the variable firing

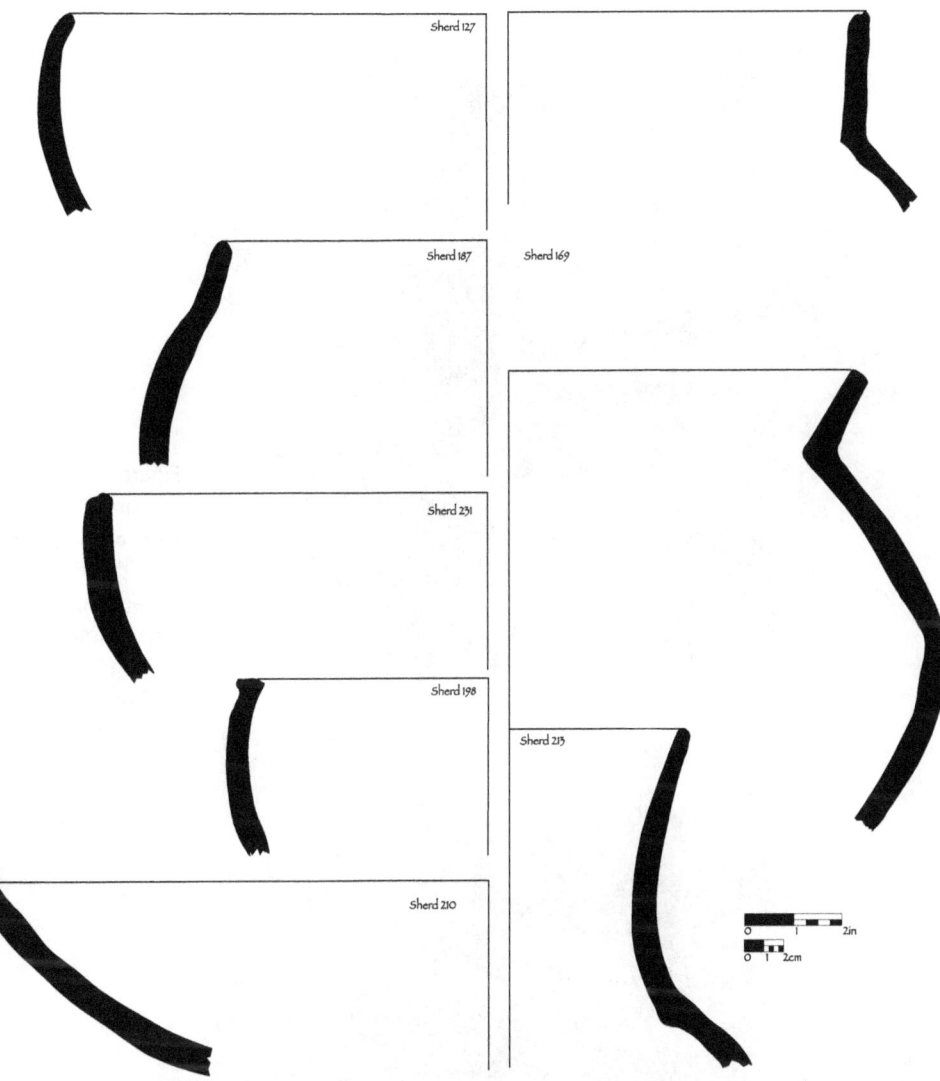

Figure 5.14. A selection of forms in which slipped yabbas are found. Illustration by Author.

environment, the slip often contained partial oxidation and clouded the surface of the vessel. The coloration of the slip varied minimally from red to reddish brown. The hematite coating is commonly applied externally, with only a few instances of an internal slip. On certain forms such as open bowls, it is also common that the slip is applied to the internal vessel (figure 5.14). Slipped yabbas were produced in a variety of forms, including vertical pots and everted pots (figure 5.15); restricted bowls and open bowls (figure 5.16).

Figure 5.15. Slipped and burnished vertical pot. Yabba from the Marx Collection, Port Royal, Jamaica. Photograph by Author.

Figure 5.16. Slipped and burnished yabba. Yabba from the Marx Collection, Port Royal, Jamaica. Photograph by Author.

Untreated Yabbas

Untreated yabbas are friable (figure 5.17). The clay is coarse and sandy. I describe it in the catalogue as irregular in texture. The clay is also well sorted. The clay is light brown. Coring is not common, and when it is present it commonly indicates a reducing environment. The clay contains fine quartz and mica inclusions. These inclusions were recorded as fine in size and subangular in texture. These pots were made into a relatively few number of forms (figure 5.18), including small everted and vertical pots (figure 5.19) or open and restricted bowls (figure 5.20).

These three types of local ceramics are found in contexts associated with eighteenth-century Jamaica. There are no modern analogues of either glazed or untreated yabbas today. As is discussed above, the introduction of the aluminum pot industry devastated the local ceramic industry. Similar changes in commodity flow most likely challenged potters in the past. In the next section, I look at the change of the ceramic tradition in Jamaica over time.

Figure 5.17. Untreated yabba with punctated decoration. Yabba from the Marx Collection, Port Royal, Jamaica. Photograph by Author.

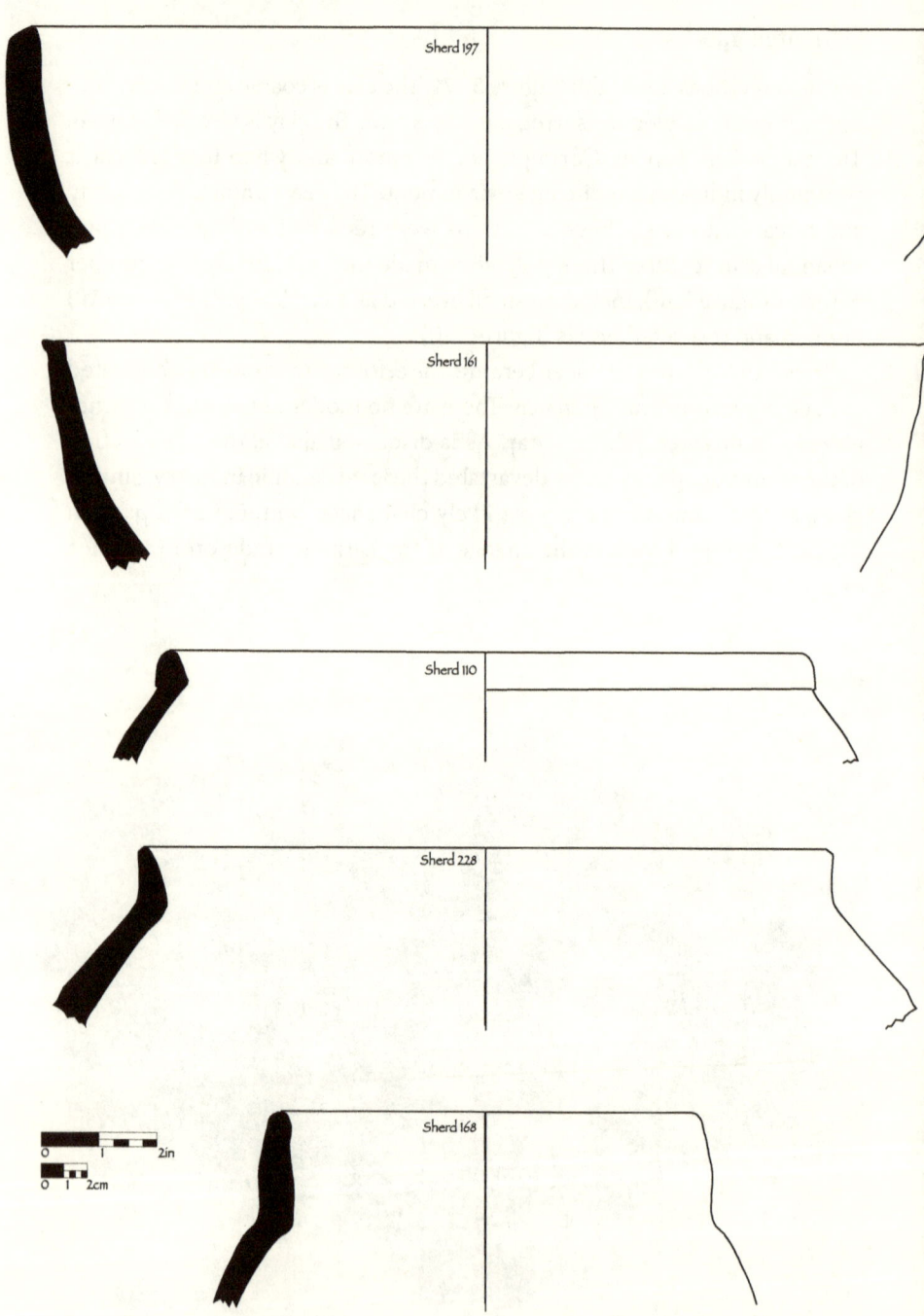

Figure 5.18. A selection of forms in which untreated yabbas are found. Illustration by Author.

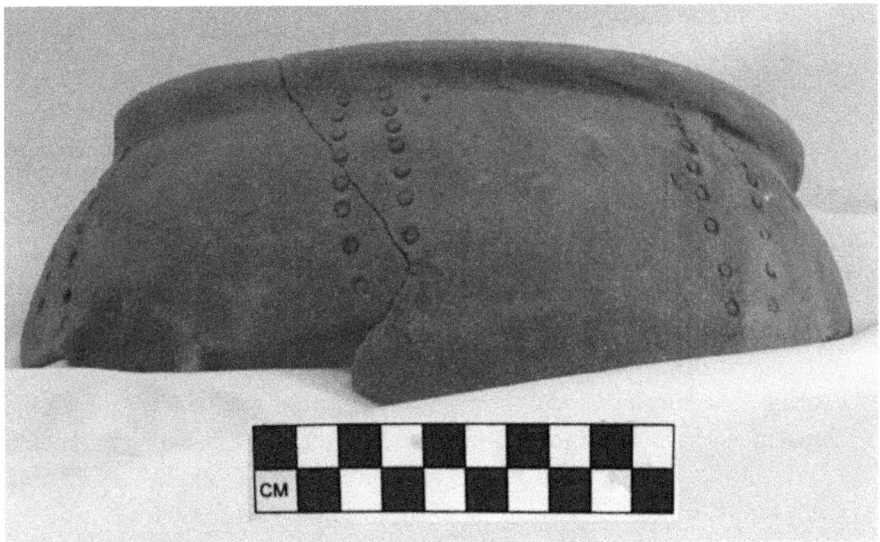

Figure 5.19. Untreated yabba with punctated decoration. Yabba from the Marx Collection, Port Royal, Jamaica. Photograph by Author.

Figure 5.20. Untreated yabba with rouletted decoration. Yabba from the Marx Collection, Port Royal, Jamaica. Photograph by Author.

Rooting the Past in the Present

Jamaican ceramic manufacture did change over time. This was in part a result of shifting tastes among consumers of the pottery, but it was also most likely a result of internal Caribbean migrations. While there is change in the decorative inventories of Jamaican-made ceramics and some reduction and florescence of forms, there is a clear analogical link between pottery manufactured by Munchie today and seventeenth-century ceramics recovered from Port Royal.

The archaeological sample I examined comprised collections gathered from Port Royal dating to the seventeenth, eighteenth, and nineteenth centuries. Specifically, I focused on the Marx collection, which dates to the seventeenth century; the Old Naval Dockyard collection, dating to the seventeenth, eighteenth, and nineteenth centuries; the Saint Peter's Church collection, which dates to the eighteenth and nineteenth centuries; and the Fort Charles collection, dated to the eighteenth century. I examined over 5,000 sherds in this collection, amounting to over 1,100 vessels. In figures 5.21 and 5.22 I have created two seriations illustrating the change in yabba types recorded as vessel count and sherd count. What is evident from these diagrams is that while there is considerable flux in percentages, there is no overall trend. It appears that glazed yabbas are dominant in the archaeological record in the seventeenth, eighteenth, and nineteenth centuries.

If we look at rim counts, however (figure 5.23), we do see that the pottery seriates nicely. While rim counts of glazed yabbas decrease steadily between the seventeenth and twentieth centuries, rim sherds of slipped yabbas are in greater abundance over those same centuries. Finally, one startling change is the increase in untreated ceramics in the twentieth century.

The preceding illustrations demonstrate that the ceramic population is in flux over time. The popularity of types of local pottery changes between the seventeenth and twentieth centuries. While there is this flux, however, the presence of specific yabba types remains constant in the archaeological record. In the twentieth century, items I identified as untreated ceramics increase dramatically in popularity. One explanation for the abrupt increase in rim, minimum vessel, and sherd counts of untreated ceramics in the twentieth century is the growing abundance of forms like flowerpots and monkey jars.

We see similar fluidity expressed in the popularity of forms over time. In figure 5.24 I have plotted a chart illustrating changes in form frequency between the seventeenth and twentieth centuries.

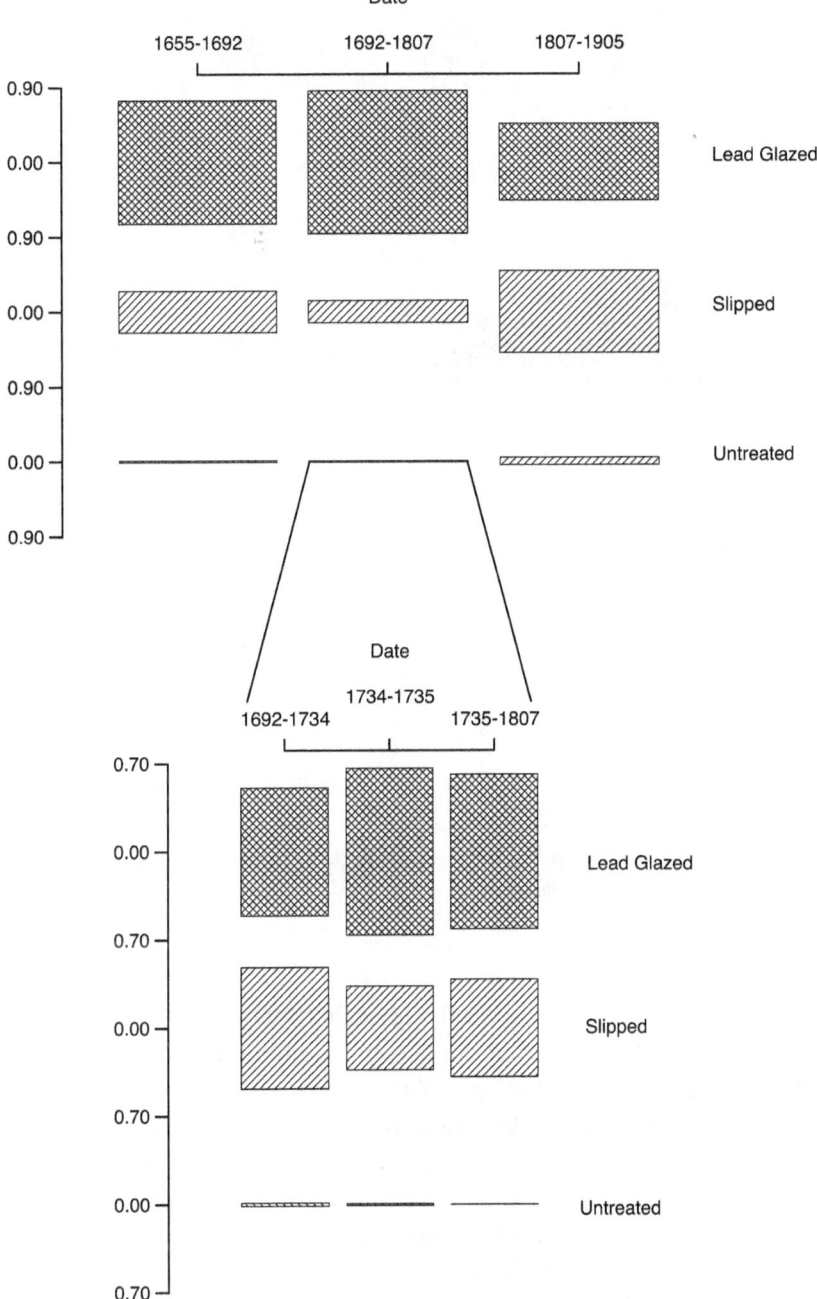

Figure 5.21. Frequency of raw sherd count of the three types of ceramics over time using Port Royal ceramic collection.

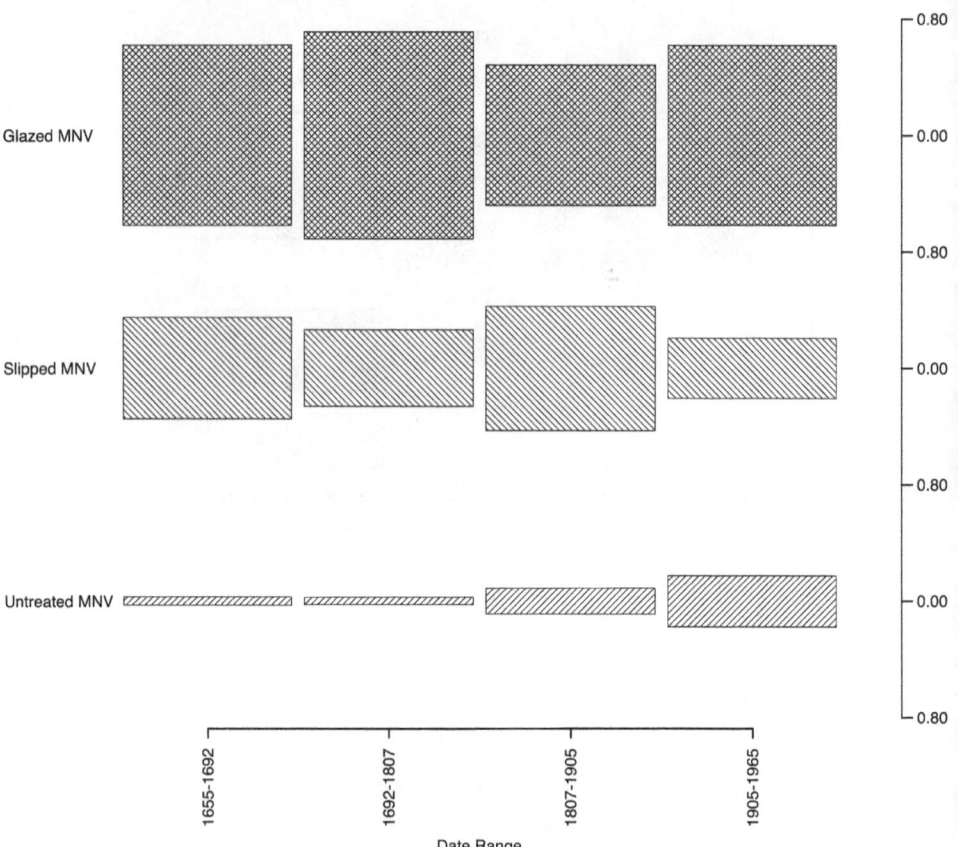

Figure 5.22. Frequency of minimum number of vessels (MNV) of the three types of ceramics over time using Port Royal ceramic collection.

Following Costin (1991, 1999) and Mills (1999), as a measure of variation, I looked at diameters of rim openings within specific forms of slipped coarse earthenware, including cooking vessels and water pots. In contexts from the seventeenth to the nineteenth century in Port Royal, I recorded the rim diameters of 183 slipped yabbas. During the seventeenth-century occupation of Port Royal, there was a considerable degree of variation in the diameter of the rims of slipped yabbas. During the eighteenth century, this variation decreased considerably. Beginning in contexts associated with occupations after 1807, the variation in rim diameter increases again (figure 5.25). While not necessarily an indication of standardization, the data do

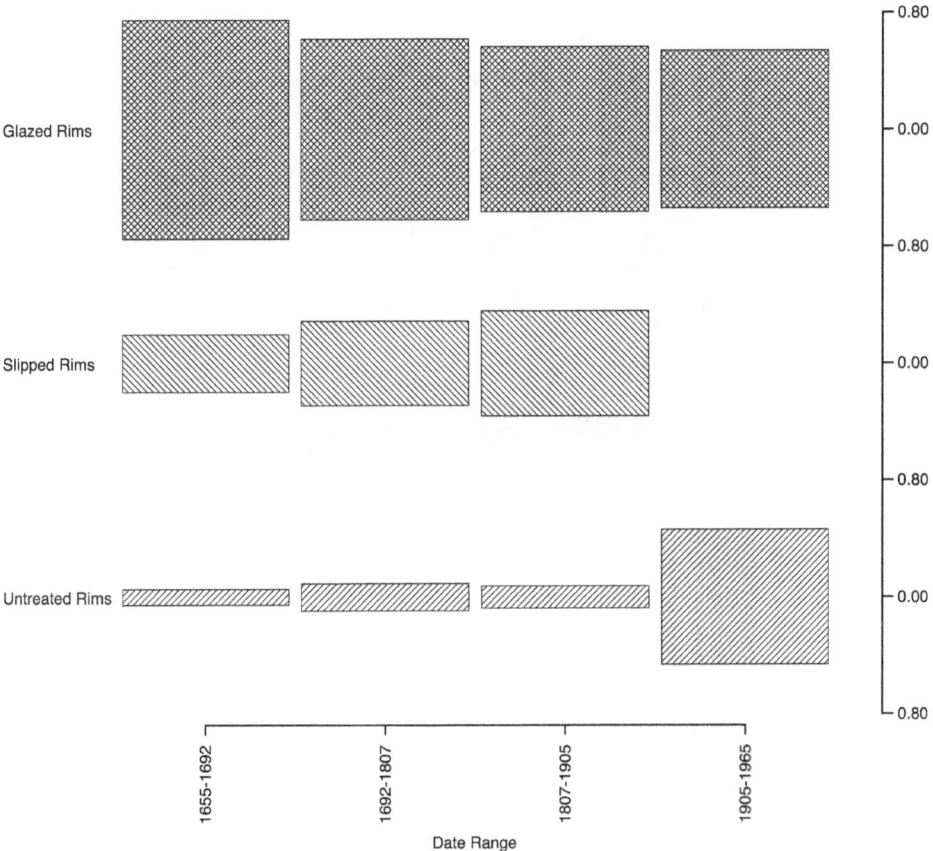

Figure 5.23. Frequency over time of rim sherds of the three types of ceramics over time from Port Royal (Fort Charles, Saint Peter's Church, Marx, Old Naval Dockyard collections).

indicate that significant transformation took place in the potting industry during the eighteenth century.

Evidence of this transformation is further buttressed by changes in the decorative inventory of the ceramic assemblage during the eighteenth century (figure 5.26). During the seventeenth century, potters used seven distinct techniques in decorating the slipped yabbas. These decorations included punctation using the end of a reed, impressions on the pottery using a rice grain, fiber rouletting, grooved incisions, fluted rims, and maker's marks. In all, 18 percent of the sherds were decorated. By the eighteenth century, there were only three decorations, which were fluted rims, grooved

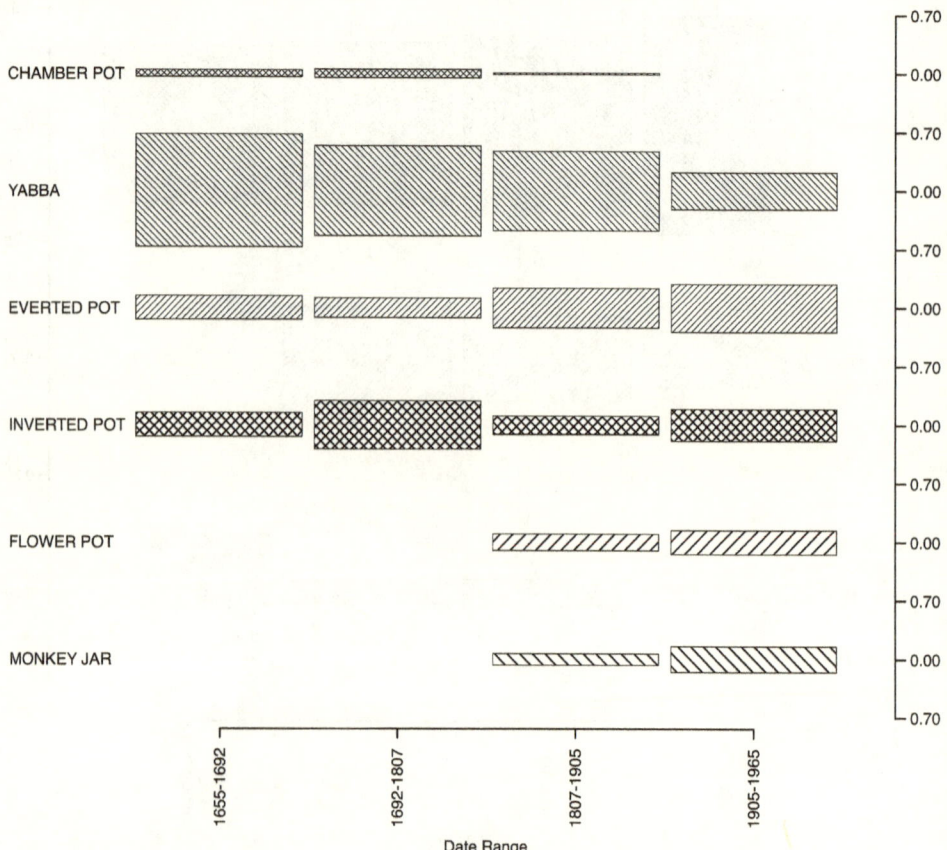

Figure 5.24. Frequency over time of rim sherds of different forms of local ceramics from Port Royal (Fort Charles, Saint Peter's Church, Marx, Old Naval Dockyard collections).

incisions, and maker's marks. The decorated sherds at this point were only approximately 1.2 percent of the overall assemblage. In the nineteenth century, there was an explosion of decorative techniques, including appliqué, perforations, fiber impressions, fluted rims, and maker's marks (6.7% of the ceramic assemblage).

These results suggest a growth and transformation of the pottery industry in Jamaica beginning in the seventeenth century and continuing through the twentieth century. While many of the slipped yabbas were not decorated in the three temporal contexts, there was a distinct reduction and then a florescence in the decorative inventory. This coincides with a decrease in the variability in rim diameters, followed by a sharp increase. It

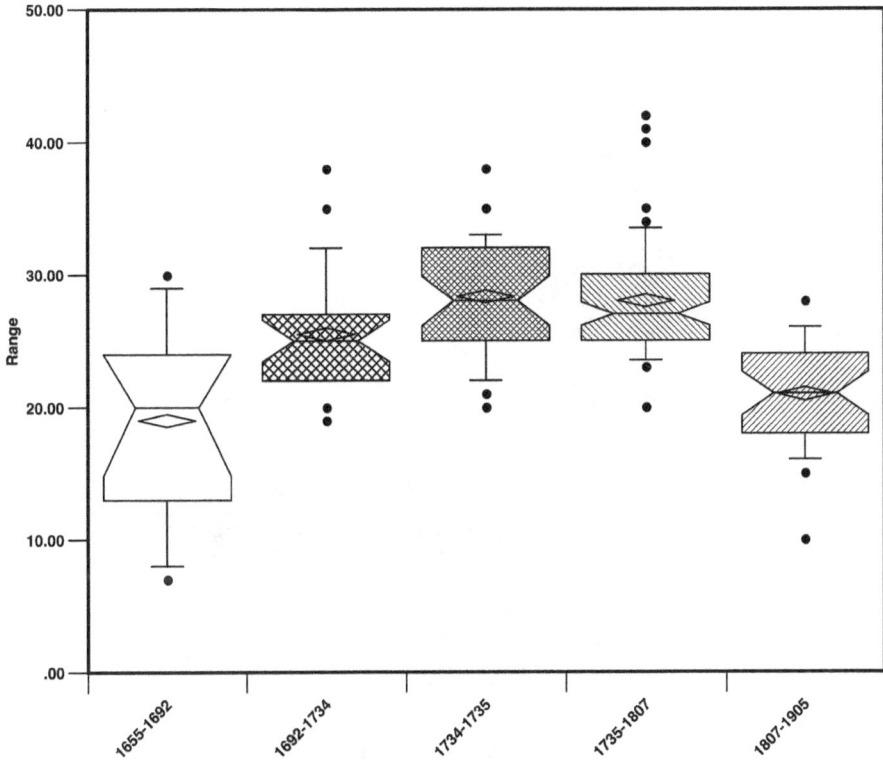

Figure 5.25. Variation in rim diameters of yabbas from Port Royal over time. This notched box and whisker chart displays the mean (diamond), the median, the 75th percentile, the half width (notch), and the 10th and 90th percentiles (whisker).

is my belief that in the eighteenth century we see the development of these yabbas as a trade item which is produced in a somewhat larger scale than suggested by domestic manufacture.

Importantly, the above data suggest that while there were changes in the ceramic industry of Jamaica, it continued to operate until the early twentieth century, when imported aluminum pots undermined the market for yabbas. The pottery produced by Munchie today is very similar in technological choices and ways of doing things as those found in the archaeological records of the seventeenth, eighteenth, and nineteenth centuries. Only after the local industry is decimated by the introduction of cheap aluminum pots do we see a change in the kinds of ceramics produced, their intended functions, and their ultimate audience.

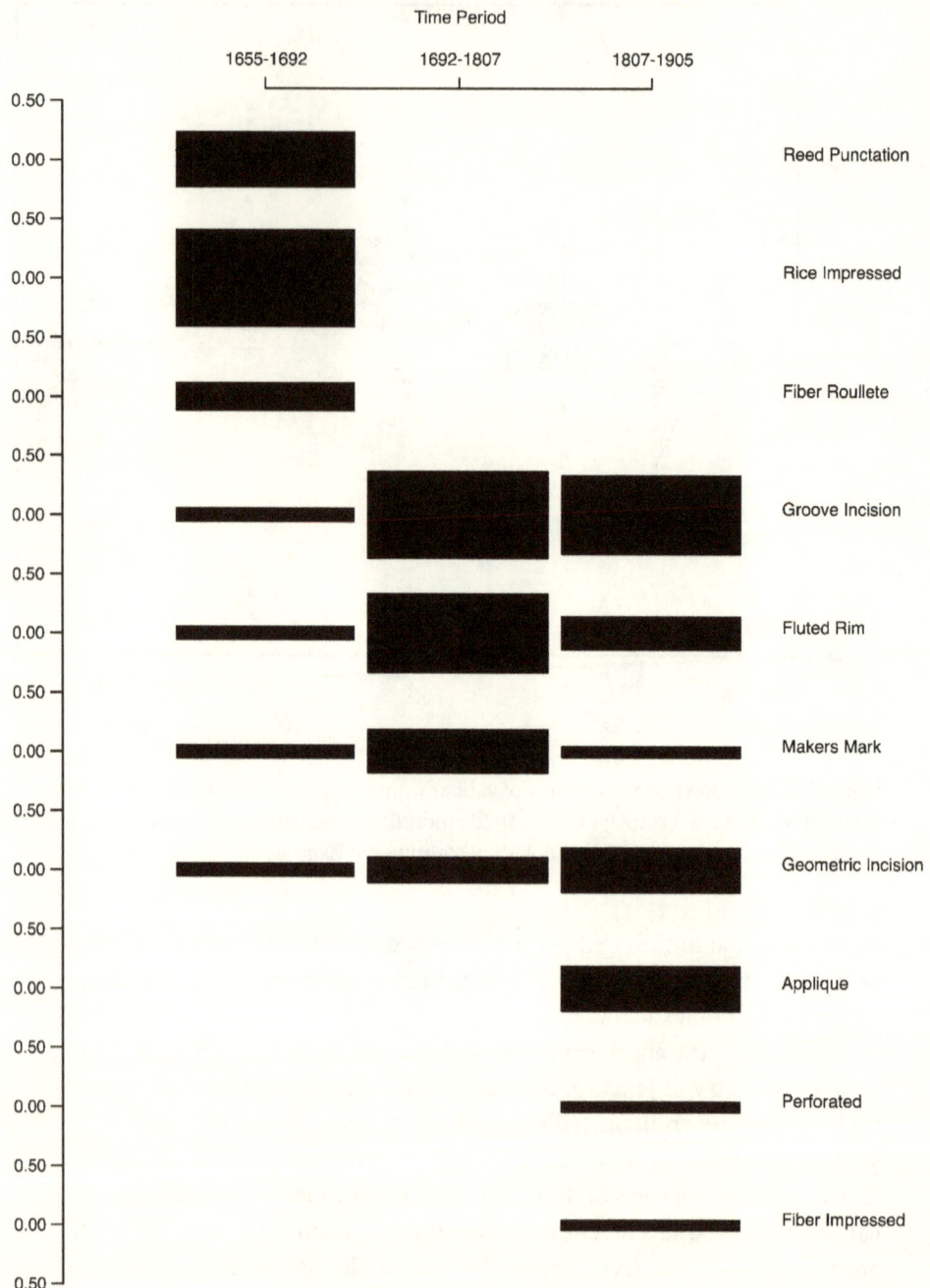

Figure 5.26. Frequency of decorated ceramics by decoration type over time from Port Royal (Fort Charles, Saint Peter's Church, Marx, Old Naval Dockyard collections).

Conclusion

To talk about a single type of yabba or colonial Jamaican ceramic misrepresents the archaeological assemblage and the variation in production strategies of eighteenth-century potters. Even if the ceramics were uniform, they would not represent the diversity of peoples arriving in Jamaica between 1655 and 1807 (figure 5.27). Low-fired ceramics have been found throughout the central region of Jamaica in contexts associated with the seventeenth, eighteenth, and nineteenth centuries. On rural sites, locally manufactured forms are commonly excavated from domestic contexts related to the houses of enslaved Africans. In urban settings, however, low-fired ceramics have been recovered from contexts associated both with palatial structures, as in the case of Old King's House (Mathewson 1972a, 1972b, 1973), and with much smaller tenements in Port Royal (Mayes 1972). In the eighteenth century, the ceramics seem to be an in-demand item of local manufacture that is relatively standardized and found in archaeological contexts across the island. This raises a question, however, about whether the lack of decoration and reduction of variation in forms mirrors a trend followed by artisans in different communities across the island of Jamaica, or whether it represents the consolidation of a single locus of ceramic manufacture.

The simplicity of the forms and the crudeness of the manufacture support a localized manufacture and distribution system. According to this hypothesis, free and enslaved persons in urban and rural contexts would obtain their ceramics from a potter in the area of their residence. It follows that ceramics in the study collection would reflect local articulations, both structurally and compositionally. The second scenario involves the centralized manufacture of pottery and island-wide distribution. The similarity of the ceramics' matrix, form, and decorative inventory suggests that a similar group of potters produced them. Evidence suggests that one such group of potters was located along the Rio Cobre River near Spanish Town, Jamaica. While ideally these strategies are mutually exclusive, archaeological evidence suggests that they are not. Both mechanisms are models representing strategies of ceramic production and distribution. They should be seen as end members between which a host of strategies are possible.

The documentary record is neutral in terms of gender and background of the people who made this pottery. There is only one source that attributes the manufacture of the pottery to people of African descent. Examination of archaeological ceramics, along with ethnographic analogues, is able to

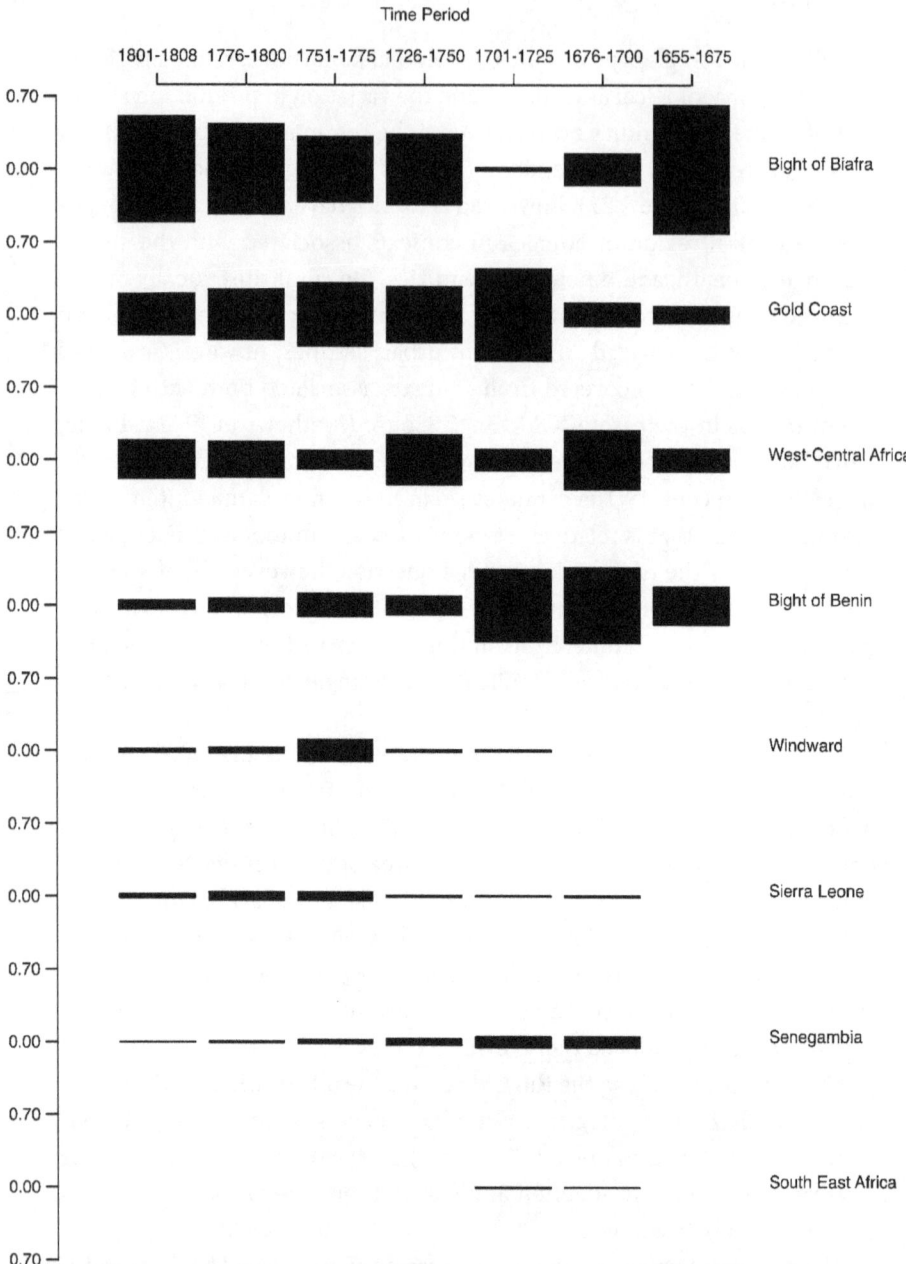

Figure 5.27. Frequency of enslaved coming from different regions of Africa into Jamaica between 1655 and 1808. Data are based on Burnard's synthesis of Eltis 2000 (Burnard 2001: 21).

shed some light on who made the pottery and the manner in which it was traded. As can be gleaned from the pictorial evidence, the pottery would have been only one item traded in this system of markets. However, that being said, because yabbas are one of the few items of material culture that survive the archaeological record and speak directly to the independent production of enslaved laborers, they can speak to the silences of the documentary record on the scale and scope of the internal economy. In so doing, they give us an idea of the extent to which social networks were refashioned beyond the plantation community.

6

Locating Enslaved Craft Production

Petrographic and Chemical Analysis of Eighteenth-Century Jamaican Pottery

> In old days the calabash and the great clay jar called "panya" (Spanish) were the common receptacles, with a gourd for a carrier poised upon the head.... Today the kerosene can is the common carrier. I have seen children of eight or ten carrying such cans of water on their heads from the brook.... Earthen bowls, hand-turned and covered with a rude glaze, are always to be had in the Kingston market, but they are more rare in the hills where the old-time "yabba" is being supplanted by tinware.
>
> Beckwith 1929: 47.

Between 1919 and 1924, Mary Beckwith visited Jamaica and chronicled the domestic routines of laboring class African Jamaicans. The above quote is an excerpt from a larger section of her description of the Kingston and Mandeville street markets. Beyond chronicling everyday "folk" activities, this passage hints at the various routes of trade and commodities in circulation at these markets. The "earthen bowls" in circulation as gleaned from the passage are only a fragment of the various items sold. I view them as a sherd of the whole vessel—significant as it provides a faint hint at the larger economic circuits in which commodities moved. These circuits and the social relations within which they are nested must be extrapolated from the sets of documentary sources detailed in the previous chapters.

The problem with using quotes like that given above as a mechanism to interpret artifacts deposited two hundred years prior to the recording of the description is that it has the danger of introducing anachronism into the analysis of the documentary record (Cooper 2005: 12) and material culture (Stahl and das Dores Giaro da Cruz 1998: 222; Stahl 2001). Christopher DeCorse (1999) has demonstrated in his work in coastal Ghana that colonial encounters were neither continuity nor change. These encounters and subsequent transformations in the material record resulted from a complex combination of conservative forms of material culture and innovation incorporated from abroad or independently developed. As Stephen Silliman (2004, 2005) has pointed out, continuity and change are part of the same interwoven processes resulting from colonial encounters. It is therefore fundamental not only that change is demonstrated as part of the archaeological understanding of time, but that continuity is equally demonstrated (Stahl 1993).

Because there are direct historical and archaeological links, discussed in the last chapter, we are able to conjure, to a certain extent, the faces of the potters in the eighteenth century. We must also use, however, the above quote as a cautionary. Certainly, the excerpt demonstrates that the pottery was involved in a circuit of commodity distribution. But it also demonstrates how technological innovations, global shifts in production, and trade had a real impact on the market for the "old-time 'Yabba.'"

The people who made this pottery, for the most part, were women of African descent. Accounts of Ma Lou and Munchie do give us some insight into the ways in which this pottery was manufactured. More important, the fact that production was focused around matrifocal house compounds organized by women raises an issue that must at least be considered in interpreting the archaeological record. As many archaeologists have pointed out, archaeology can get at those silent yet vital ways that women contributed to post-political economies through a focused examination of domestic and artisanal production (Brumfiel 1991, 1994; McCafferty and McCafferty 1991; Wright 1991; Stark 1993; Ames 1995; Costin 1998; Joyce 1993). Systems of ceramic production and distribution are nested in broader sets of social relations. In plantation societies, the "double burden" (Morgan 2004) of production and reproduction were nested in assumed capacities of women and broader ideologies of slavery. But how do systems of production and distribution they were involved in reveal how people were both encumbered by and mediated past structures of inequality? In a sense, to quote Leland Ferguson, this kind of research "enables us to see the contrast between the world the slaves built and the one they rejected" (1992: 120).

Many archaeologists studying Colono wares in the southeastern United States had argued that these ceramics were made by enslaved women during their free time and were for their own use or for use by others in the village where they lived. I would like to highlight the point that most believed, because of the fragility of ceramics and because of the assumption of the kinds of industry the enslaved women could undertake, that the manufacture and the distribution of Colono ware would be highly localized in production and distribution. Meaning they could not easily be transported and the potters could not produce enough to meet a regional demand. In part, this reasoning has been the result of poorly articulated assumptions on the part of archaeologists, but also of a vague engagement in scale. The scholars working on this issue were interested in production strategies, commodity flow, or market engagement only to the extent that it helped them identify and answer questions of ethnic affiliation.

As several archaeologists have argued (Wilkie and Farnsworth 1999, 2005; Wilkie 2000a; Delle 2000a, 2002), though admittedly in different ways, examining identity formation and community consolidation in plantation contexts requires multi-scalar analyses. These analyses require positioning of material culture in a broader network of social relations and paying greater attention to the variegated commodity chains in which the enslaved actively engaged. Tracing the circuits through which yabbas were traded can reveal the potential reach of the social networks of the enslaved. In this chapter I explore the extent of the ceramic trade in local markets through an analysis of the relative heterogeneity and homogeneity of ceramic recipes used to make yabbas recovered from the central corridor of Jamaica. The methods through which I determined the relative homogeneity and heterogeneity of this group of ceramics involved a combination of ceramic petrography and neutron activation analysis. I would first like to highlight a few things about the producers of this pottery.

Provenance and Composition: Typology or Interaction

There has been a considerable amount of scholarship highlighting the strengths and limitations of provenance studies (Wallis 1963; Bareis and Porter 1965; Wagner and Schubert 1972; Goad 1980a, 1980b; Peacock 1980; Mason and Aigner 1987; Betts 1991; Neff et al. 1992; Newman 1992; Hegmon 1995, 1998; Owen and Hansen 1996; Steponaitis, Blackman, and Neff 1996; Mallory-Greenough, Greenough, and Owen 1998; Hegmon, Nelson, and Ennes 2000; Rapp et al. 2000). The term *provenance* needs to be disambiguated from *provenience*. The former indicates the source from which constituent geological materials are derived. *Provenience* is a term which refers to the location from which the artifact was recovered. Provenance studies rely on discerning patterns of elements, minerals, and included materials which constitute the composition of the artifact (Steponaitis, Blackman, and Neff 1996; Neff 2001). Ideally, these patterns can be coordinated with naturally occurring geological formations, thus providing a direct link between the *provenience* of the artifact and the source of the material used to make it (Goad 1980a; Bishop and Neff 1989; Glascock 1992; Neff 2001). This can, in turn, be used to extrapolate commodity circuits and trade networks.

The idea that we can create fingerprints that can be used to identify geological sources is premised on the anticipation that "there exists some qualitative or quantitative chemical or mineralogical difference between natural sources that exceeds the qualitative or quantitative variation within each source" (Neff 2001: 2; see Weigand et al 1977 for original formulation of premise). Yet, as many have shown, "there is no way to know a priori the compositional difference among the sources one hopes to discriminate" (Steponaitis, Blackman, and Neff 1996: 555). Without systematic and comprehensive examination of potential sources, one can create geologically informed typologies but cannot find the kind of information required to establish provenance. In the real world, and especially with but not restricted to ceramic materials, provenance studies rely on "definitions of the sources less precise than one would like" (Rapp et al. 2000: 3).

Neutron activation analysis (NAA) and ceramic petrography have been employed with varying success to establish geochemical and mineralogical signatures of clays and ceramic materials (Freestone 1992; Middleton 1998). NAA, which determines the bulk chemistry of a ceramic, thus establishing a chemical signature (see Bishop, Rands and Holley 1982; Blackman et al 1989, 1993; Bishop and Neff 1989; Bishop et al. 1988; Arnold, Neff, and Bishop 1991; Blackman 1992; Glascock 1992) has been used successfully in numerous world areas (D'Altroy and Bishop 1990; Stahl and das Dores Giaro da Cruz 1998; Lynott et al. 2000; Vaughn and Neff 2000; Descantes et al. 2001; Olin et al. 2002; Steponaitis, Blackman, and Neff 1996; Vaughn et al. 2006). Ceramic petrography identifies included aplastic particles within the clay matrix and analyzes their relationship to one another to approximate the source conditions of the materials used to make the ceramic. It has been used in numerous areas to establish the relative provenance of ceramic manufacture (Isaacson and Aleto 1989; Vince 1989; Donahue, Watters, and Millspaugh 1990; Betts 1991; Cordell 1993; Fieller and Nicholson 1991; Stoltman 1991; Hegmon 1995; Dye 1996; Jordan, Schrire, and Miller 1999; Dickinson et al. 2001). While each technique has its own particular strength and weakness, as complementary methodologies they can reinforce archaeological inferences or complicate analytical interpretation.

Because much research (the research for this book included) employs techniques that attempt to establish physicochemical patterns in archaeological materials but do not incorporate potential source materials in an exhaustive, systematic, or statistically significant way, they are not truly provenance studies. Compositional studies, therefore, can become geologically informed, complementary forms of typology. These typologies, like any, can become abstractions, no matter how grounded in empirical data, and must be set against a social context. Ideally they should be studies which attempt not only to infer the geological constraints on the potential clay sources but also to extrapolate production zones (Monette et al. 2007) or "ceramic recipes" (Descantes et al. 2001; Mommsen 2001). In order for the relationships of trade and exchange to make any sense, these recipes are juxtaposed against a given context of interaction. In short, the question I am asking of these particular techniques is one of extent. Were the pots recovered from the south coast made in the same place as the pots recovered from the north coast?

Archaeologists working with ceramics of the African Diaspora have generally assumed that the artisans who produced this pottery were unattached specialists who manufactured their wares during their free time (Handler 1963b, 1964; Wheaton and Garrow 1985: 183; Beuze 1990: 40; England 1994) and that the pottery that made its way into urban settings was a result of links created by the planter (Crane 1993). Relying on either potential waster sherds (Wheaton and Garrow 1985) or ethnographic evidence and indirect analogy (Handler 1964; Beuze 1990: 42), there has been little evidence to date to challenge the model that local, low-fired, coarse earthenware was the product of part-time potters resulting in intermittent and indirect distribution. Higher-fired glazed ceramics, like those discussed by Handler (1963a) and England (1994), were the result of more intensive production and distribution systems. In initiating my analysis of ceramics in Jamaica, I framed, rather uncritically, my models around these dichotomous production strategies, mirroring the two predominant types of local pottery in Jamaica: slipped and glazed yabbas.

Archaeological Context

I chose to examine eight previously excavated sites dating to the eighteenth century (map 6.1). On the whole, these sites represent an occupational history that extends from the seventeenth century to the twentieth century. Ceramics were recovered from contexts associated with house yards of enslaved laborers at Seville (Armstrong 1999), Drax Hall (Armstrong

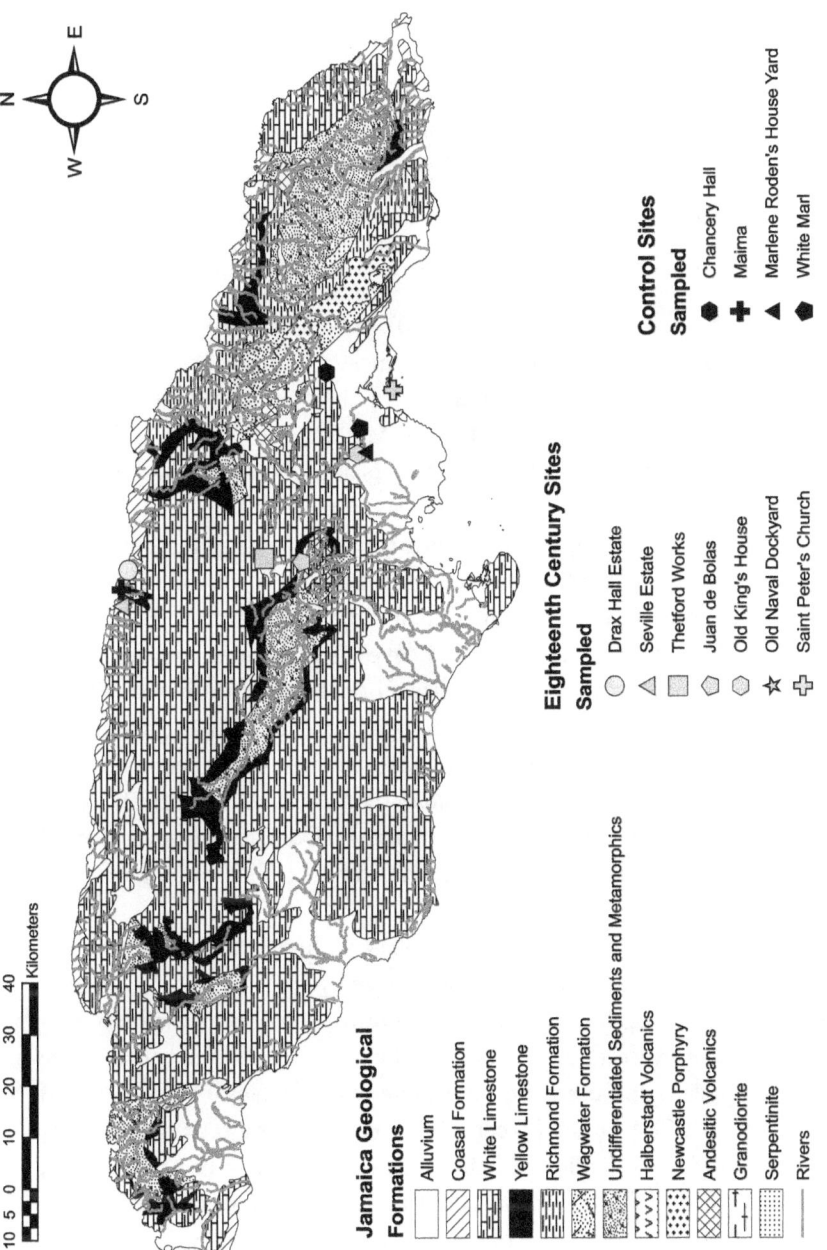

Map 6.1. Geological Map of Jamaica with the location of sites included in petrographic analysis. Adapted from the Jamaica Geological Survey (1969). Illustration by Author.

Table 6.1. Distribution of Yabba Sherds, MNVs, and Rim Sherds

Site	Glazed Sherd	MNV	Rim	Slipped Sherd	MNV	Rim	Untreated Sherd	MNV	Rim
Drax Hall	7	7	7	236	8	1	0	0	0
Juan de Bollas	20	6	4	208	32	18	0	0	0
King's House	110	41	27	629	129	76	56	11	11
Naval Dockyard	642	135	80	487	76	41	19	9	8
St. Peter's	412	169	72	654	214	55	59	33	21
Seville	124	44	6	301	122	6	15	5	1
Thetford	8	5	2	174	31	15	4	1	1
Total	1,323	407	198	2,689	612	212	153	59	42

1990: 74), Juan de Bollas (Reeves 1997: 50); provision grounds the laborers worked at Thetford (Reeves 1997: 43); domestic assemblages that the enslaved employed to cook for themselves and for their masters at Drax Hall (Armstrong 1990: 74); Old King's House (Mathewson 1972: 3); and urban residences of enslaved and enslaved laborers at St. Peter's Church (Brown 1996: 23) and Old Naval Dockyard (Mayes 1972: 6).

Each site contained discrete eighteenth-century deposits, thus permitting an analysis of contemporary ceramics. These contexts were distinguished through a combination of techniques, including associated material culture (Mayes 1972; Armstrong 1990, 1999; Reeves 1997), sealed archaeological contexts associated with known construction events (Mathewson 1972; Armstrong 1991b, 1992, 1998,), and geological events such as earthquakes (Mayes 1972; Brown 1996). To ensure those ceramics did indeed belong to the eighteenth century, *termini post quem* (namely, dates on or after which artifacts could have been manufactured) derived from associated imported materials were primary determinants in establishing chronological control.

I examined 1,417 sherds of glazed yabbas, with an estimated minimum vessel number of 403; 2,689 sherds of slipped yabbas, with an estimated minimum vessel number of 612; and 153 untreated yabbas, with an estimated minimum vessel number of 142. In examining just the various type counts, it appears that there are some general tendencies. Overall, slipped yabbas comprised a larger percentage of ceramic usage than any other type of local ceramic (table 6.1, figure 6.1). There is a degree of variability, though, in the popularity of types. On the sites of Port Royal and Spanish Town, there is a greater degree of parity between the three types of ceramics.

There are several possible reasons for the variation in numbers. First, it might simply be a result of the greater ease of access to different pottery

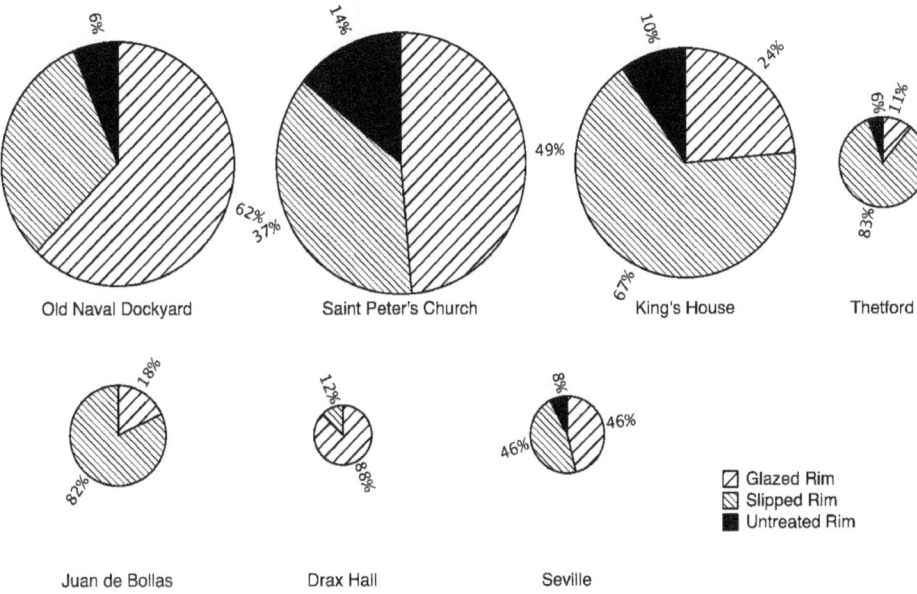

Figure 6.1. Distribution of ceramic types on analyzed sites by rim count.

producers. Second, it might represent variability in the status of consumers in urban centers and the relative poverty of plantation enslaved laborers. Finally, it could just be an artifact of uneven samples from each of the sites. As discussed in the last chapter, these types of pottery are varied in manufacture, decorative inventory, and surface treatment.

Taken as whole, the eighteenth-century Jamaican ceramic assemblage is highly varied in apparent manufacture, form, and size. Glazed, slipped, and untreated yabbas all seem to have been exposed to varying firing environments indicated in the multiple types of cores and abundant clouding observed on the vessels. While this variation might be an artifact of different skills potters adopted in attempting to incorporate technologies like glazing, it does not seem to be the result of regional variation in pottery production.

These ceramics were examined to determine the extent to which they were distributed through the market systems of eighteenth-century Jamaica. Adopting an approach in which ceramics are items of exchange in a network of market systems requires a focus on distribution and provenance. Whereas African Jamaican manufacture of locally produced pottery is fairly well accepted (Mathewson 1972a, 1972b, 1973; Mayes 1972; Armstrong 1990; Bratten 1992; Reeves 1997), the location of manufacturing sites and the distribution of the pottery are still fairly conjectural (Reeves 1997). Archaeological and historical evidence suggests one of two mechanisms for the distribution of Jamaican earthenware in the study collection. One mechanism revolves around the local production and distribution of these earthenware objects. A second mechanism is centralized production and an island-wide distribution of the earthenware. Both mechanisms are models representing strategies of ceramic production and distribution. They should be seen as ideal strategies, two ends framing a broader continuum of possible ceramic practices. Given the diversity of Jamaican clay deposits and the geographic scope of the samples, a combination of ceramic petrography and neutron activation analysis was believed sensitive enough to pick up variation in ceramic materials.

Geological Context

Jamaica is a geologically diverse island with considerable mineralogical variation in clay deposits located across the island (Bailey 1970). The island is divided into two blocks: the Cornwall-Middlesex Block and the Blue Mountain block, separated by the Wagwater trough in the area of Mona Heights (Robinson, Lewis, and Cant 1970: 2). Distinct to the north and western coasts of Jamaica is the coastal formation, which is dominated by sandy calcarenite, silts, and bedded limestones. Texturally, sediments tend to be produced by high-energy processes. Jamaica has two major limestone groups, which form a large component of Jamaica's bedrock. The Newport, the Browns Town, and the Claremont groups characterize the White Limestone formation, formed in the late Tertiary period. The Yellow Limestone formation is characterized by the Chapelton and Font Hill formations. Whereas the Chapelton and Font Hill formations are found throughout the island, rocks of the Claremont are volumetrically most abundant, followed by the Browns Town formation (Robinson et al. 1970: 2–6).

There are nine major inliers, three of which are potentially important in understanding the detrital inclusions found within alluvial clays that might have been used to make the ceramics: the Above Rocks granodiorite (Early Albian), the Blue Mountain and eastern Wagwater belt (Maastrichtian), and the Saint Ann's Inlier (Santonian) (Robinson, Lewis, and Cant 1970: 5). These inliers, which are of Cretaceous volcanic, metamorphic, and plutonic rocks, extend from Negril to St. Thomas in an east–west direction. One of the direct results of this geology is that there is only one place in Jamaica where quartz-rich sands are located. The St. Elizabeth plains contain sands of monocrystalline quartz grains that have shown some degree of mechanical deformation. Also included are the minerals magnetite, hematite, zircon, rutile, and tourmaline. Jackson and West-Thomas argue that these formations derive from the erosion of the Above Rocks cretaceous granitoids (Jackson and West-Thomas 1994).

Clays from Jamaica have been examined mineralogically by Bailey (1970). Potential sources for clay include St. Catherine's Rio Cobre alluvium (Phillippo 1843; Reeves 1997: 184), Hope River sediment in St. Andrew's, and riverine deposits in St. Ann's. Saint Catherine's contains red burning clay deposits (Bailey 1970: 1) near Bog Walk and "silty, slightly contaminated, cream colored clays" near Spanish Town (3). At Bog Walk, clays are located in the region of Tulloch. They are reported to be of high quality and contain only limestone and organics as impurities (1).

In Spanish Town, the clay was most likely extracted from an alluvial deposit known as the older Liguanea gravels. This deposit formed when the Rio Cobre, which now flows directly into Kingston Harbor, flowed into Galleon Harbor (Green and Black 1970: 8). Texturally, this alluvium is comprised of coarse gravels, sands, and clay. Mineral inclusions in these alluvial clays comprise residual clasts from the Above Rocks granodiorite inlier (Bailey 1970: 3). Sediment derived from erosion of this granodiorite should contain large simple quartz grains.

Petrography

I used petrographic analysis to establish that there was very little variation in the recipes used to produce the ceramics from eighteenth-century archaeological contexts. There is a wealth of literature showing the strength and limitations of ceramic petrography in establishing the recipe used to produce ceramics (Hegmon 1995; Dye 1996; Vince 1989; Jordan, Schrire, and Miller 1999; Dickinson et al. 2001). It has been successfully used in the Caribbean by David Watters and Jim Petersen in the analysis of Barbudian and Montserratian ceramics (Petersen and Watters. 1988; Donahue, Watters, and Millspaugh 1990). In Jamaica, this was the first systematic attempt to determine the ceramic recipe used to produce ceramic including constituent materials. I discovered through analysis of these ceramics in thin section that the inclusions in some of the recipes used to produce the ceramics seem to resemble those in clays recovered from the Rio Cobre around Spanish Town.

One hundred sixty-four sherds from the collection were examined petrographically. In my sampling strategy I concentrated on glazed, slipped, and untreated ceramics from each of the historic context sites ($n = 138$). I also included ceramics of probable English and Cuban, yet unknown, origin ($n = 12$). Initial cuts were made along the vertical axis of the pot beginning at the lip of the rim sherd at the Heroy Geological Laboratory at Syracuse University. I analyzed the ceramics qualitatively, noting mineral identity, size, angularity, alteration in the minerals, and relationship to each other, as well as point counting. I examined each sherd through a technique called point counting, which offers more informative results, described below.

Stoltman (1989, 1991, 1999) has described one method of point counting, essentially a systematic sampling technique in which the microscope stage is advanced at an arbitrary set interval. Specifically, I used a multiple intercept approach (Middleton, Freestone, and Leese 1985: 66). The petrographer records the mineral at the center of the field of view. Each grain is measured. Stoltman suggests that 100 observations be made at 1-mm intervals exclusive of voids in the clay. The question of how many observations are enough is one that plagues ceramic petrographers. There are some very important guides to point counting and the statistical significance its results reveal (van der Plas and Tobi 1965; Pettijohn et al. 1972; Howarth 1989). Whereas 100 observations is expedient in analysis and far more than the conventional wisdom of 50 counts (Peacock 1971), it is far less than the 150 suggested by Middleton, Freestone, and Leese (1985) and the 200 suggested by Fieller and Nicholson (1991: 88). I used 185 observations, exclusive of voids, to describe the mineralogical variation.

The mineralogical identity of the inclusion, its size, shape, and angularity were recorded. The relative abundance of specific minerals and their shape give some indication of the relative maturity of the source materials. Several minerals were significant in the overall analysis of the composition of the ceramics: quartz, potassium feldspar, and plagioclase feldspar.

Quartz (SiO_2) is an extremely stable mineral, both chemically and mechanically. In sedimentary rocks, immature quartz is generally angular and is identified under polarized light by its light yellow interference color. Quartz in volcanic rocks generally forms simple phenocrysts. Metamorphosed quartz generally has an undulose extinction pattern and is commonly polycrystalline. Plutonic igneous quartz forms large, simple to undulose, euhedral to anhedral crystals. Fluid inclusions in quartz are common, appearing as trains of tiny bubbles. The texture of quartz crystals can be indicative of the maturity of the source clays. Rounded quartzes are found in mature sediment that either has been exposed to a high-energy environment or has had prolonged exposure to mechanical forces such as a riverine system (Bokman 1952; Blatt 1952: 401; Moss 1972: 909; Ferring and Perttula 1987: 439). In aggregating the data, I combined recrystallized, simple, and mechanically deformed quartz crystals.

Feldspars turned out to be a relatively important class of mineral in this research. They are aluminum silicates that have varying compositions of calcium, potassium, or sodium. Potassium feldspar ($KAlSi_3O_8$) is a mechanically resistant mineral. It is subject, however, to chemical weathering (Philpotts 1989). It can be distinguished from quartz under plane-polarized light by its alteration, in which sericite film forms around the mineral. Degree of alteration was estimated on potassium feldspar inclusions by an approximation of the mineral that had been altered to sericite and the percentage of the mineral that was fresh. Size and angularity of potassium feldspar can be indicative of the sediments' maturity (Middleton, Freestone, and Leese 1985). Some potassium feldspars grow in such a manner as to produce a crosshatched pattern under cross-polarized light. This is known as microcline twinning and indicates anorthoclase feldspar. I aggregated anorthoclase feldspar, sanidine feldspar, and altered potassium feldspar together in quantifying percentages.

Plagioclase feldspars [$(Na,Ca)AlSi_3O_8$] are chemically and mechanically unstable and are susceptible to diagenesis. Oftentimes in sedimentary materials this accounts for a somewhat lower frequency. As with its potassium counterpart, alteration of the mineral was determined through an approximation of sericite that had formed as a film around the inclusion. Mechanical deformation was noted when the plagioclase feldspar was described as anhedral. In immature sediment, plagioclase maintains a euhedral, tabular texture and is generally fresh, without a sericite film. Under polarized light, it is distinguished by textural properties known as zoning, where the mineral goes extinct in a concentric fashion, and albite twinning, in which a pattern of alternating light and dark lamellae is formed by alternate extinction angles. The relative abundance of this mineral is an indication of the maturity of the sediment and the possible nature of the parent material (Grantham and Vebel 1988: 221). As with quartz and potassium feldspar, I combined chemically altered, mechanically deformed, and euhedral plagioclase feldspars as a single aggregate.

Trace minerals were also identified, and their relative percentages estimated, including two types of micas, biotite and muscovite. Biotite is a common rock-forming mineral that is found in most middle-range metamorphic rocks. It is easily distinguished by its pleochroism, cleavage, and high birefringence (Philpotts 1989: 51). Biotite is found abundantly in Jamaica's rocks, especially in the Above Rocks granodiorite and surrounding sedimentary sources (Porter, Jackson, and Robinson 1982: 56). Muscovite also has strong birefringence and cleavage. It is common in low- to medium-grade metamorphic rocks. Specifically, biotite displays a yellowish brown color under plane-polarized light. Muscovite is more rare in Jamaica and restricted to the Blue Mountain range and the rivers that drain the weathered sediment from the source material.

A final group of inclusions that were in some abundance are the lithic fragments. These include arkoses and litharkoses of varying composition and sorting. These fragments are the result of mechanical weathering of sandstones. The fragments were classified following the system introduced by Folk (1954, 1974) and Pettijohn (1975). Also included in the paste of some samples were nodules of laterite soils. These nodules are composed primarily of a very fine iron-rich soil that bears a concentric structure around a small quartz or feldspar inclusion. Finally, there were some limestone fragments found within the matrix of the pottery. These were identified through the presence of bioclasts, commonly ooids, and an iron-rich cement. Shell fragments were also found within the matrix of the ceramic, and were not associated with a cement or in any relationship to other minerals. They were, therefore, interpreted as having been purposefully included by past potters as a tempering agent.

The principal mineral components of the ceramic samples are a fine clay matrix, potassium feldspar, plagioclase feldspar, and quartz. The proportions were obtained by gaining the percentage of each mineral minus the points counting voids and the matrix (generally either clay minerals or inclusions too small to be identified at 100x). To assess the compositional variability in the parent rocks of the source material, I plotted the relative abundances of the three minerals normalized to percentage on ternary diagrams.

I first examined the pre-Columbian pottery from three sites to see if there would be significant variation in the composition based on location. I also examined three samples from waster piles at Marlene Roden's (Munchie's) house yard. One may distinguish the Maima ceramics, which have about 55 percent quartz and about 45 percent total feldspar, and the Chancery Hall and White Marl ceramics, which have from 10 to 30 percent quartz and 40 to 60 percent total feldspar (figure 6.2). What is interesting is that samples from both White Marl and Chancery Hall are heterogeneous, indicating that past potters most likely employed different source materials or recipes

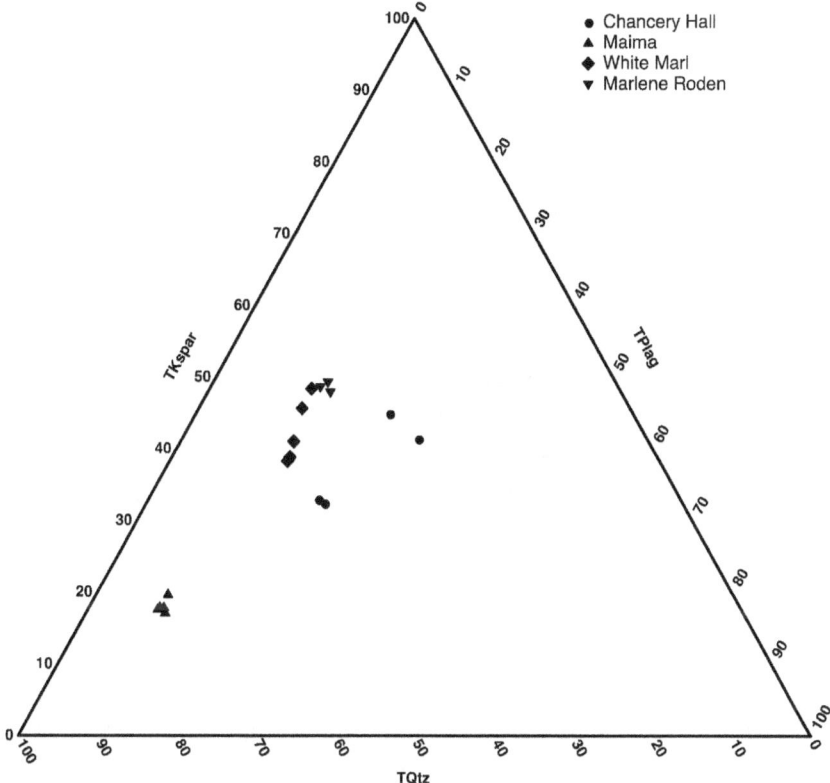

Figure 6.2. Ternary diagram showing the diversity of ceramic recipes of ceramics recovered from control samples. Quartz includes mechanically deformed, altered, and simple quartz. Potassium feldspar percentages are based on the combination of all alkali feldspars, including potassium feldspar, perthite, microcline feldspar, and sanidine. Plagioclase feldspar includes nonaltered and chemically altered plagioclase. Crystals included in foliated lithic fragments were not included in the count.

to make all nine ceramics tested. The five ceramics recovered from Maima seem to be relatively homogeneous and distinct from the White Marl and Chancery Hall ceramics. This illustrates that this particular analysis is sensitive to variation in the sediments potentially used to produce pottery in colonial Jamaica. Moreover, the sample obtained from Marlene Roden's house yard provides a baseline of information about mineral inclusions that one could expect in slipped yabbas made in the Spanish Town vicinity.

In figure 6.3 I have plotted the relative abundances of all quartz, plagioclase feldspar, and potassium feldspar crystals that were not part of lithic fragments. It is apparent that there are several distinct groups with numerous outliers or unassigned samples. While I am confident that this tech-

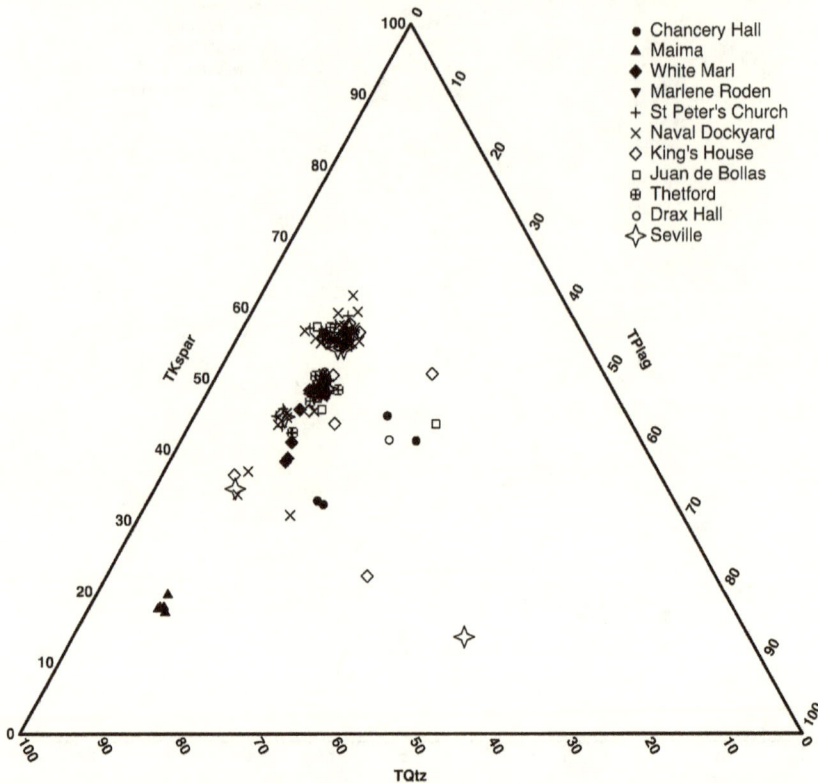

Figure 6.3. Ternary diagram showing the diversity of ceramic recipes used to make yabbas. Quartz includes mechanically deformed, metamorphically altered, and simple quartz. Potassium feldspar percentages are based on the combination of all akali feldspars, including potassium feldspar, perthite, microcline feldspar, and Sanidine. Plagioclase feldspar includes nonaltered and chemically altered plagioclase. Crystals included in foliated lithic fragments were not included in the count.

nique has identified or at least characterized each sherd, I am hesitant to suggest that these groups are statistically significant. There are many reasons why these groupings do not necessarily equate with specific sources. First, there are many factors which result in the mineral assemblage found within each sherd, including choices made by the potter in terms of temper to be added or inclusions to be removed, mixing of different clay sources, and the adding of grog. Second, and more important, I have displayed in two dimensions only three kinds of inclusions (quartz, potassium feldspar, and plagioclase feldspar). Such reduction can lead to a misrepresentation of the exact sources of materials used. These groups, rather, should be seen as indicating the kinds of recipes apparent in the ceramics. What is important

Table 6.2. A Cross-Tabulation of Groups Represented from Samples Plotted on the Ternary Diagram and Their Provenance

	St. Peters Church	Naval Dockyard	King's House	Juan de Bollas	Thetford	Drax Hall	Seville
Group 1		2	1				1
Group 2	14	16	13	1	2	6	5
Group 3	8	12	12	6	9	1	3
Group 4	2	3	4	1	1	1	1
Group 5	6	2	2	1	1	1	1
NA	1	3	3	2		1	2

in reading this diagram is that most of the groups contain samples from each of the archaeological sites (Appendix A).

Description of Ceramic Compositional Groups

While the ternary diagram is a useful visual aid to describe the heterogeneity of recipes used to make the entire suite of colonial ceramics, it is important that the clusters not be seen as anything more than that. Point counting, and its result, is a semiquantitative technique at best, in that it produces only an approximation of true values for each of the minerals recorded. I therefore did not try to draw any ellipses and mislead the reader about the significance of these clusters.

Indeed, while the ternary diagram indicates a single large cluster of samples in the upper left side, it actually belies differences in mineral size, and sorting of some of the samples from my petrographic notes. Qualitative description of thin sections is one of the strengths of petrography in that it can determine the kinds of fragments and their relationship with one another. For the most part, these ceramics were feldspar-rich, with major quartz components, exclusive of the clay matrix. Other major components included fragments of sedimentary or metamorphic rocks. There were some trace minerals present, such as biotite and muscovite. For the most part, however, these sherds could be described as rich in orthoclase, quartz, and feldspar.

Ceramic Group 1

Samples in this group are primarily composed of a fine paste that is reddish brown in color. Major minerals included in this ceramic paste are quartz (approx. 53%), potassium feldspar (approx. 34%), and plagioclase feldspar (approx. 9%). Also included in the clay matrix are biotite inclusions (approx. 2%), sandstone lithic fragments (approx. 1%) and brecciated fragments (< 1%).

The paste is a fine unstructured clay matrix (figure 6.4). There is abundant silt and very fine sand-sized inclusions (between approx. 0.01 mm and 0.05 mm) and medium-coarse sand- to granule-sized inclusions (approx. 0.3 mm and 3.2 mm). The larger inclusions are primarily quartz, potassium feldspar, and plagioclase feldspar, with smaller quantities of lithic fragments. Monocrystalline and polycrystalline quartzes range in size from silt to coarse sand (approx. 0.01 mm to 1.2 mm in diameter). They are, for the most part, elongated and are subrounded and subangular. Some monocrystalline quartzes display undulatory extinction. Potassium feldspar inclusions are also medium to very coarse sand (approx. 0.05 to 1.2 mm). They are both elongated and equant and tend to be subangular. They have experienced a small degree of chemical alteration and seemingly little mechanical deformation. Plagioclase feldspars are also large. They have an elongate shape and an angular to subangular texture. They are recognizable through lamelar extinction called polysynthetic or albite twinning.

Minor inclusions in the ceramic paste are sedimentary rock fragments, biotite crystals, and conglomerates. There are some sandstone inclusions in the matrix of the clay. These inclusions appear to be litharenites. They are primarily composed of quartz and feldspar inclusions cemented by a brown to black groundmass. They range in size from 0.03 mm to 0.6 mm. They are irregularly shaped and are generally subangular in texture. There is no preferred extinction angle among the quartz or feldspar inclusions. Biotites are generally small, between 0.02 and 0.05 mm. They are mechanically deformed. They tend to be subangular to angular in texture and elongate in shape.

I recorded only four samples with characteristics similar to those described above (see Appendix 1), which were recovered from Old Naval Dockyard, Old King's House, and Seville. They are, in general, industrial sugar wares or Spanish jars.

Ceramic Group 2

The large group of samples displayed in the ternary diagram belies a considerable amount of heterogeneity. Samples in this group are primarily composed of a fine paste that is brick red in color. Major minerals included in this ceramic paste are potassium feldspar (approx. 33%), quartz (approx. 18%), and plagioclase feldspar (8%). Also included in the clay matrix are granitic lithic fragments (approx. 15%–30%), and biotite inclusions (approx.

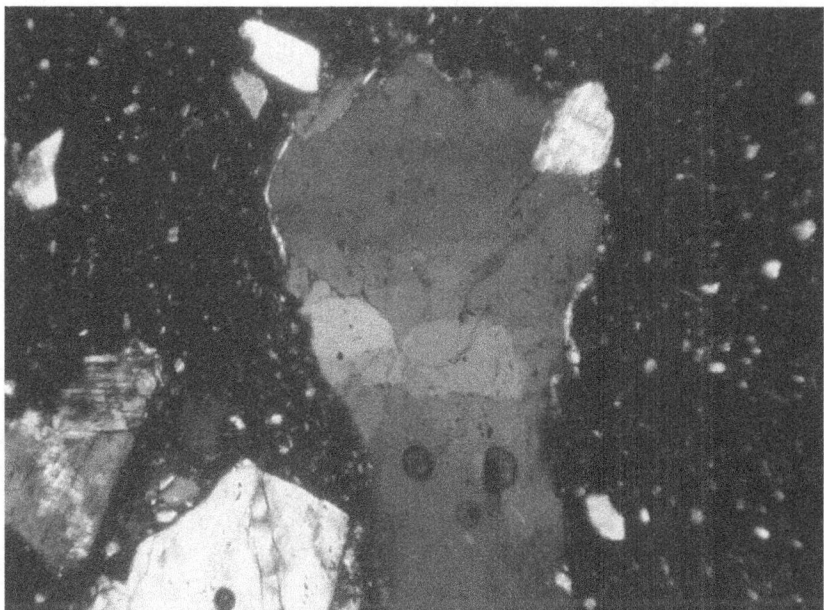

Figure 6.4. Microphotograph taken at 10x of sample 025, which belongs to ceramic group 1. This sherd contains coarse, medium fine, and fine fragments of polycrystalline and monocrystalline quartz, sericized (altered) plagioclase feldspar, and altered potassium feldspar. Anhedral plagioclase feldspar appears to have undergone some partial melting to recrystallization in the lower center of the microphotograph. Likewise, the poikilitic relationship of the feldspar and quartz also demonstrates partial melting or sequential crystallization. The plate is approximately 12 mm wide.

1%). Some samples contain fewer lithic fragments within the fine structured matrix, thus increasing the abundances of the primarily mineral components: potassium feldspar (approx. 38%), quartz (approx. 22%), and plagioclase feldspar (approx. 7%).

The paste is poorly sorted, with a normal distribution in inclusion size ranging from very fine sand to granules (approx. 0.01 mm and 2.1 mm). Potassium feldspars are irregularly shaped and are subangular and angular. Approximately 10 percent of the potassium feldspars exhibited Carlsbad twinning. The potassium feldspars, as a whole, have experienced a high degree of chemical alteration as indicated by its partial diagenesis and the presence of abundant sericite. Monocrystalline and polycrystalline quartz inclusions range in size from silt to coarse sand (approx. 0.01 mm to 0.1 mm). They are elongated and are subangular in texture. While some grains were euhedral, all exhibited undulatory extinction. Significant portions of

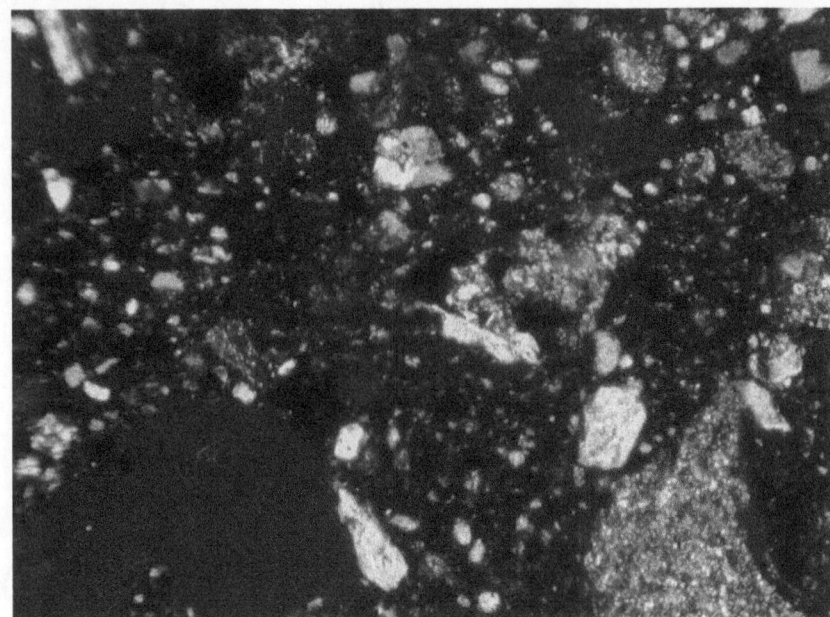

Figure 6.5. Microphotograph taken at 10x of sample 011, which belongs to ceramic group 2. This sherd contains abundant medium fine, mechanically deformed quartz with vesicules, and mechanically deformed, sericitized alkali feldspars. One feldspar in the upper left corner exhibits Carlsbad twinning. The large, subangular coarse lithic fragments are composed of very fine quartz, feldspar, and opaque fragments, possibly hematite. In the center of the field of view are two crushed sandstone fragments.

the quartzes appear to be recrystallized (approximately 20%). Some quartz are in a poikilitic relationship with potassium feldspar. Plagioclase feldspars range in size from 0.01 mm to 0.2 mm. They are tabular in shape and subangular in texture. A significant portion of the plagioclase feldspars were chemically altered (approx. 30%), while only some exhibit signs of mechanical deformation (approx. 10%). Biotites are also present in very small quantities (approx. 1%). These biotites are long, angular grains and range from silt-sized particles to medium fine sand-sized particles (approx. 0.02 mm to 0.05 mm) in maximum diameter (figure 6.5).

Other detrital inclusions in samples of this group are lithic fragments with abundant quartz, feldspar and opaque minerals. Within the samples the abundance of these inclusions are variable (up to 30%). Lithic fragments range from very fine sand to pebbles (approx. 0.05 mm to 0.6 mm). They appear broken and irregularly shaped. They appear to be composed of quartz and partially altered feldspar inclusions and are potentially derived from granitic sources. Also included in the paste of the ceramic are sandstone fragments, which I classified as litharkoses. They are predominantly weathered plagioclase feldspars and cement.

The majority of the thin sections sampled in this group were prepared from glazed yabbas. The samples were recovered from Drax Hall, Seville, Juan de Bollas, Thetford, Old King's House, St. Peter's Church, and Old Naval Dockyards. While the entire group does betray a degree of heterogeneity in the proportions of lithic fragments, it probably reflects the heterogeneity of the alluvium from which the clays were derived and represents small variations in ceramic recipes of the potters.

Ceramic Group 3

Samples within group 3 are primarily composed of a coarse red paste. Included within the matrix of this paste are potassium feldspar (approx. 42%), quartz (approx. 31%), plagioclase feldspar (approx. 12%), and biotite (approx. 1%). Also included in the paste are sandstone lithic inclusions (approx. 2%) and shell fragments (< 1%).

The paste is a coarse unstructured clay matrix with poorly sorted inclusions ranging in size from silt to granules (approx. 0.01 mm to 2.5 mm). Potassium feldspars are irregularly shaped—angular to round in texture, with the majority of the inclusions subangular. Fewer than 1 percent of the potassium feldspars exhibit Carlsbad twinning. Within some of the potassium feldspars there are zones of perthite. The potassium feldspars have experienced a high degree of chemical alteration, evident by a thick sericite film surrounding the mineral. Many of the potassium feldspar inclusions are also mechanically deformed, displaying an apparently crushed texture. These feldspars are also found in conglomerate fragments with quartz and feldspar. Quartzes are for the most part monocrystalline, and predominantly equant with some elongated inclusions. They range in texture from subangular to round with the majority being subrounded. A majority of quartzes (70%) exhibit undulatory extinction. Approximately 15 percent of the quartz inclusions appear to be recrystallized, and 10 percent of the quartzes have intergrowth textures with potassium feldspar. This texture indicates that the quartz inclusions experienced some remelting and sequential growth crystallization. Plagioclase feldspar ranged in size from 0.01 mm to 0.3 mm. They are tabular in shape and subangular in texture. Some of the plagioclase feldspars are euhedral and fresh. A portion of the plagioclase feldspars are chemically altered (approx. 10%), while many plagioclase feldspars exhibit signs of mechanical deformation (approx. 50%). Biotites are

Figure 6.6. Microphotograph of sample 052 (St. Peter's Church), which belongs to group 3. This sample contains abundant alkali feldspar that has undergone some chemical alteration, rounded angular and subangular quartz inclusions that exhibit mechanical deformation, and sandstone lithic fragments. The plagioclase feldspar, displaying polysntheitic twinning (albite), is for the most part fresh, except for a seriticized vein running across its axis. The quartz in the lower right-hand corner is exhibiting undulatory exticinction. The plate is approximately 12 mm wide.

also present in small quantities. These biotites are in the range of 0.02 mm to 0.05mm in maximum diameter. Fewer than 1 percent of biotites are on the order of 0.1 mm. These are subangular and lathlike in shape. All of the biotites exhibited a degree of mechanical and chemical deformation (figure 6.6).

Also included in the paste of the ceramic were small sandstone fragments, volcanic lithic fragments, laterite fragments, and shell fragments. The sandstone fragments are predominantly litharkoses that had been severely altered due to weathering. The volcanic lithic fragments ranged in size from 0.05 mm to 0.3 mm. They are angular to subangular and irregular in shape. There are fine-grained partially seriticized inclusions. They are predominantly composed of an iron-rich groundmass, with some quartz inclusions. They are round and subrounded in texture and are generally equant in shape. Also included in minor quantities were shell fragments.

These are predominantly broken, curved lenticular pieces, with a distinct structure. They are on the order of 0.05 mm long. They are highly altered and are recognizable only through their shape.

Samples from this group are predominantly slipped yabbas. The samples were recovered from Drax Hall, Seville, Juan de Bollas, Thetford, Old King's House, St. Peter's Church, and Old Naval Dockyard. The lithic inclusions along with the types of minerals present are consistent with the sediments from around the Rio Cobre in Spanish Town.

Ceramic Group 4

Samples within group 4 are primarily composed of a fine brown-red paste. Included within the matrix of this paste are potassium feldspar (42%), quartz (28%), plagioclase feldspar (9%), and biotite (2%). Also included in the paste are sandstone lithic inclusions (2%), microgranite lithic fragments (16%), and shell fragments (< 1%).

The paste is a fine-structured clay matrix. It is poorly sorted, with a normal distribution from silt-sized inclusions to granule-sized inclusions. Inclusions range in size from 0.01 mm to 1.6 mm. Potassium feldspar inclusions are medium in size, between 0.02 and 0.6 mm, with an average size of 0.25 mm. They are irregularly shaped. They are angular to subrounded in texture, with the majority of the inclusions subangular. Many (approx. 20%) potassium feldspars exhibited Carlsbad twinning. Most potassium feldspars have experienced a moderate degree of chemical alteration, and some have a sericite film surrounding the mineral. Many of the inclusions are also mechanically deformed. Some are cemented to plagioclase feldspars. Monocrystalline and polycrystalline quartz inclusions range in size from 0.01 mm to 0.5 mm in diameter, with an average size of 0.2 mm. They are predominantly irregular in shape. Some (approx. 10%) were recorded as euhedral. They range in texture from angular to round, with the majority being subangular. Many quartzes (at least 30%) exhibited undulatory extinction. These same quartzes appear to be recrystallized. There are rare occurrences of intergrowth between quartz and potassium feldspar and plagioclase feldspar (3%). Plagioclase feldspars range in size from 0.01 mm to 0.4 mm, with an average size of 0.2 mm. They are tabular in shape and angular to subangular in texture. A significant portion of the plagioclase feldspars were chemically altered, while none exhibit signs of mechanical deformation. Biotites are also present in small quantities (approx. 2%). These biotites are in the range of 0.01 mm to 0.2 mm in maximum diameter, with the average size 0.08 mm. They are equant grains that were angular

Figure 6.7. Microphotograph of sample 013 (Old Naval Dockyard) taken at 10x, which belongs to ceramic group 4. The paste is dominated by alkali feldspar (the large inclusion in the lower left and upper right-hand corner; note the film indicating chemical alteration), simple (mineral on top displaying extinction) and recrystallized quartz (white mineral in upper portion of microphotgraph) with undulatory extinction. There is also a plagioclase feldspar displaying diagnostic albite twinning in the center of the field and in the lower right-hand corner. The plate is approximately 12 mm wide.

in texture. All of the biotites exhibit a degree of mechanical and chemical deformation (figure 6.7).

Also included in the paste of the ceramic are a host of lithic fragments, including sandstone fragments, and shell fragments. The sandstone fragments appear to be derived from arkoses and to be primarily composed of poorly sorted quartz and feldspar. The fragments are irregular in shape and are subangular to subrounded in texture. Many of the fragments appear to be chemically altered and contain interstitial sericite. Arkose inclusions range in size from 0.05 mm to 0.6 mm. They are irregularly shaped and range in texture from subangular to subrounded. Some do exhibit a degree of alteration. One sample contained a shell fragment.

Thin sections in this group were taken from slipped yabbas. These archaeological samples were recovered from all seven historic sites. Samples within this group are located along with group 2 samples on the ternary diagram. As is evident, however, from the photomicrograph and the description, it varies significantly in composition.

Ceramic Group 5

Samples within this group are composed primarily of a light brown unstructured matrix. Also found within the matrix of these samples are potassium feldspar (approx. 41%), quartz (approx. 38%), plagioclase (approx. 11%), and biotite (approx. 4%). Also included in the paste are sandstone (27%) and shell fragments (< 1%).

Quartz and potassium feldspars dominate the paste. In many ways, the textural properties are similar to those samples belonging to group 2, while the compositional properties are more closely aligned with groups 3 and 4. This paste is better sorted than the pastes of groups 3 and 4. The feldspars are also more weathered than those in groups 3 and 4. Also included in the paste of the ceramic are arkose fragments. These range from 0.02 to 0.5 mm, with an average of 0.1 mm in maximum diameter. They are angular in texture and irregular in shape. They do show signs of weathering. The paste is a coarse, partially sorted structured matrix. Inclusions within the paste range in size from 0.01 mm to 2.9 mm. The average inclusion size, however, is around 0.08 mm. Quartz and potassium feldspar seem to be found in relatively equal quantities. Polycrystalline and monocrystalline quartzes are relatively small, ranging from 0.01 mm to 0.2 mm, with an average of 0.15 mm in maximum diameter. They are irregular in shape and exhibit no rounding or mechanical deformation. They are angular to subrounded in texture. Some quartz exhibits signs of recrystallization and undulatory extinction.

Potassium feldspars tend to be irregular in shape and angular to subangular in texture. They exhibit a moderate degree of chemical alteration and mechanical deformation. Some observed minerals exhibited Carlsbad twinning. Potassium feldspar show signs of mechanical deformation and some alteration. However, approximately 10 percent of feldspars are fresh. Biotites have also been found in some abundance. They tend to be angular to subangular in texture (figure 6.8).

In general these ceramics were derived from untreated yabbas. The archaeological samples were recovered from Old King's House, Old Naval Dockyard, St. Peter's Church, and Thetford. At this point it is difficult to estimate potential sources used in their manufacture.

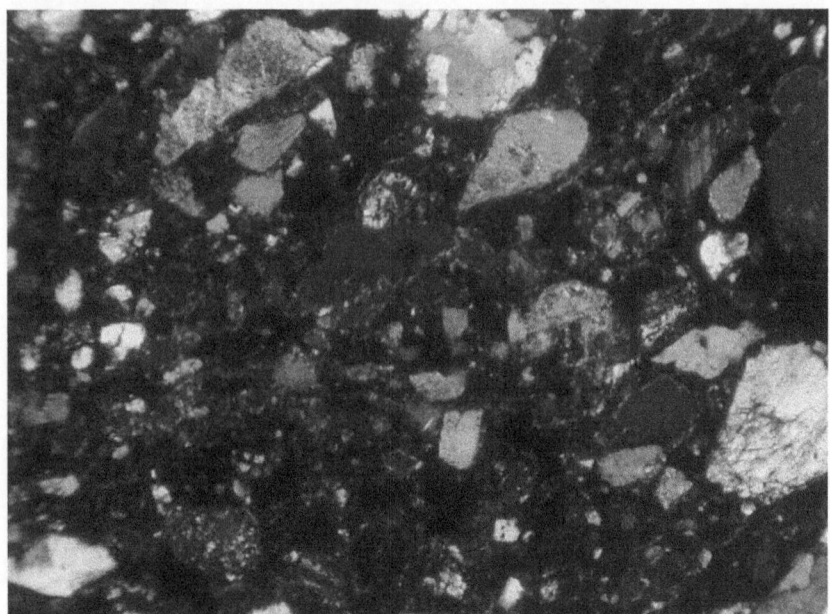

Figure 6.8. Microphotograph of sample 058 (St. Peter's Church), which belongs to group 5. This sample contains abundant weathered alkali feldspar that has undergone some chemical alteration, rounded, angular, and subangular quartz inclusions that exhibit mechanical deformation, and plagioclase feldspars. In the center of the field of view, one weathered potassium feldspar is displaying Carlsbad twinning. Toward the upper right-hand corner is a fragmented yet unweathered plagioclase feldspar exhibiting albite twinning. The quartz on the top of the image is showing signs of recrystallization. The plate is approximately 12 mm wide.

Nonassigned Samples

This is a varied group of ceramics that include ceramics of probable European manufacture (there were two samples from wheel-thrown chamber pots), possible regional manufacture (one Spanish jar), and mineralogical outliers. Some unassigned samples could potentially form a group, but with such a small sample it is difficult to interpolate. Samples within this group are composed primarily of a light brown unstructured matrix. Also found within the matrix of these samples are potassium feldspar (28%), quartz (23%), plagioclase (18%), and biotite (< 1%). Also included in the paste are arkose fragments (24%). The paste is a fine, poorly sorted structured matrix. Inclusions within the paste range in size from silt- to granule-sized inclusions. Quartz and potassium feldspar are found in relatively equal quantities. Plagioclase feldspars appear to have been mechanically and chemically

Figure 6.9. Microphotograph of paste from sample 124 (St. Peter's Church), which does not belong to any group. The lithic fragments, which dominate this paste, are angular. There is one rounded quartz in the upper part of the slide. There is one sericitized potassium feldspar in the lower part of the plate. The plate is approximately 12 mm wide.

deformed. Many of the feldspars are found within breccias. The feldspars also are surrounded by a sericite film. Quartzes are also small, ranging in size from 0.01 mm to 0.5 mm. Quartz inclusions are angular to subangular, with minor amounts of rounded quartz (see figure 6.9).

Also included in the paste of the ceramic are arkose lithic fragments. These tend to be larger than other inclusions, ranging from 0.02 and 1.5 mm with an average of 0.8 mm in maximum diameter. They are subangular in texture and irregular in shape. They do not show signs of weathering. There are conglomerate fragments included in the ceramic paste as well.

Interpretation

Four of the compositional groups (groups 2, 3, 4, and 5) interpreted from petrographic analysis contain inclusions that are consistent with the alluvial sediments from either the Rio Cobre in the region of Spanish Town or the gravels from the Liguanea plain. These include abundant potassium feldspar, quartz, plagioclase feldspar, laterite fragments, and minor amounts of biotite. Of note was the recrystallization of quartz indicating a metamorphic source material for the clays used to construct the pottery. One of the compositional groups contained inclusions that were consistent with sediments from the Liguanea Plain around Kingston. These soils had considerable feldspar and quartz but also contained high quantities of lithic and arkose fragments. Finally, there was one group which contained smaller inclusions of quartz, potassium feldspar, and plagioclase feldspar. This compositional group is significantly different from sediment in both the Liguanea and the Rio Cobre.

Neutron Activation Analysis

In 2004 I was approached by Christophe Descantes and Michael Glascock of the Missouri University Research Reactor (MURR) to subject fifty samples to neutron activation analysis (NAA) as part of a larger NSF-funded pilot project to establish a baseline of chemical data on Caribbean ceramics. The goal of this project was to see how similar some of the compositional groups were to Rio Cobre clay sources. The ethnographic samples came from the waster pile of Munchie, one of the last remaining traditional potters working in Jamaica. Clay sources used in her analysis have a known provenance in her house yard near the Rio Cobre. For archaeological samples, I decided to focus primarily on glazed and slipped yabbas and sampled fifty-one specimens from remaining samples used to prepare thin sections for petrography. In other words, I was able to analyze fifty-one of the same ceramics using both petrography and NAA. These samples were randomly selected from ceramic groups 2, 3, and 4 (DesCantes and Glascock 2005; Hauser et al. n.d.). The following description summarizes their analysis and report (see Appendix 2). The ceramic specimens comprise sherds representing three types from eight archaeological sites (Drax Hall, Juan de Bollas, Munchie, Old King's House, Old Naval Dockyard, St. Peter's Church, Seville, Thetford) in Jamaica's central corridor. These types include glazed (n = 18), slipped (n = 27), and untreated (n = 4) yabbas. Chemical characteristics for the two compositional groups are represented in figures B.2, B.3, and B.4. Group 1, a distinct compositional group, tends to be enriched in sodium relative to compositional Group 2.

Group 1 may be comprised of subgroups (see figure B.5). Group 1a is characterized by enriched sodium concentrations and depleted arsenic concentrations when compared to Group 1b. Glascock and Descantes have decided to "lump" instead of "split" compositional Group 1, because there does not appear to be any significant pattern of sample distribution on ar-

Table 6.3 Distribution of Chemical Subgroups

Site Name	Chemical Group					
	1a	1b	2	OUT	U	TOTAL
Plantation Sites						
Seville	2	1	3			6
Drax Hall	1	3	2			6
Juan de Bollas	1		4	1		6
Thetford			4		2	6
Urban Sites						
King's House	1	5	5			11
Naval Dockyard	2		4			6
St. Peter's	1	2	3			6
Ethnographic						
Marlene Roden			2	1		3
Total	8	11	27	2	2	50

Note: Cross-tabulation of compositional groups derived from Neutron Activation Analysis (see figures B.1–B.5) and the sites from which samples were excavated. The techniques for statistically reducing the data and assigning group membership is described in Appendix B.

chaeological sites. While using highly mobile elements such as sodium and other alkali metals might belie patterns derived from postdepositional environments exposed to seawater, such as Port Royal and Seville, this does not seem to be borne out in the group membership table (table 6.3) (Hauser et al. n.d.).

Compositional group 2 subsumes much chemical variability and is enriched in hafnium and thorium when compared to compositional group 1. It is highly probable that analyzing more samples will allow us to identify subgroups within group 2 (figure B.5).

At this early stage, it is difficult to ascertain what the chemical compositional groups represent. Determining whether the identified compositional groups refer to local or exotic sources will require the submission of raw clay samples for chemical analysis or the mineralogical analysis of raw clay samples. However, using the criterion of abundance, defined above, it is safe to assume that both compositional groups are of local origin and that chemical differences are attributable to different local sources of raw clay, different ceramic recipes, diverse uses, or a combination of all these potential factors.

Despite the large membership of the compositional groups, tentative patterns can be identified when investigating the decoration of the sherd members in each group.

Compositional group 1 members are predominantly yabbas with internal glazing, whereas compositional group 2 members tend to be vertical pots with slipping and burnishing for decoration. Glascock and Descantes analyzed the glazed surface of specimen JAM002, a member of compositional group 1, with a nondestructive energy dispersive X-ray fluorescence (EDXRF) spectrometer and found the glaze chemical composition to have high concentrations of lead.

Ceramic specimens from six of the eight sites have membership in both compositional groups (figure 6.10). Two sites have ceramics that belong only to compositional group 2. But for two unassigned specimens, all of the sherds collected from the enslaved village contexts of the site of Thetford have membership in compositional group 2. Except for a single specimen that was considered an outlier and not included in the NAA study, ceramic sherd specimens from the ethnographic contexts of the site of Munchie (Marlene Roden) belong only to compositional Group 2.

The NAA study had identified two distinct ceramic compositional groups. Possible tendencies or associations between the chemical compositions of the sherds, their provenience, and their ceramic decorative styles were identified. As with any project attempting to define the composition and recipe of archaeological ceramics, the overall study is incomplete, given the importance of sample size in establishing patterns where no geological standards are employed. The submission of more samples from these contexts could further test these identified patterns as well as delineate more groups and subgroups. On the whole, though, the patterns of ceramics and the delineated groups do seem to conform with groups established through petrographic description.

Turning back to the question of relative provenance, whether archaeological ceramics recovered from the south coast were made using the same recipe as archaeological ceramics recovered from the north coast, an analysis of compositional groups and their distribution across the island is telling. Samples identified as petrographic groups 2 and 3 were recovered from each of the archaeological sites in the study area. Samples identified as chemical groups 1 and 2 were also recovered from each of the historic period sites. Each of these groups does have some degree of variation.

To combine the different analyses as a measure of further precaution, we still find similar distributions. Samples identified as chemical group 1 and petrographic group 2 were recovered from the north coast (Drax Hall and Seville Estate), central (Juan de Bollas and King's House), and the south coast (Naval Dockyard and St. Peter's Church). These samples were glazed yabbas and similar to those that Cecil Baugh described as being made on Mountain View Road. The fact that there were none found in Thetford is a function of their low abundance in the overall assemblage of that excava-

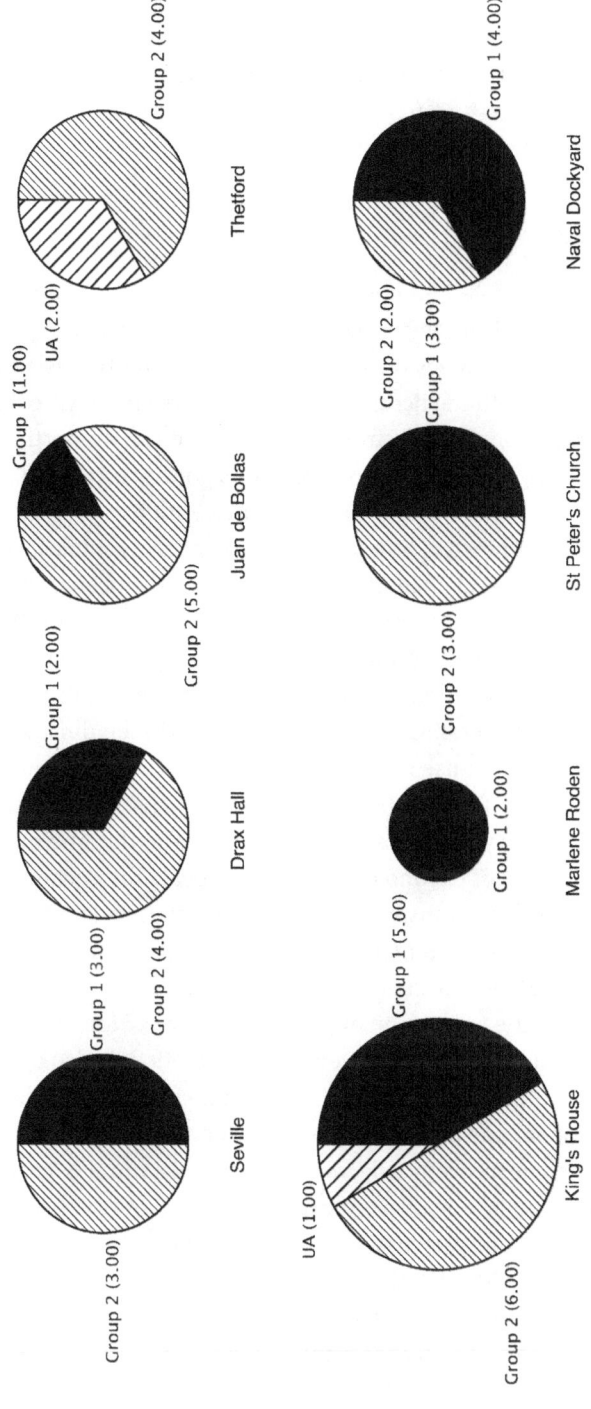

Figure 6.10. Distribution of chemical groups across sites. Pie chart areas are proportional to the size of the sample analyzed.

tion's collection. Samples identified as chemical group 2 and petrographic group 3 were recovered from all seven historic period sites sampled and the control sample from Munchie's houseyard. These samples were slipped and burnished yabbas and are similar to those described by Edward Long, Hans Sloane, and Roderick Ebanks.

Conclusion

I actually anticipated finding a considerable amount of variation in the pottery. This came from my visual inspection of the pieces and from the previously published studies on analogous pottery on other islands. Essentially, the results of both the petrographic description and NAA confirm that pots recovered archaeologically from the sites located on the north coast appear to be made using the same ceramic recipe as pottery recovered from the south coast and the central part of the island. In addition, it appears that the recipe employed by Munchie, at least in the case of two samples, is similar to the recipe used in the eighteenth century for slipped and burnished pieces.

While this does not indicate an island-wide system of distribution, the scale of production is certainly larger than I had anticipated. Many archaeologists studying Colono wares in the North American Southeast had argued that these ceramics made by enslaved women during their free time were for their own use or the use by other enslaved laborers in the village. Most believed, given the fragility of ceramics and their assumptions of the kinds of industry the enslaved could undertake, that the manufacture and the distribution of Colono ware would be local. They believed that the pots could not easily be transported between parishes and that the potters could not produce enough to meet a regional demand. Rather, what we see is that there were different potters whose ceramics were sold on the north and south coasts with little facilitation by the planting class. Not only does this give us a lens to understanding enslaved craft production, it also gives us an ability to evaluate and track the flow of commodities with the enslaved's own economic system. The pots that were in Seville and St. Peter's Church were not in and of themselves mobile, nor was there a natural conservancy in their use. They were moved by people who were, in many cases, enslaved women, and whose mobility, at least in legislative terms, was circumscribed.

In Jamaica, the partial nature of the documentary record leaves much room for the interpretation of internal market exchange and pottery production. More so, the ethnographic evidence of contemporary potters in the Caribbean producing analogous ceramics points to small-scale production. An unstable market and an early-twentieth-century crash in the demand for pottery makes these links between contemporary potters and those that produced the archaeological ceramics tentative. Still, hints about the scale of pottery production and distribution can be gleaned from contemporary oral histories. Archaeological evidence indicates that ceramic production of yabbas, though highly variable, was focused in a limited number of locations for three centuries. Note that I do not indicate an exact provenance for the production of the ceramics. We don't know necessarily where they were made; we have only a good idea that ethnographic examples retrieved from Munchie's house yard have the same chemical constituency as ceramic group 3 and chemical group 2. The analysis described above gives us an answer, though partial, about the extent of commodity flow. To speculate from this set of archaeological data, our understanding of commodity flow has an enormous impact on our understanding of Jamaica's economy as a whole.

It goes beyond a question of extent, however. Maria das Dores Giaro da Cruz (2003) in her dissertation on Banda pottery production between the fifteenth and the twentiethth century provides an excellent model on how to incorporate empirically grounded sourcing studies into an analysis of social structure and political economy. Her study, which focused on the shifting trade relationship and its effect on the circuits through which local pottery traveled, interjects many implications in understandings of history and political economy (Stahl and das Dores Giaro da Cruz 1998; das Dores Giaro da Cruz 2003)—and how they configure and transform local ceramic industries.

The local street-market system employed by the enslaved population of Jamaica had formal and informal components that fed both internal and external markets. Not only did the enslaved population participate in this system, but planters, administrators, and merchants did as well. Mobility becomes a crucial variable in thinking about the status of this group. Clearly, women entrepreneurs, oftentimes enslaved, who traveled vast distances to trade their goods, played a key role in greasing the wheels of the Jamaican economy. Through this analysis, we are able to reimagine the "geography" of the enslaved's experience.

We are also left with some unresolved or archaeologically unanswerable questions. Was it the clay traded across the island, or was it the pottery? Were the potters afforded the same kind of mobility to hawk their wares, or was this an activity monopolized by the higglers of Jamaica? If we are to take Stahl's cautionary tale about demonstrating continuities to heart, then how do we explain the production of glazed yabbas? How also do we account for the demise of the industry that made "old-time yabbas" with the introduction of tin and aluminum crockery?

Epilogue

Boundaries and Identities

> As for money I am well assured from the Merchants that 150,000 is the least Quantity that is yearly sent here, and other provision, but not much now from any drapery or dry goods, that trade being lost to us by the great quantities supplied by the Dutch and French who can under sell us 40 p Ct and therefore have caused that trade to Cieze, and in all Appearance the Flower trade and provisions will fayle us too, if some way be not found to hinder it, and the profit of the merchants, and Imployment of our sloops and vessels lost to this island and by consequence much money also.
>
> C.O. 137: 1, e 2. Cited in Pitman [1917] 1945: 148.

It is impossible to essentialize the history or people of the Caribbean basin to one event, system, or social organization. But what can be said is that during the period immediately following Spanish colonization, huge transformations in demography took place—most notably the devastation of indigenous peoples due to forced labor and disease and their subsequent replacement by enslaved Africans. The primary concern of this book has been to understand how these people adapted to and transformed the cultural landscape around them using the systems of knowledge they brought with them and refashioned as they went along.

The ubiquitous presence of yabbas on archaeological sites associated with both plantation field hands and domestic servants speaks to the necessity of these wares in everyday life, but also to their availability. In archaeological sites on the north coast of Jamaica as well as in sites located on the south coast of Jamaica, these wares are present in significant numbers. As I have argued in this book, this pottery provides material evidence for the networks of informal trade in eighteenth-century Jamaica. Informal markets were basically a grey area of economic behavior conducted outside, or in competition with, the formal, state-sponsored economy. I find the complex networks that formed the informal markets interesting because they provided a potential mechanism for information to pass between the enslaved outside of the gaze of the planter. As I have indicated, these networks, and the transactions that took place through them, were poorly documented and based on barter and cash. Women were the primary participants, a factor that might also provide a reason why such networks and exchanges were outside of the gaze of the planter. Tracing the movements of goods through these internal markets illuminates a history of persons, networks, and economic exchanges that have been sidelined in the historical record. Indeed, the archaeology of black markets allows us to rethink, reimagine, and reconstruct the silences of the past (Trouillot 1995).

As I have argued in this book, the combination of historical and archaeological analysis indicates an economic system that extended between the north and south coasts of the island. Petrographic analysis of local earthenware shows that these ceramics did flow between the north and south coasts and were involved in a network of commodity trade. The scale of this network suggests that this economy, though in part supporting the plantation economy, also extended beyond it. This is in contrast to the planters' internal marketing system that was both localized and global in scale. The internal market economy was not, as some have argued, simply ancillary to the plantation economy. Rather than being a functionary of the global economic system, the informal market system must be seen as a partially articulated local economy with its own rules. Through their own independent production and labor, enslaved peoples engaged in market activities and created an arena for the development of social networks. These arenas also became places where individuals gained symbolic and material capital among their peers.

Pots made by the same people were found in Drax Hall, Seville, Juan de Bollas, Thetford, Old King's House, Old Naval Dockyard, and St. Peter's Church. The people who lived on these sites in the eighteenth century were of varied economic and social backgrounds. The one commonality that all of the residents of these sites shared was their access to the street markets and higglers of eighteenth-century Jamaica. While some of the residents bemoaned their dependence on these markets, this economy proved to be vital to maintaining and transforming the social landscape of Jamaica.

On Boundaries

In a sense, Jamaica in the eighteenth century was a created locality, where the colonizers did not have to negotiate with preexisting realms of power. Administrators could ostensibly create and control the institutions through which the enslaved population operated. Thus, the local in Jamaica should have been a near-perfect articulation of the global. The informal economy was hardly a perfect nexus between these two spheres. Though there is relatively little information on commodity flow, through petrographic analysis of the distribution of local pottery we can see that the markets moved beyond localized functions and were more an economic system through which the enslaved were able to negotiate their existences.

Planters, like the enslaved, were very much dependent on informal, ancillary economic activities through which they could overcome shortfalls in the production of their cash crops. One mechanism through which they mediated these island contingencies was heavy reliance on contraband trade. As major players in the circum-Caribbean trade, the mention of Dutch merchants became synonymous with contraband. Long complains of the Dutch:

> If the Dutch at Curucoa purchase and ship them [mules] to Jamaica, they seldom will take anything except cash in payment.... This drains away much of the old hammered silver, and the milled ryals; and indeed renders them so scarce, that it is to be feared, the want of them must some time prove distressful to the Negroes. (Long [1774] 1970: 549)

While this trade depleted the island of silver in all denominations, it was seen as minor compared to the effects of the internal markets.

This infuriated planters and magistrates like Edward Long, who had become cash-dependent:

> One of the greatest difficulties resulting from a scarcity of coin in this island is, that, although he may possess an estate worth fifty thousand pounds, he might not procure money enough to pay a sudden demand. (Long [1774] 1970 1:560)

For Long the answer was not to get rid of the internal market, but rather to standardize the market's currency. Long suggested the minting of a coin:

> These remarks may serve to show the utility of a copper coin; if it were only calculated for the relief of these poor people; such a coin would resemble the light money in one respect; it would not pass of the country, but it would not partake in any of its bad effects. (Long [1774] 1970 1: 573)

This, Long claimed, "would prevent those secret robberies committed on the public, by *clipping villains*" (emphasis in original, Long [1774] 1970 1: 561). Indeed, there were many reforms offered. One way suggested in the

Assembly was to establish a freemen's bank (Notes of the Assembly of Jamaica 1776). Currency would be taken out of the informal markets and placed back into the formal sector. None of these suggestions attempted to get rid of these markets.

The planters felt mistrust toward the markets. There was actual fiscal danger involved for those on the island with the existence of the markets. The fact that planters permitted and in some cases encouraged the markets might suggest that the planters were somewhat dependent on them. What Edward Long is complaining about here is that planters, while having wealth in real estate and credit, were actually quite cash-poor. They began to accrue debt locally because they did not have access to smaller denominations of currency. He felt that such debt diminished their standing locally and left them subject to "the advantages of malicious crafty and knavish men to the very great detriment of the planting interest" (Long [1774] 1970, 1: 564). Long is complaining about the merchants of the three towns, who, he felt, destroyed honest trade by employing a range of itinerant peddlers and selling contraband goods. The conspiracy of merchants and higglers is something that is very much present on the minds of the planters and the assemblyman writing the laws of Jamaica. Here we have an economy initially intended to supplement the plantation but extending very much beyond it.

The significance of this is several-fold. First, it was through these markets that the enslaved were able to create a bit of financial independence from the plantation context. To help illustrate the monetary scale of this economy, by 1774, 170,000 enslaved laborers, rural and urban, had amongst them £10,437 and 10 shillings in "small silver" (Long [1774] 1970, 1: 537). This translates into £0.06 per enslaved laborer. As a corollary to the above figure, it was through this economy that the enslaved were able to transgress to a certain degree the authority of the elites over them. Most of the island's small silver was taken out of circulation in the formal market and hoarded by the enslaved.

Long writes of capital in the hands of enslaved laborers:

> ... Negroes have been known to possess from £50 to £200 at their death; and few among them, that are at all industrious and frugal, lay up less than £20 or £30. For in this island they have the greatest part of the small silver circulating among them, which they gain by sale of their hogs, poultry, fish, corn, fruits, and other commodities, at markets in town and country. (Long [1774] 1970 2: 430)

Edward Long emphasizes here what a few exceptional individuals might be able to accrue in terms of material wealth in the course of their lifetime. The fact of the matter is that much of the island's currency, large and small, was in the hands of a very small white minority. The markets were ultimately part of the indeterminacies of everyday life for the enslaved. While they could accrue substantial wealth, more likely than not their earnings from the market were relegated to small, devalued denominations of coin.

However, although their earnings may have been small in economic terms, it is important to recognize the importance of these markets in the social and economic lives of the enslaved. The planters also needed the markets, even though, and most likely because, they extended beyond the planters' control. Legislation was only partly effective in curbing the impact that these markets had on the daily lives of enslaved laborers. And though attempts were made to formalize this side of the Jamaican economy, social relationships and economic conditions never permitted the full integration of this market with more global economic factors. Attempts to control the market had only partial success. While laws regarding tickets and scheduling were operationalized, these structures of control did not curb the extent to which the markets became important in the economy of the island as a whole.

As suggested in this book, possibly the greatest threat to the planter class came in what access to the markets afforded, namely a social space in which the enslaved could pass information and (re)create social networks on their own. These networks had the potential to form different kinds of communities—lived-in and imagined—at the interstices between law and practice. Trouillot states that subjects are those with the ability to define the terms under which situations can be described (1995: 23). The 1831 rebellion discussed in the introduction of the book was certainly one such circumstance. It was definitely not the first. There was constant struggle between the Crown and the Maroon communities. The 1760 slave rebellion in St. Mary parish and Westmoreland parish later came to be called Tacky's Rebellion. In 1799, slaves revolted in St. James parish. These rebellions required organization, leadership, and a material means through which information could be passed. The markets as a center of life among the enslaved and a locus of social networks were one such place where this information could have been passed. Because these were spaces outside the gaze of the planter that operated under rules they were unfamiliar with, leaders could develop both the social and material capital necessary for leading these struggles of resistance.

There is a historical irony when we turn our focus from the purely economic to the ways in which the actors were represented in the documentary record. For the planters, the markets were an economic headache, but a necessary evil. They were places that were for the most part unmanageable and unquantifiable. For historians, they are places that were vital, active, lively, but remarkably silent. While there is a considerable amount of text spent talking about the markets by contemporary observers, there are very few words actually spent on describing the markets. The planters were concerned, but ultimately they could not act. As Douglas Eggerton has said,

> Whether one chooses to regard the great planters of the western hemisphere to be calculating agrarian capitalists who operated their "factories in the field" according to commercial demand, or whether one sees them instead as fundamentally prebourgeois lords who participated in the larger Atlantic network even as they resisted its values and ideology, there remains the possibility that the slaves who entered into rebellion better understood the power of capital and its corrosive effect on the plantation regime, than did their masters. (2006: 364)

It has been argued that identity materializes from the deployment and rejection of power (Comaroff 1985, 1996). Women, as subjects of legal and narrative descriptions, were largely silenced in the documentary record but were simultaneously the primary actors in these markets. This becomes central to our understanding of both the overt and subtle forms of agency during the eighteenth and nineteenth centuries. What are generally configured as activities caught up in the indeterminacies of everyday life become crucial points of analysis in our understanding of creole society in Jamaica. As many authors have noted (Bush 1990; Beckles 1989a, 1991, 1995, 1999; Burnard 2004), women were able to acquire an enormous amount of power through their engagement in independent production. They played a large role not only in forging the material links for rebellions to be organized, but also in the way that they shaped the economic and social landscape of eighteenth-century Jamaica.

Although we know that the planters prided themselves on taming the landscape and creating an organized plantation space, the internal market systems of the Caribbean introduced disorder into the colonial landscapes. It initiated economic instability, at least from the planters' perspective, and its participants and their practices were discordant with administrator expectations. These were spaces that introduced disorder into the landscape and anxiety into the minds of the planters. In a description of market participants in 1825, a local Anglican minister and anti-slavery proponent, Rev. Richard Bickell, gives us a clue as to why this anxiety might exist:

> Jews with shops and standings as at a fair, selling old and new clothes, trinkets and small wares at cent. per cent. to adorn the Negro person; there were some low Frenchmen and Spaniards, and people of colour, in petty shops and with stalls; some selling their bad rum, gin, tobacco, etc.; others, salt provisions, and small articles of dress; and many bartering with the slave or purchasing his surplus provisions to retail again. (Bickell 1825: 66)

Here he defines in clear and unambiguous terms what Douglas (1966: 35) refers to as "inappropriate elements." The market participants here are considered anything but outstanding members of society. They were seen as extranational/extracolonial and therefore potentially undermining the political economy of the island. But what is of greater interest is that early on, these markets were seen as transnational spaces, which underscores the need to theorize these markets beyond island-specific ways.

As I have argued, the locus of this internal trade, in Jamaica at least, was a series of Sunday markets established by law to assist in the provisioning of enslaved laborers on the plantation and to facilitate the distribution of provision-ground produce to urban populations. Yet, in the above excerpt, the Reverend Bickell reveals that these markets clearly extended beyond this mandate, and he illuminates how these markets became transnational spaces that escaped colonial control. These spaces, which became dominated by enslaved and free peoples of African descent, were simultaneously inhabited by extracolonials exposing Jamaica to economic and potential political insecurity. In short, the markets were international spaces where their participants introduced disorder into the Jamaican landscape and regional goods into the internal commodity flow of Jamaica. Quotes like Bickell's here raise the question "How internal were the internal economies of Caribbean island colonies"?

On Identities

As mentioned earlier, a central problematic faced by those tackling topics in the African Diaspora is the inherent tension between an intellectual project which focuses on developing a corrective narrative and developing a "real" history of a people. On the one hand, its goal is to pay particular attention to past actors' subjectivity situated in historical forces. In this sense positionality becomes very important. On the other hand, the intellectual project attempts to redress silences in the historical pasts used in national narratives. The great hope of historical archaeology was that it could balance the relationships of power in the construction histories, alternative or otherwise, through a focus on material culture (Schmidt and Patterson 1995; Stahl 2001). The danger of this approach lies in the ways in which material culture becomes totemic to a people or set of actions. Meanings become imbued in things that can be anachronistic, much less merely metaphorical.

In the Caribbean, every century had its own histories and counterhistories. What becomes particularly problematic is the simple fact that many of those histories are used in the construction of past narrative without reference to the counterhistories. Historical subjects in Jamaica as elsewhere continually refashion themselves, and this refashioning has implications for how their histories are constructed by them and other discourses. The situatedness of this refashioning must be understood in the interpretation of material culture.

The research for this book began when historical archaeologists working on the African Diaspora were caught in a debate revolving primarily around what these pots meant. Which identity should we ascribe to their production and use? In the case of the debate, the pottery Leland Ferguson (1992) and others were discussing was Colono ware. That does not mean, however, that analogous debates did not occur in the Caribbean basin. Certainly in Jamaica, the presence of this tradition in archaeological and modern-day contexts constitutes for some a tangible link to Africa. Similarly in Martinique, analogous pottery has been used to establish material links with an indigenous Caribbean past. As touchstones that are actively being generated, they become important signifiers in the creation of local identities. Similarly, by focusing on the origins of this and analogous pottery traditions, we had missed the point. While pottery is plastic and could potentially lead us to stylistic interpretations of an Afro-Jamaican past, it is also a historical residue of the ways people mediated a political economy that simultaneously was a technology of control and a means of agency.

Certainly, if we look at Jamaica's history, particularly in the nineteenth century, we see that the possession or use of such pottery does not automatically assign itself to one ethnic group or another. In 1907 Rev. W. Bailey provided us with some tantalizing evidence as to why we should not reify a set of social relations from material culture (figure 7.1) in this picture entitled *Indian Girls Cooking Rice outside of House*. These women were

Figure 7.1. *Indian Girls Cooking Rice outside of House* by Rev. W. Bailey 1907. Courtesy of the Jamaica National Library.

either the daughters of indentured laborers who came from India or indentured servants themselves. As many scholars have noted, this was also a time when political and economic conflict between both African Jamaican and "East" Indian laborers began to develop. In a sense, physical and social boundaries were establishing themselves around the identities of these two laboring populations. If one examines the picture closely, one sees that the two young women are cooking rice in a yabba. This in and of itself shows how we cannot conflate the use of a particular item of material culture to a single group. What becomes interesting is the way in which the local pottery and markets became identified with a single group in Jamaica and how that is used to reinforce a history.

Circuits of History

In the course of this book, I have tried to demonstrate the links between archaeology and history in helping us to write another history of Jamaica. Specifically, I suggest that a greater place needs to be made for the consideration of how material culture both reflects the lived experiences of past peoples and raises questions about historical discourse (Stahl 2001). This project, as I have tried to show, can begin with the most unassuming of objects: clay pots, clay pots that were manufactured by enslaved laborers and their descendants. There is nothing of particular interest about these clay pots—their manufacture and use were not illegal, and the trade in them was not diabolical. Rather, what sets this pottery apart is its durable embodiment of the social relations in which the enslaved operated.

This pottery offers different and unique sets of lenses on the cultural experience of enslaved Jamaicans, the scales of its expression, and the historical forces that shaped it. First, these pots embody the techniques, the practical savoir-faire, the repeated gestures and inventiveness of their makers. These knowledges, however, extend beyond the material vessels, and connect us to broader cultural narratives of the Diaspora, conjuring, on the one hand, glimpses of African cultural ancestries, their resilience and plasticity against the grain of the Middle Passage; and, on the other hand, the networks of transmission of craft traditions, their social settings, their inscription in kinship, and gendered dimensions.

Second, we should emphasize that pots did not remain confined to the matrifocal household but became embedded in broader networks of exchange. They were exchanged, purchased, traded, and consumed over wide distances. Here, compositional analysis proved instrumental in showing (if only partially) the extent of these commercial activities. The clay pots moved, but not of themselves. They did so in fields of social relations. And so we are poised to retrieve the humans and the social forces guiding the actions behind the distributions of archaeological collections on the site level, the regional level, or even the oceanic scale. This should encourage us to avoid reifying ceramics as inert containers of identity or economic rationale, and rather to seek to understand them as strategic elements in human choices and interactions.

Third, these pots bring our attention to an important area in the field of social relations: the informal economy of "black markets." Here, in conjunction with documents, they indicate faintly the vibrancy of economic activities conducted at the margins of official economic terrains. In passing, they chip another myth: the "black market" as exclusively belonging to the unregulated realm of shadowy practices and illegal activity. The "black market" maintained a symbiotic (if tense) and mutually constitutive relationship with the "formal" economy. In this context, debate over the origin of black markets—in Europe or Africa—become moot, revealing instead a quintessentially transcultural field of practice, partaken in, unevenly mastered by, and differently understood by whites, blacks, and creoles.

Last, these debates and material encounters were not solely bound to the geographic contours of Jamaica. They radiated and resonated beyond the island to intersect with similar concerns and practices in the Caribbean and the metropole. In turn, it is impossible to understand these histories without resituating the Caribbean in the political economy and power plays of an emerging capitalist world system, moving and reshaping commodities, peoples, ideas, tastes, and desires at increasing speeds and decreasing costs across the world. Again, because material culture mediated global flows, anchoring them in human practice, it opens important insights on the local shaping of these global forces. Ceramic manufacture, petty commerce, and informal markets cannot be dissociated from metropolitan economic arithmetic and the requirements of plantation agro-industrial complexes. They do present a different slant on those relations. In turn, black markets and "colono-ceramics" hint at the world of commodity circuits and spheres of influence, blurring a neat cartography of colonial/national sovereignty between Caribbean islands. Once again, a consideration of materiality encourages caution with respect to accepted historical narratives, while creating a terrain for more emancipatory—yet never definite—pasts.

In redefining a certain problem-space (Scott 2004b: 4), objects not only retrieve certain silences of the past but pose new questions about the construction of Caribbean modernities—which are inextricable from the canonical history of Western modernity (Trouillot 2003). In using objects as my points of departure and subsequently tacking back and forth between the physical/chemical structure of vessels, historic documents, and material landscapes, my intention was to outline a history of Jamaica that moved beyond tired antinomies of repression and resistance, power and rebellion, master and slave, formal and informal economies, history and tradition, structure and agency, and so forth. Rather, I sought to show that, through the looking glass of materiality, histories look a lot messier. In this respect, this book can be seen as an attempt to explode the boundaries and identities which have been the basic units of analysis in historical archaeology.

Appendix A. Assignment of Samples from Sites to Ceramic Groups

I was able to draw several conclusions from the petrographic analysis of the ceramics. First, the technique of image analysis I employed was not sensitive enough to consistently and accurately describe the granulometric properties of detrital inclusions in the paste matrix. For this analysis I relied on primarily information retrieved from the point counting technique.

A.1. Assignment of Samples from Sites to Ceramic Groups

Ceramic Group	Drax Hall	Juan de Bollas	King's House	Naval Dockyard	St. Peter's	Seville Estate	Thetford Works
NA	092	083, 146	041, 095, 138	006, 062, 120	124	087, 148	
1			025	001, 164		089	
2	011, 032, 033, 093, 094, 149	031	005, 012, 038, 040, 098, 115, 118, 122, 134, 136, 139, 140, 143	017, 021, 047, 049, 061, 065, 066, 067, 068, 069, 071, 072, 074, 075, 163, 165	009, 015, 020, 044, 051, 055, 056, 057, 059, 151, 152, 153, 161, 162	035, 037, 086, 088, 090	080, 147
3	014	002, 023, 029, 084, 085, 145	010, 099, 116, 117, 129, 131, 132, 133, 135, 137, 141, 142	008, 016, 019, 046, 048, 060, 063, 073, 076, 125, 126, 127	018, 042, 043, 052, 053, 150, 155, 158	024, 036, 091	004, 007, 026, 027, 028, 077, 078, 081, 082
4	144	030	039, 097, 119, 130	013, 050, 064	054, 159	128	079
5	022	003	096, 121	045, 070	058, 123, 156, 157, 160	034	154

The composition of mineral inclusions in the paste of the ceramic, the textural properties of those inclusions, and the overall size distributions indicate that there are multiple recipes used in pottery manufacture in Jamaica. The recorded granulometric data and the bulk composition of the ceramics show that there is heterogeneity in the source materials. It also shows, however, that this heterogeneity is not related to the sites in which the pottery was excavated. In this appendix, I have cross-tabulated the sample number, the ceramic group to which the sample belongs, and the site from which it was excavated. These ceramic groups are described in chapter 6, and the sites are described in chapter 3.

In general, the two methods employed in this analysis—petrographic analysis conducted by myself in 2000 and INAA performed by Descantes, Speakman, and Glascock in 2005—have some amount of agreement in the degree of variation and the amount of recipes (see appendix B). In general, the majority of ceramics identified as chemical group 1 were identified as petrographic group 2 (n=15). Similarly the majority of ceramics identified as chemical group 2 were identified as petrographic group 3 (n=15). The correspondence is not perfect, however. Several samples identified as chemical group 1 were identified as petrographic groups 3 (n=1), group 4 (n=1), an Outlier (n=1), and NA (n=1). Several samples identified as chemical group 2 were also identified as petrographic groups 2 (n=2), 4 (n=4), 5 (n=5), and NA (n=1). With these two analytical techniques combined, there seems to be a high correlation between compositional groups and the archaeological types of ceramics recovered. In general, chemical group 1 ceramics and petrographic group 2 ceramics are glazed yabbas. Chemical group 2 and petrographic group 3 ceramics tend to be slipped yabbas. As was indicated above, chemical group 2 was considerably varied and might contain potential subgroups. Similarly, slipped yabbas are the most varied type of ceramic material. This could be a function of sampling error, but it also could suggest potential multiple locations of manufacture. However, the fact that five of the slipped yabba samples are grouped as chemical group 2 and petrographic group 5 supports the possibility that there are potential sub groups that are captured using qualitative and semi-quantitative techniques like ceramic petrography and point-counting that are not statistically significant from the larger group. This might indicate variation in the recipes employed by the potters or the sources the potters used.

Appendix B. Instrumental Neutron Activation Analysis of Eighteenth-Century Pottery from Jamaica

Christophe Descantes and Michael D. Glascock

Introduction

Fifty-one ceramic specimens from eighteenth-century archaeological contexts in Jamaica were submitted for neutron activation analysis (NAA) at the University of Missouri Research Reactor Center (MURR). The ceramic specimens submitted by Mark Hauser of DePaul University comprise sherds representing three types from eight archaeological sites (Drax Hall, Juan de Bollas, Munchie, Old King's House, Old Naval Dockyard, Saint Peter's Church, Seville, Thetford) in Jamaica's central corridor. The goal of this analysis is to establish a baseline of chemical data for understanding the transformation of local economic behavior among enslaved and freed people of African descent. The sample preparation and analytical techniques used at MURR and the analytical results of the compositional analysis are reported here.

Sample Preparation

The ceramics were prepared for NAA using standard MURR procedures. Pieces of each sherd were burred with a silicon carbide burr to remove painted or slipped surfaces and adhering soil. The burred sherd samples were then washed with de-ionized water and allowed to dry in air. These were then crushed in an agate mortar to yield a fine powder. Where possible a portion of each specimen was retained, unpowdered, for the MURR archive of analyzed ceramic fabrics.

The powder samples were oven-dried at 100 degrees C for 24 hours. Portions of approximately 150 mg were weighed and placed in small polyvials used for short irradiations. At the same time, 200 mg of each sample were weighed into high-purity quartz vials used for long irradiations. Along with the unknown samples, reference standards of SRM-1633a (coal fly ash) and SRM-688 (basalt rock) were similarly prepared, as were quality control samples (e.g., standards treated as unknowns) of SRM-278 (obsidian rock) and Ohio Red Clay.

Irradiation and Gamma-Ray Spectroscopy

Neutron activation analysis of ceramics at MURR, which consists of two irradiations and a total of three gamma counts, constitutes a superset of the procedures used at most other laboratories (Glascock 1992; Neff 1992, 2000). As discussed in detail by Glascock (1992), a short irradiation is carried out through the pneumatic tube irradiation system. Samples in the polyvials are sequentially irradiated, two at a time, for five seconds at a neutron flux of 8×10^{13} n cm^{-2} s^{-1}.

The 720-second count yields gamma spectra containing peaks for nine short-lived elements: aluminum (Al), barium (Ba), calcium (Ca), dysprosium (Dy), potassium (K), manganese (Mn), sodium (Na), titanium (Ti), and vanadium (V). The samples encapsulated in quartz vials are subjected to a 24-hour irradiation at a neutron flux 5×10^{13} n cm^{-2} s^{-1}. This long irradiation is analogous to the single irradiation utilized at most other laboratories. After the long irradiation, samples decay for seven days, and then are counted for 1,800 seconds (the "middle count") on a high-resolution germanium detector coupled to an automatic sample changer. The middle count yields determinations of seven medium half-life elements, namely, arsenic (As), lanthanum (La), lutetium (Lu), neodymium (Nd), samarium (Sm), uranium (U), and ytterbium (Yb). After an additional three- or four-week decay, a final count of 9,000 seconds is carried out on each sample. The latter measurement yields the following 17 long half-life elements: cerium (Ce), cobalt (Co), chromium (Cr), cesium (Cs), europium (Eu), iron (Fe), hafnium (Hf), nickel (Ni), rubidium (Rb), antimony (Sb), scandium (Sc), strontium (Sr), tantalum (Ta), terbium (Tb), thorium (Th), zinc (Zn), and zirconium (Zr).

Elemental concentration data from the two irradiations and three counts (a total of 33 elements) are assembled into a single tabulation and stored in a dBASE III file along with descriptive information available for each sample.

Quantitative Analysis of the Chemical Data

The analyses at MURR described above produced elemental concentration values for 33 elements in most of the analyzed samples. As is customary in ceramic provenance studies at MURR (Bishop and Neff 1989), the data were converted to base-10 logarithms of concentrations. Use of log concentrations instead of raw data compensates for differences in magnitude between major elements, such as iron, on the one hand, and trace elements, such as the rare earth or lanthanide elements, on the other hand. Transformation to base-10 logarithms also yields a more nearly normal distribution for many trace elements.

The goal of quantitative analysis of the chemical data is to recognize compositionally homogeneous groups within the analytical database. Based on the "provenance postulate" (Weigand, Harbottle, and Sayre 1977), such groups are assumed to represent geographically restricted sources or source zones. The location of sources or source zones may be inferred by comparing the unknown groups to knowns (source raw materials) or by indirect means. Such indirect means include the "criterion of abundance" (Bishop, Rands, and Holley 1982) or arguments based on geological and sedimentological characteristics (e.g., Steponaitis, Blackman, and Neff 1996).

Initial hypotheses about source-related subgroups in the compositional data can be derived from noncompositional information (e.g., archaeological context, decorative attributes, etc.) or from application of pattern-recognition techniques to the chemical data. Principal components analysis (PCA) is one technique that can be used to recognize patterns (i.e., subgroups) in compositional data. PCA provides new reference axes that are arranged in decreasing order of variance subsumed. The data can be displayed on combinations of these new axes, just as they can be displayed relative to the original elemental concentration axes. PCA can be used in a pure pattern-recognition mode (i.e., to search for subgroups in an undifferentiated data set) or in a more evaluative mode (i.e., to assess the coherence of hypothetical groups suggested by other criteria, such as archaeological context, decoration, etc.). Generally, compositional differences between specimens can be expected to be larger for specimens in different groups than for specimens in the same group, and this implies that groups should be detectable as distinct areas of high point density on plots of the first few components.

One often-exploited strength of PCA, discussed by Baxter (1991) and Neff (1994), is that it can be applied as a simultaneous R- and Q-mode technique, with both variables (elements) and objects (individual analyzed samples) displayed on the same set of principal component reference axes. The two-dimensional plot of element coordinates on the first two principal components is the best possible two-dimensional representation of the correlation or variance-covariance structure in the data. Small angles between vectors from the origin to variable coordinates indicate strong positive correlation; angles close to 90 degrees indicate no correlation; and angles close to 180 degrees indicate negative correlation. Likewise, the plot of object coordinates is the best two-dimensional representation of Euclidean relations among the objects in log-concentration space (if the PCA was based on the variance-covariance matrix) or standardized log-concentration space (if the PCA was based on the correlation matrix). Displaying objects and variables on the same plots makes it possible to observe the contributions of specific elements to group separation and to the distinctive shapes of the various groups. Such a plot is called a "biplot" in reference to the simultaneous plotting of objects and variables. The variable interrelationships inferred from a biplot can be verified directly by inspection of bivariate elemental concentration plots (note that a bivariate plot of elemental concentrations is not a "biplot").

Whether a group is discriminated easily from other groups can be evaluated visually in two dimensions or statistically in multiple dimensions. A metric known as Mahalanobis distance (or generalized distance) makes it possible to describe the separation between groups or between individual points and groups on multiple dimensions. The Mahalanobis distance of a specimen from a group centroid (Sayre 1975; Bieber et al. 1976; Harbottle 1976; Bishop and Neff 1989; Neff 2001) is:

$$D^2_{y,X} = [y-\bar{X}]^t I_X [y-\bar{X}]$$

Also $\bar{X}$ is X

where y is $1 \times m$ array of logged elemental concentrations for the individual point of interest, X is then the $n \times m$ data matrix of logged concentrations for the group to which the point is being compared with $\bar{X}$ being its $1 \times m$

centroid, and I_x is the inverse of the m × m variance-covariance matrix of group X. Because Mahalanobis distance takes into account variances and covariances in the multivariate group, it is analogous to expressing distance from a univariate mean in standard deviation units. Like standard deviation units, Mahalanobis distances can be converted into probabilities of group membership for each individual specimen (e.g., Bieber et al. 1976; Harbottle 1976). For relatively small sample sizes, it is appropriate to base probabilities on Hotelling's T^2, which is a multivariate extension of the univariate Student's t.

Mahalanobis-distance-based probabilities of group membership may fluctuate dramatically depending on whether or not each specimen is assumed to be a member of the group to which it is being compared. Harbottle (1976) calls this phenomenon "stretchability," in reference to the tendency of an included specimen to stretch the group in the direction of its own location in the elemental concentration space. This problem can be circumvented by cross-validation (or "jackknifing"), that is, by removing each specimen from its presumed group before calculating its own probability of membership (Baxter 1994; Leese and Main 1994). This is a conservative approach to group evaluation that sometimes excludes true group members. All probabilities discussed below are cross-validated.

In the present case, all but one of the groups is smaller than the total number of variates, and this places a further constraint on use of Mahalanobis distance. With more variates than objects, the group variance-covariance matrix is singular, thus rendering calculation of I_x (and $D2$ itself) impossible. Dimensionality of the groups therefore must be reduced somehow. One approach to dimensionality reduction would be to eliminate elements considered irrelevant or redundant.

The problem with this approach is that the investigator's preconceptions about which elements should best discriminate sources may not be valid; it also squanders one of the major strengths of NAA, namely, its capability to determine a large number of elements simultaneously. An alternative approach to dimensionality reduction, used here, is to calculate Mahalanobis distances not with log concentrations but with scores on principal components extracted from the variance-covariance or correlation matrix of the complete data set. This approach entails only the assumption, entirely reasonable in light of the above discussion of PCA, that most group-separating differences should be visible on the largest several components. Unless a data set is highly complex, with numerous distinct groups, using enough components to subsume 90 percent of total variance in the data may be expected to yield Mahalanobis distances that approximate Mahalanobis distances in the full elemental concentration space.

Results and Conclusion

Exploratory data analyses were conducted on the thirty-three elemental abundance measurements of these ceramic specimens before identifying compositional groups. It was decided to drop the elemental concentrations of nickel from subsequent analyses because of its absence in most samples. The elimination of nickel measurements is not uncommon in the chemical analysis of ceramics. In addition, specimens JAM016 and JAM049 were not

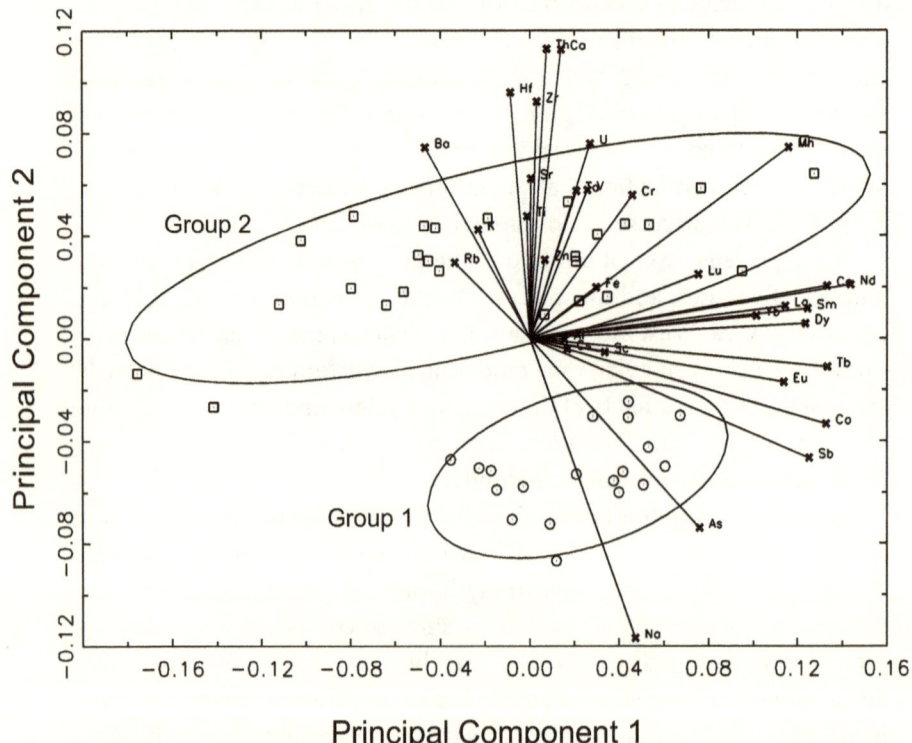

Figure B.1. Bivariate plot of principal components 1 and 2 displaying two compositional groups. Ellipses represent 90 percent confidence level for membership in the groups. Vectors denote elemental influences on the ceramic data. Unassigned specimens are not shown.

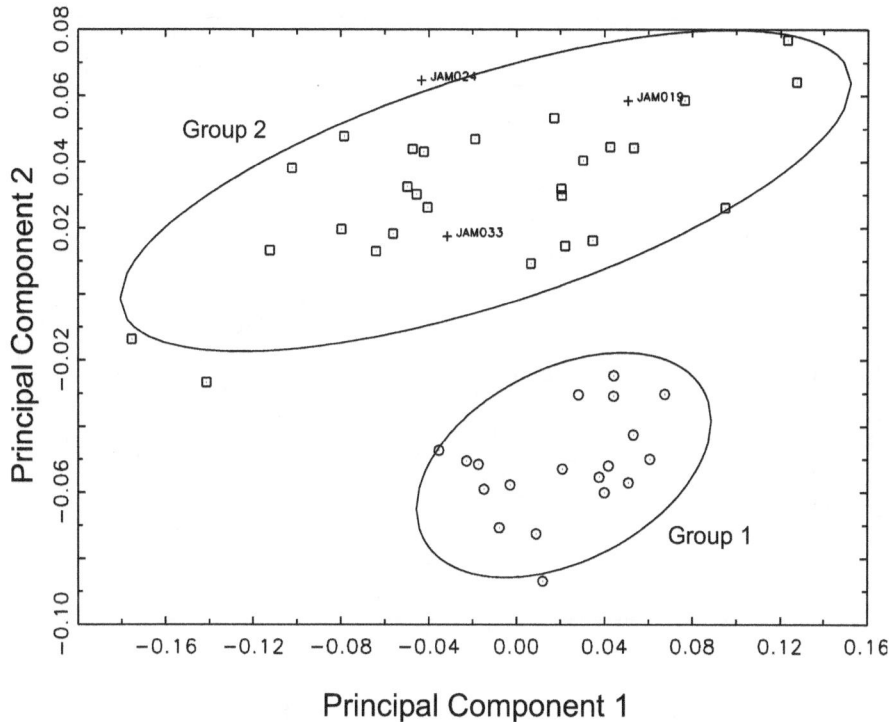

Figure B.2. Bivariate plot of principal components 1 and 2 displaying two compositional groups and labeled unassigned specimens (+). Ellipses represent 90 percent confidence level for membership in the groups.

used in the identification of compositional groups because some of their elemental abundances were considered outliers.

A two-group structure was identified in the ceramic specimens: Group 1 ($n = 19$) and Group 2 ($n = 27$). The compositional groups can be graphically represented in principal component space (see figures B.1–B.2) and in elemental space (see figures B.3–B.4). Ellipses in the figures represent 90 percent confidence intervals.

Statistical tests based on Mahalanobis-distance-derived probabilities using seven principal components were conducted subsuming 89.9 percent of the total variance (see table B.1) to support the graphical representation of the group structure (figures B.1–B.4). A cut-off of 1 percent was generally used to refine the membership of the groups; however, exceptions were made based on the graphical representation of the data. Three specimens

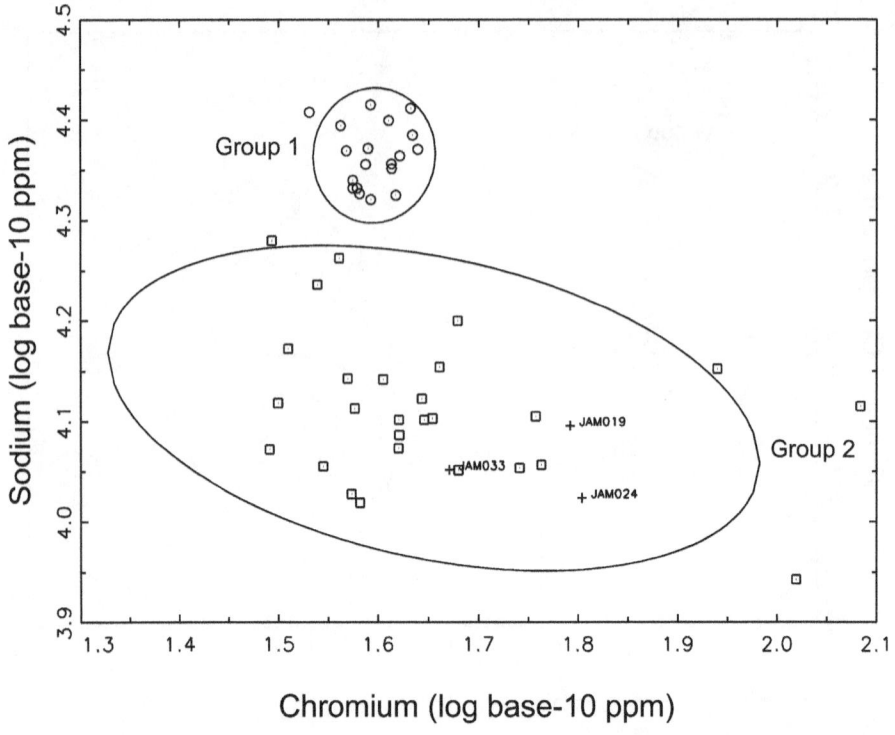

Figure B.3. Bivariate plot of base-10 logged chromium and sodium concentrations showing the chemical distinctiveness of the two compositional groups. Ellipses represent 90 percent confidence level for membership in the groups. Unclassified samples (+) are labeled.

(6%) could not be assigned to any of the identified compositional groups (see figures B.2–B.4; table B.4).

Chemical characteristics for the two compositional groups are represented in figure B.1. Group 1, a distinct compositional group, tends to be enriched in sodium relative to compositional group 2. Note that group 1 may comprise subgroups (see figure B.5). Group 1a is characterized by enriched sodium concentrations and depleted arsenic concentrations when compared to group 1b. We have decided to "lump" instead of "split" compositional group 1 because there does not appear to be any archaeological meaning to splitting this group at the moment. Compositional group 2 subsumes much chemical variability and is enriched in hafnium and thorium

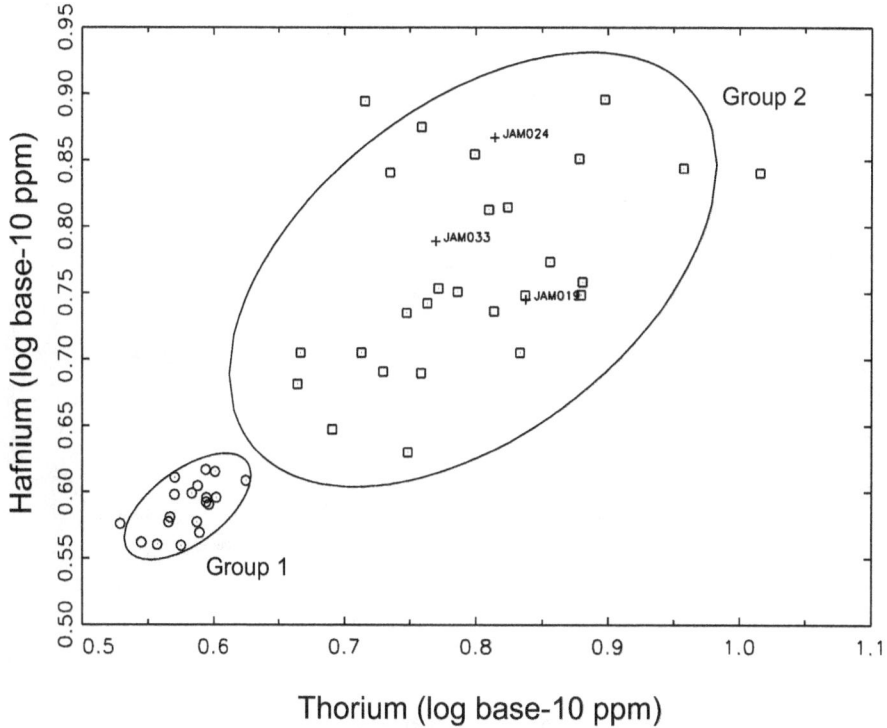

Figure B.4. Bivariate plot of base-10 logged thorium and hafnium concentrations showing the chemical distinctiveness of the two compositional groups. Ellipses represent 90 percent confidence level for membership in the groups. Unclassified samples (+) are labeled.

when compared to compositional group 1. It is highly probable that analyzing more samples will allow us to identify subgroups within group 2.

At this early stage, it is difficult to ascertain what the chemical compositional groups represent. Determining whether the identified compositional groups refer to local or exotic sources will require the submission of raw clay samples for chemical analysis or the mineralogical analysis of raw clay samples. However, using the criterion of abundance, defined above, it is safe to assume that both compositional groups are of local origin and that chemical differences are attributable to different local sources of raw clay, different ceramic recipes, diverse uses, or a combination of all these potential factors.

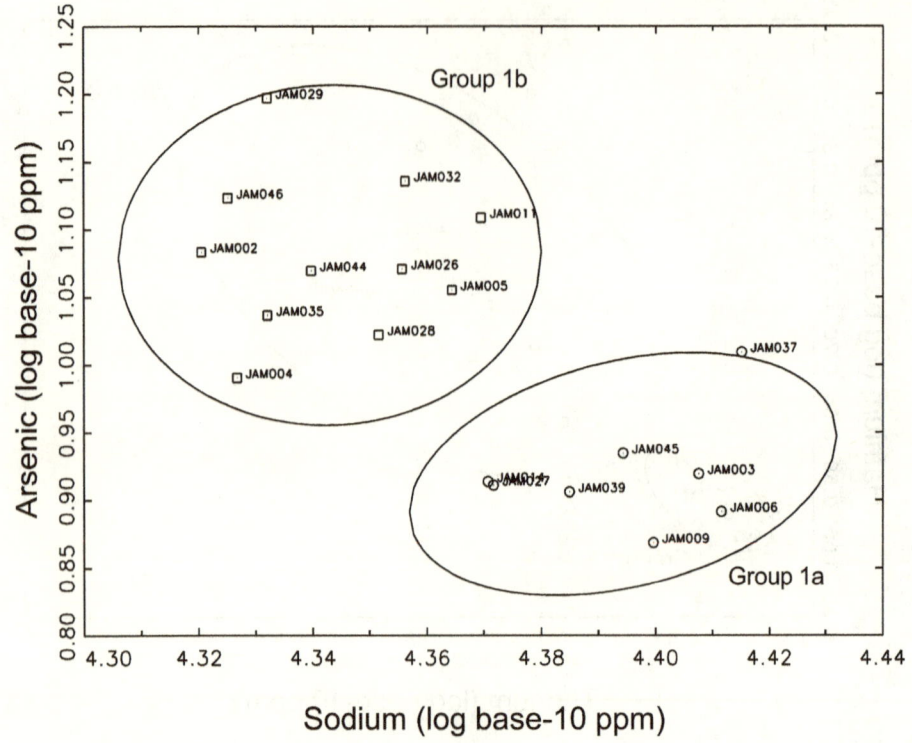

Figure B.5. Bivariate plot of base-10 logged sodium and arsenic concentrations showing two possible subgroups within compositional group 1. Ellipses represent 90 percent confidence level for membership in the groups. Unclassified samples (+) are labeled.

Despite the large membership of the compositional groups, tentative patterns can be identified when investigating the decoration of the sherd members in each group (see table B.5). Compositional group 1 members are predominantly yabbas with internal glazing, whereas compositional group 2 members tend to be vertical pots with slipping and burnishing for decoration. We analyzed the glazed surface of specimen JAM002, a member of compositional group 1, with a nondestructive energy dispersive X-Ray fluorescence (EDXRF) spectrometer and found the glaze chemical composition to have high concentrations of lead.

Ceramic specimens from six of the eight sites have membership in both compositional groups. Two sites have ceramics that belong only to compositional group 2. But for two unassigned specimens, all of the sherds collected from the slave village contexts of the site of Thetford have membership in

Table B.1. Principal Components Analysis of 49 Specimens. Simultaneous R-q Factor Analysis Based on Variance-Covariance Matrix

PCs	Eigenvalue	%Variance Cum.	%Var.
1	0.1944	37.7393	37.7393
2	0.1046	20.3006	58.0399
3	0.0634	12.3106	70.3505
4	0.0391	7.5864	77.9369
5	0.0255	4.9486	82.8854
6	0.0216	4.1891	87.0745
7	0.0148	2.8682	89.9427
8	0.0100	1.9327	91.8754
9	0.0081	1.5765	93.4519
10	0.0067	1.3053	94.7572
11	0.0046	0.8851	95.6423
12	0.0033	0.6446	96.2869
13	0.0032	0.6180	96.9049
14	0.0027	0.5262	97.4311
15	0.0021	0.4072	97.8383
16	0.0020	0.3920	98.2303
17	0.0017	0.3339	98.5642
18	0.0013	0.2507	98.8149
19	0.0013	0.2466	99.0615
20	0.0009	0.1761	99.2377
21	0.0008	0.1514	99.3891
22	0.0007	0.1424	99.5315
23	0.0005	0.1002	99.6316
24	0.0005	0.0895	99.7211
25	0.0004	0.0831	99.8042
26	0.0004	0.0706	99.8748
27	0.0002	0.0379	99.9127
28	0.0002	0.0355	99.9482
29	0.0001	0.0249	99.9731
30	0.0001	0.0125	99.9856
31	0.0001	0.0104	99.9959
32	0.0000	0.0041	100.0000

compositional group 2. Except for a single specimen that was considered an outlier and not included in the study, ceramic sherd specimens from the ethnographic contexts of the site of Munchie belong only to compositional group 2.

In sum, this study has identified two distinct ceramic compositional groups. Possible tendencies or associations between the chemical compositions of the sherds, their provenience, and their ceramic decorative styles were identified. The submission of more samples from these contexts could further test these identified patterns as well as delineate more groups and subgroups.

Table B.2. Mahalanobis-distance-calculated Probabilities and Posterior Classification for Compositional Group 1 Members Using Seven Principal Components

ID NO	Group 1	Group 2	ID NO	Group 1	Group 2
JAM002	17.973	0.066	JAM003	60.488	0.005
JAM004	65.867	0.001	JAM005	84.854	0.010
JAM006	87.167	0.007	JAM009	13.137	0.066
JAM011	0.190	0.581	JAM014	83.885	0.085
JAM026	61.527	0.080	JAM027	59.237	0.094
JAM028	90.803	0.002	JAM029	2.912	0.706
JAM032	44.096	0.050	JAM035	57.921	0.014
JAM037	33.983	0.009	JAM039	97.508	0.014
JAM044	53.612	0.001	JAM045	4.636	0.000
JAM046	82.935	0.002			

Note: Probabilities are jackknifed for specimens included in each group. Jackknifing, or cross-validation, is a conservative approach that removes each specimen from its presumed group before calculating its own probability of membership.

Table B.3. Mahalanobis-distance-calculated Probabilities and Posterior Classification for Compositional Group 2 Members Using 7 Principal Components

ID NO.	Group 1	Group 2	ID NO.	Group 1	Group 2
JAM001	0.012	89.686	JAM007	0.000	64.300
JAM008	0.003	70.879	JAM010	0.001	86.949
JAM012	0.008	46.391	JAM013	0.001	37.019
JAM015	0.001	95.267	JAM017	0.015	86.962
JAM018	0.091	5.163	JAM020	0.001	68.181
JAM021	0.044	71.173	JAM022	0.055	70.719
JAM023	0.003	84.718	JAM025	0.000	43.345
JAM030	0.000	22.161	JAM031	0.000	21.844
JAM034	0.011	8.731	JAM036	0.000	16.456
JAM038	0.000	5.028	JAM040	0.009	4.618
JAM041	0.000	19.377	JAM042	0.430	55.531
JAM043	0.000	66.382	JAM047	0.000	58.717
JAM048	0.000	64.093	JAM050	0.002	63.158
JAM051	0.001	36.263			

Note: Probabilities are jackknifed for specimens included in each group. Jackknifing, or cross-validation, is a conservative approach that removes each specimen from its presumed group before calculating its own probability of membership.

Table B.4. Mahalanobis-distance-calculated Probabilities and Posterior Classification for Unassigned Specimens into Groups 1 and 2 Using Seven Principal Components

ID NO.	Group 1	Group 2
JAM019	0.002	0.008
JAM024	0.000	0.719
JAM033	0.001	0.556

Table B.5. Compositional Group Membership and Decoration

Compositional Group	Glazed Yabba	Slipped & Burnished Yabba	Untreated Yabba
Group 1	16	3	0
Group 2	3	19	2

Bibliography

Agorsah, E. K. 1983. *An Ethnoarchaeological Study of Settlement and Behavior Patterns of a West African Traditional Society: The Nchumuru of Banda-wiae in Ghana.* Ph.D. diss., Department of Anthropology, University of California, Los Angeles. Ann Arbor, Mich.: University Microfilms.
———. 1985. Excavations in the northern Volta Basin. *West African Journal of Archaeology* 15: 11–40.
———. 1990. Ethnoarchaeology: The search for a self-corrective approach to the study of past human behavior. *African Archaeological Review* 8: 189–208.
———. 1992. Archaeology and Maroon heritage. *Jamaica Journal* 22: 2–9.
———. 1994. *Maroon Heritage: Archaeological, Ethnographic and Historical Perspectives.* Kingston: Canoe Press, University of the West Indies.
Akinade, O. 1995. Pottery production at Ogga, Kogi state. *Nigerian Heritage* 4: 113–23.
Akinwumi, O. 2001. Ceramic spheres and regional networks in the Yoruba-Edo region, Nigeria, 13th–19th centuries A.D. *Ethnohistory* 38(3): 250–75.
Allen, C. 2002. Creole: The problem of definition. In *Questioning Creole: Creolisation Discourses in Caribbean Culture*, edited by V. Shepherd and G. Richards, pp. 47–63. Kingston: Ian Randle.
Alleyne, M. 1988. *Roots of Jamaican Culture.* London: Pluto Press.
Allsworth-Jones, P. 1996. Continuity and change in Yoruba pottery. *School of Oriental and African Studies Bulletin* 59: 312–22.
Altink, H. 2005. Deviant and dangerous: Pro-slavery representations of Jamaican slave women's sexuality, c. 1780–1834. *Slavery and Abolition* 26(2): 271–88.
Ames, K. M. 1995. Chiefly power and household production on the Northwest Coast. In *Foundations of Social Inequality*, edited by T. D. Price and G. M. Feinman, pp. 155–87. New York: Plenum Press.
Anderson, J. 1971. *A Solid Sufficiency: An Ethnography of Yeoman Foodways in Stuart England.* Ph.D. diss., University of Pennsylvania Folklore and Folklife Department. Ann Arbor, Mich.: University Microfilms.
Anonymous. 1797. Characteristic traits of the Creolian and African Negroes in Jamaica. *Columbia Magazine or Monthly Miscellany* 1 (11, 12); 2 (April–June). Photocopy located at the Syracuse University Archaeological Research Center. Provided by the National Library of the Institute of Jamaica.
———. 1823. Condition of the Negroes in our colonies. *Quarterly Review* 29(58): 475–508.
Anquandah, J. 1982. *Recovering Ghana's Past.* Accra: Longman.

Anstey, R. 1975. *The Atlantic Slave Trade and British Abolition, 1760–1810*. Atlantic Highlands, N.J.: Humanities Press.

Armstrong, D. V. 1983. *The "Old Village" at Drax Hall Plantation: An Archeological Examination of an Afro-Jamaican Settlement.* Ph.D. diss., University of California, Los Angeles. Ann Arbor, Mich.: University Microfilms.

———. 1990. *The Old Village and the Great House: An Archaeological and Historical Examination of Drax Hall Plantation, St. Ann's Bay, Jamaica.* Blacks in the New World. Urbana: University of Illinois Press.

———. 1991a. The Afro-Jamaican community at Drax Hall. *Jamaica Journal* 24(1): 3–8.

———. 1991b. Recovering an early 18th-century Afro-Jamaican community: Archaeology of the slave village at Seville, Jamaica. Paper presented at the Thirteenth International Congress for Caribbean Archaeology, Curacao, Netherlands Antilles.

———. 1991c. The Afro-Jamaican house-yard: An archaeological and ethnohistorical perspective. *The Florida Journal of Anthropology* Special Publication 7: 51–63.

———. 1992. African-Jamaican housing at Seville: A study of spatial transformation. *Archaeology Jamaica* 6: 51–63.

———. 1998. Cultural transformation within enslaved labor communities in the Caribbean. In *Studies in Culture Contact: Interaction, Culture Change, and Archaeology*, edited by J. G. Cusick, pp. 378-401. Carbondale: Southern Illinois University Center for Archaeological Investigations.

———. 1999. Archaeology and ethnohistory of the Caribbean plantation. In *"I, too, am America": Archaeological Studies of African-American Life*, edited by T. A. Singleton, pp. 173–92. Charlottesville: University Press of Virginia.

———. 2003. *Creole Transformation from Slavery to Freedom: Historical Archaeology of the East End Community, St. John, Virgin Islands.* Gainesville: University Press of Florida.

Armstrong, D. V., and M. L. Fleischman. 2003. House-yard burials of enslaved laborers in eighteenth-century Jamaica. *International Journal of Historical Archaeology* 7(1): 33–65.

Armstrong, D. V., and M. W. Hauser. 2004. An East Indian laborers' household in nineteenth-century Jamaica: A case for understanding cultural diversity through space, chronology and material culture analysis. *Historical Archaeology* 38(2): 9–21.

Armstrong, D. V., M. W. Hauser, and D. Knight. 2005. The Early Shoreline Settlement at Cinnamon Bay, St. John, USVI: Before Formal Colonization to the Slave Rebellion of 1733. Paper presented at the XX Congreso International de Arqueologia del Caribe, Santo Domingo, Dominican Republic.

Armstrong, D., and K. G. Kelly. 2000. Settlement patterns and the origins of African Jamaican society: Seville Plantation, St. Ann's Bay, Jamaica. *Ethnohistory* 47(2): 369–94.

Arnold, D. E. 1985. *Ceramic Theory and Cultural Process.* Cambridge and New York: Cambridge University Press.

———. 1993. *Ecology and Ceramic Production in an Andean Community.* Cambridge and New York: Cambridge University Press.

———. 1999. Advantages and disadvantages of vertical half-molding technology: Implications for production organization. In *Pottery and People: A Dynamic Interaction*, edited by J. Skibo and G. M. Feinman, pp. 59–80. Salt Lake: University of Utah Press.

Arnold, D. E., H. Neff, and R. L. Bishop. 1991. Compositional analysis and "sources" of pottery: An ethnoarcheological approach. *American Anthropologist* 93(1): 70–90.

Arnold, P. J. 1991. *Domestic Ceramic Production and Spatial Organization: A Mexican Case Study in Ethnoarchaeology*. Cambridge and New York: Cambridge University Press.

Arthur, J. W. 2002. Pottery use-alteration as an indicator of socioeconomic status: An ethnoarchaeological study of the Gamo of Ethiopia. *Journal of Archaeological Method and Theory* 9(4): 331–55.

Atherton, J. 1983. Ethnonoarchaeology in Africa. *African Archaeological Review* 1: 75–104.

Austin, R. A., and W. Smith. 1992. Private tooth decay as public economic virtue: The slave-sugar triangle, consumerism and European industrialization. In *The Atlantic Slave Trade*, edited by J. Inikori and S. L. Engerman, pp. 183–240. Durham, N.C.: Duke University Press.

Bailey, B. V. 1970. *Jamaican Clay Deposits*. Economic Geology Report No. 3. Kingston: Geological Survey Department.

Barclay, A. [1828] 1969. *A Practical View of the Present State of Slavery in the West Indies*. Miami: Mnemosyne.

Bareis, C. J., and J. W. Porter. 1965. Megascopic and petrographic analyses of a foreign pottery vessel from the Cahokia site. *American Antiquity* 31(1): 95–101.

Barley, N. 1994. *Smashing Pots: Works of Clay from Africa*. Washington, D.C.: Smithsonian Institution Press.

Baxter, M. J. 1991. Archaeological uses of the biplot—a neglected technique? In *Computer Applications and Quantitative Methods in Archaeology*, edited by G. Lock and J. Moffett, pp. 141–48. BAR International Series S577. Oxford: Tempvs Reparatvm, Archaeological and Historical Associates.

———. 1994. Stepwise discriminant analysis in archaeometry: A critique. *Journal of Archaeological Science* 21: 59–74.

Beaudry, M. C. 2008. "Above vulgar economy": The intersection of historical archaeology and microhistory in writing archaeological biographies of two New England merchants. In *Small Worlds: Method and Meaning in Microhistory*, edited by J. F. Brooks, C. DeCorse, and J. Walton, pp. 173–98. Santa Fe, N.Mex.: School of Advanced Research.

Beckford, W. D. 1790. *A descriptive account of the island of Jamaica: With remarks upon the cultivation of the sugar-cane, throughout the different seasons of the year, and chiefly considered in a picturesque point of view; also, observations and reflections upon what would probably be the consequences of an abolition of the slave-trade, and of the emancipation of the slaves*. 2 vols. London: Printed for T. and J. Egerton.

Beckles, H. 1989a. *Natural Rebels: A Social History of Enslaved Black Women in Barbados*. New Brunswick, N.J.: Rutgers University Press.

———. 1989b. Slaves and the internal market economy of Barbados. *Historia y Sociedad* 2: 9–31.

———. 1991. An economic life of their own: Slaves as commodity producers and distributors in Barbados. In *The Slaves Economy: Independent Production by Slaves in the Americas*, edited by I. Berlin and P. D. Morgan, pp. 31–47. London: Frank Cass

———. 1995. Sex and gender in the historiography of Caribbean slavery. In *Engendering History: Caribbean Women in Historical Perspective*, edited by V. B. Shepherd, B. Brereton, and B. Bailey, pp. 125–40. New York: St. Martin's Press.

———. 1999. *Centering Women: Gender Discourses in Caribbean Slave Society*. Kingston: Ian Randle.

Beckwith, M. W. 1929. *Black Roadways: A Study of Jamaican Folk Life*. Chapel Hill: University of North Carolina Press.

Belisario, I. M. 1838. Sketches of Character, In Illustration of the Habits, Occupation, and Costume of the Negro Population, in the Island of Jamaica, Drawn from Nature and in Lithography. Kingston: Isaac M. Belisario.

Bellin, J. N. 1758. *Carte de l'Isle de Jamaique*. Paris.

Bellis, J. 1972. Archaeology and the culture history of the Akan of Ghana: A case study. Ph.D. diss., Indiana University, Bloomington.

———. 1982. *The "Place of Pots" in Akan Funerary Custom*. Bloomington: African Studies Program, Indiana University.

Bennett, J. Harry. 1964. Cary Helyar, merchant and planter of seventeenth-century Jamaica. *The William and Mary Quarterly* 21(1): 53–76.

Berlin, I., and P. D. Morgan (editors). 1995. *The Slaves' Economy: Independent Production by Slaves in the Americas*. London and Portland, Oreg.: Frank Cass.

Berns, M. C. 1993. Art, history, and gender: Women and clay in West Africa. *African Archaeological Review* 11: 129–48.

Best, L. 1998. Outlines of a model of pure plantation economy (after twenty-five years). *Marronage* 1: 27–40.

Best, L., and K. Levitt. 1967. Externally Propelled Growth in the Caribbean: Selected Essays. Mimeo. Montreal: McGill Centre for Developing Area Studies, McGill University.

Betts, I. M. 1991. Thin-section and neutron activation analysis of brick and tile from York and its surrounding sites. In *Recent Developments in Ceramic Petrology*, edited by A. Middleton and I. Freestone, pp. 39–55. British Occasional Paper No. 81. London: British Museum.

Beuze, L.-R. 1990. La poterie en Martinique. *Cahiers du patrimoine* 7: 39–46.

Bickell, Reverend R. 1825. *The West Indies as They are: Or, A Real Picture of Slavery*. Jamaica: Printed for J. Hatchard and Son [etc.].

Bieber, A.M.J., W. D. Brooks, G. Harbottle, and E. V. Sayre. 1976. Application of multivariate techniques to analytical data on Aegean ceramics. *Archaeometry* 18: 59–74.

Bishop, R. L., V. Canouts, S. P. De Atley, A. Qoyawayma, and C. W. Aikins. 1988. The formation of ceramic analytical groups: Hopi pottery production and exchange, D.C. 1300–1600. *Journal of Field Archaeology* 15: 317–37.

Bishop, R. L., and H. Neff. 1989. Compositional data analysis in archaeology. In *Archaeological Chemistry IV*, edited by R. O. Allen, pp. 576–86. Advances in Chemistry series, 220. Washington, D.C.: American Chemical Society.

Bishop, R. L., R. L. Rands, and G. R. Holley. 1982. Ceramic compositional analysis in archaeological perspective. In *Advances in Archaeological Method and Theory*, edited by M. Schiffer, pp. 275–330, vol. 5. New York: Academic Press.

Black, C.V.B. 1963. *Spanish Town, the Old Capital*. Kingston: Sangster's Press.

———. 1965. *A History of Jamaica*. 3rd ed. Kingston: Sangster's Press.

Blackburn, R. 1988. *The Overthrow of Colonial Slavery, 1776–1848*. London: Verso.

———. 1997. *The Making of New World Slavery: From the Baroque to the Modern, 1492–1800*. London: Verso.

Blackman, M. J., S. Mery, and R. P. Wright. 1989. Production and exchange of ceramics on the Oman Peninsula from the perspective of Hili. *Journal of Field Archaeology* 16: 61–77.

Blackman, M. J., G. J. Stein, and P. M. Vandiver. 1993. The standardization hypothesis and ceramic mass production: Technological, compositional, and metric indexes of craft specialization at Tell Leila, Syria. *American Antiquity* 58: 60–80.

Blackman, R. 1992. The effect of natural and human size sorting on the mineralogy and chemistry of ceramic clays. In *Chemical Characterization of Ceramic Pastes in Archaeology*, edited by H. Neff, pp. 113–24. Madison, Wisc.: Prehistory Press.

Blatt, H. 1952. Original characteristics of clastic quartz grains. *Journal of Sedimentary Petrology* 37: 401–24.

———. 1967. Provenance determinations and recycling of sediments. *Journal of Sedimentary Petrolology* 37: 1031–44.

Blome, R. 1672. A Description of the Island of Jamaica, with Other Isles and Territories in America, to Which the English Are Related. London: Milbourn.

Boa, S. 1993. Urban free black and coloured women: Jamaica 1760–1834. *Jamaica Historical Review* 18: 1–6.

Bokman, J. 1952. Clastic quartz particles as indices of provenance. *Journal of Sedimentary Petrology* 22: 17–24.

Bourdieu, P. 1977. *Outline of a Theory of Practice*. Cambridge: Cambridge University Press.

Braithwaite, E. K. 1971. *The Development of Creole Society in Jamaica*. Oxford: Clarendon Press.

Bratten, J. R. 1992. Yabba Ware, the African presence at Port Royal. Paper Presented at the annual meeting of the Society of Historical Archaeology, Jan. 9, 1992, Kingston, Jamaica.

Bravmann, R. 1980. *Islam and Tribal Art in West Africa*. Cambridge: Cambridge University Press.

———. 1983. *African Islam*. Washington, D.C.: Smithsonian Institution Press.

Bredhwa-Mensah, Y. 1996. The production and use patterns of Ga pottery in the lower Densu Valley, western Accra Plains. *Papers from the Institute of Archaeology* 7: 47–58.

Brereton, B. 1999. General problems and issues in studying the history of women. In *Gender in Caribbean Development*, edited by P. Mohammed and C. Shepherd, pp. 119–35. Kingston: Canoe Press.

Bromley, R. 1978. The urban informal sector: Critical perspectives. *World Development* 6: 9–10.

Brown, M. 1996. Examination of an inn in Port Royal, Jamaica. M.A. thesis, Department of Anthropology, University of Texas, San Antonio.

Brown, V. 1994. Higgling: The language of markets in economic discourse. In *Higgling: Transactors and Their Markets in the History of Economics*, edited by M. S. Morgan, pp. 66–93. Annual supplement to Vol. 26, *History of Political Economy*. Durham, N.C.: Duke University Press.

Browne, K. E. 2004. *Creole Economics: Caribbean Cunning under the French Flag*. 1st ed. Austin: University of Texas Press.

Browne, P. [1759] 1789. *The Civil and Natural History of Jamaica*. London: B. White and Son.

Brumfiel, E. M. 1991. Weaving and cooking: women's production in Aztec Mexico. In *Engendering Archaeology*, edited by J. Gero and M. Conkey, pp. 224–54. Oxford: Blackwell.

——— (editor). 1994. *Economic Anthropology of the State*. Lanham, Md.: University Press of America.

———. 2003. It's a material world: History, artifacts, and anthropology. *Annual Review of Anthropology* 32: 205–23.

Brumfiel, E. M., and T. K. Earle (editors). 1987. *Specialization, Exchange and Complex Societies*. Cambridge: Cambridge University Press.

Burke, H. 1999. *Meaning and Ideology in Historical Archaeology: Style, Social Identity, and Capitalism in an Australian Town*. New York: Plenum Press.

Burnard, T. 1996. Who bought slaves in early America? Purchasers of slaves from the Royal African Company in Jamaica, 1674–1708. *Slavery and Abolition* 17: 68–92.

———. 2001. E pluribus plures: African ethnicities in seventeenth- and eighteenth-century Jamaica. *Jamaican Historical Review* 21: 8–22, 56–59.

———. 2002. "The Grand Mart of the Island": The economic function of Kingston, Jamaica, in the mid-eighteenth century. In *Jamaica in Slavery and Freedom; History, Heritage and Culture*, edited by K. Monteith and G. Richards, pp. 225–41. Kingston: University of the West Indies Press.

———. 2004. *Mastery, Tyranny, and Desire: Thomas Thistlewood and His Slaves in the Anglo-Jamaican World*. Chapel Hill: University of North Carolina Press.

Burnard, T., and K. Morgan. 2001. The dynamics of the slave market and slave purchasing patterns in Jamaica, 1655–1788. *William and Mary College Quarterly* 58: 205–28.

Burton, R. 1999. *Afro-Creole: Power, Opposition, and Play in the Caribbean*. Ithaca, N.Y.: Cornell University Press.

Bush, B. 1981. White "ladies," coloured "favourites" and black "wenches"; Some considerations on sex, race and class factors in social relations in white creole society in the British Caribbean. *Slavery and Abolition* 2: 246–62.

———. 1990. *Slave Women in Caribbean Society, 1650–1838*. London: James Curry Press.

———. 1996. Hard Labor: Women, Childbirth, and Resistance in British Caribbean Slave Societies. In *More Than Chattel: Black Women and Slavery in the Americas*, edited by D. B. Gaspar and D. C. Hine, pp. 193–217. Bloomington: Indiana University Press.

Cadbury, H. J. 1971. Quakers and the earthquake at Port Royal, 1692. *Jamaican Historical Review* 7: 19–33.

Campbell, J. 1993. As "a kind of freeman"? Slaves' market-related activities in the South Carolina upcountry, 1800–1860. In *Cultivation and Culture: Labor and the Shaping of Slave Life in the Americas*, edited by I. Berlin and P. D. Morgan, pp. 243–74. Charlottesville: University Press of Virginia.

———. 1995. As "a kind of freeman"? Slaves' market-related activities in the South Carolina upcountry, 1800–1860. In *The Slaves' Economy: Independent Production by Slaves in the Americas*, edited by I. Berlin and P. D. Morgan, pp. 131–69. London: Frank Cass.

Cassidy, F. G. [1961] 1971. *Jamaica Talk. Three Hundred Years of the English Language in Jamaica*. London: Macmillan.

Cassidy, F. G., and R. Le Page. [1967] 1980. *Dictionary of Jamaican English*. Cambridge: Cambridge University Press.

Chambers, D. B. 1997. "My own nation": Igbo exiles in the Diaspora. *Slavery and Abolition* 18(1): 72–97.

———. 2000. Tracing Igbo into the African Diaspora. In *Identity in the Shadow of Slavery*, edited by P. E. Lovejoy, pp. 55–71. London: Continuum.

Chappel, E. 1994. Interpreting Bermuda's Architecture. *Bermuda Journal of Architecture and Maritime History* 6: 145–50.

Clark, W. 1823. *Drawings Made by William Clark, during a Residence of Three Years in the West Indies*. London.

Clarke, K. M. 2004. *Mapping Yoruba Networks: Power and Agency in the Making of Transnational Communities*. Durham: Duke University Press.

Clement, C. 1997. Settlement patterning on the British Caribbean island of Tobago. *Historical Archaeology* 31(2): 93–106.

Clifford, J. 1994. Diasporas. *Cultural Anthropology* 9(3): 302–37.

Cobb, C. R. 1993. Economic approaches to the political economy of non-stratified societies. In *Archaeological Method and Theory*, edited by M. B. Schiffer, pp. 43–100. Vol 5. Tucson: University of Arizona Press.

———. 2005. Archaeology and the "savage slot": Displacement and emplacement in the premodern world. *American Anthropologist* 107(4): 563–74.

Cohn, B. S. 1996. *Colonialism and Its Forms of Knowledge: The British in India*. Princeton, N.J.: Princeton University Press.

Comaroff, J. 1985. *Body of Power, Spirit of Resistance: The Culture and History of a South African People*. Chicago: University of Chicago Press.

———. 1996. The Empire's old clothes: Refashioning the colonial subject. In *Commodities and Cultural Borders*, edited by D. Howes, pp. 19–38. New York: Routledge.
Comaroff, J., and J. Comaroff. 1992. *Ethnography and the Historical Imagination*. Boulder, Colo.: Westview Press.
Conkey, M. 1990. Experimenting with style in archaeology. In *The Uses of Style in Archaeology*, edited by M. Conkey and C. Hastorf, pp. 5–17. Cambridge: Cambridge University Press.
Cook, N. D. 1998. *Born to Die: Disease and New World Conquest, 1492–1650*. New York: Cambridge University Press.
Cook, S., and W. Borah. 1971a. *Essay on Population History: Mexico and the Caribbean*. Berkeley: University of California Press.
———. 1971b. The aboriginal population of Hispaniola. In *Essay on Population History: Mexico and the Caribbean*, edited by S. Cook and W. Borah, pp. 376–410. Vol. 2. Berkeley: University of California Press.
Cooper, F. 2005. *Colonialism in Question: Theory, Knowledge, History*. Berkeley: University of California Press.
Cordell, A. 1993. Chronological variability in ceramic paste: A comparison of Deptford and Savannah period pottery in the St. Mary's River region of northeast Florida and southeast Georgia. *Southeastern Archaeology* 12(1): 33–58.
Costin, C. L. 1991. Craft specialization: Issues in defining, documenting, and explaining the organization of production. In *Archaeological Method and Theory*, vol. 1, edited by M. B. Schiffer, pp. 1–56. Tucson: University of Arizona Press.
———. 1998. Introduction to *Craft and Social Identity*, edited by C. L. Costin and R. Wright, pp. 109–22. Archaeological Papers of the American Anthropological Association.
———. 1999. Formal and technological variability and the social relations of production: Crisoles from San Jose de Moro, Peru. In *Material Meanings: Critical Approaches to the Interpretation of Material Culture*, edited by E. Chilton, pp. 85–102. Salt Lake City: University of Utah Press.
Cotter, C. S. 1948. The discovery of the Spanish Carvings at Seville. *Jamaican Historical Review* 1(3). Kingston.
———. 1953. Don Christopher's cove. *Jamaican Historical Review*, 39–43.
———. 1964. The Jamaica of Columbus. *Jamaica Historical Society Bulletin* 3(16): 252–59. Kingston.
———. 1970. Sevilla Nueva, the story of an excavation. *Jamaica Journal* 4(2): 15–22.
Council of Jamaica. 1678. Council Minutes. Vol. 2, Folio 159v, 8 (August). Jamaica Archives and Records Department.
———. 1685. Council Minutes. Volume 3a Folio 193, 11 (May). Jamaica Archives and Records Department.
Crane, B. 1993. *Colono Ware and Criollo Ware Pottery from Charleston, South Carolina, and San Juan, Puerto Rico, in Comparative Perspective*. Ph.D. diss., Department of American Civilization, University of Pennsylvania, Philadelphia. Ann Arbor, Mich.: University Microfilms.

Craton, M. 1982. *Testing the Chains: Resistance to Slavery in the British West Indies.* Ithaca: Cornell University Press.

———. 1985. Emancipation from below? The role of the British West Indian slaves in the Emancipation Movement, 1816–34. In *Out of Slavery: Abolition and After*, edited by J. Hayward, pp. 110–31. London: Frank Cass.

———. 1997. *Empire, Enslavement and Freedom in the Caribbean*, Princeton: Markus Weiner Press.

Craton, M., and J. Walvin. 1970. *A Jamaican Plantation: The History of Worthy Park, 1670–1970.* Toronto: University of Toronto Press.

Crossland, L. B. 1973. A study of Begho pottery in the light of excavations conducted at the Begho-B2 Site. Master's thesis, University of Ghana, Legon.

———. 1989. *Pottery from the Begho-B2 Site, Ghana.* African Occasional Papers, No. 4. Calgary: University of Calgary Press.

Crossland, L. B., and M. Posnansky. 1978. Pottery, people and trade at Begho. In *The Spatial Organization of Culture*, edited by I. Hodder, pp. 77–89. London: Duckworth.

Crumley, C. and W. H. Marquardt. 1990. Landscape: A unifying concept in regional analysis. In *Interpreting Space: GIS and Archaeology*, edited by K. Allen, S. Green, and E. Zubrow, pp. 73–79. London: Taylor and Francis.

Cundall, F. 1902. *Bibliographia Jamaicensis. A list of Jamaica books and pamphlets, magazine articles, newspapers, and maps, most of which are in the library of the Institute of Jamaica.* Kingston: Institute of Jamaica.

———. 1929. *A Brief Account of King's House, Spanish Town, Jamaica.* Kingston: Institute of Jamaica.

Cundall, F., and J. Pietersz. 1919. *Jamaica under the Spaniards.* Kingston: Institute of Jamaica.

Cunningham, J. J. 2005. Household vessel exchange and consumption in the Inland Niger Delta of Mali: An ethnoarchaeological study. Ph.D. diss., McGill University, Montreal.

Curet, A. 2002. The chief is dead, long live... who? Descent and succession in the protohistoric chiefdoms of the Greater Antilles. *Ethnohistory* 49(2): 259–80.

Curtin, P. D. 1969. *The Atlantic Slave Trade, a Census.* Madison: University of Wisconsin Press.

Cutsinger, L. 1991. It's Part of We: Gender and Class Identity of Hawkers in Barbados. In Paper presented at the 90th Annual Meeting of the American Anthropological Association, Chicago.

Dadzie, S. 1990. Searching for the invisible woman: Slavery and resistance in Jamaica. *Race and Class* (32): 21–38.

D'Altroy, T. 1987. Transitions in power: Centralization of Wanka political organization under Inka rule. *Ethnohistory* 34(1): 78–102.

———. 1992. *Provincial Power in the Inca Empire.* Washington, D.C.: Smithsonian Institution Press.

D'Altroy, T., and R. Bishop. 1990. The provincial organization of Inka ceramic production. *American Antiquity* 55: 120–38.

D'Altroy, T., and T. K. Earle. 1985. Staple finance, wealth finance, and storage in the Inka political economy (including comment and reply). *Current Anthropology* 25(2): 187–206.

D'Altroy, T., and C. Hastorf. 2001. *Empire and Domestic Economy*. New York: Kluwer.

Darrington, G. 1994. Analysis and reconstruction of impermanent structures in the 17th and 18th centuries. Master's thesis, Nautical Archaeology Program, Texas A&M University, College Station.

das Dores Giaro da Cruz, M. 1996. Ceramic production in the Banda area (west-central Ghana): An ethnoarchaeological approach. *Nyame Akuma* 45: 30–39.

———. 2003. *Shaping Quotidian Worlds: Ceramic Production and Consumption in Banda, Ghana, c. 1780–1994*. Ph.D. diss., Dept. of Anthropology, SUNY, Binghamton. Ann Arbor, Mich.: University Microfilms.

David, N. 1972. On the life span of pottery, type frequencies, and archaeological inference. *American Antiquity* 37(1): 141–42.

David, N., K. Gavua, J. Sterner, and S. MacEachern. 1991. Ethnicity and material culture in North Cameroon. *Canadian Journal of Archaeology* 15: 171–77.

David, N., and C. Kramer. 2001. *Ethnoarchaeology in Action*. New York: Cambridge University Press.

David, N., J. Sterner, and K. Gavua. 1988. Why pots are decorated. *Current Anthropology* 29(3): 365–89.

Deagan, K. A. 1995. *Puerto Real: The Archaeology of a Sixteenth-Century Spanish Town in Hispaniola*. Ripley P. Bullen series. Columbus Quincentenary series. Gainesville: University Press of Florida.

———. 2001. Dynamics of imperial adjustment in Spanish America: Ideology and Social Integration. In *Empires: Perspectives from Archaeology and History*, edited by S. E. Alcock, T. N. D'Altroy, K. D. Morrison and C. M. Sinopoli, pp. 179–94. New York: Cambridge University Press.

Deagan, K. A., and J. M. Cruxent. 2002a. *Archaeology at La Isabela: America's First European Town*. New Haven: Yale University Press.

———. 2002b. *Columbus's Outpost among the Taínos: Spain and America at La Isabela, 1493–1498*. New Haven: Yale University Press.

DeCorse, C. R. 1989a. Material aspects of Limba, Yalunka and Kuranko ethnicity: Archaeological research in northeastern Sierra Leone. In *Archaeological Approaches to Cultural Identity*, edited by S. Shennan, pp. 125–40. London: Unwin Hyman.

———. 1989b. *An Archaeological Study of Elmina, Ghana: Trade and Culture Change on the Gold Coast Between the Fifteenth and Nineteenth Centuries*. Ph.D. diss., Department of Anthropology, UCLA. Ann Arbor, Mich.: University Microfilms.

———. 1990. Historical archaeology. *African Archaeological Review* 8(1): 18–21.

———. 1992. Culture contact, continuity, and change on the Gold Coast, AD 1400–1900. *African Archaeological Review*. 10: 163–96.

———. 1993. The Danes on the Gold Coast: Culture change and the European presence. *African Archaeological Review* 11: 149–73.

———. 1994. The Elmina Bakatue: Evaluation, change and continuity in coastal Ghana. *Ghana Studies Council Newsletter*. St. Paul. No. 7, Spring 1994, p. 5.

———. 1996. Archaeological perspectives of culture contact and trade in West Africa. In *Aspects of African Archaeology: Papers from the 10th Congress of the PanAfrican Association for Prehistory and Related Studies*, edited by G. Pwiti and R. Soper, pp. 681–86. Harare: University of Zimbabwe Publications.

———. 1998. Culture contact and change in West Africa. In *Studies in Culture Contact: Interaction, Culture Change, and Archaeology*, edited by J. G. Cusick, pp. 358–77. Occasional Paper No. 25. Carbondale: Center for Archaeological Investigations, Southern Illinois University.

———. 1999. Oceans apart: Africanists perspectives on Diaspora archaeology. In *"I, too, Am America": Archaeological Studies of African American Life*, edited by T. A. Singleton, pp. 132–58. Charlottesville: University of Virginia Press.

———. 2001a. *An Archaeology of Elmina: Africans and Europeans on the Gold Coast, 1400–1900*. Washington, D.C.: Smithsonian Institution Press.

———. 2001b. Introduction to *West Africa during the Atlantic slave trade: Archaeological Perspectives*, edited by C. R. DeCorse, pp. 1–13. New Approaches to Anthropological Archaeology. Leicester: Leicester University Press.

Deetz, J. 1977. *In Small Things Forgotten: The Archaeology of Early American Life*. Garden City, N.Y.: Anchor Press/Doubleday.

———. 1996. *In Small Things Forgotten: An Archaeology of Early American Life*. Rev. and expanded ed. New York: Anchor Books.

DeFoe, D. [1756] 1895. *Journal of the Year of the Plague*. New York: Longmans, Green.

de Lisser, H. G. 1910. *In Jamaica and Cuba, with Hints to Tourists*. Kingston: Gleaner.

Delle, J. A. 1989. A spatial analysis of sugar plantations on St. Eustatius, Netherlands Antilles. Master's thesis, College of William and Mary, Williamsburg, Va.

———. 1994. The settlement pattern of sugar plantations on St. Eustatius, Netherlands Antilles. In *Spatial Patterning in Archaeology: Selected Studies of Settlement*, edited by D. W. Robinson and G. G. Robinson, pp. 33–61. Williamsburg, Va.: King and Queen's Press.

———. 1998. *An Archaeology of Social Space: Analyzing Coffee Plantations in Jamaica's Blue Mountains*. Contributions to Global Historical Archaeology. New York: Plenum Press.

———. 1999. The landscapes of class negotiation on coffee plantations in the Blue Mountains of Jamaica, 1797–1850. *Historical Archaeology* 33(1): 136–58.

———. 2000a. The material and cognitive dimensions of creolization in nineteenth-century Jamaica. *Historical Archaeology* 34(3): 56–72.

———. 2000b. Gender, power and space: Negotiating social relations under slavery on coffee plantations in Jamaica, 1790–1834. In *Lines That Divide: Historical Archaeologies of Race, Class and Gender*, edited by J. A. Delle, S. A. Mrozowski, and R. Paynter, pp. 168–203. Knoxville: University of Tennessee Press.

———. 2001. Race, missionaries, and the struggle to free Jamaica. In *Race and the Archaeology of Identity*, edited by C. E. Orser, pp. 177–95. Salt Lake City: University of Utah Press.

———. 2002. Power and landscape: Spatial dynamics in early-nineteenth-century Jamaica. In *The Dynamics of Power*, edited by M. O'Donovan, pp. 341–61. Center for Archaeological Investigations, Occasional Paper No. 30. Carbondale: Southern Illinois University.

———. Forthcoming. The governor and the enslaved: An archaeology of colonial modernity at Marshall's Pen, Jamaica. *International Journal of Historical Archaeology*.

Delle, J. A., S. A. Mrozowski, and R. Paynter. 2000. *Lines That Divide: Historical Archaeologies of Race, Class, and Gender*. 1st ed. Knoxville: University of Tennessee Press.

Descantes, C., H. Neff, M. D. Glascock, and W. R. Dickinson. 2001. Chemical characterization of Micronesian ceramics through instrumental neutron activation analysis: A preliminary study. *Journal of Archaeological Science* 28: 1185–90.

Descantes, C., and M. Glascock. 2005. Instrumental Neutron Activation Analysis of Eighteenth Century Pottery from Jamaica. Report prepared by C. Descantes and M. D. Glascock, Research Reactor Center University of Missouri Columbia, Mo. (March 4, 2005).

Dewolf, H. C. 1998. *Chinese Porcelain and Seventeenth-century Port Royal, Jamaica*. Ph.D. diss., Dept of Anthropology, Texas A&M University, College Station. Ann Arbor, Mich.: University Microfilms.

Dickinson, W.R.B., M. Butler, D. R. Moore, and M. Swift. 2001. Geologic source and geographic distribution of sand tempers in prehistoric potsherds from the Mariana Islands. *Geoarchaeology* 16(8): 827–54.

Diderot, D., J.L.R. d'Alembert, and P. Mouchon. 1751. *Encyclopédie, ou Dictionnaire raisonné des sciences, des arts et des métiers*. 17 vols. Paris: Chez Briasson, David, Le Breton, Durand.

———. 1762. *Recueil de planches, sur les sciences, les arts libéraux, et les arts méchaniques: Avec leur explication*. 11 vols. Paris: Chez Briasson [and 3 others].

Dietler, M. and I. Herbich. 2000. Habitus, techniques, and style: An integrated approach to the social understanding of material culture and boundaries. In *The Archaeology of Social Boundaries*, edited by M. Stark, pp. 232–63. Washington, D.C.: Smithsonian Institution Press.

Dobres, M. A. 2000. *Technology and Social Agency: Outlining an Anthropological Framework for Archaeology*. Oxford: Blackwell.

Dobres, M. A., and C. R. Hoffman. 1994. Social Agency and the Dynamics of Prehistoric Technology. *Journal of Archaeological Method and Theory* 1(3): 211–58.

Dobres, M. A., and J. Robb. 2000. Agency in archaeology: Paradigm or platitude? In *Agency in Archaeology*, edited by M. A. Dobres and J. Robb, pp. 3–17. New York and London: Routledge.

Donachie, M. J. 2001. *Household Ceramics at Port Royal, Jamaica, 1655–1692: The Building 4/5 Assemblage*. Ph.D. diss., Dept. of Anthropology, Texas A&M University, College Station. Ann Arbor, Mich.: University Microfilms.

Donahue, J., D. R. Watters, and S. Millspaugh. 1990. Thin-section petrography of northern Lesser Antilles ceramics. *Geoarchaeology* 5(3): 229–54.

Douglas, M. 1966. *Purity and Danger: An Analysis of Concepts of Pollution and Taboo*. New York: Praeger.

Dunn, R. S. 1972. *Sugar and Slaves: The Rise of the Planter Class in the English West Indies, 1624–1713*. Chapel Hill: Published for the Institute of Early American History and Culture at Williamsburg, Virginia, by the University of North Carolina Press.

———. 1993. Sugar production and slave women in Jamaica. In *Cultivation and Culture: Labor and the Shaping of Slave Life in the Americas*, edited by I. Berlin and P. D. Morgan, pp. 49–72. Charlottesville: University Press of Virginia.

Duperly, A. 1844. Daguerian Excursions in Jamaica, being a collection of views . . . taken on the spot with the Daguerreotype. Kingston: A. Duperly.

Durant-Gonzales, V. 1983. The Occupation of Higglering. *Jamaica Journal*, 16(3): 2–12.

Dye, T. 1996. Sources of sand temper in prehistoric Tongan pottery. *Geoarchaeology* 11(2): 141–64.

Ebanks, R. 1984. Ma Lou, an Afro Jamaican pottery tradition. *Jamaica Journal* 17: 31–37.

———. 2003. History of Jamaican ceramics, 1655–1840. M.Phil thesis, Department of History and Archaeology, University of the West Indies, Mona.

Edwards, B. [1793] 1972. *The History, Civil and Commercial, of the British Colonies in the West Indies*. Research Library of Colonial Americana 2. New York: Arno Press.

Effah-Gyamfi, K. 1979. *Traditional History of the Bono State*. Legon: University of Ghana, Institute of African Studies.

———. 1985. *Bono Manso: An Archaeological Investigation into Early Akan Urbanism*. Calgary: University of Calgary Press.

———. 1986. Ancient urban sites in Hausaland: a preliminary report. *West African Journal of Archaeology*, 16: 117–34.

Eggerton, D. 2006. Slaves to the marketplace: Economic liberty and black rebelliousness in the Atlantic World. *Journal of the Early Republic* 26(4): 617–39

Ellis, W. 1744. *The Timber-Tree Improved*. Printed for, and sold by T. Osborne and M. Cooper

Eltis, D. 1995. New estimates of exports from Barbados and Jamaica, 1665–1701. *William and Mary Quarterly* 52(4): 631–48.

———. 2000. *The Rise of African Slavery in the Americas*. New York: Cambridge University Press.

———. 2001. The volume and structure of the transatlantic slave trade: A reassessment. *William and Mary Quarterly* 58(1): 17–46.

Eltis, D., S. D. Behrendt, and D. Richardson. 2000. *The Transatlantic Slave Trade, 1562–1867: A Database*. New York: W.E.B. DuBois Institute, Harvard University.

Eltis, D., and D. Richardson (editors). 1997. *Routes to Slavery: Direction, Ethnicity and Morality in the Atlantic Slave Trade*. Portland, Oreg.: Frank Cass.

Emerson, T. E., and T. R. Pauketat. 2002. Embodying power and resistance at Cahokia. In *The Dynamics of Power*, edited by M. O'Donovan, pp. 105–25. Center for Archaeological Investigations. Carbodale: Southern Illinois University.

Emmer, P. C. (editor). 1998. *The Dutch in the Atlantic Economy: Trade, Slavery and Emancipation*. Ashgate, London.

England, S. 1994. Acculturation in the Creole context: A case study of La Poterie Martinique. Ph.D. diss., University of Cambridge, Cambridge.

Ewen, C. R. 1990a. Spanish colonial adaptation to the New World: Current research at Puerto Real, Haiti. *Proceedings of the International Association of Caribbean Archaeologists* 11: 448–52.

———. 1990b. The rise and fall of Puerto Real. In *Columbian Consequences*, Vol. 2: *Archaeological and Historical Perspectives on the Spanish Borderlands East*, edited by D. H. Thomas. Washington, D.C.: Smithsonian Institution Press.

———. 2000. From colonist to creole: Archaeological patterns of Spanish colonization in the New World. *Historical Archaeology* 34(3): 36–45.

Farnsworth, P. 1992. Comparative Analysis in Plantation Archaeology. The Application of a Functional Classification. In the 25th Annual Meeting of the Society for Historical Archaeology, Kingston, Jamaica.

Ferguson, L. 1992. *Uncommon Ground: Archaeology and Early African America, 1650–1800*. Washington, D.C.: Smithsonian Institution Press.

Ferring, C. R., and T. K. Pertulla. 1987. Defining the provenance of red slipped pottery from Texas and Oklahoma by petrographic methods. *Journal of Archaeological Science* 14: 437–56.

Fielding, H. 1791. *The History of Tom Jones: A Foundling*. Printed for J. L. Legrand.

Fieller, N. R., and P. Nicholson. 1991. Grain size analysis of archaeological pottery: The use of statistical models. In *Recent Developments in Ceramic Petrology*, edited by A. Middleton and I. Freestone, pp. 71–111. Occasional Papers 81. London: British Museum.

Folk, R. L. 1954. The distinction between grain size and mineral composition in sedimentary rock nomenclature. *Journal of Geology* 62: 344–50.

———. 1974. *The Petrology Of Sedimentary Rocks*. Austin: Hemphill.

Foucault, M. 1972. *The Archeology of Knowledge*, translated by A. M. Sheridan-Smith. London: Tavistock

Foulks, T. 1833. Defining the provenance of red slipped pottery from Texas. London.

Fox, G. L. 1998. *The Study and Analysis of the Kaolin Clay Tobacco Pipe Collection from the Seventeenth-Century Archaeological Site of Port Royal, Jamaica*. Ph.D. diss., Nautical Archaeology Program, Texas A&M University, College Station. Ann Arbor, Mich.: University Microfilms.

Francis-Brown, S. 1983 [2002]. Ma Lou. In *A Tapestry of Jamaica: the Best of Skywritings*, edited by L. Gambrill. Oxford: Macmillan Caribbean.

Frank, B. 1993. Reconstructing the history of an African ceramic tradition: Technology, slavery, and agency in the region of Kadiolo (Mali). *Cahiers d'études africaines* 33(3): 381–401.

Frank, B. E. 1998. *Mande Potters and Leather-Workers: Art and Heritage in West Africa*. Washington, D.C.: Smithsonian Institution Press.

Franklin, M. A. 1992. Wrought-iron hand tools in Port Royal, Jamaica: A study based upon a collection of the tools recovered from archaeological excavations and listed in the probate records of colonial Port Royal, c. 1692. Master's thesis, Nautical Archaeology Program, Texas A&M University, College Station.

Franklin, M. 1997a. "Power to the People": Sociopolitics and the archaeology of Black Americans. *Historical Archaeology* 31(3): 36–50.

———. 1997b. Why are there so few black American archaeologists? *Antiquity* 71: 274.

Franklin, M., and G. Fesler. 1999. *Historical Archaeology, Identity Formation, and the Interpretation of Ethnicity*. Colonial Williamsburg Research Publications. Colonial Williamsburg, Va.: Colonial Williamsburg Foundation.

Freestone, I. A. 1992. Ceramic petrography. *American Journal of Archaeology* 99: 111–15.

Friedman, J. 2002. From roots to routes: Tropes for trippers. *Anthropological Theory* 2(1): 21–36.

Gabriel, I. 2003. Poterie de Grande Baie. *Bilan scientifique de la région Guadeloupe.* 8: 47–61.

García-Arévalo, M. 1978. La arqueologia Indo-Hispana en Santo Domingo. In *Unidad y variedad, esayos antropologicas en homenaje a Jose a Cruxent*, edited by E. Wagner and A. Zucchi, pp. 77–127. Caracas: Institute Venezolano Investigaciones Cientificas.

———. 1986. *El Maiel de Jose Leta: Evidencias arqueologicas de un posible cimarron en el religion sud oriental de la isla de Santo Domingo*. Cimmaron no. 18. Santo Domingo: Fundacion Garcia Arevalo.

Gardner, W. J. 1873. *A History of Jamaica from Its Discovery by Christopher Columbus to the Present Time*. London: Elliot Stock.

Gartley, R. 1979. Afro-Cruzan pottery: A new style of colonial earthenware from St. Croix. *Journal of the Virgin Islands Archaeological Society* 8: 47–61.

Gaspar, D. B. 1996. From "the sense of their slavery": Slave women and resistance in Antigua, 1632–1763. In *More Than Chattel: Black Women and Slavery in the Americas*, edited by D. B. Gaspar and D. C. Hine, pp. 218–38. Bloomington: Indiana University Press.

Gaspar, D. B., and D. C. Hine (editors). 1996. *More Than Chattel: Black Women and Slavery in the Americas*, Bloomington: Indiana University Press.

Giddens, A. 1979. *Central Problems in Social Theory: Action, Structure and Contradiction in Social Analysis*. London: Macmillan.

———. 1981. *A Contemporary Critique of Historical Materialism* Berkeley: University of California Press

Gilroy, P. 1993. *The Black Atlantic: Modernity and Double Consciousness*. Cambridge: Harvard University Press.

———. 1994. Diaspora. *Paragraph* 17(3): 207–12.

Glascock, M. D. 1992. Characterization of archaeological ceramics at MURR by neutron activation analysis and multivariate statistics. In *Chemical Characterization of Ceramic Pastes in Archaeology*, edited by H. Neff, pp. 11–26. Madison: Prehistory Press.

Glover, R. [1775] 1909. Petition of the West India planters to the Commons respecting the American Non-Importation Agreement, February 2, 1775. In *Selections from the Economic History of the United States, 1765–1860*, edited by G. S. Callender. Boston: Ginn and Company.

Goad, S. I. 1980a. Chemical analysis of native copper artifacts from the southeastern United States. *Current Anthropology* 21: 270–71.

———. 1980b. Patterns of Late Archaic exchange. *Tennessee Anthropologist* 5(1): 1–16.

Gomez, M. A. 1998. *Exchanging Our Country Marks: The Transformation of African Identities in the Colonial and Antebellum South*, Durham: University of North Carolina Press.

———. 2005. *Reversing Sail: A History of the African Diaspora*, New York: Cambridge University Press

Goodwin, W. B. 1940. *The Lure of Gold: Being the Story of the Five Lost Ships of Christopher Columbus*. Boston: Meador Publishing Company.

———. 1946. *Spanish and English Ruins in Jamaica*. Boston: Meador Publishing Company.

Gosden, C., and L. Head. 1994. Landscape—usefully ambiguous concept. *Archaeology in Oceania* 29: 113–16.

Gosse, P. H. 1851. *A Naturalist's Sojourn in Jamaica*. London: Longman, Brown, Green and Longmans.

Gosselain, O. P. 1992a. Bonfire of the enquiries: Pottery firing temperature in archaeology: What for? *Journal of Archaeological Science* 19: 243–59.

———. 1992b. Technology and style: Potters and pottery making among the Bafia of Cameroon. *Man* 27: 559–86.

———. 1998. Social and technical identity in a clay crystal ball. In *The Archaeology of Social Boundaries*, edited by M. Stark, pp. 78–106. Washington, D.C.: Smithsonian InstitutionPress.

———. 1999. In pots we trust. The processing of clay and symbols in Sub-Saharan Africa. *Journal of Material Culture* 4: 205–30.

———. 2000. Materializing identities: An Africanist perspective. *Journal of Archaeological Method and Theory* 7: 187–217.

Gotelipe-Miller, S. 1990. Pewter and pewterers from Port Royal, Jamaica: Flatware before 1692. Master's thesis, Nautical Archaeology Program, Texas A&M University, College Station.

Goucher, C. 1990. John Reeder's foundry: A study of 18th-century African-Caribbean technology. *Jamaica Journal* 23: 39–43.

———. 1993. African metallurgy in the New World. *African Archaeological Review* 11: 197–215.

———. 1999. African-Caribbean metal technology: Forging cultural survivals in the Atlantic world. In *African Sites Archaeology in the Caribbean*, edited by J. B. Haviser, pp. 143–56. Princeton. N.J.: Markus Wiener.

Goveia, E. V. 1965. *Slave Society in the British Leeward Islands at the End of the Eighteenth Century*. Caribbean series 8. New Haven: Yale University Press.

———. 1980. *A Study on the Historiography of the British West Indies to the End of the Nineteenth Century*. Washington, D.C.: Howard University Press.

———. [1960] 1991. The West Indian Slave Laws of the Eighteenth Century. In *Caribbean Slave Society and Economy: A Student Reader*, edited by V. Shepherd, pp. 346–62. New York: New Press.

Grantham, J. H., and M. A. Vebel. 1988. The influence of climate and topography on rock-fragment abundance in modern fluvial sands of the southern Blue Ridge Mountains, North Carolina. *Journal of Sedimentary Petrology* 58(2): 219–27.

Green, G. W., and C.D.G. Black (editors). 1970. *The Geology of the Hellshire Hills Quadrangle.* Geological Survey Bulletin No. 7. Kingston, Jamaica.

Greene, S. 1994. From whence they came: A note on the influence of West African ethnic and gender relations on the organizational character of the 1733 St. John slave rebellion. In *The Danish West Indian Slave Trade: Virgin Islands Perspectives,* edited by G. Tyson and A. Highfield, pp. 47–68. Charlotte Amalie, St. Thomas: Virgin Islands Humanities Council.

Gronenborn, D. 1998. Archaeological and ethnohistorical investigations along the southern fringes of Lake Chad, 1993–1996. *African Archaeological Review* 15(4): 225–59.

Gronenborn, D., and C. Magnavita. 2000. Imperial expansion, ethnic change and ceramic traditions in the southern Chad basin. *International Journal of Historical Archaeology* 4(1): 35–70.

Hailey, T. I. 1994. *The Analysis of 17th- , 18th- and 19th-Century Ceramics from Port Royal, Jamaica, for Lead Release: A Study in Archaeotoxicology.* Ph.D. diss., Nautical Archaeology Program, Texas A&M University, College Station. Ann Arbor, Mich.: University Microfilms.

Hair, P.E.H. 1967. Ethnolinguistic continuity on the Guinea coast. *Journal of African History* 8: 247–68.

———. 1989. *The Atlantic Slave Trade.* Liverpool: Liverpool University Press.

———. 1994. *The Founding of the Castelo de Sao Jorge da Mina: An Analysis of the Sources.* Madison: African Studies Program, University of Wisconsin.

Hall, D. 1959. *Free Jamaica.* New Haven: Yale University Press.

———. 1999. *In Miserable Slavery: Thomas Thistlewood in Jamaica, 1750–1786.* Kingston: University of the West Indies Press.

Hall, M. 2000. *Archaeology of the Modern World: Colonial Transcripts in South Africa and the Chesapeake.* New York: Routledge.

Hall, N.A.T. 1977. Slave laws of the Danish Virgin Islands in the later eighteenth century. *Annals of the New York Academy of Sciences* 292(1): 174–86.

———. 1980. Slaves' use of their "free" time in the Danish Virgin Islands in the later eighteenth and early nineteenth century. *Journal of Caribbean History* 13: 21–43.

———. 1985. Maritime Maroons: "Grand Marronage" from the Danish West Indies. *The William and Mary Quarterly,* 3rd Ser., 42(4): 476–98

———. 1994. *Slave society in the Danish West Indies: St. Thomas, St. John, and St. Croix. Johns Hopkins Studies in Atlantic History and Culture.* Baltimore: Johns Hopkins University Press.

Hall, S. 1996. Introduction: Who Needs "Identity"? In *Questions of Cultural Identity,* edited by S. Hall and P. du Gay, pp. 1–17. London: Sage.

Handler, J. S. 1963a. Pottery making in rural Barbados. *Southwestern Journal of Anthropology* 19: 314–34.

———. 1963b. A historical sketch of pottery manufacture in Barbados. *Journal of the Barbados Museum and Historical Society* 30: 129–53.

———. 1964. Notes on pottery making in Antigua. *Man* 64: 184–85.

Handler, J., and Lange, F. W. 1978. *Plantation Slavery in Barbados: An Archaeological and Historical Investigation*, Cambridge, Mass.: Harvard University Press.

Haour, A. 2000. The former Kano? Ethnoarchaeology of Kufan Kanawa, Niger. *Antiquity* 74: 767–68.

———. 2005. Power and permanence in precolonial Africa: A case study from the central Sahel. *World Archaeology* 37(4): 552–65.

Haour, A., and R. Galpine. 2005. Culture and technology in the pottery of the medieval Sahel: A preliminary view from the Makarauci valley, Niger. *Journal of African Archaeology* 3(1): 127–37.

Harbottle, G. 1976. Activation analysis in archaeology. *Radiochemistry* 3: 33–72.

Harley, J. B. 1966. The bankruptcy of Thomas Jefferys: An episode in the economic history of eighteenth century map-making. *Imago Mundi: A Review of Early Cartography* 20: 27–48.

Hart, K. 1973. Informal income opportunities and urban employment in Ghana. *Journal of Modern African Studies* 11: 61–89.

Hauser, M. 1998. Embedded identities: Seeking economic and social relations through compositional analysis of low-fired earthenwares. Master's thesis. Dept. of Anthropology, Syracuse University, Syracuse, New York.

———. 2001. *Peddling Pots: Determining the Extent of Market Exchange in Eighteenth Century Jamaica Through the Analysis of Local Coarse Earthenware*. Ph.D. diss., Dept. of Anthropology, Syracuse University, Syracuse, New York. Ann Arbor, Mich.: University Microfilms.

———. 2006. Hawking your wares: Determining the scale of informal economy through the distribution of local coarse earthenware in eighteenth-century Jamaica. In *African Re-Genesis: Confronting Social Issues in the Diaspora*, edited by K. C. MacDonald, pp. 160–75, R. Torrence, general editor. New York: Left Coast Press.

———. 2007. Between urban and rural: Organization and distribution of local pottery in eighteenth-century Jamaica. In *Archaeology of Atlantic Africa and the African Diaspora*, edited by A. Ogundiran and T. Falola, pp. 292–310. Bloomington: Indiana University Press.

Hauser, M., and D. Armstrong. 1999. Embedded identities: Piecing together relationships through compositional analysis of low-fired earthenwares. In *African Sites: Archaeology in the Caribbean*, edited by J. B. Haviser, pp. 65–93, 313–64. Princeton, N.J.: Markus Weiner.

———. 2004. Determining Social Relations at Cinnamon Bay, St. John, USVI. Paper presented at the annual meeting of the Society of Historical Archaeology, Saint Louis, Mo.

Hauser, M., and C. R. DeCorse. 2003. Low-fired earthenwares in the African Diaspora: Problems and prospects. *International Journal of Historical Archaeology* 7(1): 67–98.

Hauser, M., C. Descantes, and M. Glascock. Under review. Locating enslaved craft

production: Chemical analysis of eighteenth century Jamaican pottery. *Journal of Caribbean Archaeology.*
Heath, B. J. 1988. *Afro Caribbean Ware: A Study of Ethnicity on St. Eustatius.* Ph.D. diss., Dept. of American Civilization, University of Pennsylvania. Ann Arbor, Mich.: University Microfilms.
———. 1990. "Pots of earth": Forms and functions of Afro-Caribbean ceramics. In *Topics in Caribbean Anthropology,* edited by J. G. Cusick and K. Barnes, pp. 33–50. *Florida Journal of Anthropology* Special Publication 16(7).
———. 1999. Yabbas, monkeys, jugs, and jars: A historical context for African Caribbean potterys on St. Eustatius. In *African Sites Archaeology in the Caribbean,* edited by J. B. Haviser. Kingston: Ian Randle.
Hegmon, M. 1995. Pueblo I ceramic production in southwest Colorado: Analyses of igneous rock temper. *Kiva* 60(3): 371–90.
———. 1998. Technology, style, and social practices: Archaeological approaches. In *The Archaeology of Social Boundaries,* edited by M. Stark, pp. 264–77. Washington, D.C.: Smithsonian Institution Press.
Hegmon, M., M. C. Nelson, and M. J. Ennes. 2000. Corrugated pottery, technological style, and population movement in the Mimbres region of the American Southwest. *Journal of Anthropological Research* 56: 217–40.
Heidtke, K. 1992. Jamaican red clay pipes. Master's thesis, Nautical Archaeology Program, Texas A&M University, College Station.
Helms, M. W. 1983. Miskito slaving and culture contact: Ethnicity and opportunity in an expanding population. *Journal of Anthropological Research* 39(2): 179–97.
———. 1986. Of kings and contexts: Ethnohistorical interpretations of Miskito political structure and function. *American Ethnologist* 13(3): 506–23.
———. 1988. *Ulysses' sail: An ethnographic odyssey of power, knowledge, and geographical distance.* Princeton, N.J.: Princeton University Press.
———. 1993. Esoteric knowledge, geographical distance, and the elaboration of leadership status: Dynamics of resource control. In *Profiles in Cultural Evolution,* edited by T. Rambo and K. Gillogly, pp. 233–350. Ann Arbor: Museum of Anthropology, University of Michigan.
Herskovits, M. J. 1933. Race, cultural groups, social differentiation: On the provenance of New World Negroes. *Journal of Social Forces* 7: 247–56.
———. 1936. The significance of West Africa for Negro research. *Journal of Negro History* 21: 15–30.
———. [1941] 1990. *The Myth of the Negro Past.* Boston: Beacon Press.
Higman, B. W. (editor). 1976. *Characteristic Traits of the Creolian and African Negroes in Jamaica.* Mona, Jamaica: Caldwell Press Originally Published by an anonymous author in *Columbian Magazine or Monthly Miscellany,* April–Oct., 1797. Kingston, Jamaica: William Smith Publisher.
———. 1986a. Plantation maps as sources for the study of West Indian ethnohistory. In *Ethnohistory: A Researcher's Guide,* edited by D. Wiedman, pp. 107–36. Studies in Third World Societies, Publication No. 35. Williamsburg, Va.: Department of Anthropology, College of William and Mary.

———. 1986b. Jamaican coffee plantations, 1780–1860: A cartographic analysis. *Caribbean Geography* 2: 73–91.

———. 1987. The spatial economy of Jamaican sugar plantations: Cartographic evidence from the 18th and 19th centuries. *Journal of Historical Geography* 13(1): 17–19.

———. 1988. *Jamaica Surveyed: Plantation Maps and Plans of the Eighteenth and Nineteenth Centuries*. Jamaica and San Francisco: Institute of Jamaica Publications.

———. 1991. Jamaica port towns in the early nineteenth century. In *Atlantic Port Cities: Economy, Culture, and Society in the Atlantic World, 1650–1850*, edited by F. W. Knight and P. K. Liss, pp. 117–48. Knoxville: University of Tennessee Press.

———. 1995. *Slave Population and Economy in Jamaica, 1807–1834*. Barbados: University of the West Indies Press.

———. 1996. Patterns of exchange within a plantation economy: Jamaica at the time of emancipation. In *West Indies Accounts: Essays on the History of the British Caribbean and the Atlantic Economy in Honour of Richard Sheridan*, edited by R. A. McDonald, pp. 211–31. Kingston: The Press, University of the West Indies.

———. 1998. *Montpelier, Jamaica: A Plantation Community in Slavery and Freedom, 1739–1912*. Mona, Jamaica: The Press, University of the West Indies.

———. 2002. The internal economy of Jamaican pens, 1760–1890. In *Slavery without Sugar: Diversity in Caribbean Economy and Society since the 17th Century*, edited by V. Shepherd and K. Monteith, pp. 63–81. Gainesville: University Press of Florida.

———. 2005. *Plantation Jamaica, 1750–1850: Capital and Control in a Colonial Economy*. Kingston: University of the West Indies Press.

Hill, J. N. 1970. *Broken K Pueblo: Prehistoric Social Organization in the American Southwest*. Anthropological Papers No. 18. Tucson: University of Arizona.

Hill, M. 1987. Ethnicity lost? Ethnicity gained? Information functions of "African Ceramics" in West Africa and North America. In *Ethnicity and Culture: Proceedings of the Eighteenth Annual Chacmool Conference*, edited by R. Auger, M. F. Glass, S. MacEachern and P. McCartney, pp. 135–39. Calgary: Archaeological Association, University of Calgary.

Hiskett, M. 1984. *The Development of Islam in West Africa*. New York: Longman.

Hodder, I. 1982. *Symbols in Action: Ethnoarchaeological Studies of Material Culture*. London: Cambridge University Press.

Hodges, W. H. 1995. How we found Puerto Real. In *Puerto Real: The Archaeology of a Sixteenth-Century Spanish Town in Hispaniola*, edited by K. Deagan, pp. 9–32. Gainesville: University Press of Florida.

Hofman, C. L., and A. J. Bright. 2004. From Suazoid to folk pottery: Pottery manufacturing traditions in a changing social and cultural environment on St. Lucia. *New West Indian Guide* 78(1 and 2): 73–104.

Honychurch, L. 2003. Chatoyer's artist: Agostino Brunias and the Depiction of St Vincent. Paper presented at the University of the West Indies' St Vincent Country Conference, St. Vincent.

Howard, H., and E. L. Morris. 1981. *Production and Distribution: A Ceramic Viewpoint*. British Archaeological Reports, International Series, No. 120, Oxford.

Howarth, R. 1989. Improved estimators of uncertainty in proportions, point-counting and pass-fail test results. *American Journal of Science* 298: 564–607.

Howson, J. 1990. Social relations and material culture: A critique of the archaeology of plantation slavery. *Historical Archaeology* 24(4): 78–91.

———. 1995. *Colonial Goods and the Plantation Village: Consumption and the Internal Economy in Montserrat from Slavery to Freedom*. Ph.D. diss., Dept. of Anthropology, New York University. Ann Arbor, Mich.: University Microfilms.

Inikori, J. E. (editor). 1982. *Forced Migration: The Impact of the Export Slave Trade on African Societies*. New York: Africana Publishing.

Insoll, T. 2003. *The Archaeology of Islam in Sub-Saharan Africa*. Cambridge: Cambridge University.

Isaacson, J., and T. Aleto. 1989. Petrographic analysis of ceramic thin sections from La Puna Island, Ecuador. *Archaeomaterials* 3: 61–67.

Jackson, T., and J. West-Thomas. 1994. The genesis of the silica sands of Black River, St. Elizabeth, Jamaica. *Sedimentology* 41(4): 777–86.

Jamaica. 1684. *The Laws of Jamaica Passed by the Assembly and Confirmed by His Majesty in Council, April 17, 1684: to Which Is Added, The State of Jamaica as it Is Now under the Government of Sir Thomas Lynch: with a Large Mapp of the Island*. [2], xix, [3], 151 , [1] leaf of plates (folded).

———. 1716. *The Laws of Jamaica, Pass'd by the Governours, Council and Assembly in That Island, and Confirm'd by the Crown*. London.

———. 1735. *Acts of Assembly, passed in the island of Jamaica; from 1681, to 1734, inclusive*.

———. 1738. *Acts of Assembly, passed in the island of Jamaica; from 1681, to 1737, inclusive*. London, 1738 [1739]. In Eighteenth Century Online, St Jago de la Vega.

———. 1743. *Acts of Assembly, passed in the Island of Jamaica; from 1681, to 1737, Inclusive*.

———. 1756a. *An Abridgment of the Laws of Jamaica, in manner of an index. To which is prefixed, a table*... Eighteenth Century Collections Online. London: Curtis Brett. printers, booksellers, and stationers, in Jamaica, 1756.

———. 1756b. *Acts of Assembly, passed in the Island of Jamaica; from 1681, to 1754, inclusive*. Eighteenth Century Collections Online. London: Curtis Brett and Com printers, booksellers, and stationers, in Jamaica, 1756.

———. 1761. *Acts of Assembly, Passed in the Island of Jamaica; from . . . 1681, to . . . 1754, . . .* In two volumes. . . . Eighteenth Century Collections Online. Saint Jago de la Vega, Jamaica: Lowry and Sherlock, 1769–71.

———. 1786. *An Abridgment of the Laws of Jamaica: comprehending the subject-matter of each Act and clause, . . . To which is prefixed, by way of index, a table . . . .* In Eighteenth Century Collections Online, Kingston, Jamaica.

———. 1787. *Acts of Assembly, Passed in the Island of Jamaica, from the Year 1681 to the year 1769 Inclusive*. 2 vols. . . . Eighteenth Century Collections Online 2. Kingston, Jamaica.

———. 1790. *Acts of Assembly Passed in the Island of Jamaica, in the Years 1789 and 1790*. Eighteenth Century Collections Online; Gale Group.

———. 1792. *The Laws of Jamaica: Comprehending all the Acts in force, passed between the thirty-second year of the reign of King Charles the Second, and the thirty-third year of . . . George the Third*. Eighteenth Century Collections Online; Gale Group 2. St. Jago de la Vega, Jamaica.

———. 1793. *An Abridgment of the Laws of Jamaica; Being an alphabetical digest of all the public Acts of Assembly now in force, from the thirty-second year of King Charles II. to the thirty-second year of . . . George III.* Inclusive, as published in two volumes. . . . Eighteenth-Century Collections Online. St. Jago de la Vega, Jamaica.

———. 1797. *The Laws of Jamaica, Passed in the Thirty-Seventh Year of the Reign of King George the Third.* . . . Eighteenth Century Collections Online. St. Jago de la Vega, Jamaica.

Jamaica Geological Survey. 1969. *Map and Brief Explanation of Geology.* Jamaica Geological Survey Department. Kingston, Jamaica.

James, C.L.R. 1963. *Black Jacobins: Toussaint L'Ouverture and the San Domingo Revolution.* 2nd ed. revised from 1963. New York: Vintage.

Jefferys, T. 1771. *A General Topography of North America and the West Indies. Being a Collection of all the Maps, Charts, Plans, and Particular Surveys, that have been published of that Part of the World, either in Europe or America.* London.: Sayer

———. [1768] 1776. A New and Correct Map of Jamaica. In *A General Topography of North America and the West Indies. Being a Collection of all the Maps, Charts, Plans, and Particular Surveys, that have been Published of that Part of the World, either in Europe or America.* Printed for Robert Sayer . . . and Thomas Jefferys, London.

Johnson, M. 1989. Conceptions of agency in archaeological interpretation. *Journal of Anthropological Archaeology* 8(2): 198–211.

———. 1996. *The Archaeology of Capitalism.* Oxford: Blackwell.

Johnson, M. V. 2006. *Ideas of Landscape.* London: Blackwell.

Jones, S. 1997. *The Archaeology of Ethnicity: Constructing Identities in the Past and Present.* New York: Routledge.

———. 1999. The Praxis of Archaeology. In *Historical Archaeology, Back from the Edge*, edited by P. Funari, M. Hall and S. Jones, pp. 219–32. One World Archaeology series. New York: Routledge.

Jordan, S. C., C. Schrire, and D. Miller. 1999. Petrography of locally produced pottery from the Dutch colonial Cape of Good Hope, South Africa. *Journal of Archaeological Science* 26: 1327–37.

Joyce, R. A. 1993. Women's work: Images of production and reproduction in prehispanic Southern Central America. *Current Anthropology* 34(3): 255–74.

Katzin, M. F. 1959a. Community organization in rural Jamaica. *Social and Economic Studies* 8(4).

———. 1959b. The Jamaican country higgler. *Social and Economic Studies* 8(4): 421–40.

———. 1960. The business of higglering in Jamaica. *Social and Economic Studies* 9(3): 297–331.

———. 1971. The business of higglering in Jamaica. In *Peoples and Cultures of the Caribbean*, edited by M. M. Horowitz, pp. 340–81. New York: American Museum of Natural History.

Kea, R. 1996. "When I die, I shall return to my own land." In *The Cloth of Many Colored Silks: Papers on History and Society Ghanaian and Islamic in Honor of Ivor Wilks*, edited by J. Hunwick and N. Lawler, pp. 159–93. Evanston, Ill.: Northwestern University Press.

Kellar, E. 2004. *The Construction and Expression of Identity: An Archaeological Investigation of the Laborer Villages at Adrian Estate, St. John, USVI*. Ph.D. diss., Syracuse University, Syracuse, New York. Ann Arbor, Mich.: University Microfilms.

Kelly, K. G. 1996. Trade contacts and social change: The archaeology of the Hueda Kingdom, Republic of Bénin. In *Aspects of African Archaeology*, edited by R. Soper and G. Pwiti, pp. 687–91. Harare: University of Zimbabwe Press.

———. 1997a. The archaeology of African-European interaction: Investigating the social role of trade, traders, and the use of space in the seventeenth- and eighteenth-century Hueda Kingdom, Republic of Benin. *World Archaeology* 28(3): 351–69.

———. 1997b. Using historically informed archaeology: Seventeenth and eighteenth century Hueda / European interaction on the coast of Bénin. *Journal of Archaeological Method and Theory* (3/4): 353–66.

———. 2001. Change and continuity in coastal Bénin. In *West Africa During the Atlantic Slave Trade: Archaeological Perspectives*, edited by C. R. DeCorse, pp. 81–100. Leicester: Leicester University Press.

———. 2002. Indigenous responses to colonial encounters on the West African Coast: Hueda and Dahomey from the 17th through 19th centuries. In *The Archaeology of Colonialism*, edited by C. L. Lyons and J. Papadopoulos, pp. 96–120. Issues and Debates series, Getty Research Institute, Los Angeles, Calif.

———. 2004. The African Diaspora starts here: Historical archaeology in coastal West Africa. In *African Historical Archaeologies*, edited by P. Lane and A. Reid, pp. 219–41. Kluwer Academic/Plenum Press, New York.

Kelly, K. G., and M. W. Hauser. In Press. Cabotage or contraband: Compositional analysis of French colonial ceramics. *Journal of Caribbean Archaeology* (submitted).

Kelly, K. G., and N. Norman. 2006. Medium vessels and the Longue Durée: The endurance of ritual ceramics and the archaeology of the African Diaspora. In *African Re-Genesis: Confronting Social Issues in the Diaspora*, edited by J. B. Haviser and K. C. MacDonald, pp. 223–34. New York: Left Coast Press.

Kiple, K. 1984. *The Caribbean Slave: A Biological History*. New York: Cambridge University Press.

Kiple, K., and V. Kiple. 1991 [1980]. Deficiency diseases in the Caribbean. In *Caribbean Slave Society and Economy: A Student Reader*, edited by V. Shepherd, pp. 173–82. New York: New Press.

Kiple, K., and K. C. Ornelas. 1996. After the encounter: Disease and demographies in the Lesser Antilles. In *The Lesser Antilles in the Age of European Expansion*, edited by R. L. Paquette and S. L. Engerman, pp. 50–69. Gainesville: University Press of Florida.

Klein, H. S., and S. L. Engerman. 1978. Fertility differentials between slaves in the United States and the British West Indies: A note on lactation practices and their possible implications. *William and Mary College Quarterly* 35(2): 357–74.

Klein, M. A. 2002. The slave trade and decentralized societies. *Journal of African History* 42: 49–65.

Knight, F. W. 1990. *The Caribbean: The Genesis of Fragmented Nationalism*. New York: Oxford University Press.

Knight, F. W., and P. K. Liss. 1991. *Atlantic Port Cities: Economy, Culture, and Society in the Atlantic World, 1650–1850*. 1st ed. Knoxville: University of Tennessee Press.

Knight, J. 1726. *The State of the island of Jamaica. Chiefly in Relation to Its Commerce, and the Conduct of the Spaniards in the West-Indies. Address'd to a Member of Parliament*. London: Printed for H. Whitridge.

Kopytoff, I., and S. Miers. 1977. *Slavery in Africa: Historical and Anthropological Perspectives*. Madison: University of Wisconsin Press.

Kouwenberg, S. Forthcoming. The problem of multiple substrates: The case of Jamaican Creole. In *Creoles between Substrates and Superstrates*, edited by S. Michaelis. Amsterdam: John Benjamins.

———. In press. *Africans in Early English Jamaica: The Akan-Dominance Myth*.

Krause, R. A. 1978. Toward a formal account of Bantu ceramic manufacture. In *Archaeological essays in honor of Irving B. Rouse*, edited by R. A. Dunnell and E. S. Hall, pp. 87–120. The Hague: Mouton.

———. 1985. *The Clay Sleeps: An Ethnoarchaeological Study of Three African Potters*. Tuscaloosa: University of Alabama Press.

Kroeber, A. L. 1916. *Zuñi Potsherds*. Anthropological Papers of the American Museum of Natural History, Vol. 18, Pt. 1. New York: The Trustees.

Kropp Dakubu, M. E. 1988. *The Languages of Ghana*. London: Kegan Paul.

La Rosa Corzo, G. 1988. *Los cimarrones de Cuba. Historia de Cuba*. Havana: Editorial de Ciencias Sociales.

———. 1991. *Los palenques del oriente de Cuba. Resistencia y acoso*. Havana: Editorial Academia.

La Rosa Corzo, G., and M. T. Gonzalez. 2004. *Cazadores de esclavos: Diarios*. Havana: Fundación Fernando Ortiz.

LaViolette, A. J. 1995. Women craft specialists in Jenné: The manipulation of Mande social categories. In *Status and Identity in West Africa: Nyamakalaw of Mali*, edited by D. C. Conrad and B. E. Frank, pp. 171–81. Bloomington: Indiana University Press.

———. 2000. *Ethno-Archaeology in Jenné, Mali: Craft and status among smiths, potters and masons*. British Archaeological Reports, International Series 838. Oxford: Archaeopress.

Leese, M. N., and P. L. Main. 1994. The efficient computation of unbiased Mahalanobis distances and their interpretation in archaeometry. *Archaeometry* 36: 307–16.

Lefebvre, H. 1991. *The Production of Space*. New York: Oxford University Press.

Lenik, S. 2004. Historical archaeological approaches to Afro-Cruzan identity at Estate Lower Bethlehem, St. Croix, U.S. Virgin Islands. Master's thesis, University of South Carolina, Columbia.

Leone, M. P. 1984. Interpreting ideology in historical archaeology: Using the rules of perspective in the William Paca Garden in Annapolis, Maryland. In *Ideology, Repre-*

sentation and Power in Prehistory, edited by C. Tilley and D. Miller, pp. 25–35. New York: Cambridge University Press.

———. 1988. The relationship between archaeological data and the documentary record: Eighteenth-century gardens in Annapolis, Maryland. *Historical Archaeology* 22(1): 29–35.

———. 1995. A historical archaeology of capitalism. *American Anthropologist* 97: 251–68.

Leslie, C. 1740. *A New and Exact account of Jamaica, wherein the antient and present state of that colony, its importance to Great Britain, laws, trade, manners and religion, together with the most remarkable and curious animals, plants, trees, &c. are described: with a particular account of the sacrifices, libations, &c. at this day in use among the negroes.* . . . 3rd ed. Edinburgh: R. Fleming.

———. 1741. *A New History of Jamaica . . . In thirteen letters from a gentleman to his friend.*. Dublin: Oliver Nelson.

Lightfoot, K. G. 2005. The archaeology of colonization: California in cross-cultural perspective. In *The Archaeology of Colonial Encounters: Comparative Perspectives*, edited by G. Stein, pp. 207–35. School of American Research Advanced Seminar Series, G. J. Gumerman, general editor. Santa Fe: School of American Research Press.

Lilly, W. 1647. *Christian Astrology: Modestly Treated of in Three Books.* London: Printed by Tho. Brudenell for John Partridge and Humph. Blunden

Little, B. 1994. People with history: An update on historical archaeology in the United States. *Journal of Archaeological Method and Theory* 1(1): 540.

———. 2004. Archaeology, history, and material culture: Grounding abstractions and other imponderables. *International Journal of Historical Archaeology* 1(2): 179–87.

Loftfield, T. C. 2001. Creolization in seventeenth-century Barbados. In *Island Lives: Historical Archaeologies of the Caribbean*, edited by P. Farnsworth, pp. 207–33. Tuscaloosa: University of Alabama Press.

Long, E. [1774] 1970. *The history of Jamaica; or, General survey of the antient and modern state of that island: with reflections on its situations, settlements, inhabitants, climate, products, commerce, laws, and government. New, with a new introd.* by George Metcalf. Cass library of West Indian studies, No. 12. [London]: F. Cass.

Longacre, W. A., and School of American Research (Santa Fe). 1970. *Reconstructing Prehistoric Pueblo Societies.* 1st ed. Albuquerque: University of New Mexico Press.

———. 1991. *Ceramic Ethnoarchaeology.* Tucson: University of Arizona Press.

Lovejoy, P. E. 1981. Slavery in the context of ideology. In *The Ideology of Slavery in Africa*, edited by P. E. Lovejoy, pp. 11–38. Beverly Hills: Sage Publications.

———. 1982. Volume of the Atlantic slave trade. *Journal of African History* 23: 473–501.

———. 1983. *Transformations in Slavery: A History of Slavery in Africa.* African studies series, 36. Cambridge and New York: Cambridge University Press.

———. 1989. The impact of the slave trade on West Africa, a review of the literature. *Journal of African History* 30: 365–94.

Lovejoy, P. E., and J. C. Curto. 2004. *Enslaving Connections: Changing Cultures of Africa and Brazil during the Era of Slavery.* Amherst, N.Y.: Humanity Books.

Lowenthal, D. 1972. *West Indian Societies.* New York: Oxford University Press.

———. 1977. The bicentennial landscape: A mirror held up to the past. *Geographical Review* 67(3): 253–67.

Lynott, M. J., H. Neff, J. E. Price, J. W. Cogswell, and M. D. Glascock. 2000. Inferences about prehistoric ceramics and people in southeast Missouri: Results of ceramic compositional analysis. *American Antiquity* 65(1): 103–26.

MacEachern, S. 1994. "Symbolic reservoirs" and cultural relations between ethnic groups: West African examples. *The African Archaeological Review* 12: 203–22.

———. 1996. Foreign countries: The development of ethnoarchaeology in sub-Saharan Africa. *Journal of World Prehistory* 10(3): 243–304.

———. 1998. Scale, style and cultural variation: Technological traditions in the northern Mandara Mountains. In *The Archaeology of Social Boundaries*, edited by M. Stark, pp. 107–31. Washington, D.C.: Smithsonian Institution Press.

Magana, C. 1999. Criollo pottery from San Juan de Puerto Rico. In *African Sites Archaeology in the Caribbean*, edited by J. B. Haviser, pp. 131–42. Kingston: Ian Randle.

Mallory-Greenough, L. M., J. D. Greenough, and J. V. Owen. 1998. Provenance of temper in a New Kingdom Egyptian pottery sherd: Evidence from the petrology and mineralogy of basalt fragments. *Geoarchaeology* 13: 391–410.

Manning, P. 1990. *Slavery and African Life: Occidental, Oriental, and African Slave Trades.* New York: Cambridge University Press.

Marcus, G. E. 1998. *Ethnography through Thick and Thin.* Princeton, N.J.: Princeton University Press.

Marcus, G. E., and F. R. Myers. 1995. *The Traffic in Culture: Refiguring Art and Anthropology.* Berkeley: University of California Press.

Marcus, J. 1991. Another pinch of salt: A comment on Mackinnon and Kepecs. *American Antiquity* 56(3): 526–27.

Marquardt, W. H. 1992. Dialectical archaeology. In *Archaeological Method and Theory*, vol. 4, edited by M. B. Schiffer, pp. 101–40. Tucson: University of Arizona Press.

Marshall, W. K. 2003. The post-slavery problem revisited. In *Slavery, Freedom, and Gender: The Dynamics of Caribbean Society*, edited by B. L. Moore, B. W. Higman, C. Campbell, and P. Bryan, pp. 115–32. Kingston: University of the West Indies Press.

Mason, O., and J. Aigner. 1987. Petrographic analysis of basalt artifacts from three Aleutian sites. *American Antiquity* 52(3): 595–607.

Mathewson, R. D. 1972a. History from the earth: Archaeological excavations at Old King's House. *Jamaica Journal* 6: 3–11.

———. 1972b. Jamaican ceramics: An introduction to 18th century folk pottery in West African tradition. *Jamaica Journal* 6: 54–56.

———. 1973. Archaeological analysis of material culture as a reflection of sub-cultural differentiation in 18th century Jamaica. *Jamaica Journal* 7: 25–29.

Mayes, P. 1972. *Port Royal Jamaica: Excavations 1969–1970.* Kingston, Jamaica: Jamaica National Trust Commission.

Mbembe, A. 2002. *On the Postcolony*. Berkeley: University of California Press.
McCafferty, S., and G. McCafferty. 1991. Spinning and weaving as female gender identity in post-classic Central Mexico. In *Textile Traditions of Mesoamerica and the Andes: An Anthology*, edited by M. Schevill, J. C. Berlo, and E. Dwyer, pp. 19–44. New York: Garland.
McClenaghan, P. E. 1988. Drinking glasses from Port Royal, Jamaica c. 1630–1840: A study of styles and usage. Master's thesis, Texas A&M University, College Station.
McDonald, R. A. 1993. *The Economy and Material Culture of Slaves: Goods and Chattels on the Sugar Plantations of Jamaica and Louisiana*. Baton Rouge: Louisiana State University Press.
———. 1995. Independent economic production by slaves on antebellum Louisiana sugar plantations. In *The Slaves' Economy: Independent Production by Slaves in the Americas*, edited by I. Berlin and P. D. Morgan, pp. 182–208. New York: Routledge.
———. 1996. *West Indies Accounts: Essays on the History of the British Caribbean and the Atlantic Economy in Honour of Richard Sheridan*. Barbados: The Press, University of the West Indies.
McEwan, B. 1995. Spanish precedents and domestic life at Puerto Real: The archaeology of two Spanish homesites. In *Puerto Real: The Archaeology of a Sixteenth-Century Spanish Town in Hispaniola*, edited by K. Deagan, pp. 195–230. Gainesville: University Press of Florida.
McGuire, R. H. 1982. The study of ethnicity in historical archaeology. *Journal of Anthropological Archaeology* 1(2): 159–78.
———. 1992. *A Marxist Archaeology*. San Diego: Academic Press.
McIntosh, S. K. 1995. Excavations at Jenne-jeno, Hambarketolo, and Kaniana (Inland Niger Delta, Mali), the 1981 season. In *University of California Publications in Anthropology*, vol. 20. Berkeley: University of California Press.
McIntosh, S. K., and H. Bocoum. 2000. New perspectives on Sincu Bara, a first millennium site in the Senegal Valley. *African Archaeological Review* 17(1): 1–43.
McIntosh, S. K., and I. Thiaw. 2001. Tools for understanding transformation and continuity in Senegambian society: A.D. 1500–190. In *West Africa during the Atlantic Slave Trade: Archaeological Perspectives*, edited by C. R. DeCorse, pp. 14–37. Leicester: Leicester University Press.
McKee, L. 1999. Food supply and plantation social order: An archaeological perspective. In *"I, too, am America": Archaeological Studies of African-American Life*, edited by T. A. Singleton, pp. 218–39. Charlottesville: University Press of Virginia.
McKusick, M. B. 1960. *Distribution of Ceramic Styles in the Lesser Antilles, West Indies*. Ph.D. diss., Yale University, New Haven. Ann Arbor, Mich.: University Microfilms.
Meillassoux, C. 1991. *The Anthropology of Slavery: The Womb of Iron and Gold*. Chicago: University of Chicago Press.
Meskell, L. 1999. *Archaeologies of Social Life: Age, Sex, Class, etc. in Ancient Egypt*. Oxford: Blackwell.
———. 2002a. *Private Life in New Kingdom Egypt*. Princeton, N.J.: Princeton University Press.

———. 2002b. The intersections of identity and politics in archaeology. *Annual Review of Anthropology* 31: 279–301.

Meyers, A. D. 1999. West African tradition in the decoration of colonial Jamaican folk pottery. *Journal of Historical Archaeology* 3(4): 201–24.

Middleton, A. P. 1998. *Ceramic Petrography*. Revista do Museu de Arqueologia e Etnologia, Sao Paulo, Suplemento 2, 73–79.

Middleton, A. P., I. C. Freestone, and M. N. Leese. 1985. Textural analysis of ceramic thin sections: Evaluation of grain sampling procedures. *Archaeometry* 54(1): 147–60.

Miller, D. 1985. *Artefacts as Categories: A Study of Ceramic Variability in Central India*. Cambridge and New York: Cambridge University Press.

Mills, B. J. 1999. Ceramics and the social contexts of food consumption in the northern Southwest. In *Pottery and People, A Dynamic Interaction*, edited by J. Skibo and G. Feinman, pp. 99–114. Salt Lake City: University of Utah Press.

Mintz, S. W. 1955. The Jamaican internal marketing pattern. *Social and Economic Studies* 4: 95–103.

———. 1960. Peasant markets. *American Scientific* 203(2): 112–22.

———. 1971a. Men, Women, and Trade. *Comparative Studies in Society and History* 13(3): 247–69.

———. 1971b. Toward an Afro-American history. *Cahiers d'histoire mondiale* 13(2): 317–32.

———. 1978. Caribbean marketplaces and Caribbean history. *Nova Americana* 1(1): 333–44.

———. 1983. Caribbean marketplaces and Caribbean history. *Radical History Review* 27: 110–20.

———. 1985. *Sweetness and Power: The Place of Sugar in Modern History*. New York: Viking.

———. [1974] 1992. *Caribbean Transformations*. Chicago: Aldine.

Mintz, S. W., and D. Hall. [1970] 1991. The origins of the Jamaican internal marketing system. In *Caribbean Slave Society and Economy: A Student Reader*, edited by V. Shepherd, pp. 319–34. New York: New Press.

Mintz, S. W., and R. Price. 1992. *The Birth of African-American Culture: An Anthropological Perspective*. Boston: Beacon Press.

Mintz, S. W., and S. Price. 1985. *Caribbean Contours*. Johns Hopkins Studies in Atlantic History and Culture. Baltimore: Johns Hopkins University Press.

Mitchell, W.J.T. 1994a. Introduction. In *Landscape and Power*, edited by W.J.T. Mitchell, pp. 1–5. Chicago: University of Chicago Press.

———. 1994b. Imperial landscapes. In *Landscape and Power*, edited by W.J.T. Mitchell, pp. 6–34. Chicago: University of Chicago Press.

Mohammed, P. 1996. Writing gender into history: The negotiation of gender relations among Indian men and women in post-indenture Trinidad society, 1917–1945. In *Engendering History: Caribbean Women in Historical Perspective*, edited by V. Shepherd, B. Brereton, and B. Bailey, pp. 20–47. New York: St. Martin's Press.

Moitt, B. 2005. Freedom from bondage at a price: Women and redemption from slavery in the French Caribbean in the nineteenth century. *Slavery and Abolition* 26(2): 247–56.

Mommsen, H. 2001. Provenance determination of pottery by trace element analysis: Problems, solutions and applications. *Journal of Radioanalytical and Nuclear Chemistry* 247(3): 657–62.

Monette, Y., M. Richer-LaFlèche, M. Moussette, and D. Dufournier. 2007. Compositional analysis of local redwares: Characterizing the pottery productions of 16 workshops located in Southern Québec dating from late 17th to late 19th-century. *Journal of Archaeological Science* 34(1): 123–40.

Morgan, D. 1989. *Ma Lou: Profile of a Potter*. Kingston: Petroleum Corporation of Jamaica.

Morgan, J. 2002. Slavery and the slave trade. In *A Companion to American Women's History*, edited by N. A. Hewitt, pp. 20–34. New York: Blackwell.

———. 2004. *Laboring Women: Reproduction and Gender in New World Slavery*. Philadelphia: University of Pennsylvania Press.

———. 2006. Accounting for the women in slavery: Demography and the transatlantic slave trade. Paper given at the University of Notre Dame, Sept. 14, 2006.

Morgan, P. D. 1995. Slaves and livestock in eighteenth-century Jamaica: Vineyard pen, 1750–1751. *William and Mary Quarterly* 52(1): 47–76.

———. 1997. *The Cultural Implications of the Atlantic Slave Trade: African Regional Origins, American Destinations and New World Developments*, edited by D. Richardson and D. Eltis, pp. 122–45. London: Routledge.

———. 1998. *Slave Counterpoint: Black Culture in the Eighteenth-Century Chesapeake and Lowcountry*. Chapel Hill: University of North Carolina Press.

———. 2002. Conspiracy scares. *The William and Mary Quarterly* 59(1): 159–66.

Morrison, K. D., and M. T. Lycett. 1997. Inscriptions as Artifacts: Precolonial South India and the Analysis of Texts. *Journal of Archaeological Method and Theory* 3(3–4): 215–37.

Morrison, K. D., and C. M. Sinopoli. 1992. Economic diversity and integration in a precolonial Indian empire. *World Archaeology* 23(3): 335–52.

Moss, A. J. 1972. Initial fluviatile fragmentation of granitic quartz. *Journal of Sedimentary Petrology* 42: 905–916.

Muller, J. 1997. *Mississippian Political Economy*. New York: Kluwer/Plenum Press.

Mullin, M. 1994. *Africa in America: Slave Acculturation and Resistance in the American South and the British Caribbean*. Bloomington: Indiana University Press.

Mullins, P. R. 1998. Expanding archaeological discourse: Ideology, metaphor, and critical theory in historical archaeology. In *Annapolis Pasts: Historical Archaeology in Annapolis, Maryland*, edited by P. A. Shackel, P. R. Mullins, and M. S. Warner, pp. 7–34. Knoxville: University of Tennessee Press.

Mullins, P. R., and R. Paynter. 2000. Representing colonizers: An archaeology of creolization, ethnogenesis, and indigenous material culture among the Haida. *Historical Archaeology* 34(3): 73–84.

Murdock, G. P. 1959. *Africa: Its Peoples and Their Culture History*. New York: McGraw-Hill.

Neff, H. 1992. Introduction. In *Chemical Characterization of Ceramic Pastes in Archaeology*, edited by H. Neff, 1–10. Madison: Prehistory Press.

———. 1994. RQ-mode principal components analysis of ceramic compositional data. *Archaeometry* 36: 115–30.

———. 2000. Neutron activation analysis for provenance determination in archaeology. In *Modern Methods in Art and Archaeology*, edited by E. Ciliberto and G. Spoto, pp. 81–134. Chemical Analysis series, Vol. 55. New York: John Wiley and Sons.

———. 2001. Quantitative techniques for analyzing ceramic compositional data. In *Ceramic Production and Circulation in the Greater Southwest: Source Determination by INAA and Complementary Mineralogical Investigations*, edited by D. Glowacki and H. Neff, pp. 15–36. Monograph 44. Los Angeles: Cotsen Institute of Archaeology.

Neff, H., J. W. Cogwell, L. J. Kosakowsky, F. E. Belli, and F. J. Bove. 1999. A new perspective on the relationships among cream paste ceramic traditions of southeastern Mesoamerica. *Latin American Antiquity* 10(3): 281–99.

Newman, R. 1992. Applications of petrography and electron microprobe analysis to the study of Indian stone sculpture. *Archaeometry* 34(2): 163–74.

Nicholson, D. 1990. Afro-Antiguan folk-pottery and emancipation. In *Proceedings of the 11th Congress for Caribbean Archaeology*, edited by A. Vargas and M. Sanoja, pp. 433–37. San Juan: La Fundacion Arquelologica, Antropologica, y Historica de Puerto Rico.

Norman, N. 2004. The serpent ditch and the rainbow: Landscape politics in West Africa. Master's thesis, University of South Carolina, Columbia.

Norman, N. and K. G. Kelly. 2004. Landscape politics: The serpent ditch and the rainbow in West Africa. *American Anthropologist* 106(1): 89–110.

Northrup, D. 2000. Igbo and Myth Igbo: Culture and ethnicity in the Atlantic world, 1600–1850. *Slavery and Abolition* 21(3): 1–20.

Norton, A., and R. Symanski. 1975. The internal marketing systems of Jamaica. *Geographical Review* 65(4): 461–75.

O'Donovan, M. 2002. *The Dynamics of Power*. [Carbondale]: Center for Archaeological Investigations, Southern Illinois University, Carbondale.

Ogundiran, A. 2001. Ceramic spheres and regional networks in the Yoruba-Edo Region, Nigeria, 13th–19th centuries A.C. *Journal of Field Archaeology* 28(1/2): 27–43.

———. 2002. Of small things remembered: Beads, cowries, and cultural translations of the Atlantic experience in Yorubaland. *The International Journal of African Historical Studies*, 35(2/3): 427–57.

Olin, J., J. Blackman, J. Mitchem, and G. Waselkov. 2002. Compositional analysis of glazed earthenwares from eighteenth-century sites on the northern Gulf Coast. *Historical Archaeology* 36(1): 79–96.

Ollman, B. 1993. *Dialectical Investigations*. London: Routledge.

Olwell, R. 1996. "Loose, idle and disorderly": Slave women in the eighteenth-century Charleston marketplace. In *More Than Chattel: Black Women and Slavery in the Americas*, edited by D. B. Gaspar and D. C. Hine, pp. 97–110. Bloomington: Indiana University Press.

Olwig, K. F. 1977. *Households, Exchange and Social Reproduction: The Development of a Caribbean Society.* Ph.D. diss., University of Minnesota, Minneapolis. Ann Arbor, Mich.: University Microfilms.

———. 1985. *Cultural Adaptation and Resistance on St. John: Three Centuries of Afro-Caribbean Life.* Gainesville: University of Florida Press.

———. 1987. Village, Culture and Identity on St. John, V.I. In *Afro-Caribbean Villages in Historical Perspective*, edited by C. V. Carnegie, pp. 20–44: African-Caribbean Institute of Jamaica.

———. 1990. Cultural Identity and Material Culture: Afro-Caribbean Pottery. *Folk* 32: 5–22.

Olwig, K. R. 1996. Nature—Mapping the ghostly traces of a concept. In *Concepts in Human Geography*, edited by C. Earle, K. Mathewson, and M. Kenzer, pp. 63–96. Savage, Md.: Rowman & Littlefield.

Ong, A. 1999. *Flexible Citizenship: The Cultural Logics of Transnationality.* Durham, N.C.: Duke University Press.

Orser, C. E. 1996. *A Historical Archaeology of the Modern World. Contributions to Global Historical Archaeology.* New York: Plenum Press.

———. (editor). 2001. *Race and the Archaeology of Identity.* Salt Lake City: University of Utah Press.

Ortiz, F. 1940. *Contrapunteo cubano del tabaco y el azucar.* Havana: Ediciones Ciences Sociales.

———. 1994. *Cuban Counterpoint: Tobacco and Sugar.* Durham, N.C.: Duke University Press.

Osborne, F. J. 1974. Spanish church, St. Ann's Bay. *Jamaica Journal* 8: 33–35.

Owen, J. V., and D. Hansen. 1996. Compositional constraints on the identification of eighteenth-century porcelain sherds from Fort Beausejour, New Brunswick and Grassy Island, Nova Scotia, Canada. *Historical Archaeology* 30(4): 88–100.

Palmié, S. 2006. Creolization and its discontents. *Annual Review of Anthropology* 35: 433–56.

Paquette, R. L., and S. L. Engerman (editors). 1996. *The Lesser Antilles in the Age of European Expansion.* Gainesville: University Press of Florida.

Pares, R. 1956. *Yankees and Creoles: The Trade between North America and the West Indies before the American Revolution.* Cambridge: Harvard University Press.

Parrent, J., and M. Brown Parrent. 1993. The search continues for Columbus's caravels: 1992 field report. *INA Newsletter* 20(1): 8–14.

Parrent, J., J. Neville, and B. Neyland. 1991. The search for Columbus's last ships: The 1991 field season. *INA Newsletter* 18(4): 16–19.

Pasquariello, R. 1995. An analysis of Non-European, coarse earthenware from Port Royal, Jamaica. Master's thesis, Dept. of Anthropology, Syracuse University, Syracuse, New York.

Paton, D. 1996. Decency, dependence and the lash: Gender and the British debate over slave emancipation, 1830–34. *Slavery and Abolition* 17(3): 163–84.

———. 2001. Punishment, crime, and the bodies of slaves in eighteenth-century Jamaica. *Journal of Social History* 34 (4): 923–54.

Patterson, O. 1969. *The Sociology of Slavery; An Analysis of the Origins, Development, and Structure of Negro Slave Society in Jamaica*. 1st American ed. Rutherford, N.J.: Fairleigh Dickinson University Press.

———. 1982. *Slavery and Social Death: A Comparative Study*. Cambridge: Harvard University Press.

Patterson, T. C. 1999. The political economy of archaeology in the United States. *Annual Review of Anthropology* 28: 155–74.

Pauketat, T. R. 2000. The tragedy of commoners. In *Agency in Archaeology*, edited by M. A. Dobres and J. Robb, pp. 113–29. New York and London: Routledge.

———. 2004. The economy of the moment: Cultural practices and Mississippian chiefdoms. In *Archaeological Perspectives on Political Economies*, edited by L. M. Nicholas, pp. 25–39. Foundations of Archaeological Inquiry, J. Skibo, general editor. Salt Lake City: University of Utah Press.

Pawson, M., and D. Buisseret. [1975] 2001. *Port Royal, Jamaica*. Oxford: Clarendon Press.

Peacock, D.P.S. 1970. The scientific analysis of ancient ceramics: A review. *World Archaeology* 1: 375–89.

———. 1977. Ceramics in Roman and medieval archaeology. In *Early Commerce*, edited by D.P.S. Peacock, pp. 21–34. London: Academic Press.

———. 1980. The Roman millstone trade: A petrological sketch. *World Archaeology* 12(1): 43–53.

———. 1982. *Pottery in the Roman World: An Ethnoarchaeological Approach*. London: Longman.

Pedley, M. S. 1979. The subscription list of the 1757 Atlas Universal; A study in cartographic dissemination. *Imago Mundi* 31: 66–77.

Petersen, J., and D. Watters. 1988. Afro-Montserratian ceramics from the Harney site Cemetery, Montserrat, West Indies. *Annals of the Carnegie Museum* 67: 167–87.

Petersen, J., D. Watters, and D. Nicholson. 1999. Continuity and syncretism in Afro-Caribbean ceramics from the northern Lesser Antilles. In *African Sites Archaeology in the Caribbean*, edited by J. B. Haviser, pp. 157–220. Kingston: Ian Randle.

Pettijohn, F. J. 1975. *Sedimentary Rocks*. 3rd ed. New York: Harper & Row.

Pettijohn, F. J., P. E. Potter, and R. Siever. 1972. *Sand and Sandstone*. Berlin: Springer-Verlag.

Petty, W. [1669] 1970. *The Political Anatomy of Ireland*. Shannon: Irish University Press.

Phillippo, J. M. [1843] 1969. *Jamaica: Its Past and Present State*. 1st ed. reprinted. With a new introduction by Philip Wright. London: Dawsons.

Philpotts, A. R. 1989. *Petrography of Igneous and Metamorphic Rocks*. Clifton Heights, N.J.: Prentice Hall.

Piot, Charles. 1996. Of slaves and the gift: Kabre sale of kin during the era of the slave trade. *Journal of African History* 37: 31–49.

Pitman, F. [1917] 1945. *The Development of the British West Indies, 1700–1763*. New Haven: Yale University Press.

Plog, S. 1980. *Stylistic Variation of Prehistoric Ceramics: Design Analysis in the American Southwest*. Cambridge: Cambridge University Press.
Pope, P. H. 1969. *Cruzan Slavery: An Ethnohistorical Study of Differential Responses to Slavery in the Danish West Indies*. Ph.D. diss., University of California, Davis. Ann Arbor, Mich.: University Microfilms.
Porter, A. R. D., T. A. Jackson, and E. Robinson. 1982. *Minerals and Rocks of Jamaica*. Kingston: Longman.
Posnansky, M. 1961. Pottery types from archaeological sites in East Africa. *Journal of African History* 2: 177–98.
———. 1973. Aspects of early West African trade. *World Archaeology* 5: 149–62.
———. 1976a. New radiocarbon dates from Ghana. *Sankofa* 2: 60–63.
———. 1976b. Archaeology and the origins of the Akan society in Ghana. In *Problems in Economic and Social Archaeology*, edited by G. de G. Sieveking, I. H. Longworth, and K. E. Wilson, pp. 49–59. London: Duckworth.
———. 1979. Archaeological aspects of the Brong-Ahaf o Region. In *A profile of Brong Kyempim: Essays on the Archaeology, History, Language and Politics of the Brong Peoples of Ghana*, edited by K. Arhin, pp. 22–35. Accra, Ghana: Afram Publications.
———. 1982. African archaeology comes of age. *World Archaeology* 13(3): 345–58.
———. 1984. Toward an archaeology of the Black Diaspora. *Journal of Black Studies* 15: 195–205.
———. 1987. Prelude to Akan civilization. In *The Golden Stool: Studies of the Asante Center and Periphery*, edited by E. Schildkrout, pp. 14–22. Anthropological Papers, Vol. 65., Pt. 1. New York: American Museum of Natural History.
———. 1999. West Africanist reflections on African–American archaeology. In *"I, too, Am America": Archaeological Studies of African American Life*, edited by T. A. Singleton, pp. 21–38. Charlottesville: University of Virginia Press.
Posnansky, M., and P. de Barros. (1980). An Archaeological Reconnaissance of Togo, August 1979. Prepared for The Minister of National Education for Scientific Research of under the sponsorship of the U.S. International Communication Agency.
Pratt, M. L. 1992. *Imperial Eyes: Travel Writing and Transculturation*. New York: Routledge.
Pratt Puig, F. 1980. *Significad De Un Conjuito Ceramico Hispano Del XVI Santiago de Cuba*. Cuba: De Santiago De Cuba, Editorial Oriente.
Price, S. and R. Price. 1980. *Afro-American Arts of the Suriname Rainforest, Museum of Cultural History*. Los Angeles: University of California.
———. 1999. *Maroon Arts: Cultural Vitality in the African Diaspora*. Boston: Beacon Press.
Pulsipher, L. 1990. They have Saturdays and Sundays to feed themselves. *Expedition Magazine* 32(2): 24–33.
———. 1991 Galways Plantation, Montserrat. In *Seeds of Change*, edited by H. J. Viola and C. Margolis, pp. 139–59. Washington, D.C.: Smithsonian Institution Press.
———. 1994. The landscapes and ideational roles of Caribbean slave gardens. In *Ar-*

chaeology of Garden and Field, edited by N. Miller and K. Gleason, pp. 202–21. Philadelphia: University of Pennsylvania Press.

Pulsipher, L., and M. Goodwin. 1999. Here where the old time people be: Reconstructing the landscapes of the slavery and post-slavery era on Montserrat, West Indies. In *African Sites Archaeology in the Caribbean*, edited by J. B. Haviser, pp. 9–37. Kingston: Ian Randle.

Rampini, C. 1873. *Letters from Jamaica. The Land of Streams and Woods*. Edinburgh.

Rapp, G., J. Allert, V. Vitali, Z. Jing, and E. Henrickson. 2000. *Determining Geologic Sources of Artifact Copper: Source Characterization Using Trace Element Patterns*. New York: University Press of America.

Rapp, G., and C. L. Hill. 2006. Raw materials and sources. In *Geoarchaeology: The Earth-Science Approach to Archaeological Interpretation*, pp. 195–221. New Haven: Yale University Press.

Rawley, J. A. 1981. *The Transatlantic Slave Trade: A History*. New York: Norton.

Reddock, R. 1985. Women and slavery in the Caribbean: A feminist perspective. *Latin American Perspectives* 12(1): 63–80.

———. 1988. Women and the slave plantation economy in the Caribbean. In *Retrieving Women's History: Changing Perceptions of the Role of Women in Politics and Society*, edited by J. S. Kleinberg, pp. 105–32. New York: Berg/UNESCO.

Redfield, R., R. Linton, and M. J. Herskovits. 1935. A memorandum for the study of acculturation. *Man* 35: 145–48.

Reeves, M. 1997. "By Their Own Labor": Enslaved Africans' Survival Strategies on Two Jamaican Plantations. Ph.D. diss., Department of Anthropology, Syracuse University, Syracuse, New York. Ann Arbor, Mich.: University Microfilms.

Reitan, E. A. 1985. Expanding horizons: Maps in the "Gentleman's Magazine," 1731–1754. *Imago Mundi* 37: 54–62.

Reitz, E. J., and B. G. McEwan. 1995. Animals, environment, and the Spanish diet at Puerto Real. In *Puerto Real: The Archaeology of a Sixteenth-Century Spanish Town in Hispaniola*, edited by K. Deagan. pp. 285–335, Gainesville: University Press of Florida.

Rice, P. 1988. *Pottery Analysis: A Sourcebook*. Chicago: University of Chicago Press.

Richard, F. 2007. From Cosaan to colony: Exploring archaeological landscape formations and socio-political complexity in the Siin (Senegal), A.D. 500–1900. Ph.D. diss., Department of Anthropology, Syracuse University.

Robertson, G. 1985. Some early Jamaican postcards, their photographers and publishers. *Jamaica Journal* 18(1): 13–22.

Robertson, J. 2001. Jamaican architectures before Georgian. *Winterthur Portfolio* 36(2/3): 73–95.

———. 2005. *Gone Is the Ancient Glory: Spanish Town, Jamaica 1534–2000*. Kingston: Ian Randle.

Robinson, E., J. Lewis, and R. Cant. 1970. *Field Guide to Aspects of the Geology of Jamaica. Guidebook to the Caribbean Island Arc System*. Washington D.C.: American Geological Institute.

Rodney, W. 1969. Gold and slaves on the Gold Coast. *Transactions of the Historical Society of Ghana* 10: 13–28.

Roitman, J. 2004. *Fiscal Disobedience: An Anthropology of Economic Regulation in Central Africa.* Princeton, N.J.: Princeton University Press.

Rouse, I. 1964. *Prehistory in Haiti.* [New Haven]: Reprinted by Human Relations Area Files Press.

———. 1992. *The Tainos: Rise and Decline of the People Who Greeted Columbus.* New Haven: Yale University Press.

Sackett, J. 1990. Style and ethnicity in archaeology: The case for isochrestism. In *The Uses of Style in Archaeology,* edited by M. Conkey and C. Hastorf, pp. 32–43. Cambridge: Cambridge University Press.

Sayre, E. V. 1975. *Brookhaven Procedures for Statistical Analyses of Multivariate Archaeometric Data.* Brookhaven National Laboratory Report BNL-23128.

Schlotterbeck, J. 1995. The internal economy of slavery in rural piedmont Virginia. In *The Slaves' Economy: Independent Production by Slaves in the Americas,* edited by I. Berlin and P. D. Morgan, pp. 170–81. New York: Routledge.

Schmidt, P. R. 2006. *Historical Archaeology in Africa: Representation, Social Memory, and Oral Traditions.* African Archaeology Series. Oxford: AltaMira Press.

Schmidt, P. R., and T. C. Patterson. 1995a. Introduction: From constructing to making alternative histories. In *Making Alternative Histories: The Practice of Archaeology and History in Non-Western Settings,* edited by P. R. Schmidt and T. C. Patterson, pp. 1–24. Santa Fe, N.Mex.: School of American Research Press.

——— (editors). 1995b. *Making Alternative Histories: The Practice of Archaeology and History in Non-Western Settings.* 1st pbk. ed. School of American Research Advanced Seminar series. Santa Fe, N.M.: School of American Research Press.

Schrire, C. 1988. The historical archaeology of the impact of colonialism in 17th-century South Africa. *Antiquity* 62: 214–25.

Scott, D. 2003. Political rationalities of the Jamaican modern. *Small Axe* 14: 1–22.

———. 2004a. Modernity that predated the modern: Sidney Mintz's Caribbean. *History Workshop Journal* 58: 191–210.

———. 2004b. *Conscripts of Modernity: The Tragedy of Colonial Enlightenment.* Durham, N.C.: Duke University Press.

Scott, J. 1985. *Weapons of the Weak: Everyday Forms of Peasant Resistance.* New Haven: Yale University Press.

———. 1992. *Domination and the Arts of Resistance: Hidden Transcripts.* New Haven: Yale University Press.

Shackel, P. A., P. R. Mullins, and M. S. Warner. 1998. *Annapolis Pasts: Historical Archaeology in Annapolis, Maryland.* 1st ed. Knoxville: University of Tennessee Press.

Shaw, R. 2002. *Memories of the Slave Trade: Ritual and the Historical Imagination.* Chicago: University of Chicago Press

Sheller, M. 2003. *Consuming the Caribbean: From Arawaks to Zombies.* New York: Routledge.

Shennan, S. 1989. Introduction to archaeological approaches to cultural identity. In

Archaeological Approaches to Cultural Identity, edited by S. Shennan. London: Unwin Hyman.

Shepard, A. 1954. *Ceramics for the Archaeologist*. Publication 609. Washington, D.C.: Carnegie Institution of Washington.

Shepherd, V. 1993. Alternative husbandry: Slaves and free labourers on livestock farms in Jamaica in the eighteenth and nineteenth centuries. *Slavery and Abolition* 14(1): 41–66.

———. 1996. Slavery without sugar in Caribbean plantation societies: Examples from Jamaica. In *Slaves with and without Sugar*, edited by A. Viera, pp. 207–25. Madeira: Atlantic Study Centre.

———. 2000. Trade and exchange in Jamaica in the period of slavery. In *Caribbean Slavery in the Atlantic World: A Student Reader*, edited by V. Shepherd and H. Beckles, pp. 355–63. Kingston: Ian Randle.

——— (editor). 2002. *Slavery without Sugar: Diversity in Caribbean Economy and Society since the 17th Century*. Gainesville: University Press of Florida.

Shepherd, V., and K. Monteith. 2000. Nonsugar proprietors in a sugar-plantation society. *Plantation Society in the Americas* 5(2–3): 205–25.

———. 2002. Penkeepers and coffee farmers in a plantation society. In *Slavery without Sugar: Diversity in Caribbean Economy and Society since the 17th Century*, edited by V. Shepherd, pp. 82–101. Gainesville: University Press of Florida.

Sheridan, R. 1965. The wealth of Jamaica. *Economic History Review* 18(2): 292–311.

———. 1968. The wealth of Jamica: A rejoinder. *Economic History Review* 21(1): 46–61.

———. 1973. *Sugar and Slavery: An Economic History of the British West Indies, 1623–1775*. Baltimore: Johns Hopkins University Press.

———. 1976. The crisis of slave subsistence in the British West Indies during and after the American Revolution. *William and Mary Quarterly* 33(4): 615–41.

Silliman, S. 2001. Theoretical perspectives on labor and colonialism: Reconsidering the California missions. *Journal of Anthropological Archaeology* 20: 379–407.

———. 2004. Social and Physical Landscapes of Contact: 273–96.

———. 2005. Culture contact or colonialism? Challenges in the archaeology of Native North America. *American Antiquity* 70(1): 55–74.

Simmonds, L. E. 1987. Slave higglering in Jamaica, 1780–1834. *Jamaica Journal* 20: 31–38.

———. 2004. The Afro-Jamaican and internal marketing systems: Kingston, 1780–1834. In *Jamaica in Slavery and Freedom: History, Heritage and Culture*, edited by K. Monteith, pp. 274–90. Kingston: University of West Indies Press.

Singleton, T. A. 1990. The archaeology of the plantation South: A review of approaches and goals. *Historical Archaeology* 24(4): 70–77.

———. 1995. The archaeology of slavery in North America. *Annual Review of Anthropology* 24: 119–40.

———. 1998. Cultural interaction and African American identity in plantation archaeology. In *Studies in Culture Contact: Interaction, Culture Change, and Archaeology*, edited by J. G. Cusick, pp. 172–87. Carbondale: Southern Illinois University, Center for Archaeological Investigations.

———. 2001. Slavery and spatial dialectics on Cuban coffee plantations. *World Archaeology* 33(1): 98–114.

———. 2006. African Diaspora archaeology in dialogue. In *Afro-Atlantic Dialogues*, edited by K. A. Yelvington, pp. 249–88. Santa Fe, N.Mex.: School for American Research.

Singleton, T. A., and M. Bograd. 1995. The African experience in America: A brief overview. In *The Archaeology of the African Diaspora in the Americas*, by T. A. Singleton and M. Bograd, pp. 5–12. Guides to Archaeological Literature of the Immigrant Experience in America, No. 2. [Glasboro, N.J.]: Society for Historical Archaeology.

Sinopoli, C. M. 1986. *Material Patterning and Social Organization: The Archaeological Ceramics of Vijayanagara, South India*. Ph.D. diss., University of Michigan, Ann Arbor. Ann Arbor, Mich.: University Microfilms.

———. 1988. The organization of craft production at Vijayanagara, South India. *American Anthropologist* 90(3): 580–97.

———. 1991. *Approaches to Archaeological Ceramics*. New York: Plenum Press.

———. 1994a. The archaeology of empires. *Annual Review of Anthropology* 23: 159–80.

———. 1994b. Political choices and economic strategies in the Vijayanagara empire. In *The Economic Anthropology of the State*, edited by E. M. Brumfiel, pp. 223–43. Monographs in Economic Anthropology, No. 11. Lanham, Md.: University Press of America.

———. 2003. *The Political Economy of Craft Production: Crafting Empire in South India, c. 1350–1650*. Cambridge and New York: Cambridge University Press.

Sinopoli, C. M., and K. D. Morrison. 1995. Dimensions of imperial control: The Vijayanagara capital. *American Anthropologist* 97(1): 83–96.

Skibo, J. 1992. *Pottery Function: A Use-Alteration Perspective*. New York: Plenum Press.

Sloane, H. S. 1707–1725. *A voyage to the islands Madera, Barbados, Nieves, S. Christophers and Jamaica, with the natural history of the herbs and trees, four-footed beasts, fishes, birds, insects, reptiles, &c. of the last of those islands; to which is prefix'd an introduction, wherein is an account of the inhabitants, air, waters, diseases, trade, &c. of that place, with some relations concerning the neighbouring continent, and islands of America. Illustrated with figures of the things described, which have not been heretofore engraved; in large copper-plates as big as the life*. London: Printed by B. M. for the author.

Smith, A. [1776] 1994. Edited by E. Cannan. *An Inquiry into the Nature and Causes of the Wealth of Nations*. New York: Modern Library.

Smith, A. T. 2003. *The Political Landscape: Constellations Of Authority in Early Complex Polities*. Berkeley: University of California Press.

Smith, C. W. 1995. *Analysis of the Weight Assemblage of Port Royal, Jamaica*. Ph.D. diss., Texas A&M University, College Station. Ann Arbor, Mich.: University Microfilms.

Smith, F., and K. Watson. Forthcoming. Urbanity, sociability, and commercial exchange in the Barbados sugar trade: A comparative colonial archaeological perspective on Bridgetown and Holetown Barbados in the seventeenth century. In *Scale Locality and the Caribbean Historical Archaeology: A Special Volume for the International Journal of Historical Archaeology*, edited by M. W. Hauser and K. G. Kelly.

Smith, M. E. 2004. The archaeology of ancient state economies. *Annual Review of Anthropology* 33: 73–102.

Smith, R., D. Lakey, T. Oerthing, B. Thompson, and R. Woodward. 1982. *Sevilla la Nueva: a site survey and historical assessment of Jamaica's first European town*. Project report, Institute of Nautical Archaeology, Texas A&M University, College Station, Texas.

Smith, S. D. 2002. Coffee and the "poorer sort of people" in Jamaica during the period of African enslavement. In *Slavery without Sugar: Diversity in Caribbean Economy and Society since the 17th Century*, edited by V. Shepherd, pp. 102–28. Gainesville: University Press of Florida.

Smith, W. D. 2004. The topology of autonomy: Markets, states, soil and self-determination in Totonacapan. *Critique of Anthropology* 24(4): 403–29.

Socolow, S. M. 1996. Economic roles of the free women of color of Cap Francais. *More than Chattel: Black Women and Slavery in the Americas*, edited by D. B. Gaspar and D. C. Hine, pp. 279–97. Bloomington: Indiana University Press.

Spyer, P. 2000. *Memory of Trade: Modernity's Entanglements on an Eastern Indonesian Island*. Durham, N.C.: Duke University Press.

Stahl, A. B. 1993. Concepts of time and approaches to analogical reasoning in historical perspective. *American Antiquity* 58(2): 235–60.

———. 1999. The archaeology of global encounters viewed from Banda, Ghana. *African Archaeological Review* 16(1): 5–81.

———. 2001. *Making History in Banda: Anthropological Visions of Africa's Past*. New Studies in Archaeology. New York: Cambridge University Press.

———. 2002. Colonial entanglements and the practices of taste: An alternative to logocentric approaches. *American Anthropologist* 104(3): 827–45.

———. 2004. Political economic mosaics: Archaeology of the last two millennia in tropical sub-Saharan Africa. *Annual Review of Anthropology* 33: 145–72.

Stahl, A. B., and M. das Dores Giaro da Cruz. 1998. Men and women in a market economy: Gender and craft production in West Central Ghana ca. 1775–1995. In *Gender in African Prehistory*, edited by S. Kent, pp. 205–26. Walnut Creek, Calif.: Alta Mira.

Stark, M. 1993. *Ceramic Production and Distribution: An Ethnoarchaeological Case Study of the Kalinga*. Ph.D. diss., Department of Anthropology, University of Arizona, Tucson. Ann Arbor, Mich.: University Microfilms.

———. 1998. Technical choices and social boundaries in material culture patterning: An introduction. In *The Archaeology of Social Boundaries*, edited by M. Stark, pp. 1–11. Washington, D.C.: Smithsonian Institution Press.

Stark, M., M. M. Elson, and J. Clark. 1998. Social boundaries and technical choices in Tonto Basin prehistory. In *The Archaeology of Social Boundaries*, edited by M. Stark, pp. 78–119. Washington, D.C.: Smithsonian Institution Press.

Stein, G. 1998. Heterogeneity, power, and political economy: Some current research issues in the archaeology of Old World complex societies. *Journal of Archaeological Research* 6(1): 1–44.

———. 2002. From passive periphery to active agents: Emerging perspectives in the archaeology of interregional interaction. *American Anthropologist* 104: 903–16.

———. 2005. The comparative archaeology of colonial encounters. In *The Archaeology of Colonial Encounters: Comparative Perspectives*, edited by G. Stein, pp. 3–31. School of American Research Advanced Seminar Series, G. J. Gumerman, general editor. Santa Fe: School of American Research Press.

Steponaitis, V., J. Blackman, and H. Neff. 1996. Large-scale compositional patterns in the chemical composition of Mississippian pottery. *American Antiquity* 61: 555–72.

Sterner, J. 1991. Who is signalling whom? Ceramic style, ethnicity and taphonomy among the Sirak Bulahay. *Antiquity* 63: 451–59.

———. 1992. Sacred pots and "symbolic reservoirs" in the Mandara Highlands of Northern Cameroon. In *An African Commitment: Papers in Honour of Peter Lewis Shinnie*, edited by N. David, pp. 171–79. Calgary: University of Calgary Press.

Sterner, J., and N. David. 1991. Gender and caste in the Mandara Highlands: Northeastern Nigeria and Northern Cameroon. *Ethnology* 30(4): 355–69.

———. 2003. Action on matter: the history of the uniquely African tamper and concave anvil pot-forming technique. *Journal of African Archaeology* 1 (1):3–38.

Stewart, J. [1808] 1971. *An Account of Jamaica*. Freeport, N.Y.: Books for Libraries Press.

Stewart, R. 2003. Akan ethnicity in Jamaica: A re-examination of Jamaica's slave imports from the Gold Coast, 1655–1807. *Maryland Historian* 28: 69–107.

Stoller, P. 1996. Spaces, places, and fields: The politics of West African trading in New York City's informal economy. *American Anthropologist* 98(4): 776–88.

———. 2001. *Money Has No Smell: The Africanization of New York City*. Chicago: University of Chicago Press.

Stoltman, J. 1989. A quantitative approach to the petrographic analysis of ceramic thin-sections. *American Antiquity* 54(1): 147–60.

———. 1991. Ceramic petrography as a technique for documenting cultural interaction: An example from the Upper Mississippi Valley. *American Antiquity* 56(1): 103–20.

———. 1999. The Chaco-Chuska connection: In defense of Anna Shepard. In *Pottery and People: A Dynamic Interaction*, edited by J. M. Skibo and G. M. Feinman, pp. 9–24. Salt Lake City: University of Utah Press.

Sweezy, N. 1984. *Raised in Clay: The Southern Pottery Tradition*. Washington, D.C.: Smithsonian Institution.

Tadman, M. 2000. The demographic cost of sugar: Debates on slave societies and natural increase in the Americas. *American Historical Review* 105(5): 15–34.

Taylor, D. 1991. Transculturating Transculturation. *Performing Arts Journal* 13(2): 90–104.

Taylor, J. 1637. *Carriers Cosmologie or a Brief Relation, of the Innes, Ordinaries, Hostelries and other Lodgings in, and near London, where the Carriers, Waggons, Foote posts & Higglers, doe usually come, from any partes, townes, shires and counties of the Kingdomes of England, Principality of Wales, as also from the Kingdomes of Scotland and Ireland*. London: A.G.

———. 1688. Second Part of the Historie of His Life and Travels in America. Manuscript on file, Institute of Jamaica, Kingston, Jamaica.

Taylor, S.A.G. 1965. *The Western Design: An Account of Cromwell's Expedition to the Caribbean*. Kingston: Institute of Jamaica.

Terrell, J. 2006. Commentary. In the 71st annual meeting of the Society of American Archaeology Meetings, opening session, San Juan, Puerto Rico.

Tetrault, T., and C. R. DeCorse. 2001. *Continuity and Innovation: Pottery and Manufacture among the Coastal Akan*. Rockville, Md.: Allaire Archaeological Enterprises.

Thomas, D. H. 2000. *Skull Wars*. New York: Basic Books.

Thomas, H. 1999. *The Slave Trade: The Story of the Atlantic Slave Trade, 1440–1870*. 1st Touchstone ed. New York: Simon & Schuster.

Thomas, N. 1991. *Entangled Objects: Exchange, Material Culture and Colonialism in the Pacific*. Cambridge: Harvard University Press.

Thompson, R. F. 1969. African Influences on the Art of the United States. In *Black Studies in the University: A Symposium*, edited by A. Robinson, C. C. Foster, and D. H. Ogilvie, pp. 122–70. New Haven: Yale University Press.

———. 1974. *African Art in Motion*. Los Angeles: University of California Press.

———. 1984. *Flash of the Spirit: African and Afro-American Art and Philosophy*. New York: Vintage Press.

———. 1990. Kongo influences on African-American artistic culture. In *Africanisms in American Culture*, edited by J. Holloway, pp. 148–84. Bloomington: Indiana University Press.

———. 1993. *Face of the Gods: Art and Altars of Africa and the African Americas*. New York: Museum for African Art.

Thornton, A. P. 1955. The organization of the slave trade in the English West Indies, 1660–1685. *William and Mary College Quarterly* 12(3): 299–409.

———. 1998. *Africa and Africans in the Making of the Atlantic World, 1400–1680*. New York: Cambridge University Press.

Tomich, D. W. 1990. *Slavery in the Circuit of Sugar: Martinique and the World Economy, 1830–1848*. Baltimore: Johns Hopkins University Press.

———. [1990] 1991. The other face of slave labor: Provision grounds and internal marketing in Martinique. In *Caribbean Slave Society and Economy: A Student Reader*, edited by V. Shepherd, pp. 304–18. New York: New Press.

———. 1993. Une petite Guinée: Provision ground and plantation in Martinique, 1830–1848. In *Cultivation and Culture: Labor and the Shaping of Slave Life in the Americas*, edited by I. Berlin and P. D. Morgan, pp. 221–42. Charlottesville: University Press of Virginia.

———. 1994. Small islands, large comparisons. *Social Science History* 18(3): 339–58.

———. 1995. Une petite Guinée: Provision ground and plantation in Martinique, 1830–1848. In *The Slaves' Economy: Independent Production by Slaves in the Americas*, edited by I. Berlin and P. D. Morgan, pp. 68–91. New York: Routledge.

———. 2004. *Through the Prism of Slavery: Labor, Capital, and World Economy*. World Social Change. Lanham, Md.: Rowman & Littlefield.

Tomich, T. P., P. Kilby, and B. F. Johnston. 1995. *Transforming Agrarian Economies: Opportunities Seized, Opportunities Missed*. Ithaca, N.Y.: Cornell University Press.

Trigger, B. G. 1980. Archaeology and the image of the American Indian. *American Antiquity* 45: 662–76.

———. 1981. Archaeology and the ethnographic present. *Anthropologica* 23: 3–17.
———. 1995. Expanding middle range theory. *Antiquity* 69: 449–58.
Trimingham, J. S. 1978. *Islam in West Africa*. Oxford: Clarendon Press.
Trouillot, M.-R. 1988. *Peasants and Capital: Dominica in the World Economy*. Johns Hopkins Studies in Atlantic History and Culture. Baltimore: Johns Hopkins University Press.
———. 1992. The Caribbean region: An open frontier in anthropological theory. *Annual Review of Anthropology* 21: 19–42.
———. 1995. *Silencing the Past: Power and the Production of History*. Boston: Beacon Press.
———. 2002. Culture on the edges: Caribbean creolization in historical context. In *From the Margins: Historical Anthropology and Its Futures*, edited by B. K. Axel, pp. 189–210. Durham, N.C.: Duke University Press.
———. 2003. *Global Transformations: Anthropology and the Modern World*. 1st ed. New York: Palgrave Macmillan.
Trussel, T. D. 1994. Artifacts of ambition: How the 17th-century middle class at Port Royal, Jamaica, foreshadowed the consumer revolution. Master's thesis, Texas A&M University, College Station.
Turner, M. 1991. Slave workers, subsistence and labour bargaining: Amity Hall, Jamaica, 1805–1832. In *The Slaves' Economy: Independent Production by Slaves in the Americas*, edited by I. Berlin and P. D. Morgan, pp. 92–106. London: Frank Cass.
———. (editor). 1995. *From Chattel Slaves to Wage Slaves: The Dynamics of Labour Bargaining in the Americas*. London: James Curry.
———. [1982] 1998. *Slaves and Missionaries: The Disintegration of Jamaican Slave Society, 1787–1834*. Urbana: University of Illinois Press.
Tylor, S. 2002. The letters of Simon Tylor of Jamaica to Chaloner Arcedekne, 1765–1775. In *Travel, Trade and Power in the Atlantic*, edited by B. Wood and M. Lynn. Cambridge: Cambridge University Press.
Ulysse, G. 1999. *Uptown Ladies and Downtown Women: Informal Commercial Importing and the Social/Symbolic Politics of Identities in Jamaica*. Ph.D. diss., University of Michigan, Ann Arbor. Ann Arbor, Mich.: University Microfilms.
Usman, A. 2004. Ceramic seriation, sites chronology, and Old Oyo factor in Northcentral Yorubaland, Nigeria. *African Archaeological Review* 20(3): 149–69.
Usman, A., R. Speakman, and M. D. Glascock. 2005. An initial assessment of prehistoric ceramic production and exchange in northern Yoruba, North Central Nigeria: Results of ceramic compositional analysis. *African Archaeological Review* 22(3): 141–68.
Van Dantzig, A. 1980. *Forts and Castles of Ghana*. Accra: Sedco.
van den Boogaart, E. 1998. The Dutch participation in the Atlantic slave trade, 1596–1650. In *The Dutch in the Atlantic Economy, 1580–1880. Trade, Slavery and Emancipation*, edited by P. C. Emmer. London: Ashgate.
van der Plas, L., and A. C. Tobi. 1965. A chart for judging the reliability of point counting results. *American Journal of Science* 263: 87–90.
Vaughn, K., C. A. Conlee, H. Neff, and K. Schreiber. 2006. Ceramic production in an-

cient Nasca: Provenance analysis of pottery from the Early Nasca and Tiza cultures through INAA. *Journal of Archaeological Science* 33(5): 681–89.

Vaughn, K., and H. Neff. 2000. Moving beyond iconography: Neutron activation analysis of ceramics from Marcaya, Peru, an early Nasca domestic site. *Journal of Field Archaeology* 27(1): 75–90.

Vega, B. 1979. Arqueologia de los cimarrones del Maniel de Bahorucu. *Bolet'n Museo del Hombre Dominicano* 12: 11–48.

———. 1981. *La herencia indigena en la cultura dominicana de hoy*. Santo Domingo: Museo del Hombre Dominicano.

Vega, M. M. 2000. Interlocking African Diaspora cultures in the work of Fernando Ortiz. *Journal of Black Studies* 31(1): 39–50.

Vérin, P. 1961. Les Caraïbes à Sainte Lucie depuis les contacts coloniaux. *Nieuwe West-Indische Gids* 41: 66–82.

———. 1963. La Pointe caraibe. Master's thesis, Yale University, New Haven.

———. 1967. Quelques aspects de la culture matérielle de la région de Choiseul (Ile de Sainte-Lucie, Antilles). *Journal de la Société des Américanistes* 56(2): 460–94.

Vince, A. 1989. The petrography of Saxon and early medieval pottery in the Thames Valley. In *Scientific Analysis in Archaeology*, edited by J. Henderson, pp. 163–77. Oxford: University of Oxford Committee for Archaeology.

Vincentelli, M. 2004. *Women Potters: Transforming Traditions*. New Brunswick, N.J.: Rutgers University Press.

Vlach, J. M. 1990. *The Afro-American Tradition in Decorative Arts*. Athens, Ga.: Brown Thrasher Books.

Vogt, J. 1973. The early Sao Tome-Principe slave trade with Mina, 1500–1545. *International Journal of African Historical Studies* 6(3): 453–67.

Voss, B. L. 2005. From Casta to Californio: Social identity and the archaeology of culture contact. *American Anthropologist* 107(3): 461–74.

Wadley, C. A. 1985. Historical Analysis of Pewter Spoons Recovered from the Sunken City of Port Royal, Jamaica. Unpublished M.A., Texas A&M University, College Station.

Wagner, E., and C. Schubert. 1972. Pre-Hispanic workshop of serpentinite artifacts, Venezuelan Andes, and possible raw material source. *Science* 175: 888–90.

Wallis, F. S. 1963. Petrological examination. In *The Scientist and Archaeology*, edited by E. Pyddoke, pp. 80–100. New York: Roy Publishers.

Watters, D. 1987. Excavations at Harney Slave Cemetery, Montserrat, West Indies. *Annals of the Carnegie Museum* 56: 289–318.

———. 1988. Afro-Montserratian ceramics from the Harney Site Cemetery, Montserrat, West Indies. *Annals of the Carnegie Museum* 57: 167–87.

———. 1997. Historical documentation and archaeological investigation of Codrington Castle Barbuda, West Indies. *Annals of the Carnegie Museum* 66: 229–88.

Watts, D. 1987. *The West Indies, Patterns of Development, Culture, and Environmental Change since 1492*. Cambridge Series in Historical Geography, No. 8. Cambridge: Cambridge University Press.

Watts, N. 1815. *A Plan of His Majesty's Yard, at Port Royal [Kingston], Jamaica*. Dedicated by Watts to Admiral William Perry, London. British Library, Shelfmark Add. 57717, 7.

Weigand, P. C., G. Harbottle, and E. V. Sayre. 1977. Turquoise sources and source analysis: Mesoamerica and the southwestern U.S.A. In *Exchange Systems in Prehistory*, edited by T. K. Earle and J. E. Ericson, pp. 15–34. New York: Academic Press.

Wheaton, T. R., and P. H. Garrow. 1985. Acculturation and the archaeological record in the Carolina lowcountry. In *Archaeology of Slavery and Plantation Life*, edited by T. A. Singleton, pp. 239–59. Orlando, Fla.: Academic Press.

Wiessner, P. 1990. Is there a unity to style? In *The Uses of Style in Archaeology*, edited by C. Hastorf and M. Conkey, pp. 105–12. Cambridge: Cambridge University Press.

Wilkie, L. A. 1999. Evidence of African continuities in material culture of Clifton Plantation, Bahamas. In *African Sites: Archaeology in the Caribbean*, edited by J. Haviser, pp. 264–75. Kingston, Jamaica: Ian Randle Publishers.

———. 2000a. Culture bought: Evidence of creolization in the consumer goods of an enslaved Bahamian family. *Historical Archaeology* 34(3): 10–26.

———. 2000b. *Creating Freedom: Material Culture and African American Identity at Oakley Plantation, Louisiana 1840–1950*. Baton Rouge: Louisiana State University Press.

———. 2003. *The Archaeology of Mothering: An African-American Midwife's Tale*. New York: Routledge.

Wilkie, L. A., and K. Bartoy. 2000. A critical archaeology revisited. *Current Anthropology* 41(5): 747–77.

Wilkie, L. A., and P. Farnsworth. 1999. Trade and the construction of Bahamian identity: A multiscalar exploration. *International Journal of Historical Archaeology* 3(4): 283–320.

———. 2005. *Sampling Many Pots: An Archaeology of Memory and Tradition at a Bahamian Plantation*. Gainesville: University of Press of Florida.

Williams, C. 1826. *A Tour through the Island of Jamaica*. London: Hunt and Clarke.

Williams, E. E. 1970. *From Columbus to Castro: The History of the Caribbean*. New York: Vintage Books.

———. [1944] 1994. *Capitalism and Slavery*. Chapel Hill: University of North Carolina Press.

Williams, J. 2001. *Narrative of Events, since the first of August, 1834, by James Williams, an apprenticed labourer in Jamaica*. Durham, N.C.: Duke University Press.

Wilmot, S. R. 1988. *Adjustments to Emancipation in Jamaica*. Mona, Kingston, Jamaica: Social History Project, Department of History, Univ. of the West Indies.

Wilson, S. M. 1990. *Hispaniola: Caribbean Chiefdoms in the Age of Columbus*. Tuscaloosa: University of Alabama Press.

———. 1993. The cultural mosaic of the indigenous Caribbean. *Proceedings for the British Academy* 81: 37–66.

———. (editor). 1997. *The Indigenous People of the Caribbean*. Gainesville: University Press of Florida.

Winslow, D. 2000. Analysis of the Holloware pewter from Port Royal, Jamaica. Master's thesis, Texas A&M University, College Station.

Wood, B. 1987. Some aspects of female resistance to chattel slavery in low country Georgia, 1763–1815. *The Historical Journal* 30: 603–22.

———. 1995. *Women's Work, Men's Work: The Informal Economies of Lowcountry Georgia*. Athens: University of Georgia Press.

Woodward, R. P. 1988. The Charles Cotter collection: A study of the ceramic and faunal remains. Master's thesis, Texas A&M University, Institute of Nautical Archaeology.

———. 2006a. Medieval legacies: The industrial archaeology of an early sixteenth century sugar mill at Sevilla la Nueva, Jamaica. Ph.D. diss., Dept. of Archaeology, Simon Fraser University, Vancouver.

———. 2006b. Taino artifacts from Post-Contact Jamaica. In *The Earliest Inhabitants: The Dynamics of the Jamaican Taino*, edited by L.-G. Atkinson. Kingston: UWI Press.

Wright, R. P. 1991a. Women's labor and pottery production in prehistory. In *Engendering Archaeology*, edited by J. M. Gero and M. W. Conkey, pp. 194–223. Oxford: Basil Blackwell.

Wu, Y. 1995. *Jamaican Trade, 1688–1769: A Quantitative Study*. Ph.D. diss., Johns Hopkins University, Baltimore. Ann Arbor, Mich.: University Microfilms.

Wurst, L. 1991. Employees must be of moral and temperate habits: Rural and urban elite ideologies. In *The Archaeology of Inequality*, edited by R. H. McGuire and R. L. Paynter, pp. 125–49. Oxford: Basil Blackwell.

———. 1999. Internalizing class in historical archaeology. *Historical Archaeology* 33(1): 7–21.

Wylie, A. 1985. The reaction against analogy. *Advances in Archaeological Method and Theory* 8: 63–111.

Yentsch, A. E. 1994. *A Chesapeake Family and Their Slaves: A Study in Historical Archaeology*. New Studies in Archaeology. Cambridge and New York: Cambridge University Press.

Yentsch, A. E., M. Beaudry, and J. Deetz. 1992. *The Art and Mystery of Historical Archaeology: Essays in Honor of James Deetz*. Boca Raton, Fla.: CRC Press.

Young, A. L. 2000. *Archaeology of Southern Urban Landscapes*. Tuscaloosa: University of Alabama Press.

Zahedieh, N. 1986a. The merchants of Port Royal, Jamaica, and the Spanish contraband trade, 1655–1692. *William and Mary Quarterly* 43(4): 570–93.

———. 1986b. Trade, plunder, and economic development in early English Jamaica, 1655–89. *The Economic History Review* 39 (2): 205–22.

———. 1994. London and the colonial consumer in the late seventeenth century. *Economic History Review* 47(2): 239–61.

———. 2002. The wickedest city in the world. Port Royal, commercial hub of the seventeenth century Caribbean. In *Working Slavery, Pricing Freedom. Essays in Honour of Barry W. Higman*, edited by V. Shepherd, pp. 3–20. Kingston: Ian Randle.

Zug, C. G., III. 1986. *Turners and Burners: The Folk Potters of North Carolina*. Chapel Hill: University of North Carolina.

Index

Page numbers in italics refer to illustrations.

Above Rocks granodiorite, *165*, 169
Actors (past), 4–5, 14, 15, 25, 37, 52, 59, 61, 119, 197–98
Africa, *99*; archaeology in, 98–101; and Atlantic period, 101; retentions in the Americas, 5, 10, 30, 43, 95, 97, 100, 117, 122, 124; trade, 105
African Diaspora, 10, 11, 15, 41, 52, 94, 96, 117, 118, 126, 164, 198, 199
Africanism, 100, 124
Agency, 4–5, 6, 14, 29, 31, 35, 38, 40, 66, 67, 68, 197, 199, 202
Agents, 4, 119
Aggregation, 77, 94, 107, 119, 201
Agro-industry, 9, 16, 22, 25, 119
Akan languages, 103
Alterity, 63, 65, 198
Aluminum pots, 131
Analogy (ethnographic), 164; direct historical approach, 125–27, 150, 190, 199; limitations of, 96, 105, 123–24, 140, 147, 164, 188; transatlantic, 96–97, 124
Archaeological sites, 11, 205; and chronology, 11, 75, *77*, 82; location of, 75, *76*; provenance of local ceramics, 175, 203–4. *See also* Chancery Hall; Drax Hall; Juan de Bollas; Maima; Old King's House; Old Naval Dockyard; Saint Peter's Church; Seville Estate; Thetford; White Marl
Armstrong, Douglas, 31–32, 77–78, 79
Ashanti (Asante), 106. *See also* Twi
Atlantic trade in Africans (slave trade), 15, 25, *26*, 39, 95, 103, 105, 106; database of, *103*, 125, *158*; effects in coastal Africa, 40; English Jamaica, 102, 125–26; Gold Coast (Ghana), 106; Spanish Jamaica, 21
Attribute analysis, 150–51

Bakongo cosmogram, 97
Bami, 16, 20
Banda (Ghana), 67, 98, 101, 191
Barracone, 29
Beckford, William, 13, 67, 71, 73, 132
Beckwith, Mary, 30, 123, 160
Begho, 99
Belisario, Isaac, 34, 54, 137–39, *138*
Best, Lloyd, 24
Black Atlantic, 3. *See also* Gilroy, Paul; Thompson, Robert Ferris
Black markets, 4, 6, 201
Bollas, Juan de (maroon leader), 22
Boundaries, 6, 193, 200
Browne, Kathleen, 8, 42
Browne, Patrick, 47–48, 50, 51, 58, 95

Cabotage (intercoastal trade), 43, 64, 70, 74, 80
Cafetal del Padre, 29, 94
Canoes, 69–70, 87
Capitalism, 9, 14, 22, 28
Caribbean, 16, *109*; historiography of, 1, 23, 24, 41, 42–43, 65, 197; and Spanish colonization, 17, 19
Caribbean peasantry, 9
Caribbean pottery, 11, 107, 108, 117; Antigua, 108, 112–13; Barbados, 126–27; Barbuda, 108, 114; Canari, 111; Christophe plain ware, 110; Cuba, 116–17, 137; Dominican Republic, 109–10; El Morro ware, 115–16; Guadeloupe, 111–12; Haiti, 109–10; Le Leschwit, 111; Jamaica, 16, 131 (*see also* New Seville ware; Yabba [type]); Martinique, 111; Montserrat, 113–14; Nevis, 112; Puerto Rico, 115–16 (*see also* Criollo ware); Saint Eustatius, 113; Saint Lucia, 110–11; Virgin Islands (U.S.), 114–15

Cassava, 20, 50
Ceramica Ordinaria, 116, 140
Ceramicas de transculturacion, 116
Ceramic petrography, 163, 169, 172, 175
Ceramics: assemblage, 139, 167; ceramic recipe, 164, 188; classification of, 94, 107, 119, 122, 201; studies of, 8, 96, 98, 100–102, 114, 124, 160, 163, 191; traditions, 94, 100–101, 111, 118, 123, 131. *See also* Pottery
Chamber pots, 80, 135, *135*, 140, 142, *142*, 143, *143*, *154*, 184
Chancery Hall, 165, 172
Cinnamon Bay (St. John, USVI), 114–15
Clark, William, 34
Class: defined by Browne, 47; dependents, 47, 58, 60; merchants, 47, 58, 63; "negroes," 47, 51, 56–58; planters, 47; settlers, 47, 50
Clay, 168, 169; Jamaica, 129, 130, 132–33; matrix, 175, 176; preparation (*see* Potters)
Coal pots, 113, 140
Coarse earthenware, 10, 140. *See also* Caribbean pottery; Yabba (type)
Codrington Castle (Barbuda), 116
Codrington Estate (Barbados), 126
Coffee estate, 27, 28–29, 82
Colonialism, 5, 9, 13–14, 27, 28, 40, 67–68, 198
Colono ware (colonoware), 5, 93–94, 97, 98, 117, 161, 189, 190, 199, 202
Columbian Magazine, 39, 129–30
Columbus, Christopher, 16, 20
Commodity, 96, 117; circuits, 2, 3, 7, 12, 33, 36, 43, 47, 91, 162, 189, 190, 191, 193; valuation, 12, 41–42, 65, 96
Community, 5, 7, 15, 30, 33, 37, 52, 63, 66, 69, 117, 120, 122, 202
Complex society, 13
Compositional groups (NAA), 186–87; distribution of, *189*
Compositional groups (petrography), *175*, 203–4; group 1, 175, *175*, *177*; group 2, *175*, *178*, 179; group 3, *175*, 180; group 4, *175*, 181, 182, 183; group 5, *175*, 184; NA, *175*, 184, 185
Consumption, 9, 90
Continuity and change, 100, 102, 108, 118, 160–61
Contraband: goods, 194–95; trade, 23, 43, 49, 87, 194
Control samples, 172
Cooper, Frederick, 5, 15, 160

Coromante, 106
Cotter, Charles, 21
Credit, 195
Creole: as born in the Americas, 23, 37, 52, 78, 85, 87, 88; identity implying hybridity, 14–15, 37, 51, 52, 85, 202; language, 111, 123
Creole economy, 51
Creolization, 10, 24, 31, 36, 37; and material culture, 5, 93–94, 95, 97, 117, 123. *See also* Materiality
Criollo ware, 93, 115
Criteria of abundance, 187, 213
Cross Church, *45*
Cruz, Maria, 100–101, 160, 191
Currency, 134, 194–96; cash transactions, 36, 48, 60, 66, 51, 54, 60, 63, 66, 193–94; coins, 194, 196; clipping, 194; freemen's bank, 194–95

Daguerreotype, 54–55
Data reduction, 209
Deagan, Kathleen, 17
Debt, 195
Decoration. *See* Pottery: decoration
DeCorse, Christopher, 94, 96–98, 101–3, 105, 106
Delle, James, 28–29, 53, 77
Dichotomies, 38, 202; urban vs. rural, 75, 157
Diderot, Denis, 26, 27
Disorder, 2, 51, 66, 196, 197
Douglas, Mary, 6, 65, 198
Drax Hall, *18*, 29, 32, 75, 90, *165*, 166, *174*, *175*, 179, 180, 181, 186, *187*, 193, 203; assemblage, 79; history, 78; location, *76*, 78
Dual economy, 51. *See also* Internal economy
Dunn, Richard, 25
Duperly, Adolphe, 1, 2, 34, 54–56, *55*

Earthquake of 1692, 23, 88, 89
Ebanks, Roderick, 130, 131, 133
Edwards, Bryan, 36, 93, 134
Efficiency, 27, 32
Elements: arsenic, 186, 214; chromium, 213; hafnium, 213; sodium, 187, 212, 214; thorium, 213; volatiles, 187
Elmina, 99, 103, 106, 107, 124
Emancipation War, 1, 2, 4–5, 33, 37, 196
Energy dispersive X-ray fluorescence (EDXRF), 188, 214

Esquival, Juan de, 22
Ethnicity, 96, 118, 162; diversity of Jamaica, 84, 85, 87; ethnolinguistic diversity in Ghana, 101–2, *104*; and material culture, 85, 96
Ethnoarchaeology, 100–101, 122, 124
Ewe, 105
Ewen, Charles, 17

Factoria system, 20
Falmouth, *18, 46, 55*
Farnsworth, Paul, 14, 37
Ferguson, Leland, 94, 97, 117, 161, 199
Feudal system, 21
"Free-time," 36
Free village, 47

Galways Plantation (Montserrat), 35, 113
Gamma-ray spectroscopy, 206
Gardens, 35, 50–51
Gender, 8–9, 63, 64–65, 78, 79, 157
Ghana, 103, *104*, 106; coastal Ghana, 100, 102
Gilroy, Paul, 3–4
Gold Coast. *See* Ghana
Goveia, Elsa, 53
Guanaboa Vale, 82
Guanabacoa (Havana), 116

Haggling, 62. *See also* Higgler(s)
Hakewill, James, 2, 34–35, *35*, 54
Hall, Douglas, 43, 49, 50, 52, 53, 62
Hall, Martin, 5
Hamilton, Donny, 23
Handler, Jerome, 112, 126, 134
Hart, Keith, 42
Hawking, 57–60, 62–63, 137, 191. *See also* Higgler(s)
Herskovits, Melville, 95
Higgler(s), 7–8, 41–42, 48, 51, 55, 59, 61–66, 68, 74, 75, 83–84, 90, *136*, 191, 193, 195; of pottery, 134–35, *135*, *136*, 137–39, *138*; history of term in Jamaica, 63; movement, 64; perception of, 7, 39, 41, 62, 63, 65, 201; higgling, 61–62
Higman, Barry, 1, 26–27, 32–33, 47–48, 74, 83
Historical archaeology, 13, 31, 77
Historicity, 4, 5, 6, 52, 101, 119, 160, 190, 192, 193, 198, 199, 201, 202
Honychurch, Lennox, 34
House yard. *See under* Plantations

Housing, 157; condition of, 87; and rent, 83. *See also* Free village; Laws; Plantations

Identity, social, 56, 61, 96, 124, 162, 198, 199
Inclusions, 169; bioclasts, 172; mineral, 183 (*see also* Minerals)
—lithic fragments, 177, 178, 181, 183; arkose, 182, 185; laterites, 180, 185; litharkose, 172, 180; litharenite, 176
Indentured laborer, 199, *200*. *See also* South Asians
Independent production, 1, 7, 190. *See also* Provision grounds
Internal economy, 4, 7, 9, 37, 40, 42, 48, 91, 122, 164, 192; and acquisition of material wealth, 1, 5, 36, 54, 65, 67, 68, 70, 74, 79, 91; analysis through material culture, 6
—informal economy, 9, 42, 48, 49, 52–53, 65–66, 74, 91; and contraband (*see* Contraband); sector of trade, 6, 48–49, 53, 54, 60, 74, 80, 87, 90, 119, 122, 191, 192, 193, 195, 201, 202; and theft by enslaved; 13, 57, 60, 64, 65; and theft by planters, 36
—island contingencies, 11, 43–44; organization of, 40–41, 47, 48; participation in, by enslaved laborers, 9, 10–11, 40–43, 49–50, 68; participation in, by planters, 43, 48, 49, 50–51, 74, 82

Jamaica, 18, 76; cities and settlements of, *18*; demography of, 28, 81, 83–84, 125, 158; diversity of (*see* Ethnicity); geology of, *165*, 168–69; and newspapers, 63, 64; patois, 107; and Spanish period, 20; topography of, 16, *17*
Jamaican potters, 120, 124–25, 128–30, 133–34, 157, 161–62, 167, 186, 190; Cecil Baugh, 131, 134; Louisa Jones (*see* Ma Lou); maker's mark, 131–32, 155; Marlene Roden (*see* Munchie); Mountainview (Kingston), 134; Spanish Town (contemporary), 123, 130–32
James, C.L.R., 24
Jobbing, 48
Jones, Louisa. *See* Ma Lou (Louisa Jones)
Juan de Bollas (archaeological site), 71, 75, 78, 81, 82, *83*, *165*, *174*, 179, 181, 186; assemblage, 82, *83*; history of, 82; location, *76*

Kingston, 69, 134, *135*
Kingston Harbor, 22, 23, 87, 169

Kinship, 77, 105, 131, 161, 201
Knowledge: embodied, 7, 67, 83; esoteric, 61; transmission of, 7, 10, 118, 120, 126, 131, 192; technical, 120, 122, 124, 132, 201

La Isabella, 19
Landscape: as analytical frame, 26, 32, 34, 56, 68, 74, 197; paintings, 2, *27*, 34, *35*
Laws: housing, 84; and licensing, 60, 64; markets, 49, 50, 54, 57; peddling, 57–58, 59, 134 (*see also* Higgler[s]); provisions, 57, 59; race, 59; slave, 36, 53; and taxing, 64; and tickets, 57, 59–60, 196
Lawyers, 48
Legality, 4, 6, 7, 40, 44, 48, 52, 53, 58, 61, 81, 87, 90, 96, 201. *See also* Laws
Liguanea Gravels, 169, 185
Liguanea Plain, *18*, 185
Linstead, *46*, 71
Livestock, 48, 49
Long, Edward, 56–57, 65, 71, 87, 130, 133, 194, 195; calculations based on, 70, 72, *73*, 83, 84

Maima, *165*, 172
Ma Lou (Louisa Jones), 120, 121, 123, 130–31, 133, 142, 161
Markets, 34, 55, 129, 159; growth of legal, 43, *44*, *45*, *46*, 47, 48–50 (*see also* Laws); informal, 7, 9–10, 11, 25, 52, 53, 54, 65, 90, 91, 122, 133, 134, 198; institution, 40, 50, 53–54, 135, 136; legal provisions, 57, 58, 59, 60, 64; licensing for, 64; sellers (*see* Higgler[s]); Sunday markets, 2, 6, 13, 36, 43, 47, 51, 54, 64, 66, 67, 70, 93, 129, 198. *See also* Internal economy
Maroons, 127
Material culture, 6, 8, 10, 12, 15, 23, 30, 31, 69, 78, 84, 92, 93, 95–98, 101–3, 159, 197, 199–200, 201, 202; limitations of, 5–6, 7
Materiality, 3–4, 5–6, 9, 68, 94–95, 101, 160, 192, 197–98, 199, 200–202
Mathewson, Duncan, 85–86, 123
Mayes, Philip, 88, 123
Mercantilism, 21, 23
Metaphor, 3
Mica, 171
Mina. *See* Elmina
Minerals, 170; biotite, 171, 175, 176, 178, 179, 180, 181, 182, 183, 184, 186; evidence of remelting, 179, 182; evidence of partial melting, 179; muscovite, 171; orthoclase feldspar, 171, 173, 174, 175, 177, 179, 181, 182, 183, 184, 185; perthite, 179; phenocryst, 170; plagioclase feldspar, 171, 173, 174, 175, 177, 178, 179, 181, 182, 183, 184, 185; quartz, 169, 170, 175, 177, 179, 180, 181, 182, 183, 184; sericite, 178, 179, 180
—texture, 170; alteration, 171, 177, 182; anhedral, 177; euhedral, 179; monocrystalline, 176, 183; poikalitic, 177; polycrystalline, 176, 177, 181, 182, 183; recrystallization, 184; seriticization, 178; undulatory extinction, 176, 180, 181, 182, 184
—twinning: microcline, 171, 180; polysynthetic (albite), 171, 176, 180, 182, 184; carlsbad, 177, 178, 179, 181, 182, 183, 184
Mintz, Sidney, 9–10, 24, 28, 30, 31, 40, 41, 43, 49–50, 52–53, 62, 68, 95–96
Mobility, 7, 64, 65, 191
Modernity, 3, 4, 24, 28, 202
Modern world, 10, 13–15, 28, 96–97, 202
Monkey jars, 113, 121, *138*, 138–39, 140, 150
Montego Bay, *45*, 69
Montserrat, 36
Montpelier Estate, 2, 33
Munchie (Marlene Roden), 120–21, 123, 131–33, 142, 150, 155, 161, 172, 186, 188

Negation, 10
Neutron Activation Analysis (NAA), 163, 186, 187, 188, 205
New Seville ware, 127–28, *128*

Old Harbor, *44*, *45*, *46*, 81
Old King's House, 75, 84, 85, 90, 157, *165*, *174*, 176, 179, 181, 183, 186; assemblage of, 85, *90*; history of, 85; location of, *76*, 85, *86*; and midden, 85
Old Naval Dockyard, 75, 90, *165*, *174*, 176, 179, 181, 183, 186; assemblage of, *90*; history of, 88; location of, *76*, 89
Ollman, Bertell, 4, 14
Order, 34, 197
Oristan, 18, 20
Ortiz, Fernando, 24, 31

Pallisadoes. *See* Port Royal
Passage Fort, 22, 44, 54, 87
Paths, 39. *See also* Roads
Peddler, 7, 8, 47, 48, 51, 57, 58, 60, 62, 63, 64, 80, 90. *See also* Higgler(s)

Pepper pots, 134
Phibba (in Thomas Thistlewood), 60, 63
Phillipo, James, 87, 128, 130
Piot, Charles, 40
Plantains. *See* Provisions
Plantation economy, 2, 25, 38, 69
Plantations, 13, 37; archaeological analysis of, 3, 26–27, 29, 31–32, 33, 69, 77; and estate house, 78, 79; and house yard, 32, 79, 80, 82, 132, 133; industrial aspects of, 9, 14, 16, 20, 21–22, 26, 28, 33, 74, 75; and laborer village, 26, 27, 29, 30–31, 32, 78, 79, 80, 82, 84, 87, 188–89, 190; spatial layout of, 34–35, 55, 77, 78, 79
Plantation society, 69
Platts, 26
Point counting, 170, 172, 175
Polinks. *See* Provision grounds
Political arithmetic, 59–60, 202
Political economy, 8, 10, 42, 50, 68, 117, 122, 161, 202
Port Royal, 23, *44, 45, 46*, 83, 87, 88, *89*, 123, 150
Posnansky, Merrick, 98, 105
Postal rates, 72, *73*
Potters: in Nevis, 118; in Saint Anne (Madame Trime), 112; in Saint Lucia, 111; in Trois Islet, 111. *See also* Jamaican potters
Pottery: afro-Caribbean ware, 5, 93, 97, 108; afro-Cruzan ware, 114; afro-Jamaican ceramics, 120 (*see also* Yabba [type]); chamber pot (*see* Chamber pots); chimney pot (*see* Chamber pots); coal pot (*see* Coal pots); compositional analysis, 157, 163, 164 (*see also* Ceramic petrography); and decoration, 125; maker's mark, 132; manufacture, 125; monkey jar (*see* Monkey jars); Spanish jars (*see* Spanish jars); sugar wares (*see* Sugar wares)
—analysis of: change in popularity, 150; foodways, 80; minimum number of vessels (MNV), 150, *166*; rim sherds, *150*; sherd count, 150
—techniques: carination, 106; clay preparation, 132; coil, 105, 133; pinch-pulling, 133; polishing, 133; scraping, 133; slab, 105; slipping, 133
Pottery sellers, in Kingston, *135*, 138
Power, 3, 8, 38, 40, 53, 56, 68, 118, 193, 194
Price, Richard, 95

Price inflation, 60–61
Principal components analysis (PCA), 206–8
Problem spaces, 5
Production, 9
Provenance, 12, 162, 163, 186, 189
Provenience, 162
Provision grounds, 35, 36, 43, 57, 62, 68, 70–71, 72, 73, 129
Provisioning, 16
Provisions: imported, 36, 43, 44, 48, 50, 70, 93, 129, 198; from provision grounds, 20, 24, 36, 43, 50, 53, 54, 57, 59, 60, 62, 66, 67, 70, 93, 129, 198
Puerto Real, 19
Pulsipher, Lydia, 35, 82
Pure Plantation Model, 24–25

Quantitative analysis, 205

Race: racism, 57; racializing, 56, 57, 58–59
Rebellion, 6, 197, 202; Baptist War (*see* Emancipation War); organization of, 1, 197; provisions against (Cuba), 29; Tacky's Rebellion, 196
Reeves, Matthew, 78, 81–83
Resistance, 1, 10, 12, 29–30, 37–38, 196, 202; everyday forms of, 8, 9, 29, 37–38, 40, 65–66; armed, 9, 37–38. *See also* Rebellion
Rio Cobre, 130, 132, 157, 169, 181, 185, 186
Roads, 39, 64, 66, 69, 71–74, *72*, 75, *76*, 81, 91, 134, 139
Roden, Marlene. *See* Munchie (Marlene Roden)
Roehampton estate, 2, 34, *35*
Roitman, Janet, 7

Saint Ann's Bay, 69, 70, 73–74, 78–81, 83
Saint Ann's Bay ware. *See* New Seville ware
Saint Ann's Inlier, 168
Saint Ann's Parish, 74, 75, 169
Saint Jago de la Vega. *See* Spanish Town
Saint Peter's Church, 75, *165, 174,* 179, 181, 183, 186, 190; assemblage of, *90*; history of, 88; location of, *76*, 88, *89*
Sampling strategy, 166, 170, 186
San Domingue, 27
Savanna-la-Mar (Savanna La Mar), 45, 50–51, 54, 64, 70, 73, 83
Savi, 99
Scale, 11, 14, 15, 33, 36, 37, 68, 74–75, 155, 161

Scott, David, 5, 28, 202
Semi-quantitative analysis, 175
Seriation: form, *154*; minimum number of vessels, *152*; rim count, *153*; sherd count, *151*
Sevilla Nueva, 18, 21. *See also* Seville Estate
Seville Estate, 32, 75, 78–80, 82, 90, 164, *165*, *166*, *174*, *175*, 176, 179, 181, 186, *187*, 190, 193, 203; assemblage of, *80*; functional analysis of, *80*; history of, 79; location of, *76*, 80
Sharpe, Sam, 2
Sheller, Mimi, 34
Singleton, Theresa, 29, 94, 96
Slavery, 27; African slavery, 39–40, 95, 103, 106–7, 124; early Caribbean, 17–19, 20, 21; plantation slavery, 3, 8, 9, 24, 26–27, 29–30, 35, 40, 53, 61, 63–64, 66, 67, 77, 94, 197; and artisans, 78, 81–82; and organization of labor, 78, 79, 81, 82; and caloric demands on labor, 43–44; rural, 74; urban, 74, 83, 85; women and, 9, 63–66, 77, 81–82, 93, 122, 161–62, 190, 197
Slave trade. *See* Atlantic trade in Africans (slave trade)
Sloane, Hans, 35–36, 126, 127, 129
Sloop (small boat) traffic, 70, 79–80
Smith, Adam, 14, 25, 61–62
Social networks, 2, 3, 7, 33, 68, 92, 159, 191, 196
Social relations, 28, 33, 74, 77, 93, 160
South Asians (east Indians), 199
Spanish jars (water storage ceramics), 79, 80, 82, 83, 90, *135*, 137, 138, *138*, 140, 176, 184
Spanish Town, 18, 44, *45*, 78, 83, 84, *86*, 185
Spatiality, 15, 20, 27, 28, 29, 32, 55, 74, 77, 191
Stahl, Ann, 5, 67–68, 100–101, 199, 201
Stoller, Paul, 52–53
Structure, 38
Style, 96, 100, 106, 137, 188
Subjects (structural position), 4–5, 6, 29, 35, 40, 52, 56–57, 67, 68, 196, 197, 198
Sugar estate, 26, 27, 78, 79, 80, 81
Sugar wares, 127; drip jar, 111, 126, 130, 176; sugar cone, 111, 126
Symbolic capital, 1, 5, 6, 9, 39, 53, 96, 193
Syncretism, 123

Tainos, 16–17, 19, 44, 115, 123, 127–28; pottery, 110, 127, 172

Ternary diagram, 172, *173*, *174*
Thetford, 75, 78, 81, 82, 83, *165*, 166, *174*, 181, 183, 186; assemblage of, 82, *83*; demography of, 81; history of, 81; location of, *76*, 81
Thistlewood, Thomas, 50–51, 54, 60, 63, 70
Thompson, Robert Ferris, 3, 30
Tomich, Dale, 28
Tourism, 118, 133
Tracks (path). *See* Roads
Transculturation, 31
Transformation, 31
Transgression, 8, 53, 61
Transients, 64. *See also* Higgler(s)
Transportation, 69, 71. *See also* Roads
"Triangle trade," 25
Twi, 123

University of Missouri Research Reactor Center, 186, 205

Vestries, 60, 64
Victoria Jubilee Market, 135, *136*
Villa de la Vega, 22. *See also* Spanish Town
Village. *See* Free village; Plantations

Wagwater Formation, *165*, 168
Water storage, 139. *See also* Monkey jars; Spanish jars
Western design, 22
West India Company (Danish), 107
White Marl, *165*, 172
Wholesalers, 47
Wilkie, Laurie, 14, 29, 37, 68
Women: agency, 30, 66, 161; historiography (anglophone Caribbean), 8–9, 63; enslaved, 63, 65, 77, 78, 84, 161; free, 63, 64, 65; marketing, 64–65 (*see also* Higgler[s]); reproduction, 161; resistance, 8, 12, 29, 30, 196
Woodward, Robyn, 21
Worthy Park, 81

Yabba (form) 4n.3, *121*, 122, 133, 134, 135, *135*, 136, *141*, *142*, *143*, *145*, *146*, *147*, *148*, *154*; variation in rim diameters, 152, *153*
Yabba (type), 4n.3, 6, 7–8, 12, 91, 93, 97, 120–23, 127, 130–35, 140, 155, 157, 159, 160, 161, 162, 191, 192, 200, 214, 217; and deco-

ration, 124; decorative inventory, 123, 140, *146*, 147, *147*, *149*, 150, 153–54, *156*, 157, 167, 187–88; disambiguation, 4n.3; distribution, *167*; frequency of treatments over time, 150, *151*, *152*, *153*; frequency of forms, 150, *154*; glazed, 123, 130, 134–35, 140, *141*, *142*, 144, 147, 150, 160, 164, 166, 167, 170, 179, 186, 188, 191, 214, 217; historic references to, 93, 128, 129, 130, 134, 137, 160; slipped, 132–34, 138, 139, 140, 142–46, *144*, *145*, *146*, 150, 152, 153, 154, 164, 166, 167, 170, 173, 181, 182, 186, 188, 205, 214, 217; untreated, 137, 138, 140, 147–49, *147*, *148*, *149*, 150, 166, 167, 170, 183, 186, 217; variation of, 152, *153*, 167

Yams. *See* Provisions

Mark W. Hauser began his career as an archaeologist in the Caribbean in 1992 when he participated in his first field school in Barbados. Since then he has conducted research in St. John, Martinique, Guadeloupe, Dominica, and Jamaica. He has researched the impact of the 1733 slave rebellion in St. John and has begun to look at contraband and cabotage trade in the Eastern Caribbean. Hauser has written on issues of identity and material culture, the political economy of the African Diaspora, colonial landscapes, and ceramic analysis. He is assistant professor of anthropology at Northwestern University.

Ripley P. Bullen Series
Florida Museum of Natural History

Tacachale: Essays on the Indians of Florida and Southeastern Georgia during the Historic Period, edited by Jerald T. Milanich and Samuel Proctor (1978)
Aboriginal Subsistence Technology on the Southeastern Coastal Plain during the Late Prehistoric Period, by Lewis H. Larson (1980)
Cemochechobee: Archaeology of a Mississippian Ceremonial Center on the Chattahoochee River, by Frank T. Schnell, Vernon J. Knight Jr., and Gail S. Schnell (1981)
Fort Center: An Archaeological Site in the Lake Okeechobee Basin, by William H. Sears, with contributions by Elsie O'R. Sears and Karl T. Steinen (1982)
Perspectives on Gulf Coast Prehistory, edited by Dave D. Davis (1984)
Archaeology of Aboriginal Culture Change in the Interior Southeast: Depopulation during the Early Historic Period, by Marvin T. Smith (1987)
Apalachee: The Land between the Rivers, by John H. Hann (1988)
Key Marco's Buried Treasure: Archaeology and Adventure in the Nineteenth Century, by Marion Spjut Gilliland (1989)
First Encounters: Spanish Explorations in the Caribbean and the United States, 1492–1570, edited by Jerald T. Milanich and Susan Milbrath (1989)
Missions to the Calusa, edited and translated by John H. Hann, with an introduction by William H. Marquardt (1991)
Excavations on the Franciscan Frontier: Archaeology at the Fig Springs Mission, by Brent Richards Weisman (1992)
The People Who Discovered Columbus: The Prehistory of the Bahamas, by William F. Keegan (1992)
Hernando de Soto and the Indians of Florida, by Jerald T. Milanich and Charles Hudson (1993)
Foraging and Farming in the Eastern Woodlands, edited by C. Margaret Scarry (1993)
Puerto Real: The Archaeology of a Sixteenth-Century Spanish Town in Hispaniola, edited by Kathleen Deagan (1995)
Political Structure and Change in the Prehistoric Southeastern United States, edited by John F. Scarry (1996)
Bioarchaeology of Native Americans in the Spanish Borderlands, edited by Brenda J. Baker and Lisa Kealhofer (1996)
A History of the Timucua Indians and Missions, by John H. Hann (1996)
Archaeology of the Mid-Holocene Southeast, edited by Kenneth E. Sassaman and David G. Anderson (1996)
The Indigenous People of the Caribbean, edited by Samuel M. Wilson (1997; first paperback edition, 1999)
Hernando de Soto among the Apalachee: The Archaeology of the First Winter Encampment, by Charles R. Ewen and John H. Hann (1998)
The Timucuan Chiefdoms of Spanish Florida, by John E. Worth: vol. 1, *Assimilation*; vol. 2, *Resistance and Destruction* (1998)
Ancient Earthen Enclosures of the Eastern Woodlands, edited by Robert C. Mainfort Jr. and Lynne P. Sullivan (1998)

An Environmental History of Northeast Florida, by James J. Miller (1998)
Precolumbian Architecture in Eastern North America, by William N. Morgan (1999)
Archaeology of Colonial Pensacola, edited by Judith A. Bense (1999)
Grit-Tempered: Early Women Archaeologists in the Southeastern United States, edited by Nancy Marie White, Lynne P. Sullivan, and Rochelle A. Marrinan (1999)
Coosa: The Rise and Fall of a Southeastern Mississippian Chiefdom, by Marvin T. Smith (2000)
Religion, Power, and Politics in Colonial St. Augustine, by Robert L. Kapitzke (2001)
Bioarchaeology of Spanish Florida: The Impact of Colonialism, edited by Clark Spencer Larsen (2001)
Archaeological Studies of Gender in the Southeastern United States, edited by Jane M. Eastman and Christopher B. Rodning (2001)
The Archaeology of Traditions: Agency and History Before and After Columbus, edited by Timothy R. Pauketat (2001)
Foraging, Farming, and Coastal Biocultural Adaptation in Late Prehistoric North Carolina, by Dale L. Hutchinson (2002)
Windover: Multidisciplinary Investigations of an Early Archaic Florida Cemetery, edited by Glen H. Doran (2002)
Archaeology of the Everglades, by John W. Griffin (2002)
Pioneer in Space and Time: John Mann Goggin and the Development of Florida Archaeology, by Brent Richards Weisman (2002)
Indians of Central and South Florida, 1513–1763, by John H. Hann (2003)
Presidio Santa Maria de Galve: A Struggle for Survival in Colonial Spanish Pensacola, edited by Judith A. Bense (2003)
Bioarchaeology of the Florida Gulf Coast: Adaptation, Conflict, and Change, by Dale L. Hutchinson (2004)
The Myth of Syphilis: The Natural History of Treponematosis in North America, edited by Mary Lucas Powell and Della Collins Cook (2005)
The Florida Journals of Frank Hamilton Cushing, edited by Phyllis E. Kolianos and Brent R. Weisman (2005)
The Lost Florida Manuscript of Frank Hamilton Cushing, edited by Phyllis E. Kolianos and Brent R. Weisman (2005)
The Native American World Beyond Apalachee: West Florida and the Chattahoochee Valley, by John H. Hann (2006)
Tatham Mound and the Bioarchaeology of European Contact: Disease and Depopulation in Central Gulf Coast Florida, by Dale L. Hutchinson (2006)
Taino Indian Myth and Practice: The Arrival of the Stranger King, by William F. Keegan (2007)
An Archaeology of Black Markets: Local Ceramics and Economies in Eighteenth-Century Jamaica, by Mark W. Hauser (2008; first paperback edition, 2013)
Mississippian Mortuary Practices: Beyond Hierarchy and the Representationist Perspective, edited by Lynne P. Sullivan and Robert C. Mainfort Jr. (2010; first paperback edition, 2012)
Bioarchaeology of Ethnogenesis in the Colonial Southeast, by Christopher M. Stojanowski (2010; first paperback edition, 2013)

French Colonial Archaeology in the Southeast and Caribbean, edited by Kenneth G. Kelly and Meredith D. Hardy (2011)

Late Prehistoric Florida: Archaeology at the Edge of the Mississippian World, edited by Keith Ashley and Nancy Marie White (2012)

Early and Middle Woodland Landscapes of the Southeast, edited by Alice P. Wright and Edward R. Henry (2013)

Trends and Traditions in Southeastern Zooarchaeology, edited by Tanya M. Peres (2014)

New Histories of Pre-Columbian Florida, edited by Neill J. Wallis and Asa R. Randall (2014)

www.ingramcontent.com/pod-product-compliance
Lightning Source LLC
Chambersburg PA
CBHW020832160426
43192CB00007B/615